RURAL EDUCATION

SOURCE BOOKS ON EDUCATION
(VOL. 25)

GARLAND REFERENCE LIBRARY
OF SOCIAL SCIENCE
(VOL. 473)

SOURCE BOOKS ON EDUCATION

RURAL EDUCATION
Issues and Practice

edited by
Alan J. DeYoung

GARLAND PUBLISHING, INC. • NEW YORK & LONDON
1991

129818

© 1991 Alan J. DeYoung
All rights reserved

Library of Congress Cataloging-in-Publication Data

Rural education : issues and practice / edited by Alan J. DeYoung.
     p.   cm. — (Source books on education ; vol. 25) (Garland
reference library of social science ; vol. 473)
     Includes index.
     ISBN 0–8240–5649–3
     1. Education, Rural—United States. 2. Rural schools—United
States—Administration. I. DeYoung, Alan J. II. Series: Garland
reference library of social science ; vol. 473. III. Series:
Garland reference library of social science. Source books on
education ; vol. 25.
LC5146.R846   1991
370.19'346'0973—dc20   90–24845
                                                             CIP

Printed on acid-free, 250-year-life paper
Manufactured in the United States of America

TO THE CHILDREN OF APPALACHIA

CONTENTS

129818

PREFACE

Collections of essays on rural education in the United States are relatively rare, particularly ones whose primary focus is on highlighting the available research literature on rural schools and their contexts. And to the best of my knowledge, even the several very good books on rural education written in the 1970s were written primarily by educators located outside of the university, where the location of educational scholarship ought logically to reside (since we are usually the only ones with the time and ostensible incentives for such undertakings).

Yet, the editor and authors of this book are hardly surprised by the comparative absence of rural education readers, or on rural education research. One of the "unadvertised" features of university life is that a highly structured status system exists, in which rural issues have typically been relegated to Colleges of Agriculture, which themselves have less prestige among university colleges.

Traditionally, scholars accorded most worth in academe have been of two types: those whose work is more theoretically oriented; and (more recently) those whose work garners the most extramural funding. Unfortunately, professors of education are accorded less status in universities because much of their work, of necessity, deals with real people in real settings. Moreover, the people with whom educational scholars are primarily concerned (i.e., children) are also of low status in our culture. Thus, few internal academic rewards are typically forthcoming for those who choose to devote their time and efforts to investigating teaching and learning in the public schools, particularly in rural settings.

Should one doubt the validity of such a claim, I urge the reader to investigate just how many prestigious universities actually have viable and visible programs for those who deal on a daily basis as practitioners with our nation's schools and its children. In such places it is behind the semi-respectable theoretical specializations (like cognitive *theory*, organizational *theory*, or, most recently, critical *theory*), where the educational professorate takes refuge from critics eager to decry the "educationists."

This analysis is not to suggest that no field-based scholarship is available at the university on educational topics, for clearly this is not the case. Rather, the second source of academic prestige in academe, money, has become increasingly available to education faculty during the twentieth century. As a number of educational historians have pointed out, ample funds targeted at researching the ameliorative possibilities of schooling for disadvantaged children in our culture became readily available in the 1960s and 1970s. In this era, achieving the good life in the "great society" was deemed possible for all under scientifically informed social and educational policies.

Truth be told, many academics made good late twentieth century careers in the quest for understanding the parameters and factors associated with urban poverty as it related to the public school. Rural educational issues, however, still rarely attracted the attention of prestigious colleges of education and their professorates. In the first place, of course, rural America has typically been the site for (first) agriculture and (second) low-wage manufacture. These are places and cultures imbued with traditions of labor and of working. By contrast, the demand for intellectual understanding and for abstract scholarship removed from the demands of work has rarely led to systematic inquiry on rural education or about the relationships between rural communities and rural schools. Furthermore, as previously stated, when research monies did become available for educational research, most of these funds were targeted at urban, rather than rural issues.

The bottom line, then, is that comparatively little scholarship on rural schools is available in the national context; and much of what is there is to be found not in the (arguably few) prestigious academic journals of education but rather in state department documents and/or in Vo-Ag Journals seldom read by mainstream educators or those who have trained them.

In recent history there have nonetheless been slight, periodic resurgences of interest in some issues of rural schooling. During the 1950s and early 1960s, "community education" was a popular theme in the national education literature, and much of this literature made reference to rural communities and rural life. A decade later, equal educational opportunity advocates in the countryside were able to convince some policymakers that urban inequality had its equivalents in many rural regions, and "reassessments of the conventional wisdom" became rallying cries in some rural locales. Unfortunately, these cries were still only rarely heard or investigated by academics (see for example Jonathan Sher's *Education in Rural America: A Reassessment of the Conventional Wisdom*, Boulder, Colo.: Westview Press, 1977).

More recently, numerous observers have "discovered" that rural life might be saved or improved, at least in part, by better education (or training) for rural children. This discovery actually echoes a late nineteenth century hope for rural schooling. As a result, new educational policy interests, new or expanded rural education associations, and some new scholarly interests in rural education have emerged. Unfortunately, even these research efforts (and systematic discussions of it) are hard to find in one place. Rural education research is still not a burning interest among most educational scholars. And it may never be.

On the other hand, those of us who work in this area (from disparate directions and intellectual traditions) believe that a literature on rural education contexts, practices and issues is available and interesting. Specifically, many of us believe that the history, sociology, and political economy of rural education tell a much greater story of the evolving social issues and social problems of this nation. Which is also one of the reasons we have put this book together.

We would like to thank Garland Publishing for allowing us the opportunity to assemble and put this volume together and into your hands. We hope you will find some or all of the following discussions and guides to further reading of interest and/or use. We think a volume like this is long overdue.

Alan DeYoung
Lexington, Ky.
April 1990

ACKNOWLEDGMENTS

In addition to the many authors who contributed to this book, I would like to also thank Valerie Saunders and Todd Strohmenger at the Appalachia Educational Laboratory for their editorial assistance on the last version of this manuscript.

Thanks are also due to Nichole Barker, Sharon Hamilton and Ann Bostrum of my own department who helped me print the final document from which this book is reproduced. Without their combined assistance on details of this manuscript, it might never have reached the camera-ready stage of production.

INTRODUCTION

Rural schools and rural education in "developed" nations are rarely written about or studied, except perhaps as anomalies. In the rush to "modernize" all private and public institutions, most national political and educational leaders are thoroughly convinced that creating a modern and efficient school organization is a key building block in the "march of progress."

In the United States, however, we are faced with what many national leaders perceive as an embarrassing dilemma. Just as children in our nation are increasingly coming to be viewed as national "human resources" in the race for continued economic development, our (admirable) eighteenth century political system has located the organization and control of public education at more local governmental levels. This fact, of course, may perform successfully in enabling our democratic political system to survive: but it creates great difficulty for those who would "globalize" our economy by "developing our human resources" for impersonal and far-flung "information age" occupations in ever changing urban/suburban settings.

Put another way, numerous leading economists currently argue that regaining American economic "competitiveness" importantly depends upon the ability of American workers to better "invest" in their "human capital" and subsequently to adapt with ease to the increasing geographic mobility that the future economic opportunities in this country are predicted to "make possible."

Yet, in the United States, we have no national ministry of education to establish national school curricular and administrative policies for better facilitating and coordinating the "training" of the future American workforce. Such a training function, therefore, remains more problematic than it does in other advanced countries. Thus, the ideology of education for economic development continues to depend upon school "reform" initiatives organized at national and state levels and frequently spearheaded by "citizen task forces" located in urban centers of the United States.

One of the most basic contradictions in rural schooling today, then, is that local schools in rural areas are charged with nurturing local children and providing skill training for them, so that one day they can leave forever the communities in which they were born and grew up. At the same time, since many (if not most) rural places in the United States have weak or declining local economies, the resources (including both monetary and community support services) available to local school districts for educating children also continue to decline.

Meanwhile, the children of the urban and suburban middle class in economically more stable communities are typically able to receive the extra support and curricular opportunities less available in the countryside. This inequity in the distribution of resources tends to provide already socially/culturally advantaged youth additional advantages in the competition for occupational entry as young adults.

In this introductory chapter, I was going to make more explicit the arguments supporting some of the above assertions, and some of those in the preface. And, in fact, I have already written on a variety of these themes in other places (e.g., DeYoung, 1989a; DeYoung, 1989b; DeYoung, 1987; DeYoung, 1985; Silver and DeYoung, 1986). However, after reading through the essays I solicited for this volume, I have decided to forego an extensive theoretical discussion of the aforementioned perspectives and will let the individual authors air issues, concerns and findings related to these topics. Importantly, since many, if not most, readers of this volume will no doubt be rural educators "in the field," a good portion of this collection of essays deals with more practical matters associated with teaching and learning in rural areas.

Furthermore, since the intention of this text (and the larger Garland series) is to serve as a guide to scholarship in areas covered, it is my hope that each of the chapters to follow will spur readers to continue their readings in each content area as guided by the resources suggested in this collection. While little national scholarship is available on rural education in America, the low status of rural education and rural issues generally should by no means suggest that "nothing is happening" out there or that research and writing on rural schools and their communities lack scholarly interest. We would argue exactly the opposite is true, and we hope this collection of essays demonstrates this point.

Part One of this book contains three essays on the historical and social contexts in which rural education did and does take place. As various experts in rural education have suggested, a great deal of variety exists in the rural regions of this country, and such variations likewise exist among their schools. In Chapter One, Paul Theobald attempts to illustrate some of the divergent eighteenth and early nineteenth century educational traditions that came to different regions of what would eventually became the United States.

What might have been in Part One of this book—but isn't—is a history of late nineteenth and early twentieth century school reforms that had the net effect of reorganizing, consolidating, and centralizing many rural schools around the nation. On the one hand, good discussions of such dynamics are already available in other widely available works on rural education (e.g., DeYoung, 1987; Sher, 1977; Tyack, 1974). Furthermore, some limited discussion on these developments is also provided in other chapters in this collection.

Instead of retelling the history of rural school consolidation in Part One, I have chosen to include an essay on an equally fascinating history of rural education phenomenon made invisible by contemporary educational preoccupations. Specifically, "modern" education is a story importantly tied up with the nineteenth and early twentieth century "discovery of childhood." A key transformation of formal learning occurred in America when "behavioral science" discovered the developmental and cognitive stages of childhood. This development provided school reformers with keys to institutionalizing education into a setting for the instruction of children rather than adults. And, since many adult education programs and initiatives were politically charged in the late nineteenth and early twentieth centuries, public schools for children were argued to be politically neutral. This forgotten history of adult rural education is presented by Harvey Neufeldt and James Akenson in Chapter Two.

The current economic and sociological contexts of rural education are discussed by Craig Howley in Chapter Three. And, while the implications of this essay for rural school "reform" or enhancement may be bleak, the analysis provided may be necessary to balance much of the more optimistic rhetoric of many rural educators who rally around hopes that one day rural schools will, in effect, serve as models for national school improvement agendas.

For practically minded educators already working in rural schools, Part One's historical and theoretical perspectives are less central (although still important) in Part Two. The theme of rural school organization and reorganization mentioned above is made current in Chapter Five by David Monk, and current concerns in identifying, recruiting, selecting, inducting and supervising teachers in rural teacher labor markets are thoroughly discussed by Dwight Hare in Chapter Four.

One of the few advantages arguably wrought by the modern age for the improvement of rural education involves the possibility of video and audio technology delivery systems for small and remote schools. A description of such modern technological innovations, which are becoming available around the United States, is presented by Bruce Barker in Chapter Six. Similarly, printed materials that might make rural school teachers and administrators more effective in their instructional efforts are increasingly becoming available, and such resources are profiled by Teri Lipinski in Chapter Nine.

Given the political economy of rural life in the United States, in which many of the most able, willing, and affluent citizens are able to relocate to cities for enhanced economic opportunities, problems of educating the poor and the handicapped appear disproportionally to fall upon rural schools and rural educators. Therefore, an increasing amount of scholarship on educational issues, dynamics, and practice among those working with such disadvantaged populations is becoming available. Chapters Seven and Eight deal specifically with such concerns. Chapter Seven, by Terry Berkeley and Barbara Ludlow, specifically deals with existing scholarship on education for special needs students in rural settings. In Chapter Eight, Margaret Phelps and George Prock deal more generally with the literature on economically disadvantaged populations in rural America.

Given all of the apparent problems in rural education in the United States (many of them covered in the first nine chapters of this collection), Part Three, on alternative visions of future developments in rural education, might suggest that easy ways out of our current difficulties will be presented. Unfortunately, while one or two authors in this section hold out either implicit or explicit hopes that rural schools will be substantially improved in the future, other less sanguine interpretations are also visible here.

Providing an intriguing glimpse of how rural schools might be able to use social and administrative science to refashion their operations, Bob Stephens and Willis Perry present a discussion in Chapter Ten of what a forward-looking policy agenda for rural schools in the United States ought to look like in the coming decade. What these authors basically argue is that there exist well-thought-out and well-fashioned programs to facilitate better teaching and learning in rural areas currently and that such programs and available scholarship on rural school "problems" and solutions to them make should make possible the systematic improvement of rural education in the decade ahead.

On the other hand, Paul Nachtigal reminds us in Chapter Eleven that rural schools and the social forces that affect them typically operate in a politicized arena, where conflicting rather than consensual goals may be important to understand. More specifically, Nachtigal discusses how grassroots school organizations have been responsible for much of the resistance to urban inspired school "improvement" plans in the late twentieth century and that urban agendas and rural ones may never be attained within an increasingly centralized public school system.

This last theme, of course, was also central to Craig Howley's discussion in Part One of the book. Yet, while Howley's assessment of the future of rural education appears rather bleak, a more optimistic note is sounded in Chapter Twelve by Toni Haas. Haas believes that a "New Story" about the differences and possibilities in rural education will be required before further talk of improvement can be fashioned. And she believes such a story is both imperative and possible.

REFERENCES

DeYoung, A. "Economic Development and Educational Status in Appalachian Kentucky." *Comparative Education Review, 29,* no. 1 (1985): 47–67.

DeYoung, A. "The Status of American Rural Education Research: An Integrated Review and Commentary." *Review of Education Research, 57,* no. 2 (1987): 123–148.

DeYoung, A. *Economics and American Education: A Historical and Critical Overview of the Impact of Economic Theories on Schooling in the United States.* New York: Longman, 1989a.

DeYoung, A. "The Erosion of 'Social Capital' in Rural America: Are all Rural Children 'At Risk?'" *Rural Special Education Quarterly, 10,* no. 1 (1989b): 38–45.

Sher, J. *Education in Rural America: A Reassessment of Conventional Wisdom.* Boulder, Colo.: Westview Press, 1977.

Silver, R., and DeYoung, A. "The Ideology of Rural/Appalachian Education, 1895-1935: The Appalachian Education Problem as

Part of the Appalachian Life Problem." *Educational Theory, 36,* no. 1 (Winter 1986): 51–65.

Tyack, D. *The One Best System.* Cambridge, Mass.: Harvard University Press, 1974.

PART I
HISTORICAL AND SOCIAL
CONTEXTS OF RURAL EDUCATION

Historical Scholarship in Nineteenth Century Rural Education

Paul Theobald

During the nineteenth century and even the first few decades of the twentieth century, the schooling experience of most Americans was rural. Yet when historians began to chronicle educational developments in the United States shortly after the turn of the century, they clearly chose to analyze the urban school experience. It was not so much that they did not recognize rural one-room schools as the dominant mode, it was mostly a matter of the availability of the "stuff" of history: the speeches, the statistics, the legislation, the bureaucracies, it all belonged to the city. As a result, traditional American educational history has been marked by a very undue clarity of focus. An informal survey of the research published in the *History of Education Quarterly* since its inception shows that 80% of the topics have been related to urban education. It remains quite difficult to find critically informing work on the experience of rural schooling. But this is changing.

"New rural historians" are currently about the business of reinterpreting the American rural past released from the constraint of an industrial view of the world. Labor historians such as E. P. Thompson, Eric Hobsbawm, and David Montgomery have opened up the values, attitudes, and belief system of preindustrial, agrarian political economies. Clearly patterns of work, worship, and recreation were substantially changed by the imposition of

3

industrial culture in the rural community. The task which now lies
before education historians is to show how tenets of agrarianism
affected rural conceptions of education and practices of schooling.
What follows is an essay designed to acquaint the reader
with historical education scholarship to date that deals with the
rural experience while giving special emphasis to work that treats
rural schooling as an outgrowth of rural political economy and
ideology. I make no pretense to offer an exhaustive account of the
available literature. Surely there will be oversights and omissions
of some consequence. But I believe that what I have presented
here is a reliable overview of the major works concerned with
nineteenth century rural education. The chapter will be divided
into four sections for each of the following geographic regions: the
Northeast, the South, the Midwest, and the West. Since American
public education began in the Northeast, we begin there.

The Northeast

The connection between religion and education was an
intimate one for most of the nineteenth century. For the purposes
of this study it is safe to assume that a "Protestant paideia" (to use
the phrase made popular by Lawrence Cremin) pervaded the
American institutional enterprise that was public schooling. But
this puts us ahead of the story and, indeed, oversimplifies the issue
of religion and education. To sort things out, certain seventeenth
and eighteenth century developments require brief explication.

The British Puritan tradition that accompanied colonists to
New England held formal schooling in high regard. Though the
skills learned in America's first schools were valuable tools for the
seaboard mercantilist class that emerged in the eighteenth century,
the learning which took place was never meant to be separate
from religious and moral training. And had the Puritan tradition
remained strong and unquestioned throughout the eighteenth
century, the educational history of the United States may have
been quite different.

The social and intellectual developments of seventeenth and
eighteenth century Europe were not kind to American Puritanism.

Collectively, these developments became known as the Enlightenment, and they changed forever the circumstances of the medieval "Dark Ages." Although there were great variations in patterns of thought, a few ideas were so pervasive that they can confidently be discussed as intellectual components of the Enlightenment. For instance, scientific discoveries led to widespread acceptance of something called "natural law." It was thought that human reason could discern the mechanisms that God set in motion at the moment of creation. That is, through the study of the world around them, man could identify these natural laws. A few of these "laws" which became quite popular were the notions that Christianity ought to be reasonable (burning witches at the stake was not deemed reasonable), and that the government of the state ought to represent the people, serve at their will, and not be in the business of prescribing religious or economic policy.

The deistic tradition that grew out of Enlightenment tenets led to an increase in the reliance of reason and scholarly inquiry in order to come to understand the nature of man. Deism, as a strand of religious thought, was a direct outgrowth of Enlightenment tenets. It was often referred to as "natural religion" for its defining characteristic was that man could discover religious truths through inferences from the world around him. For deists, God created a world governed by natural law and thereafter did not intervene in the affairs of the world. Though the impact of deistic Unitarianism in American education is significant, it is frequently overemphasized because Horace Mann, founder of the common school movement, was a devout Unitarian.

The eighteenth century movement of most significance was clearly the Great Awakening of the 1730s and 40s. The Puritan tradition in America was strictly Calvinist in nature. A central component of Calvinism was the notion of predestination. An all-knowing God determined one's religious fate at the moment of birth. God predestined an elect group for salvation, another for damnation. However, a Dutch theologian by the name of Jacobus Arminius disputed Calvin's strict determinism and suggested that Christ died for all men and not only for an elect. This "free will theology," clearly subordinate among English Reform traditions, found its way to the American colonies in the first half of the eighteenth century.

Historians agree that the Calvinist-Arminian controversy came to America via George Whitefield, a minister with close connections to John and Charles Wesley of England. The religious excitement and fervor he provoked by suggesting that individuals could choose to repent and prove their membership among the elect through Christ-like behavior was continued by American clerics with Arminian propensities such as William and Gilbert Tennent, James Davenport, and Jonathan Edwards. To bring the people to God, America's first generation of evangelicals rejected the intellectualism of Edinburgh, Cambridge, and New Haven, for they believed sophisticated Biblical exegesis alienated the common farmer and shopkeeper. It was precisely for this reason that William Tennent created his "log college" in Neshaminy, Pennsylvania. He intended to train ministers who could communicate God's message in simple terms. Part of the evangelical tradition that unseated Puritanism as the dominant strand of American Protestant thought by the 1850s was a clear tendency toward anti-intellectualism (Hofstadter, 1964; Miyakawa, 1963). A fundamental tension existed between reason and faith witnessed by such thinkers as Immanuel Kant who maintained that he needed "to destroy reason to make room for faith" (Ahlstrom, 1972, p. 587).

Though outside the scope of this chapter, American colonial education has been studied in some detail. Lawrence Cremin's *American Education: The Colonial Experience, 1607–1783* (1970) would benefit any student of education history trying to understand the interconnected nature of religion and the schooling experience. Delving all the way back to the Christianization of Britain, Cremin chronicles the religious propensity for education, including the boost it received from Renaissance thinkers such as Desiderius Erasmus and William Tyndale along with the "Protestant heroes" of the English Reformation such as John Wycliffe and Hugh Latimer. James Axtell in *The School Upon a Hill: Education and Society in Colonial New England* (1974) referred to his work as a "waist-high view of education." In other words, whenever possible he tried to recreate the social side of colonial schooling from the viewpoint of the students as opposed to Cremin's reliance on the impact of intellectuals. An important theme in Axtell's work is the New England concern for the spiritual welfare of Puritan children. Using the musings of John Winthrop and the sermons of various Boston Mathers, Axtell persuasively describes this as the foundation for feverish school building among Puritan colonials.

However, while recognizing the rural colonial experience as arduous, there seems to be a lack of appreciation in the work of both Cremin and Axtell for the perennial problem facing small freeholding yeomanry—how to provide land for the next generation. If it is fair to suggest that correct religious socialization required formal instruction, it may also be fair to suggest that the realities of an agrarian lifestyle, including the amount and patterns of labor required, put limits on the utility of formal schooling. In other words, though Axtell, and to some extent Cremin, adequately relay the Puritan desire to provide for the spiritual needs of youth, they inadequately treat the Puritan desire to provide for their material needs. Clearly, both concerns shaped the colonial school experience.

Concern with how the children would succeed the parents went well beyond religious and moral questions. The sustenance of life was derived from the soil. That there be enough soil to "land" the next generation was seemingly just as important as there being enough religious instruction to save them. Timothy Breen's (1975) study of "persistent localism" and the exclusive dimension of New English communities speaks of xenophobic concern for the utilization of local land resources. Stephen Innes' (1978) study of land tenancy in seventeenth century Massachusetts suggests that the burden of landing the next generation was not always accomplished and, in fact, land tenancy as opposed to ownership was the norm for most young men until they approached their forties. Given the primacy of intensive labor on New England farms, I believe it is fair to suggest that the preindustrial *mentalite*, as described by James Henretta (1978), circumscribed limits on the value of formal schooling.

When Horace Mann tried to centralize control over a unified public school system, he received staunch resistance from the Massachusetts countryside. This pattern, of course, would repeat itself throughout the Middle West and South. Picking up on the institution building rhetoric of America's Enlightenment-bound founding fathers, Mann promoted a free public school system as a prerequisite for a nation of free men. A Unitarian, Mann was promoting the tenets of classical liberalism at a time when those tenets were being rejected by politicians and intellectuals alike.

The best account of the foundational circumstances beneath the creation of the common school movement is clearly Michael Katz's *The Irony of Early School Reform: Educational Innovation in Mid-Nineteenth Century Massachusetts* (1968). Katz demonstrates the connection between urbanization, industrial-ization, and immigration on one hand and the creation of the common school movement on the other. Regimented, systematized public instruction had clear similarities to regimented, systematized industrial labor. Mann tried to overcome inter-Protestant opposition to free schools by reducing religious instruction to Bible reading without comment on controversial issues. In response to growing Jewish and especially Catholic numbers on the east coast, this Unitarian's answer to the legacy of church and school connectedness was largely accepted by the main body of New England's Protestants (though the question of which version of the Bible would be an issue of great importance as witnessed by "Bible riots" in New York and Philadelphia in the 1840s). In the Midwest and South, however, this did not immediately prove to be the case. Inter-Protestant sectarianism remained emotional and divisive on the frontier until after the Civil War. In part this was due to the rhythmic labor requirements of an agrarian political economy, the localism required to enhance the ability of small freeholders to land their children, and the religious ideology which rejected the educated rationality of Presbyterianism, Congregationalism, and Anglicanism, which dominated New English religious thought.

If Kant found it necessary near the end of the eighteenth century to dismiss reason to make room for faith, there were many European intellectuals reacting to the changing political economy in the first half of the nineteenth century who saw in the Age of Reason a philosophy that deserved outright rejection. The disillusionment provided by the collapse of the French republic into the Terror and military despotism was enough to trigger a wave of inward speculation in literature, philosophy, art, politics, religion, and education. If disciplined rationality did not produce predictability in life, why should man repress the emotionality inherent in the strange, the old, and the mystical? For many romantics, particularly in England which industrialized so early, lives led before the Age of Reason ushered in "Satanic mills" seemed more purposeful, more in tune with nature, and more interesting. The awesome power of the Holy Spirit of medieval faith seemed preferable to theological bantering over doctrinal heresies of whatever stripe.

In the works of Carlyle, Coleridge, Scott, Chateaubriand, Hugo, Irving, and Goethe, a Romantic Age was born, and the "reasonableness" of Puritanism, Anglicanism, and the Enlightenment itself was called into question.

As the central figure of the Enlightenment in America, Thomas Jefferson's inconsistencies are often puzzling. To some extent, this may be explained by recognizing that by the end of the eighteenth century, Jefferson was accommodating two world views. To be sure, he was devoted to the classical liberal notion of progress, but at the same time he was fascinated by romantic historicism which maintained that feudalism was a Norman import—that prior to 1066 England was a nation of yeoman farmers. Jefferson's vision for America, in part, was a throwback to medieval England with its freedom from feudalism and extremes in wealth and poverty (Horsman, 1981, pp. 18–23).

If America was born amid the Enlightenment, the Middle West and South were born amid the Romantic movement. The interior plains states were created just after America concluded its hostilities with Britain and Britain concluded its hostilities with Napoleon. The rejection of Enlightenment ideals (many dimensions of which were so persuasively chartered by the French) was matched in intensity only by the acceptance of Romantic ideals—and this would have no small impact on distinguishing later regional identities. The bloody contestation with Indians for the Middle West and the shackles restraining blacks in the South shattered the Enlightenment legacy as persuasively as the Terror of Paris and the Napoleonic Empire.

While Enlightenment spokesmen had turned their attention to the development of institutions that might produce "republican machines," Middle Westerners turned toward the development of the *Volkgeist*, the national spirit created by the achievement of "individual men, of individual nations, and of individual races"

(Horsman, 1981, p. 41). The historicism of the Romantic era glorified Anglo-Saxonism and dismantled Enlightenment notions of equality and the primacy of institution-building. For Romantics, history and tradition not reason and science, were the determinants of social order.

However, the *social* science impulse developed in the nineteenth century in the service of the Romantic intellectual agenda. Phrenologists and craniometrists were kept busy rejecting tenets of the Enlightenment during the first half of the nineteenth century. Transylvania University's famous phrenologist Charles Caldwell contended that blacks and Indians were destined for extinction due to inferior mental abilities. Said Caldwell, "When the wolf, the buffalo, and the panther shall have been completely domesticated, like the dog, the cow, and the household cat, then, and not before, may we expect to see the full-blooded Indian civilized" (Horsman, 1981, p. 118). Samuel George Martin's *Crania Americana* (1839) was immensely popular and purported undisputed proof of Caucasian superiority.

The emerging scientific racism that developed in response to the historiographic idolization of Anglo-Saxon origins was clearly welcome on the interior plains as frontiersmen ceaselessly encroached on Indian land. This racial ideology provided a way of thinking that would mix with frontier religion and education and help shape them. The tension, of course, was that the new historicism was vital in one sense but clearly troublesome in another as it came close to an assault on the veracity of the Bible. How could separate races of men evolve from Adam and Eve? In the end, the tension was resolved by the ascendancy of unquestioning faith (or something John Stuart Mill referred to as "the deep slumber of decided opinion"), a faith that continues to be an important element of the ethos of the interior plains. It is not without some justification that the area is frequently referred to as the "Bible belt." Certainly man is not in a position to question the Lord's will manifested in a hierarchy of peoples? In the United States Congress, Illinois Representative Orlando B. Ficklin commented in 1850 that "the people of my state, and the people of Indiana, and other of the Northwestern states, have no more desire to see the negroes raised to an equality with the whites than have the people of South Carolina, Louisiana, or the rest of the ultra slaveholding states." In a similar vein, Indiana Senator John Petit remarked, "I hold it to be a self-evident lie that all men are created equal" (Horsman, 1981, p. 274).

The growth of two of the smaller religious sects during the Revolutionary era, the Methodists and Baptists, into the two largest denominations in the country by 1840 is indicative of both the growth of the interior plains states and the ascendancy of Romanticism. Clearly, the path to salvation and the acceptance of Jesus Christ as savior can be accomplished both by an appeal to reason or to emotion. The ascendancy of the Romantic era doomed deistic Unitarianism, literally, to the Boston seaboard. The tradition of combining reason with emotionalism begun by Edwards and continued subsequently by Dwight and later Lyman Beecher was only marginally successful in interior America. However, the emotional appeal of revivalistic Arminianism among Methodists and popular Baptists provided fertile ground for Middle Western and Southern conversions, creating an expansion no one could have predicted in 1789.

Before turning to a discussion of historical scholarship dealing with rural education in the South, it is important to point out that rather glaring inadequacies in the history of education in the Northeast are beginning to be addressed. The education of blacks, Indians, women, and the rural poor in the Northeast has not been particularly well studied. Margaret Connell Szasz recently added a valuable contribution which begins to fill part of this void, *Indian Education in the American Colonies, 1607–1783* (1988). The black experience in the Northeast has largely been urban and, consequently, is outside the scope of this chapter. The interested reader will find Vincent Franklin's work (1979) on the education of blacks in Philadelphia to be the best in this area. Dominated as the Northeast is by large urban centers, it is not surprising that the region's educational history has focused on urban schooling.

Thomas Woody's early work on the history of Quaker education in Pennsylvania (1920) is still one of the best treatments of this topic. Woody's greater contribution, however, is his two volume work, *A History of Women's Education in the United States* (1929). Barbara Miller Solomon's *In the Company of Educated Women* (1985) also deals with women but primarily with upper class New England female academies and seminaries. Joseph Moore (1989) recently traced the educational history of a small Vermont town that provides a perspective on the schooling experience in the rural villages of New England with special emphasis on local relations with the state of Vermont. One fascinating study that deserves mention here is William Gilmore's *Reading Becomes a Necessity of Life: Material and Cultural Life in Rural New England, 1780–1835* (1989). In a very innovative fashion, Gilmore explored the impact of reading on the lives of the rural poor in New England. His work is a perceptive foray into preindustrial tradition and patterns of thought. Persuasively, Gilmore contends that reading was not the liberating activity that many believe it to be today.

The South

The intellectual and religious milieu in the days of the founding of the interior plains states had much to do with the shape of public education in the South and the Middle West. Though there are similarities, the Southern political economy based on chattel slavery necessitated marked differences in the practice of public schooling. As a consequence, the legacy of African slavery has resulted in two separate systems of education for the historian to chronicle. One for blacks, the other for whites.

Most "white" histories of Southern education purport to include historical analysis of the black experience. Prominent among them is Charles Dabney's two volume study of *Universal Education in the South* (1936). However, the central theme of almost all of the early work on Southern educational history is that the drive and the incentive to establish postbellum black schools was attributable to Northern philanthropy and foundational support such as Rockefeller's General Board of Education and the Julius Rosenwald Fund. Even books purported to be exclusively about the black experience such as Robert Morris' *Reading, 'Riting, and Reconstruction: The Education of the Freedmen in the South, 1861–1870* (1976) have failed to recognize the legacy of antebellum black striving for education and their belief that it held the key to real freedom. However, Thomas Webber's *Deep Like A*

River: Education in the Slave Quarter Community, 1831–1865
speaks of "a strong belief in the desirability of learning to read and
write among the slave community" (1978, p.131). Most recently,
James Anderson's *The Education of Blacks in the South, 1860–
1930* (1988) has demonstrated that the philanthropic movement to
dominate the black educational agenda actually displaced a strong
black school movement founded by the ex-slaves themselves. As a
consequence, Anderson's work sheds new light on the Booker T.
Washington-W.E.B. DuBois debate. As well, he relays the history
of black education in the South on its own terms. That is to say,
the book reports the story of the development of black education
within appropriate ideological and political economic contexts. It
is largely rural history since this was the predominant nineteenth
century black experience. The reader interested in black rural
schooling in the South will find no better treatment than
Anderson's contribution. However, two other volumes deserve
mention. Carter Woodson's *The Education of the Negro Prior To
1861* (1919) is an old but useful study that complements Webber's
work. Ronald Butchart's *Northern Schools, Southern Blacks, and
Reconstruction* (1980) is an admirable treatment of freedmen's
education during Reconstruction and is clearly superior to Morris'
book.

Emphasis on the rural white experience in the South is only
beginning to receive scholarly attention. The best work in this area
is William Link's study of rural education in Virginia prior to 1920,
A Hard Country and a Lonely Place (1986). Link describes Virginia
rural schools as products of an agrarian political economy with the
religious and racial ideologies that accompany the slave state
legacy of suspicion regarding public education. Juxtaposed against
Link's book, Thad Sitton and Milam Rowold's story of Texas
country schools, *Ringing The Children In* (1987), leaves a great
deal to be desired. In terms of understanding the role of schools in
rural society, the interplay between religion and education, and
the dynamics of racial coexistence, the book is of little help.
However, if the reader is interested in day to day life within Texas
country schools, he or she will find plenty of interesting
recollections from former students and teachers.

The educational history of the South is a maze of various
racial, religious, and political ideologies that interact with, and are

a part of, a pervasive attachment to preindustrial agrarian tenets. Understanding education in such a society requires thorough training in Southern history of the kind which Anderson and Link seem to possess. By contrast, the educational history of the Middle West seems straightforward, progressive, and easy to interpret. But this is at first glance. A closer look reveals that the educational history of the Midwest has been anything but onward and upward. In fact, some of the undemocratic trends of the South were replicated, in subtle ways, in the states of the Old Northwest.

The Midwest

The student about to undertake the study of rural educational history in the Midwest would do well by beginning with a few books only tangentially related to schooling. Traditional American history often leaves the impression that racism and its associated problems were the near exclusive province of the South throughout the nineteenth century. Reginald Horsman's *Race and Manifest Destiny* (1981) ably dispels this myth by documenting the impact of racial Anglo-Saxonism of the Romantic age on the states of the interior plains. V. Jacque Voegeli's *Free But Not Equal: The Midwest and the Negro During the Civil War* (1967) and Leon Litwack's *North of Slavery: The Negro in the Free States 1790–1860* (1961) both described the Middle West as a place where Enlightenment notions of equality were completely shattered. These historians agree with Tocqueville's observation in 1835 that racial prejudice is no where as prevalent "as in the states where slavery never existed" (the states of the Midwest).

T. Scott Miyakawa's *Protestants and Pioneers* (1964) and Sydney Ahlstrom's *A Religious History of the American People* (1971) analyze the impact of nineteenth century romanticism on American religious thought and discuss the implications of this on the development of an ethos on the interior plains. Miyakawa's work, in particular, deals with frontier Protestantism and its attitudes toward formal schooling.

Once again, in the Midwest, the problem of landing the next generation faced by yeoman freeholders has profound implications for the shape and scope of schooling in rural communities. The mobility of settlers who moved across the plains states has puzzled historians for nearly half a century. The traditional explanation for this mobility, of course, has been that the pioneers had a nose for profits and were therefore constantly on the move to a better situation. The reality, according to the work of "new rural historians" such as John Mack Faragher and James Henretta is that the transient nature of the Middle West pioneer experience was structural, a majority of the settlers were kept landless and on the move by a landed minority that used local institutions as instruments of exclusion. In light of their evidence, of course, traditional interpretations of rural resistance to state department initiatives as the laudable exercise of local democracy are called into serious question.

Solidified by the evidence of Populist strength there, the states of the trans-Mississippi west can be seen as holding zones of the excluded—those people who after several moves through the states of the Old Northwest found themselves at the very limits of consequential rainfall agriculture. It is a fact of some significance that the issue of free text books for public school children became a national campaign issue for Populists whose stronghold was in the Great Plains states. Frequently, the inability to purchase texts kept the children of the excluded in frontier society from successfully participating in the school. Lawrence Goodwyn's *Democratic Promise: The Populist Moment in America* (1976) should be required reading for anyone who wishes to understand the dynamics of frontier settlement and the implications of this for formal schooling. Faragher's *Sugar Creek: Life on the Illinois Frontier* (1986) and Kathleen Neils Conzen's "Peasant Pioneers: Generational Succession among German Farmers in Frontier Minnesota" (1985) along with James Henretta's "Families and Farms: *Mentalite* in Pre-Industrial America" (1978) and Michael Merrill's "Cash is Good to Eat: Self-Sufficiency and Exchange in the Rural Economy of the United States" (1977) also provide a basis for interpreting the history of the rural Midwest and consequently a new way to look at the role of rural schools in the region.

Wayne Fuller's overview of rural education in the Midwest, *The Old Country School* (1982), provides insight into the everyday lives of students, teachers, and school board members in small countryside districts. However, Fuller's contention that one room schools were "invaluable laboratories of democracy" and the springboard for "the majority of the Midwest's political and professional leaders" is terribly misleading for it ignores how the schools functioned for most children in rural society (Theobald, 1988). Regrettably, good work of the sort provided by Link and Anderson for the South has yet to be done for the Midwest.

Historian Lloyd Jorgenson has long been aware of the rather undemocratic nineteenth century trend of promoting "Protestant" religious instruction of the sort that caused disaffection among Catholics and other Protestants outside the English Reform tradition, such as German or Scandinavian Lutherans. His book *The Founding of Public Education in Wisconsin* (1956) stands as one of the best in an otherwise poor line of state educational histories across the Middle West. But of more value is his latest book, *The State and the Nonpublic School, 1825–1925* (1987) which persuasively delineates some of the troublesome trends of the common school movement ignored by more famous historians of education, such as Lawrence Cremin in *American Education: The National Experience, 1783–1876* (1980) and Carl Kaestle's *Pillars of the Republic* (1983). Kaestle's work, in particular, is lacking from the standpoint of rural education. Purported to be a history of American schooling between 1780 and 1860, a time when perhaps 90% of all schools were rural, Kaestle devotes a chapter of a mere 17 pages to rural education and follows it with a 31-page chapter on urban education.

Even Jorgenson's work, however, falls short of describing the impact of Middle Western religious history on the common schools of the region. As noted earlier, sectarianism in the Midwest was often bitter. Common schools were seen as something one religious denomination or another could control and direct. Often in the antebellum Midwest there would be a "Calvin" school only a short distance from a "Methodist" school. The anti- intellectual impulse of the evangelical denominations that so heavily populated the rural Midwest blended with agrarian household economics creating a preindustrial ethos with little room for formal education beyond reading, writing, and arithmetic. Attendance at rural schools was atrocious, school terms were short, and schooling careers often terminated at age ten, twelve, or earlier.

Teachers, of course, were often little better educated than their students. Polly Welts Kaufman's *Women Teachers on the Frontier* (1984) provides a rare glimpse of Middle Western attitudes concerning schooling through the eyes of outsiders; teachers who were born, raised, and trained in the Northeast and sent west by Catherine Beecher's National Board of Popular Education. This organization was Catherine's response to her father Lyman, whose anti-Catholic tract *A Plea for the West* (1836) contained a call for common schools to save the West as a bastion of Protestantism far removed from the Irish hordes on the east coast. In diaries and correspondence of many of these missionary teachers, Kaufman relates the anti-intellectualism of the antebellum Northwest. Kaestle, however, has warned that because these teachers "were trained to be missionaries, they got a rather dim view of frontier culture. Their reports should therefore not be taken as typical of the region." (Cremin, 1987, p. 39) However, Kaufman's work is very well researched and of great value.

Joanna Stratton's *Pioneer Women: Voices from the Kansas Frontier* (1981) includes a short chapter detailing the lives of Kansas "schoolmarms." Paul Mattingly's *The Classless Profession: American Schoolmen in the Nineteenth Century* (1975) is largely concerned with teachers on the east coast and in urban settings. Kathryn Kish Sklar's "Female Teachers: 'Firm Pillars' of the West" is a solid chapter although she covers much of the same ground as Kaufman. It appears in an edited volume dealing with the history of education in the Old Northwest, *Schools and the Means of Education* (Mattingly and Stevens, 1987).

The nineteenth century educational history of blacks and Indians in the Midwest is a serious void in the field—serious because its absence has hindered our understanding of the schooling experience of the majority by allowing the traditional "onward and upward" story of "democratic" schooling to be told and retold without critical examination. Robert McCaul's *The Black Struggle For Public Schooling in Nineteenth Century Illinois* (1987) is an attempt to address this shortcoming. McCaul relates part of the story of rural black exclusion from schools in southern Illinois but, as is true for most books dealing with that state, the Chicago story dominates. Arnie Cooper's "A Stony Road: Black Education in Iowa, 1838–1860" (1985) is a brief but valuable account of the black quest for education in Iowa's Mississippi valley communities.

The West

The days when concern with the American west dominated discussion in university history departments have been gone for some time. When the initial propensity to critique or defend Frederick Jackson Turner's frontier thesis faded after World War II, so, too, did rigorous examination of western history. Patricia Nelson Limerick's book, *The Legacy of Conquest: The Unbroken Past of the American West* (1987) has reversed this trend by evocatively describing the West as a region crucial to understanding larger themes in American history. The notion that the West was "won" is an interesting one, and it is in the study of the "winning" that nineteenth century American history can be better understood.

Taking Indian land and subordinating Mexican American and Asian American labor required ideological commitments at odds with constitutional rhetoric. As noted earlier, the Romanticism that followed the collapse of the Age of Reason provided a foundation for pseudo-scientific claims of a racial hierarchy. Many veterans of the Civil War who went west did so because they were no longer needed on the land they had previously rented or sharecropped. Excluded by settlement patterns and burgeoning agricultural technology, these individuals were able to bolster their own sense of self worth by utilizing the prevailing racial ideology in their conquest of the West.

The educational history of the region, particularly rural educational history, is largely yet to be told. Andrew Gulliford's *America's Country Schools* (1984) is the best single source of information about western rural schools and contains a lengthy, detailed bibliography. Additionally, Gulliford has started "Country School Legacy Collections" in state university libraries in Kansas, Colorado, Nebraska, Utah, North Dakota, South Dakota, Wyoming, and Nevada. These collections represent a valuable source of primary data dealing with western country schools.

In California and the Pacific Northwest the urban experience, once again, dominates the existing body of educational history. Scholarship dealing with the schooling experience of rural Japanese and Chinese Americans is needed. For background information on these populations, Lucie Cheng and Edna Bonacich's *Labor Immigration under Capitalism: Asian Workers in the United States before World War II* (1984) represents a good source. Paul Theobald and Kristin Lindholm (1989) have more recently contributed a study of the schooling experience of "Okies" on the west coast.

The educational history of native Americans in the West is lacking. Margaret Connell Szasz's *Education and the American Indian* (1977) is perhaps the most comprehensive work available. Robert Havighurst and Estelle Fuch's *To Live on This Earth: American Indian Education* (1972) also represents a valuable contribution to the field. Further insights may be drawn from comprehensive journal articles by Guy Senese (1985) and David Wallace Adams (1988).

Histories of the schooling experiences of Mexican Americans are also quite limited. Most of the information available deals with the state of Texas. David Montejano's *Anglos and Mexicans in the Making of Texas, 1836–1986* (1987) provides an excellent background on the interplay of racial ideology and the subordination of labor. A twentieth century study, Guadalupe San Miguel's *Let Them All Take Heed* (1987) admirably integrates the schooling experience of Mexican Americans into the Texas political economy described by Montejano.

A study of the Mormon influence on rural education in Utah and Idaho would be a valuable contribution. At present the best source of background information on Mormonism and education is Jan Shipps' *Mormonism: The Study of a Religious Tradition.* (1985). David Tyack's "The Kingdom of God and the Common School" (1966) describes the impact of the English religious Reform tradition on the common schools of the West utilizing Oregon as a case study. However, Tyack overemphasizes the notion of a unified Protestant *paideia* within the common school movement to the extent that inter-Protestant animosity is not recognized as a significant variable in establishment of public schools. The Sunday School tradition in America, particularly in the postbellum years, was the development that allowed common schools to develop a homogenized version of Protestantism which gradually became acceptable to the rural resistance that looked upon public education as a vehicle for certain denominations to proselytize or corrupt. The best source concerned with the development of the American version of Sunday School is Anne Boylan's *Sunday School: The Development of an American Institution* (1988).

Conclusion

Those interested in rural education are temporarily handicapped by the paucity and quality of historical scholarship that serves as the foundation for understanding current issues. On the bright side, however, it is a hopeful sign to recognize that labor, economic, political, and even church historians are turning their attention to the experiences of common men and women and everyday life. Given nineteenth century American demographics, this can only mean that rural America will receive the historical analysis it deserves. In time, it may be hoped, education historians will succumb to this propensity within the discipline. There is no need to be limited by the traditional "stuff" of history. If one is creative, "stuff" can be redefined. With new definitions, doubtless, new questions will be asked and the answers may lead to a better understanding of rural education in America.

REFERENCES

Adams, D. "Fundamental Considerations: The Deep Meaning of Native American Schooling, 1880–1900." *Harvard Educational Review, 48* (1988): 1–28.

Ahlstrom, S. *A Religious History of the American People.* New Haven: Yale University Press, 1972.

Anderson, J. *The Education of Blacks in the South, 1860- 1935.* Chapel
    Hill: University of North Carolina Press, 1988.

Axtell, J. *The School Upon a Hill: Education and Society in Colonial New
    England.* New Haven: Yale University Press, 1974.

Boylan, A. *Sunday School: The Formation of an American Institution,
    1790–1880.* New Haven: Yale University Press, 1988.

Breen, T. "Persistent Localism: English Social Change and the Shaping of
    New England Institutions." *William and Mary Quarterly, 32,* Third
    Series (1975): 3–28.

Butchart, R. *Northern Schools, Southern Blacks, and Reconstruction:
    Freedmen's Education, 1862–1875.* Westport, Conn.: Greenwood
    Press, 1980.

Conzen, K. "Peasant Pioneers: Generational Succession Among German
    Farmers in Frontier Minnesota. In *The Countryside in the Age of
    Capitalist Transformation: Essays in the Social History of Rural
    America.* Edited by S. Hahn and J. Prude. Chapel Hill: University of
    North Carolina Press, 1985.

Cooper, A. "A Stony Road: Black Education in Iowa, 1838- 1860." *The
    Annals of Iowa 48* (1985): 113–134.

Cremin, L. *American Education: The Colonial Experience 1607–1783.*
    New York: Harper and Row, 1970.

Cremin, L. *American Education: The National Experience 1783–1876.*
    New York: Harper Colophon Books, 1980.

Dabney, C. *Universal Education in the South.* 2 vols. Chapel Hill:
    University of North Carolina Press, 1936.

Faragher, J. *Sugar Creek: Life on the Illinois Prairie.* New Haven: Yale
    University Press, 1986.

Franklin, V. *The Education of Black Philadelphia: The Social and
    Educational History of a Minority Community, 1900–1950.*
    Philadelphia: University of Pennsylvania Press, 1979.

Fuller, W. *The Old Country School: The Story of Rural Education in the Middle West.* Chicago: University of Chicago Press, 1982.

Gilmore, W. *Reading Becomes a Necessity of Life: Material and Cultural Life in Rural New England, 1780–1835.* Knoxville: University of Tennessee Press, 1989.

Goodwyn, L. *Democratic Promise: The Populist Moment in America.* New York: Oxford University Press, 1976.

Gulliford, A. *America's Country Schools.* Washington, D.C.: The Preservation Press, 1984.

Hahn, S., and Prude, J. *The Countryside in the Age of Capitalist Transformation: Essays in the Social History of Rural America.* Chapel Hill: University of North Carolina Press, 1985.

Havighurst, R., and Fuchs, E. *To Live on this Earth: American Indian Education.* New York: Doubleday, 1972.

Henretta, J. Families and Farms: *Mentalite* in Pre- Industrial America. *William and Mary Quarterly, 35,* Third Series (1978): 3–32.

Hofstadter, R. *Anti-intellectualism in American Life.* New York: Knopf, 1963.

Horsman, R. *Race and Manifest Destiny: The Origins of Racial Anglo-Saxonism.* Cambridge: Harvard University Press, 1981.

Innes, S. "Land Tenancy and Social Order in Springfield, Massachusetts, 1652–1702." *William and Mary Quarterly, 35,* Third Series (1978): 33–56.

Jorgenson, L. *The Founding of Public Education in Wisconsin.* Madison: State Historical Society of Wisconsin, 1956.

Jorgenson, L. *The State and the Nonpublic School, 1825- 1925.* Columbia: University of Missouri Press, 1987.

Kaestle, C. *Pillars of the Republic: Commons Schools and American Society 1780–1860.* New York: Hill and Wang, 1983.

Kaestle, C. "The Development of Common School Systems in the States of the Old Northwest." *Schools and the Means of Education: A History of Education in the Old Northwest, 1787–1880.* Edited by P. Mattingly and E. Stevens. Athens: Ohio University Libraries, 1987.

Katz, M. *The Irony of Early School Reform: Educational Innovation in Mid-Nineteenth Century Massachusetts.* Cambridge: Harvard University Press, 1968.

Kaufman, P. *Women Teachers on the Frontier.* New Haven: Yale University Press, 1984.

Limerick, P. *The Legacy of Conquest: The Unbroken Past of the American West.* New York: W. W. Norton and Co., 1987.

Link, W. *A Hard Country and a Lonely Place: Schooling, Society, and Reform in Rural Virginia, 1870–1920.* Chapel Hill: University of North Carolina Press, 1986.

Litwack, L. *North of Slavery: The Negro in the Free States, 1790–1860.* Chicago: University of Chicago Press, 1961.

Mattingly, P. *The Classless Profession: American Schoolmen in the Nineteenth Century.* New York: New York University Press, 1975.

Mattingly, P., and Stevens, E., eds. *Schools and the Means of Education: A History of Education in the Old Northwest, 1787–1880.* Athens: Ohio University Libraries, 1987.

McCaul, R. *The Black Struggle for Public Schooling in Nineteenth Century Illinois.* Carbondale: Southern Illinois University Press, 1987.

Merrill, M. "Cash is Good to Eat: Self-Sufficiency and Exchange in the Rural Economy of the United States." *Radical History Review 3* (1977): 42–71.

Miyakawa, T. *Protestants and Pioneers: Individualism and Conformity on the American Frontier.* Chicago: University of Chicago Press, 1964.

Montejano, D. *Anglos and Mexicans in the Making of Texas, 1836–1986.* Austin: University of Texas Press, 1987.

129818

Moore, J. "Developing a School Bureaucracy: The Influences of the State of Vermont and the Town of Newbury, Vermont, on the Newbury School System." Paper presented at the American Educational Research Association convention, San Francisco, April 1989.

Morris, R. *Reading, 'Riting, and Reconstruction: The Education of Freedmen in the South 1861–1870.* Chicago: University of Chicago Press, 1981.

San Miguel, G. *Let Them All Take Heed: Mexican Americans and the Campaign for Educational Equality in Texas 1910- 1981.* Austin: University of Texas Press, 1987.

Senese, G. "Self-Determination and American Indian Education: An Illusion of Control." *Educational Theory, 36* (Spring 1986): 153–164.

Shipps, J. *Mormonism: The Story of a Religious Tradition.* Urbana: University of Illinois Press, 1985.

Sitton, T., and Rowold, M. *Ringing the Children In: Texas Country Schools.* College Station: Texas A+M University Press, 1987.

Sklar, K. "Female Teachers: 'Firm Pillars' of the West." *Schools and the Means of Education: A History of Education in the Old Northwest, 1787–1880.* Edited by P. Mattingly and E. Stevens, E. Athens: Ohio University Libraries, 1987.

Solomon, B. *In the Company of Educated Women: A History of Women and Higher Education in America.* New Haven: Yale University Press, 1985.

Stratton, J. *Pioneer Women: Voices from the Kansas Frontier.* New York: Simon and Schuster, 1981.

Szasz, M. *Education and the American Indian: The Road to Self-Determination Since 1928.* Second Edition. Albuquerque: University of New Mexico Press, 1977.

Szasz, M. *Indian Education in the American Colonies, 1607–1783.* Albuquerque: University of New Mexico Press, 1988.

Theobald, P. "Democracy and the Origins of Midwest Rural Education." *Educational Theory, 38* (Summer 1988): 363–368.

Theobald, P., and Lindholm, K. "Children of the Harvest: Class Formation and the Schooling Experience of America's Depression Era Migrants." Unpublished manuscript, College of Education, University of Illinois at Urbana/Champaign, 1989.

Tyack, D. "The Kingdom of God and the Common School." *Harvard Educational Review, 36* (Fall 1966): 447–476.

Voegeli, V. *Free But Not Equal: The Midwest and the Negro During the Civil War.* Chicago: University of Chicago Press, 1967.

Webber, T. *Deep Like the Rivers: Education in the Slave Quarter Community 1831–1865.* New York: W. W. Norton and Co., 1978.

Woodson, C. *The Education of the Negro Prior to 1861.* Second edition. Washington, D.C.: The Associated Publishers, 1919.

Woody, T. *Early Quaker Education in Pennsylvania.* New York: Columbia University Press, 1920.

Woody, T. *A History of Women's Education in the United States.* 2 vols. New York: The Science Press, 1929.

Adult Education and Rural America:
An Analysis of
Selected Topics and Sources

Harvey G. Neufeldt
and
James E. Akenson

Education for rural adults beguiles one with its apparent simplicity of purpose and delivery of services. Beneath surface simplicity, however, lies an enterprise replete with a variety of rural adult target audiences, assumptions concerning the needs of rural adults and motives of rural adult learners. This discussion seeks to address the wide range of programs, motives, explicit and implicit assumptions, and history of rural adult education in the United States during the twentieth century. A discussion of rural adult education on a global scale or a longer chronology suggests a complexity and scope beyond the limits of a single chapter. Analysis will suggest that adult rural education possesses a complex history, reflects specific value assumptions set within specific cultural contexts, targets specific audiences, and attempts to redeem non-collegiate rural adults from their perceived deficiencies. Accordingly, this discussion will identify major twentieth century programmatic thrusts for rural adults.

Long (1983) suggested that adult education demonstrates the attributes of creativity, pragmatism, volunteerism, pluralism, and dynamism. Such concepts may well describe overt characteristics of adult rural education. However, a review and critique of research concerning adult rural education must integrate other conceptual tools. The context of societal structure, advocacy, power, powerlessness, and resource allocation suggests assumptions about the needs of the rural adult audience.

Analysis of rural adult education in the United States during the twentieth century thus addresses major uses of education to solve problems of rural America as depicted in historical, educational, and agricultural literature. Specifically, focus will be brought upon agricultural education and home demonstration work, literacy training programs, adult training programs related to the New Deal and World War II, and human and community development programs since 1960. Attention will also be given to the impact of programs upon minorities, especially blacks and women. While emphasis will be placed on twentieth century developments, some mention will be made of educational efforts by the Grangers and the Farmers Alliance in the late nineteenth century. Both private and public sector bureaucracies will be scrutinized as they represent the rationalized efforts of organizations which systematize educational experiences.

A wide range of other quasi-educational endeavor might conceivably be considered as rural adult education. Religious revivals, political campaigns, and social movements all represent activities which include educational dimensions. Such activities, however, broaden the definition of adult education beyond a scope appropriate to the confines of this analysis. Only when such activities include formalized efforts to educate rural adults will their efforts be included. Thus, the citizenship schools in South Carolina and the Highlander School in Tennessee definitely merit inclusion. Likewise, farm wagons or farm literature designed to convey important principles of cultivation and animal husbandry may be considered within this analytical framework. A broader inclusionary framework also raises conceptual questions regarding the boundaries between conventional educational activity and other disciplines. The boundaries suggested by concepts such as socialization, enculturation, recruitment, advertising, propaganda, conflict, and alienation imply adult learning in a multitude of contexts. Adult education for this discussion focuses on narrower parameters suggested by concepts such as media, teaching, training, schools, interests, needs, curricula, goals, objectives, and learning activities. However, the contextual meanings in which rural adult education occurs will be taken into account.

Adult Education and the Agricultural Sector: Modernizing the "Reluctant Farmer"

In an early twentieth century report, "The Colleges and Rural Life," Frederick Gates, a Baptist minister and personal assistant of John D. Rockefeller responsible for organizing the oil tycoon's philanthropies, presented his assessment of the problems facing many rural southern communities. What he described were "one room hovels" for schools, better "fitted to be an engine of torture," villages with "emaciated . . . misshapen or bloated bodies," and "sad, pale, listless, hopeless faces." On the landscape he saw "worn out soil . . . abandoned fields overgrown with bushes . . . tumbledown houses" all "loudly proclaiming disease, poverty, thriftlessness, neglect." This picture should not have become a reality. The victims were of Anglo-Saxon lineage; the southern communities were disproportionately Christian when compared to other regions of the country. Clearly something had gone wrong in the agrarian community (Neufeldt, 1984; Maxey, 1981).

Gates' picture provides a convenient backdrop from which to analyze twentieth century educational activities for rural adults. Much of rural education, especially agricultural and home demonstration efforts, have been undertaken to solve the contradiction between rural realities and the agrarian myth. The agrarian myth depicted the rural life as one of supreme virtue, superior culture, and free of want and poverty. It also had an idealized version of the farmer, self-sufficient and devoid of greed. Unfortunately, the agrarian myth did not fit many rural realities, not only in the southern states but in much of the nation. Migration of rural folk to metropolitan centers should never have occurred. After all, cities in Thomas Jefferson's agrarian image were devoid of sanitation, virtue, beauty, and wholesome living. The displacement of farmers, the recurring farm crises, the commercialization of agriculture all stood in stark contrast to the agrarian image. And if one added to these problems the loneliness, drabness, toil, and drudgery experienced by rural women, it was clear that something had gone wrong in the agricultural garden. Adult education has been one suggested solution to right the wrongs suffered by rural Americans.

In 1908 Theodore Roosevelt's Country Life Commission issued its state of rural America report. This was not the first attempt to discover rural problems and assess blame for their existence. Grangers, Farmers Alliances, and Populists had blamed excessive railway rates, political corruption, and restrictive money supplies for various aspects of late nineteenth century rural decline (Saloutos, 1960; Clevenger, 1945; Mitchell, 1987). Others blamed an outdated rural church or the one-room rural school (Ellsworth, 1960). The Country Life Commission's significance rested in its attempt to examine agriculture in the context of an industrialized and urbanized society (Danborn, 1975; Ellsworth, 1960).

The Country Life Commission was part of a larger phenomenon, the Country Life Movement. Several characteristics of the movement, as highlighted by William Bowers, are important for an analysis of adult education. The Country Life Commission held an "unbounded faith in the efficacy of education . . . especially agricultural education" as an instrument for regenerating rural America. Another characteristic was the attempt to incorporate two groups with two differing images of rural America. One group, representing an "agriculture as business" viewpoint, called for the creation of efficient and scientific farmers. Advocates of this position were instrumental in founding the American Farm Bureau Federation.

The other group, indebted to an older agrarian image, envisioned farming as a superior way of life. This second group basically initiated the Country Life Movement, and its members importantly included urban based religious leaders, academicians, and social workers who called for a rejuvenation of social and cultural life in rural society. The Country Life Movement reflected an urban perspective with recommendations for school consolidation, farm mechanization, and rural electrification: this despite its romanticized image of the agrarian ideal. Race, ethnicity, and farm tenancy were viewed primarily from a white, Anglo-Saxon perspective (Ellsworth,1960; Bowers,1974).

The Country Life Commission was not the first group to discuss problems and propose solutions for rural America. The Grangers, The Farmers Alliance, Populists, and the Chautauqua movement all made efforts to address rural ills and all engaged in adult rural education to some degree. Gould (1961) discussed the manner in which the Chautauqua movement provided a wide variety of adult education opportunities for rural adults. Smith (1941) highlighted the efforts of Texas Grangers to educate members concerning crop diversification, the use of new machinery, new methods of cultivation, improved public schools, and the need for new methods of cooperative financing. The Grangers utilized reading rooms, set up libraries, Granger Halls, and sponsored lectures. Crompton (1965), Clevenger (1945), and Saloutos (1960) provide discussions of the Farmers Alliances efforts of the late nineteenth and early twentieth centuries to provide adult education activities. Such educational efforts ranged from the dissemination of newsletters to conferences and camps.

The most extensive study of the educational activities of late nineteenth century farm organizations is Theodore Mitchell's *Political Education in the Southern Farmers' Alliance, 1887–1900.* Mitchell (1987) argues that the Alliance sought to educate rural adults to enable them to participate in a culture created by the Alliance. Its leaders sought to unite farmers and rural producers and thereby strengthen class identification and highlight class conflict. The Alliance sought to demystify government by providing farmers with the basic tools of literacy and political analysis. Because of the high illiteracy rate among rural farmers, the Alliance emphasized the use of lectures. Mitchell's study, unlike Clevenger's or Smith's, goes beyond describing what was taught to analyzing what was learned. The Alliance emphasized the need for a new education in the public schools. In the end, however, public school reform took place on terms and agenda set by the Southern Education Movement and not by the Alliance. Its educational campaign ignored blacks. Such a blindspot is evident in twentieth century farm movements as well (Loomis, 1953). Mitchell's study raises serious questions as to the efficacy of forays by farm organizations into adult education as a viable solution for problems facing rural America.

The efforts of Grangers, Farm Alliances, and farm demonstration work at agricultural colleges were finally recognized by the Federal government in its passage of the Smith-Lever Act in 1914. The Smith Lever Act institutionalized extension work as a major twentieth century form of adult education (Scott, 1970). Smith-Lever included extension work for adults males and females through the use of county and home demonstration agents. It sought to balance local, state, and national interests in agricultural education. Scott analyzed the rise of extension as a tool of adult education in *The Reluctant Farmer: The Rise of Agricultural Extension to 1914.* Scott's work can be supplemented by True's (1928) earlier description. Scott describes various attempts to provide adult education for farmers prior to 1914. Institutes, fairs, farm wagons and trains, involvement in agricultural corporations, and the activities of agricultural colleges and experiment stations all provided rural adult education.

Scott highlights the respective efforts of Seaman Knapp and William J. Spillman in the South and the North to legitimate the extension agent concept as a teaching resource. Scott also notes the reluctance of the farmer to accept advice and change farming methods. Farmers' institutes, farm wagons, and farm trains served an important function in rural adult education. They communicated information concerning the use of technology and new cultivation methods for increasing productivity (Moss, 1988; Lass, 1953; Scott, 1960; Loomis, 1953).

Farmers' institutes sought to educate rural women as well. Tuskegee Institute used the farm wagon and the farm truck to educate black adults. Studies which focus on Tuskegee Institute and its adult education efforts convey the up-beat, positive images promoted by Booker T. Washington (James, 1971; McGee, 1984; Campbell, 1970).

In the early twentieth century few individuals had a greater impact in defining adult education than Seaman Knapp. Northern philanthropic organizations, such as the General Education Board, used Knapp's methods to guide their effort in attempting to make the agrarian myth become a reality in the South. A former president of Iowa State College, Knapp was appointed special agent for the Promotion of Agriculture in the South in 1903. Knapp concluded that rural adult education must bring the college to the farmer through farm demonstrations. If the farmer could only accept the new demonstration methods then neither poverty, farm tenancy, nor the boll weevil could undermine the agrarian myth (Neufeldt, 1984; Bailey, 1945). Knapp's work also reflected the racial attitudes of the period. The General Education Board, which underwrote much of Knapp's work, made only one grant for demonstration work among black farmers (Fosdick, 1962; Neufeldt, 1984; Rasmussen, 1989).

Farm demonstration under the Smith Lever Act envisioned the agent as the key to rural adult education. Gender biases were evident in the emergence of two types of agents. The county agent, a male, worked with farmers (Sachs, 1983). The home demonstration agent, a female, worked with housewives. Gladys Baker's 1930 study of the agent in Iowa, New York, and Alabama is a landmark effort. Although limited in its analysis of the agents' educational activities, it provides a strong political analysis of the county agent system. Baker was sensitive to the tensions between national and local interests in the agent system as well as the agents' subservience to the interests of wealthier farmers active in the Farm Bureau. By the 1930s, the agents' educational efforts shifted from engaging in a broad form of agricultural education to disseminating specialized reports of interest to the Farm Bureau. Baker showed remarkable sensitivity to racial practices within the agent system. Neither black nor white agents tended to work or identify with one third of the farmers. The poor tenant farmers and small, poor farmers were effectively ignored. In the end the poor farmers identified with the United States Department of Labor rather than with the Department of Agriculture (Baker, 1920; Rasmussen, III, 1975).

The black agricultural agent has received minimal review from scholars. At first, only two black agents were appointed at Tuskegee and Hampton Institutes. And it is primarily Tuskegee agent Thomas Campbell who has received any attention at all (James, 1971; Jones, 1976; Crosby, 1982, 1986). James' work is primarily descriptive, highly laudatory, and based heavily upon Campbell's interpretation of his own work. Jones and Crosby provide greater analytical rigor, exploring the work of the black agent within an historical and a racial context. Some black farmers benefitted economically from the activities of county agents.

Crosby points out, however, the black agent was unable to alter the "basic situation of black abject poverty and exploitation" (Crosby, 1983, p. 288).

If the county agent were to improve the farmers' economic status, the home demonstration agent sought to improve the quality of life for the rural homemaker. Cynthia Sturgis (1986) overviewed the assumption of many policy makers that the flight from the country side to the city was led by women seeking to avoid the loneliness and drudgery associated with the rural home. And, it appears that home demonstration agents were of little help in stemming the tide of rural poor women, as their efforts primarily benefitted the more economically successful farm women (Galleys, 1958; Fessenden, 1958).

Home demonstration agents tended to be disproportionately white and worked primarily with white farm families. An experiment by the Penn School did focus upon blacks in the Sea Islands of South Carolina and Georgia (Cooley, 1930; Jacaway 1980; Robbins, 1964). Home and farm demonstrations, corn and tomato clubs, and a revitalized rural school provided the focal point for the Sea Islands effort. Northern philanthropists funded such education in response to fears of black migration to northern urban centers. There is also some evidence of home demonstration work among native American and Hispanic households in the southwest prior to World War II (Jensen, 1986).

A follow-up of Scott's work which traces county extension work from 1914 to the present remains to be written. Rasmussen's (1989) *Taking the Universities to the People: Seventy Five Years of Cooperative Extension* summarizes the various extension activities since the passage of the Smith-Lever Act. However, Rasmussen's work lacks critical analysis and appears to be a status report which defends the extension concept. More useful is Rasmussen's multi-volume *Documentary History of Agriculture*, particularly volumes two and three. Here are several descriptive studies of institutional efforts in farm extension and home demonstration work. Tuskegee Institute has received much of the attention due to George Washington Carver's work in agricultural experimentation (Harlan, 1972; McGee, 1984; Gardner, 1975; McMurray, 1981). Booker T. Washington presented his concept of self-reliance, uplift, and education in *Working With Hands* (1904). Harlan (1972) points out that Negro Conferences emphasized racial accommodation, thrift, self-help, and crop diversification to showcase Tuskegee ideology.

The New York State College of Agriculture at Cornell University provides a white counterpart in farm demonstration and experimentation to that of Tuskegee. Coleman (1963) provides a useful institutional biography of Cornell's efforts in organizing farmer's institutes in the late nineteenth century, the use of farm trains in the early twentieth century, the use of the radio in the 1920s, and the development of short courses and institutes after World War II. Coleman's study delineates the difficulties created by the close ties between the county agents and the Farm Bureau, suggesting that Cornell's activities disproportionately benefitted more prosperous farmers.

Studies of state efforts at farm extension and home demonstration also tend to be more descriptive and laudatory than analytical. Burlingame's (1977) description of Montana's extension efforts prior to 1930 offers proof that local communities could effectively design and administer programs. Montana apparently demonstrated that democratically oriented cooperative efforts could combine local, state, and national constituencies to discover solutions in times of crisis. Similarly, other laudatory accounts of experimental research and demonstration in Manitoba (Canada), Minnesota, North Dakota, Utah, and New Hampshire suggested positive results (Murray, 1967; Rasmussen, 1975). Yet, such laudatory studies point to problems associated with the evaluation of demonstration and extension work. They describe what was attempted but failed to systematically assess what rural adults actually learned and internalized. Recently, Malcolm Knowles (1977) concluded that "rural adult education . . . provided a demonstration that adult education—when in step with technological progress—can make a difference in the life of a nation" (p. 94). However, Knowles' "understanding" of the historical record to substantiate much of his own current work is overly simplistic, as it, too, is built primarily upon assumptions rather than evidence.

Hurt's (1981) social history of the dustbowl includes descriptions of fourteen soil conservation demonstration projects. The impact on the actual behavior of farmers is not actually known. In a similar manner Schweiber (1986) concludes that the Iowa State College's Department of Home Economics must have had a significant impact on thousands of Iowa women. They apparently prepared more nutritious meals, established more efficient kitchens, raised work to a more efficient level, and raised women's self concept. Yet, Schweiber did not provide the data necessary to justify such conclusions.

More formal and technical approaches to evaluation of extensions' work have been attempted by Hoffman (1978) and Araji, Sim, and Gardner (1978). Both studies conclude that extension work did have a significant impact on farming methodology. The success stories of extension work fail to deal with several basic objectives inherent in rural adult education. It is clear that extension work did not help to reclaim the agrarian myth nor did it stop migration to urban centers. Extension work has consistently favored the larger commercial farmer (Araji, Sim, & Gardner, 1978). Even Tuskegee's highly publicized demonstration activities did not significantly alter poverty and exploitation experienced by the majority of black farmers.

Mass media have also historically played a role in rural adult education. Scholars have been especially sensitive to the role of the agricultural press. The Grangers and Farmers Alliances published their own papers. The southern farmers' press has received the most attention (Beck, 1952; Osborne, 1955; Scruggs & Smith, 1979; Socolofski, 1957). Yet, the South's high illiteracy rate suggests that the press relied upon a selective readership.

Beck provides perhaps the most comprehensive study of the southern agricultural press prior to 1900. What emerges from his analysis of the *Progressive Farmer* and other publications was an emphasis upon modernization, progressive reform, and white supremacist attitudes. Assessments of the agricultural press suggest that editors of farm magazines were simplistic in their view of farm life. Editors focused their attention on farmers engaged in commercial agriculture and ignored poor subsistence farmers (Ferrell, 1977). Farm magazines thus bought into an optimistic view of the agrarian myth. Only the periodicals published by radical farm organizations consistently recognized the plight of the subsistence farmers and sharecroppers (Dyson, 1971).

In a similar manner radio and library addressed the needs of commercial farmers yet ignored the plight of subsistence farmers and sharecroppers and painted a simplistic view of farm problems. Wik (1988) and Hyde (1929) analyzed the early development of radio to aid in farm extension work. In 1929 the United States Department of Agriculture accepted the offer of the National Broadcasting Company to transmit daily agricultural radio programs. Loomis (1953) analyzed the role of public libraries as vehicles for rural adult education.

With the exception of black adult education, the role of the church and religious institutions for educative purposes has been largely ignored. The March 1912 issue of the *American Academy of Political and Social Sciences* was devoted to problems of rural America. Roberts and Israel (1912) provided a brief glimpse at the work of the YMCA in rural areas. Loomis devoted a chapter to the church in rural America and described self-help and educational activities of Jewish, Roman Catholic, and Protestant churches. Discussion of rural education efforts of the Roman Catholic church have been primarily focused in Nova Scotia and Canada (MacLellan, 1935).

Adult Education: The Great Depression and World War II

The great Depression put the agrarian dream into further jeopardy. Several themes reemerged. Education, including adult education (along with relief), was proposed as a solution for the problems of drought, dust farming, and poverty. Once again the limited success of education for remedying problems of economic dislocation became evident. Agricultural recovery probably stemmed less from governmental initiatives in education than from the outbreak of World War II. Yet, depression era programs once again reflected gender and racial bias, and influenced which groups received what kinds of educational assistance. The federal government became a major participant in these educational programs, but in the end power and economic relationships changed very little.

One smaller program of the New Deal, however, did carry within it a vision of possible change. Paul Conklin (1959) described the attempt to establish some one hundred New Deal communities as a "fascinating adventure in idealism and disillusionment" (p. 6). Designed as settlement communities for carefully selected homesteaders, farm supervisors, cooperative specialists, extension teachers, vocational agricultural teachers, and specialists in handicrafts and the arts carefully planned and guided the experiments. Borrowing heavily from progressive educational ideas, the homestead communities sought to enrich rural adults, providing education from the cradle to the grave. Their forays into ceramics, landscaping, woodworking, and metalworking were intended to rebuild community spirit and restore pride in workmanship. Yet, part of their eventual failure stemmed from the romanticized concept of rural life brought to the countryside by planners from America's cities (Conklin, 1959). Meanwhile, black settlement communities reflected very little romanticism. Based on the assumption that integration was impossible, four black settlements were organized and carefully separated from neighboring communities (Holby, 1971).

Resettlement programs met opposition from wealthier farmers and the Farm Bureau. The clash between the Department of Agriculture and the Farm Bureau came to a head by 1936. The Department of Agriculture programs operated on the assumption that rural America required relief, recovery, and land reform. The settlement communities reflected a strong commitment to this last factor. Yet, the Farm Bureau called for relief and recovery only, never questioning land ownership practices (Campbell, 1962).

The Civilian Conservation Corp (CCC) and the National Youth Administration (NYA) provided training programs for young adults, especially white male adults. The CCC operated as a rural based program drawing participants from both rural and urban sectors, male, female, black, and white. Frank Hill's study of the CCC camps reveals that a wide variety of educational activities took place but depended upon the attitude of the camp commander. Some camps had extensive literacy and vocational training programs while others functioned primarily as labor camps (Hill, 1935). Kincheloe (1985) described the literacy training programs in considerable detail. The CCC camps reflected a gender and racial bias. New Deal administrators assumed the male to be the head of the home. Consequently it was the unemployed male who needed assistance. Aside from literacy training, female camps provided little vocational training until administrative changes placed them under the National Youth Administration in 1935 (Kornbluth, 1984). Similarly, blacks enrolled in limited numbers and were primarily given literacy training, elementary level schooling, and some vocational training for low skill jobs such as janitor, chauffeur, waiter, and dishwasher (Grant, forthcoming; Salmond, 1965; Daniel and Miller, 1938; Wright, 1940).

The Tennessee Valley Authority (TVA) also became heavily involved in rural adult education. Its programs of electrification, flood control, and fertilizer production offered a solution for the problems of rural southern poverty and isolation. TVA programs sought to modernize as well as maintain a viable rural community. TVA viewed rural adult education as essential if southern rural adults were to participate in a modernized South. Furthermore, TVA required a trained work force to construct dams. Under the leadership of Arthur Ernst Morgan, TVA launched an ambitious adult education apprenticeship programs at dam construction sites (Clayton, 1975; Grant, 1981). Skilled labor training programs for blacks, were nonexistent. Like other federal programs, blacks received training in janitorial service, housework, agriculture, and semi-skilled jobs traditionally open to blacks. Unable and unwilling to resolve the conflict between its own promises of non-discrimination and its respect for local customs, the TVA provided future oriented programs for white adults. As Grant (1989; forthcoming) and Bond (1938) point out, TVA programs for blacks once again helped perpetuate the status quo in the South.

The literature on governmental initiatives in adult education during the 1930s is limited. Historians have been interested primarily in the political and economic aspects of the New Deal and TVA programs. Education has rarely been their major interest. Consequently, treatments of educational activities remain peripheral and sketchy, descriptive but not analytical. Exceptions include studies such as Joyce Kornbluth's (1987) analysis of New Deal workers' education programs. Kornbluth's interest in workers' education programs and their relationship to the American

Federation of Labor reflects an urban perspective. Workers' education programs had to resolve the problem of possible conflict between local, state, and national educational policies. Such programs struggled to resolve tensions between federally funded programs and the wishes of the national labor leadership as well as resolve tensions created between federally funded programs and conservative political realities. Kornbluth's evidence suggests that workers' programs were somewhat successful; that labor unions and workers were involved in the planning of educational projects; and that many progressive teaching methods which had been developed by adult educators during the 1920s were utilized.

Yet, despite Kornbluth's positive evaluation, the overall significance of New Deal workers' educational programs remains in doubt. The primary goal of the New Deal was recovery and relief, not education. This was especially true of the Emergency Education Program, the major purpose of which sought to provide employment for qualified teachers. These teachers presumably received employment in rural elementary schools, provided vocational training for handicapped adults, and taught adults to become self-supporting citizens. Nursery schools functioned as a form of rural adult education by providing special programs of benefit to the entire family. Stated goals for workers' educational programs were written as broadly as possible to create a constituency for adult education which transcended literacy training. Some of the vocational programs prepared women for low-skilled positions as household maids. Many of the literacy programs bypassed the rural black adults in southern states (Punke, 1929; Punke, 1935; Woodward, 1929, Smith & Donald, 1935; Chalmers, 1935).

Currently, New Deal programs for women are beginning to receive the attention of scholars. Kornbluth's study of the "She-She-She Camps," analyzes the political and social restraints placed upon CCC camps set aside for females. Women's CCC camps remain of secondary interest because policy makers presumed the male to be in need of relief payments. Furthermore, females were typically not even allowed to be taken off the campsites for training for limited work and apprenticeship opportunities (Kornbluth, 1984; Kornbluth, 1987; Ware, 1985). Most educators assumed women were not the major decision makers on farms.

Consequently, females were seldom offered vocational training in agriculture. The introduction of science to rural America legitimated existing practices. Men were instructed in scientific agricultural knowledge at agricultural colleges, while females were taught "scientific" homemaking skills (Sachs, 1983; Smith & Wilson, 1930).

On the other hand, the Summer School for Women Workers envisioned a more radical approach to female education. From 1927 until World War II, Sweet Briar College hosted the sessions in which participants came from farms, sharecropper homes, and small towns. The Summer School for Women Workers set forth a more radical agenda, seeking to recruit workers and leaders for labor unions in textile industries (Fredrickson, 1984).

Educational activities for rural black adults continue to receive the attention of several scholars. Private religious, philanthropic, and fraternal organizations played the major role in black adult education prior to 1930. Federal governmental funding became increasingly important during the 1930s (Franklin, forthcoming; Williams, forthcoming; Bullock, 1945; Height, 1945; Moorland, 1924; Muraskin, 1976). Just what these governmental initiatives meant for the future of blacks in America is not clear. Howard Sitkoff (1985) provides a positive assessment of the New Deal's impact on black adults, arguing that New Deal initiatives gave hope for the future that was different from the past. Reid (1945), Reddick (1945), Weis, (1983) and Grant (forthcoming) offer more negative conclusions. Grant concludes that if governmental initiatives indicated future opportunities, then the future would greatly resemble the past. Substantial evidence supports Grant's conclusion: in the agricultural sector, rural southern blacks gained little despite the increase of governmental funding. Southern states often used federal funds to expand research programs at white colleges and hire additional white county agents. Only Tuskegee and Hampton Institute participated in the research programs. The minority of black farmers who received assistance from these programs did benefit. The Farm Security Administration provided some training for black farmers by selecting interns at experimental farms. These farms, designated as adult education centers served some 1700 black families (Grant, forthcoming; McAlister and McAlister, 1945; Herbert, 1945, Wilkerson, 1938). Similarly, war industries and the armed forces reflected racial discrimination during World War II (Evans, 1945; Lane, 1964; Reddick, 1947; Grant, forthcoming). Governmental efforts to promote the hiring of blacks in skilled vocational training programs met with only limited success (Wilkerson, 1942;, Branson, 1943; Caliver, 1937; Wilkerson and Penn, 1938; Thompson, 1938; Grant, forthcoming, and Hill, 1985).

Literacy and Civic Education

The literature reviewed in preceding sections points to a rich lode of knowledge regarding adult rural education. Many of the studies, however, were the work of trained historians whose domain often remains separate from the domain of adult education specialists. Indeed, adult educators sometimes refer to what appears to be the ahistorical and nonphilosophical nature of the discipline (Hill, 1981). However, the previous literature identified assumptions concerning the parameters of which groups should benefit from rural adult education. Closely linked to visions of modern rural life stand related assumptions about how adults should behave as citizens in modern rural society. Assumptions about citizenship behavior merit elaboration to further understand many hopes for rural adult education. Studies which address adult literacy instruction and civic participation point toward root assumptions upon which rural adult education justifies and defines itself.

Literacy still represents the key through which a variety of civic virtues, vices, and cures may be addressed and achieved. Specific historical studies have examined the role of adult literacy instruction in relationship to perceived needs and deficits designed to empower adults or to integrate them into the dominant economic and social mainstream. Such historical studies, however, differ in scope and thoroughness. Cook's (1971) comprehensive, broad brushed discussion of adult literacy instruction since 1900 focuses on programs without examining underlying cultural assumptions. Cook identified basic goals of adult literacy instruction and changing definitions of literacy. However, his work (among others) assumes a deficit model, with a focus on integrating and retrofitting adults into the job market and/or helping to Americanize immigrants. Yet, the actual characteristics of such rural residents relevant to understanding their "deficits" are rarely forthcoming in such scholarship. In addition, the nature of resource allocation provides a theme worthy of further analysis in conjunction with seemingly cyclical discovery of illiteracy as a shocking societal ill.

Akenson and Neufeldt (1984; 1985a; 1985b, 1986, forthcoming), Estes, Neufeldt, and Akenson (1988), and Kincheloe (1985) have all examined the southern literacy campaign in the early twentieth century, using combinations of oral history, primary documents, and statistical data. The southern literacy campaign evolved in the context of the progressive movement and a heightened awareness of literacy needs for a modern agricultural and industrial South. Literacy became likened to a malady, a blight, upon the illiterate individual and upon society which contributed to crime, impaired physical health, hindered social and economic development, and weakened national defense.

Akenson and Neufeldt (1983) reported on the social pathological view of illiteracy. Publications produced by agencies such as the Illiteracy Commission of Alabama discussed illiteracy in terms of a "black stain" and implied crime could be reduced through literacy and the process of aided modernization. Akenson and Neufeldt also examined statistical data to determine the actual impact of the southern literacy campaign on illiteracy. Despite the rhetoric, the actual data suggest that rural adult education failed to make the desired impact. The reduction in illiteracy resulted from other factors such as death and increased schooling opportunities for children. Such analyses parallel those cited earlier regarding extension and its actual impact, as opposed to the uncritical perceptions of the rural adult educators.

Descriptive memoirs and laudatory biographies of the Kentucky Moonlight Schools (Stewart, 1922) and Wil Lou Gray of South Carolina (Montgomery, 1963) reflect the important missionary zeal and belief in the ultimate triumph of a righteous cause characteristic of the early twentieth century literary campaigns. Yet, the evangelistic rhetoric, unrealistic expectations, and limited resources identified in historical analyses have yet to be expunged from adult literacy education in the late twentieth century.

The southern literacy campaign witnessed instruction through Moonlight schools, Cotton Mill schools, Lay-By schools, and Opportunity schools delivered through specific curricula to rural southern adults. The early twentieth century saw emphasis upon a wide range of basic literacy instruction which emphasized everyday applications such as reading the Bible, newspapers, letters, and road signs. In addition, basic arithmetic skills found practice in word problems based upon the cost of cotton, groceries, and clothing. On the periphery stood lessons in nutrition, history, civics, and personal hygiene which addressed a mixed bag of civic virtues. Cleanliness, knowledge of government, and healthful living supported civic goals. Knowledgeable, literate adults, it was argued, would participate in progressive government, defend the United States, and advance the cause of a progressive agricultural and industrial South. The heart of the southern literacy campaign curricula, however, remained a basic emphasis upon reading instruction, writing, and arithmetic skills.

Rural adult literacy instruction, however, cannot be understood outside of the context of assumptions concerning citizenship or civic education. During the southern literacy campaign civic education materials received the attention of South Carolina and Kentucky leaders (Akenson & Neufeldt, 1986). Wil Lou Gray (1927) published *Elementary Studies in Civics*, a text which stressed good citizenship in terms of voting and the need for taxes to pay for roads and schools. Cora Wilson Stewart (1915, 1917) published *Country Life Readers* designed to help adults realize the necessity of good roads, taxes, voting, and related concepts. Akenson and Neufeldt's analysis pointed out its inherent patriotic purposes and desire to upgrade the New South. Stubblefield (1973) analyzed the civic participation concept in adult education from Colonial times to the present. Stubblefield defined civic participation as education for political understanding and participation in the political process and the maintenance and strengthening of those elements essential for a democratic society" (p. 176).

Akenson and Neufeldt's analysis, however, suggested that participants in Opportunity Schools attended because of rather simple reasons—reading the Bible or newspaper, being with friends, or learning new skills which would help in their employment. Yet in the eyes of southern literacy campaigners, politically conservative ends appear to have been central, i.e., that illiterates might fit into the emerging New South.

Akenson's 1984 analysis further suggests that the literacy campaigns of the late twentieth century exhibit many of the same assumptions and characteristics of the earlier literacy campaigns. One only need examine contemporary documents such as "The Design and Administrative Management of Literacy Training Programs in South Carolina" (Harris, 1984) and "State Models for Literacy Partnerships" (Harris, 1984) to realize the continuity of literacy instruction throughout the twentieth century. Previous analysis in this chapter identified similar, parallel forces in the impact of the Farm Bureau and wealthy farmers on the extension agents carried with it similar assumptions concerning the good of modern technology and the implied need for citizens to support the existing set of social and economic relationships.

Literacy instruction represented an important component of one institution with a specific civic mission. Less centralist, and fraught with their own problems, stand several alternative rural adult education initiatives such as that represented by the Highlander Folk School in Tennessee. Horton (1971), Glenn (1988), and Oldendorf (1987, 1989) dealt with the work of Myles Horton to develop the Highlander Folk School as a social reconstructionist institution tied into the "history of dissent and reform and the American South . . . " (Glenn, p. 220).

Highlander's initial activities addressed the needs of the mountain poor in Grundy County, Tennessee. Highlander subsequently focused upon a multitude of political activities designed to help educate workers and minorities to advance their interests against the dominant system. Highlander received the endorsement of John Dewey and George Counts, who sympathized with the reconstructionist orientation of the school. Such civic education concepts stand in stark contrast to most of the previously reviewed adult education programs, and the eventual closing of places like Highlander suggests the inherent difficulty of defining adult civic education outside dominant educational, cultural, political, and economic structures. Stated simply, adult rural education exists as an activity supported by state mandated bureaucratic systems or interest groups that essentially support existing institutional relationships.

The concepts associated with adult civic education point to a broader range of issues based upon the entire adult education enterprise. Long's (1983) concepts of activity, volunteerism, pragmatism, creativity, and dynamism provide overt, global descriptions of programmatic attributes. Long's concepts reflect the surface neutrality of adult education work that focuses upon the identification of needs and tendency for apparently technical studies to focus upon the specifics of programmatic content, the outcomes of instruction, and the needs of the targeted adult audience. Jacobs (1966) dealt with an analysis of farmstead mechanization as it related to farmers and related agribusinesses. As a result, Jacobs suggested specific implications for inclusion in the vocational-technical agriculture curriculum. Kroupa (1970) analyzed basic agricultural information which farmers encountered on radio and television. Analysis of such information and comprehension level of such information pointed to specific ways in which agricultural content could be structured for maximum understanding.

Omer (1987) analyzed factors which correlated with the participation of young Iowa farmers in agricultural extension programs. Such an analysis helps program planning by including content which addresses the needs of the target audience. In turn, the likelihood of participation in agricultural extension by the target audience may be increased. Such studies take the concept of need as a pivotal given. If needs can be identified, then rural adult education services may be structured and delivered. Meeting the needs of the rural adult suggests that a larger portion of the target audience will avail themselves of the services.

Overt characteristics as identified by Long reflect deeper conceptual underpinnings. Hill (1981) critiqued dominant concepts related to adult education focusing upon utility, individualism, empiricism, self-fulfillment, and curriculum. Such an analysis demands substantive depth of discussion and should contextualize adult education in the historical and cultural matrix of assumptions which define it. The nuances of such concepts and their relationship to socio-political power certainly merit further elaboration as do the tensions inherent between self-fulfillment, individualism, and responsible action to benefit society.

Hill concluded that adult education should bring about the "cultivation of the intellect and the civilized emotions" which make students "ever more conscious of the true unity of humankind" (p. 100). Civic education, the role of liberal arts, literacy instruction, extension and demonstration work, as well as vocational training require greater analysis of nuances to successfully critique and integrate the adult education enterprise. In addition, the manner in which such concepts differ in application to rural adult education as opposed to urban settings also merit consideration.

A more complicated line of inquiry relates to the manner in which concepts may be appropriated out of one discipline or educational context and applied to another educational context. Apple (1972) pointed out the manner in which the borrowing of biological/business metaphors such as *system* result in educational applications with specific applications unintended in their original disciplinary context. Examining the manner in which a system maintains itself often keeps one from raising questions of justice and equity. The model used to analyze, describe, and direct programs, instruction, or research exerts a powerful influence not evident when concepts are borrowed. Likewise, Gouldner's (1970) analysis of the origin of Talcott Parsons' functionalist sociological theory points to the manner in which apparently objective knowledge hides a variety of sentiments, subjective predispositions embedded in the life and times of the researcher.

Two examples relate to rural adult education and questions of borrowing. First, works by Paulo Friere such as *The Pedagogy of the Oppressed* (1970) appeal to literacy educators and bureaucrats. Department of adult education officials in one southern state routinely refer to Friere and empowerment and make available video tapes based upon the Highlander Folk School experience. Literacy instruction supposedly should be a vehicle for empowerment. However, other routine statements (consistent with national literature analyzing the needs of illiterate adults) point to the need for a positive self-concept and literate workers who can function successfully in the existing workplace. Such goals hardly seem consistent with Friere's social reconstructionist equation designed to transform political structures.

Adult education which helps newly literate adults find jobs within the existing economic system hardly represents a transformative education that challenges existing inequities. Adopting terms such as "empowerment" mean little when removed from the totality of Friere's theory and the third world context of the 1960s from which it evolved. White and Rose (1988) reveal the ultimate in removing the empowerment concept from its contextual meaning. Empowerment is reduced to guidelines in community education to ". . . contact senior citizen groups to determine what educational programs or services are provided . . . " and to "appoint older adults to current community education advisory committee (White and Rose, p. 22). Similarly, Kovel-Jarboe (1987) viewed the use of satellites, videotapes, interactive videodiscs, and computer networks as bringing about empowerment.

Kovel-Jarboe dealt with the application of technology for empowerment in rural adult learners on topics such as mastitis prevention, suicide prevention, selecting and working with a lawyer, and consumer information systems. Such very limited empowerment expectations which now fill the rhetorical world in adult education are easy to find. For example, the *Rural Adult Education FORUM* (1989) titled a news item "Empowerment Through Education-Tillamook Bay Community College." The article described the community college service district as a ". . . way for rural residents to empower themselves through education" (p.6).

Wrongly adopting the politically charged Highlander and Friere social reconstructionist terminology to adult rural adult education points to an additional question regarding the adoption of models and concepts: Do the actual results of the model justify the enthusiasm of the advocates desiring its adoption? Language from Friere may well have worked itself into the vocabulary of literacy educators. However, did the actual track record of Friere's equation (including the interdisciplinary study teams) result in the transformational results claimed? One need not expect Friere's model to be adopted on a wide scale in Brazil. Specific evidence beyond anecdotal descriptions, however, would be appropriate to expect before opting for borrowing such concepts.

In the case of Highlander, the entire nature of success for social reconstructionist activities may be open to question. Highlander shifted priorities many times. Such shifts may well reflect the ability of less complex organizations to be flexible in the face of newly emergent needs. It might also mean the lack of a clearly defined mission beyond the conceptual focus "that education could be used to push for fundamental social, economic, and political change leading to what they saw as a more democratic and humane society" (Glenn, p. 221). One may admire and sympathize with the Highlander thrust, yet realize the validity of Glenn's observation that Highlander methods often lacked coherence or produced lasting results (p. 222). At the very least, Highlander's social reconstructionist approach to civic education is difficult to execute, even in the hands of committed persons. Enthusiasm and commitment may not produce the clear evidence to justify adopting and adapting a specific model from a different setting.

The southern literacy campaign as well as the Friere and Highlander Folk School examples raise a variety of interesting observations and vexing questions. The predominantly rural southern literacy campaign raises points regarding the distinctions which may be drawn regarding uniqueness of rural education. The participation of southern leaders in national organizations such as the American Association for Adult Education as well as formal training and professional relationships with major urban universities minimized rural and regional characteristics. Reading specialist and University of Chicago dean William S. Gray (1932) published an analysis of the predominantly rural South Carolina Opportunity Schools through the American Association of Adult Education. Supervisor of Adult Education, Wil Lou Gray, maintained close professional ties with Columbia University faculty as well as the Adult Education Association. Future studies dealing with rural adult education should address the degree to which rural adult education actually differs from adult education in urban areas. Questions of distance and resource allocation appear to be major concerns in all of rural education. Technical problems, however, do not necessarily equate to actual differences in the instructional process or curriculum content. Thus, questions arise: What is rural adult education and how does it differ from adult education in urban settings? Does a national network of educators working on a common task result in a uniformity of content and delivery regardless of the setting? To what extent can educational concepts be borrowed from setting to setting, discipline to discipline, and applied to rural adult education without altering the outcomes anticipated by those who borrow?

Foundational studies, carefully structured for substantive depth and analytical vigor, legitimately address such questions. Such analyses must place concepts in a detailed context of time and culture such that the subtleties and nuances may be explicated.

Human and Community Development

Post–World War II initiatives in rural education have faced, in part, problems created by the success of mechanized agriculture. From 1947–1969, farm output per worker hour increased 260%, while non-farm output increased 82%. While farm output increased, the number of farms and farm workers decreased, leading to the displacement of a significant number of adults. Blacks and other minorities' percentage of farm population dropped from 16% in 1950 to 10% in 1969 (Marshall, 1974).

Human and community development in non-metropolitan counties can be defined in different ways. Smith and Anschel (1987) call for strategies which will facilitate the industrialization of rural communities. Such a strategy probably will also facilitate urbanization. It calls for communities to make concessions to attract industrial firms and the movement of surplus workers to these plants. An alternative approach advocates rural development providing it preserves the rural community and the rural life style (Spears, 1985; Dunne, 1981). The alternative approach envisions the creation of jobs in nearby settings, thus enabling a farmer to maintain his home and farm (Spears, 1987). Common to both definitions is the assumption that development activities must move beyond job training to job creation.

Human and community development programs have been stimulated by federal legislation and funding in the 1960s and 1970s. The Manpower Development and Training Act (MATA) of 1962 and the Rural Development Act of 1961 sought to deal with unemployment by providing extensive on-the-job training. The economic Opportunities Act of 1964 was a major part of the federal government's War on Poverty, calling for job creation and job training. In addition, the Adult education Act of 1966 supported programs in basic adult education (Hamilton, forthcoming). The Comprehensive Employment and Training Act of 1973 (CETA), amended in 1978, reflected revenue sharing concepts which provided assistance to states and local communities to operate manpower programs. The Job Training Partnership Act (JTPA) of 1982 shifted job training programs from the Department of Labor to state governors. Title IV of JTPA included funding for programs such as the Job Corps as well as programs to migrant workers and native Americans.

The war on poverty recognized the existence in many rural places of a "culture of poverty." This culture of poverty was multifaceted, including deficiencies in health care, housing, income, and education. People in poverty were also assumed to lack appropriate values and attitudes necessary for success in school and on the job. Presumably, one could attract the culture of poverty by addressing any one of these deficits.

Federally funded programs supporting human and community development in rural areas can be divided into three major divisions. First, the Office of Education administered vocational and career educational programs. Second, CETA programs promoted employment training. Third, extension centers moved into community resource development. Since the mid 1970s, 50% of extension center funding went to metropolitan counties. The Concerted Services in Training and Education (CSTE) program was designed especially for rural areas. CSTE focused upon an integrated approach to increasing rural employment through economic development and education (Mirengoff and Rindler, 1976).

Rural advocates have criticized the war on poverty programs for their urban bias. The neglect of rural areas is attributed to several factors. Rural areas tend to remain invisible in a society where mass media is urban based. Historically, it has been difficult to organize rural populations for concerted action. The agribusiness sector has not shown a great deal of interest in problems facing sparsely populated communities. Many manpower training programs were based on unemployment rather than poverty statistics. Rural workers tend to be underemployed, often seasonally employed, but not listed with the chronic unemployed. Yet a larger percentage of rural families are listed as poor compared to their urban counterparts. Urban workers, on the other hand, have a larger percentage classified as unemployed (Marshall, 1972; Levitan, Mangum and Marshall, 1981).

It has been argued that rural adult learners also differ from their counterparts in urban areas. Many of the rural unemployed are either too young or too old to be sought by employers. Also, many have completed fewer years of formal schooling than have urban adults. However, evidence suggests that the uniqueness of rural adults has been overemphasized. McCannon (1985) surveyed rural adult students and found substantial resemblance to urban adults in terms of reasons for enrolling in class, age, and gender. Rural adults may not be unique but do experience difficulties in terms of distance required to travel for education and declining rural income. In addition, sparsely settled areas increase the expense of delivering educational and training programs (McDaniel et al., 1986).

It is difficult to evaluate the success of human and community development programs in rural education. There appears to be no scarcity of potential providers. Extension and demonstration centers, community colleges, universities, public schools, 4-H clubs, and business-school partnerships provide potential delivery of services. A diversity of programs exists in the form of continuing education at colleges and universities, community resource development, and adult basic education with specialized information for farmers, literacy training, and preparation for the GED (McCorkle, 1988; Schweitzer, 1974; Fraeto, 1979). Cooperation between programs rather than new programs is probably the greatest need. Operation Hitchhike illustrated cooperative efforts by using existing services and community organizations (Fraeto, 1979).

Central to community development programs is job creation. For rural areas, this means attracting jobs in the non-agricultural sector. Industrialization of rural communities assumed that importing workers with relatively high educational levels would stimulate educational interest in the local population. Smith and Anschel (1987) suggested that this may have only limited success. In the rural South many new industries have depended upon low or semi-skilled labor. Nevertheless, community development remains a much discussed topic into the 1990s. The 1990 conference of the Southern Rural Education Association has a theme of "Questing the Good Life in the Rural South: Educational Agenda for the 90's" with a primary theme focused upon "Linking Rural Education and Rural Economic Development." References to job creation, community development, and school/business partnerships abound in this emerging literature.

Even so, human development programs for black adults and for women continue to be limited. Levitan et al. (1975) and Hamilton (forthcoming) focus on black adult education but do not differentiate rural and urban programs. It is important to remember that in 1970 some 25% of blacks lived in rural areas and small towns. Evidence suggests that Neighborhood Youth Programs, Work Incentive Programs, and CETA have provided some long term benefits for blacks (Hamilton, forthcoming). It is also evident that the shift to revenue sharing has had a negative impact upon programs for black adults. The 1980s presidential rhetoric of market economics will not solve problems facing rural black adults. Emphasis upon self-reliance has some merit for the black landowner who has, however, become a vanishing breed in the rural South (Shimkin, 1974; McGee, 1977).

On the other hand, there is evidence that some efforts are being undertaken to break out of the gender tracking programs in adult education. For example, the Mountain Women's Exchange sought to organize the Rural Communities Educational Cooperative (RCEC) in Campbell County, Tennessee, and Whitley County, Kentucky. The RCEC set up clinics, a child care center, a community land trust, a development council, and promoted post secondary educational opportunities for women (Conto et al., 1986).

Conclusion

This discussion set forth technical and conceptual aspects of the history and contemporary status of rural adult education in the United States during the twentieth century. Most significantly, rural adult education carries with it a variety of sentiments that determine the focus of the educational content delivered to the target audience. In no sense can rural adult education be thought of in simplistic terms. A host of assumptions about the nature of society, the nature of what constitutes rural life, the directions in which society will and ought to be moving, the validity of racial and sexual perceptions, and the nature of citizenship undergird the content delivered to adults. Goals, objectives, curriculum materials, and delivery systems take their form from the spoken and unspoken assumptions that arise from the complicated cultural milieux in which rural adults live.

Rural education exists as an activity with a rich history. However, the actual impact of the rural educational enterprise frequently remains clouded in evangelistic zeal and impressionistic beliefs which may not be supported by rigorous analysis. Rural adult education will continue to reflect a myriad of agencies and delivery services for a variety of targeted audiences. One wishes for the rural adult learner to find life changing and life enhancing experiences from these enterprises; yet our analysis of previous programs, particularly in the South, suggest the problematic nature of such hopes.

REFERENCES

Akenson, James E. "The Southern Literacy Campaign, 1910–1935: Lessons for Adult Learning in an Information Society." *Resources in Education, 20* (Spring 1985): 189–195.

Akenson, James E., and Neufeldt, Harvey G. "A Southern Campaign Against Illiteracy: The Adult Opportunity Schools in Alabama

1915–1935." Paper presented to the Southern History of Education Society, Atlanta, Georgia, November 1983.

Akenson, James E., and Neufeldt, Harvey G. "Alabama's Illiteracy Campaign for Black Adults." *Journal of Negro Education, 54* (Spring 1985): 189–195.

Akenson, James E., and Neufeldt, Harvey G. "The Social Studies Component of the Southern Literacy Campaign: 1915–1930." *Theory and Research in Social Education, 14* (Summer 1986): 187–200.

Akenson, James E., and Neufeldt, Harvey G. "The Southern Literacy Campaign for Black Adults in the Early Twentieth Century." In *The Education of the African American Adult: An Historical Overview.* Edited by Harvey Neufeldt and Leo McGee. Westport, Conn.: Greenwood Press, forthcoming.

Apple, Michael W. "The Adequacy of Systems Management Procedures in Education." *Journal of Educational Research, 66* (September 1972): 10–18.

Araji, A. A., Sim, R. J., and Gardner, R. L. "Return to Agricultural Research and Extension Programs: An Ex-Ante Approach." *Journal of Agricultural Economics, 60* (December 1978): 964–968.

Bailey, Joseph C. *Seaman A. Knapp: Schoolmaster of American Agriculture.* New York: Columbia University Press, 1945.

Baker, Gladys. *The County Agent.* Chicago: University of Chicago Press, 1939.

Barker, Bruce. "Adult Education in Rural America: A Review of Recent Research and Identification of Further Research Needs." Paper presented at the Annual Meeting of the Texas Association for Community Service and Continuing Education, Lubbock, Texas, November 1985a. ERIC Document ED 265 994.

Barker, Bruce. "Understanding Rural Adult Learners: Characteristics and Challenges." *Lifelong Learning, 9* (October 1985b): 4–7.

Beck, Oscar, Jr. "The Agricultural Press and Southern Rural Development, 1900–1940." Doctoral dissertation. George Peabody College for Teachers, 1952.

Bond, Max. "The Educational Program for Negroes in the TVA." *Journal of Negro Education, 6* (April 1937): 144–151.

Bond, Max. "The Training Program of the Tennessee Valley Authority for Negroes." *Journal of Negro Education, 7* (July 1938): 383–389.

Bowers, William A. "Country Life Reform, 1900–1920: NeglectedAspects of Progressive Era History." *Agricultural History, 45* (July 1971): 211–221.

Bowers, William A. *The Country Life Movement in America, 1900–1920.* Port Washington, N.Y.: Kennikat Press, 1974.

Bransom, Herman. "The Training of Negroes for War Industries in World War II." *Journal of Negro Education, 12* (Summer 1943): 376–385.

Bullock, Ralph W. "The Adult Education Programs of the YMCA Among Negroes." *Journal of Negro Education, 14* (Summer 1945): 385–389.

Burlingame, Merill G. "National Contributions of the Montana Extension Service, 1893–1930." *Agricultural History, 51* (January 1977): 229–243.

Caliver, Ambrose. *Vocational Education and Guidance of Negroes: Report of a Survey Conducted by the Office of Education.* 1937. Reprint Westport, Conn.: Negro University Press, 1970.

Campbell, Christian M. *The Farm Bureau and the New Deal: A Study of the Making of National Farm Policy, 1933–1940.* Urbana: University of Illinois Press, 1962.

Campbell, Thomas M. *The Moveable School Goes to the Negro Farmer.* Tuskegee, Ala.: Tuskegee Institute Press, 1939.

Chalmers, Ruth A. "Training for Household Workers: A Work Relief Project." *Journal of Home Economics, 27* (June-July 1935).

Clayton, Ronald K. "Arthur Ernest Morgan and the Development of an Adult Education Enterprise Within the Tennessee Valley Authority, 1933–1938." Doctoral dissertation. Michigan State University, 1975.

Clevenger, Homer. "The Teaching Techniques of the Farmers' Alliance: An Experiment in Adult Education." *Journal of Southern History, 11* (November 1945): 504–518.

Coleman, Gould P. *Education and Agriculture: A History of the New York State College of Agriculture at Cornell University.* Ithaca, N.Y.: Cornell University Press, 1963.

Conklin, Paul. *Tomorrow A New World: The New Deal Community Program.* Ithaca, N.Y.: Cornell University Press, 1959.

Cook, Wanda D. *A History of Adult Literacy Education in the United States.* Doctoral dissertation. Florida State University, 1971.

Cooley, Rossa B. *School Acres: An Adventure in Rural Education.* New Haven: Yale University Press, 1930.

Couto, Richard, et al. "For a Sharing of Life's Glories: An Evaluation of the Rural Competencies Curriculum Development Project of the Rural Communities Educational Cooperative." 1986. ERIC Document ED 277–503.

Crompton, John A. *The National Farmers Union: Ideology of a Pressure Group.* Lincoln: University of Nebraska Press, 1965.

Crosby, Earl W. "Limited Success Against Long Odds: The Black County Agent." *Agricultural History, 57* (July 1983): 277–288.

Crosby, Earl W. "The Struggle for Existence: The Institutionalization of the Black County Agent System." *Agricultural History, 60* (Spring 1986): 123–136.

Danbom, David B. *The Resisted Revolution: Urban America and the Industrialization of Agriculture: 1910–1930.* Ames, Iowa: Iowa State University Press, 1979.

Daniel, Walter G., and Miller, Carol L. "The Participation of the Negro in the National Youth Administration Program." *Journal of Negro Education, 7* (July 1938): 357–365.

Dunbar, Anthony P. *Against the Grain: Southern Radicals and Prophets, 1929–1959.* Charlottesville: University of Virginia Press, 1981.

Dunne, Faith. "Reform and Resistance: Rural School Improvement Projects in the United States." In *Rural Education in Urbanized Nations: Issues and Innovations.* 325–346. Edited by Johnathon Sher. Boulder, Colo.: Westview Press, 1981.

Dyson, Lowell. "Radical Farm Organizations and Periodicals in America, 1920–1960." *Agricultural History, 45* (April 1971): 11–20.

Eiger, Norman. "Toward a National Commitment to Workers Education: The Rise and Fall of the Campaign to Establish a Labor Extension Service, 1942–1950." *Labor Studies Journal, 1* (Fall 1976): 130–150.

Ellsworth, Clayton. "Theodore Roosevelt's Country Life Commission." *Agricultural History, 39* (October 1960): 155–172.

Estes, Florence, Neufeldt, Harvey G., and Akenson, James E. "Appalachian and Southern Literacy Campaigns in the Early Twentieth Century: Historical Perspectives in Two Keys." In *Education in Appalachia: Proceedings from the 1987 Conference on Appalachia.* 81–94. Edited by Alan J. DeYoung. Lexington, Ky.: University of Kentucky Press, 1987.

Evans, James C. "Adult Education Programs for Negroes in the Armed Forces." *Journal of Negro Education, 45* (Summer 1945): 437–442.

Ferrell, Richard T. "Advice to Farmers: The Content of Agricultural Newspapers." *Agricultural History, 51* (January 1977): 209–217.

Fesseden, Jewell G. "What Do We Know About What Home Economics Extension Is Doing Today?" *National Symposium on Home Demonstration Work: Report of Proceedings.* 89–97. East Lansing, Mich.: Kellogg Center, Michigan State University, 1958.

Fitzharris, Joseph C. "Science for the Farmer: The Development of the Minnesota Agricultural Experiment Station, 1868–1910." *Agricultural History, 48* (January 1974): 202–214.

Fosdick, Raymond. *Adventure in Giving: A Story of the General Education Board.* New York: Harper, 1962.

Franklin, Vincent P. "Education for Life: Adult Education Programs for African Americans in Northern Cities, 1900–1942." In *The Education of the African American Adult: An Historical Overview.* Edited by Harvey Neufeldt and Leo McGee. Westport, Conn.: Greenwood Press, forthcoming.

Frato, Frank. "Education Training Programs and Rural Development." Paper presented at the Rural Education Seminar, College Park, Md., May 1979. ERIC Document ED 172 967.

Fredericksen, Mary. "Recognizing Regional Differences: The Southern Summer School for Women Workers." In *Sisterhood and Solidarity: Workers' Education for Women, 1914–1984.* 149–186. Edited by Joyce Kornbluth and Mary Fredericksen. Philadelphia: Temple University Press, 1984.

Freire, P. *The Pedagogy of the Oppressed.* New York: The Seabury Press, 1970.

Galleys, Gladys. *The Effectiveness of the Home Demonstration Program of the Cooperative Extension Service of the United States Department of Agriculture in Reaching Rural People and in Meeting Their Needs.* Doctoral dissertation. George Washington University, 1943.

Galleys, Gladys. "What Do We Know About What Home Economics Extension is Doing Today?" In *National Symposium on Home Demonstration Work.* 75–87. East Lansing, Mich.: Kellogg Center, Michigan State University, 1958.

Gardner, Booker T. "The Educational Contributions of Booker T. Washington." *Journal of Negro Education, 44* (Fall 1975): 502–518.

Glen, John M. *Highlander: No Ordinary School*. Lexington, Ky.: The University of Kentucky Press, 1988.

Goodenow, Ronald K., and White, Arthur, eds. *Education and the Rise of the New South*. Boston: G. K. Hall, 1981.

Gould, Joseph E. *The Chautauqua Movement*. New York: State University of New York, 1961.

Gouldner, Alvin W. *The Coming Crisis of Western Sociology*. New York: Basic Books, 1970.

Grant, Nancy. "Government Social Planning and Education for Blacks: The TVA Experience 1933–1945." In *Education and the Rise of the New South*. 215–236. Edited by Ronald K. Goodenow and Arthur White. Boston: G. K. Hall, 1981.

Grant, Nancy. *TVA and Black Americans: Planning for the Status Quo*. Philadelphia: Temple University Press, 1989.

Grant, Nancy. "Adult Education for Blacks During the New Deal and World War II: The Federal Program." In *The Education of the African American Adult: An Historical Overview*. Edited by Harvey G. Neufeldt and Leo McGee. Westport, Conn.: Greenwood Press, forthcoming.

Gray, Wil Lou. Elementary Studies in Civics. Revised Edition. Columbia, S.C.: The State Company, 1927.

Gray, William S. *The Opportunity School of South Carolina: An Experimental Study*. New York: American Association for Adult Education, 1932.

Hamilton, Edwin. "Post World War II Manpower Training Programs." In *The Education of the African American Adult: An Historical Overview*. Edited by Harvey Neufeldt and Leo McGee. Westport, Conn.: Greenwood Press, forthcoming.

Harlan, Louis R. *Booker T. Washington: The Making of a Black Leader, 1865–1901*. New York: Oxford University Press, 1972.

Harris, Joan E. "The Design and Administrative Management of Literacy Training Programs in South Carolina." Unpublished paper, South Carolina Literacy Association. Columbia, S.C., n.d.

Harris, Joan E. "State Models for Literacy Partnerships." Paper presented to the National Adult Education Conference, Louisville, Ky., November 1984.

Height, Dorothy J. "The Adult Education Program of the YWCA Among Negroes." *Journal of Negro Education, 14* (Summer 1945): 390–395.

Herbert, Giles. Some Recent Developments in Adult Education Among Negroes in Agriculture. *Journal of Negro Education, 14* (Summer 1945): 337–340.

Hildreth, R. J., and Armbruster, Walter. "Extension Program Delivery-Past, Present, and Future: An Overview." *Journal of Agricultural Economics, 63* (December 1961): 853–858.

Hill, Frank Ernest. *The School in the Camps: The Educational Program of the Civilian Conservation Corps.* New York: American Association for Adult Education, 1935.

Hill, Fred D. *Critique of Some Dominant Ideas in Contemporary Adult Education.* Doctoral dissertation. Auburn University, 1981.

Hill, Herbert. *Black Labor and the American Labor System.* Madison: University of Wisconsin Press, 1985.

Holby, Donald. "The Negro in the New Deal Settlement Programs." *Agricultural History, 45* (July 1971): 179–194.

Hone, Karen. "Serving the Rural Adult: Inventory of Model Programs in Rural Adult Postsecondary Education." 1984. ERIC Document ED 256 527.

Horton, Aimee I. *The Highlander Folk School: A History of the Development of its Major Programs Related to Social Movements in the South, 1932–1961.* Doctoral dissertation. University of Chicago, 1971.

Huffman, Wallace. "Assessing Returns to Agricultural Extension." *Journal of Agricultural Education, 60* (December 1978): 969–975.

Hurt, Douglas, R. *The Dust Bowl: An Agricultural and Social History.* Chicago: Nelson Hall, 1981.

Jacobs, Clinton O. "An Analysis of Activities in Farmstead Mechanization Experienced by Selected Farmers and Associated Business with Implications for Vocational-Technical Education in Agriculture." Doctoral dissertation. University of Missouri, 1966.

Jacoway, Elizabeth. *Yankee Missionaries in the South: The Penn School Experiment.* Baton Rouge: Louisiana State University Press, 1980.

James, Felix. "The Tuskegee Institute Moveable School, 1906–1923." *Agricultural History, 45* (July 1971): 201–209.

James, Felix. "Booker T. Washington and George Carver: A Tandem of Adult Educators at Tuskegee." In *The Education of the African American Adult: An Historical Overview.* Edited by Harvey Neufeldt and Leo McGee. Westport, Conn.: Greenwood Press, forthcoming.

Jensen, Joan. "Crossing Ethnic Barriers in the Southwest: Women's Agricultural Extension Education, 1914–1940." *Agricultural History, 60* (Spring 1986): 169–181.

Jones, Allen W. "The South's First Black Farm Agents." *Agricultural History, 50* (October 1976): 636–644.

Kincheloe, Teresa S. "An Examination of Adult Literacy Efforts in Louisiana for 1910–1940." Doctoral dissertation. Northwestern State University of Louisiana, 1985.

Knowles, Malcolm S. *A History of the Adult Education Movement in the United States.* Revised. Malabar, Fla.: Robert E. Krieger, 1977.

Kornbluth, Joyce L. "The She-She-She Camps: An Experiment in Living and Learning, 1934–1937." In *Sisterhood and Solidarity: Workers Education for Women, 1919–1984.* 255–283. Edited by Joyce Kornbluth and Mary Fredericksen. Philadelphia: Temple University Press, 1984.

Kornbluth, Joyce L. *A New Deal for Workers' Education: The Workers' Service Program, 1933–1942.* Urbana: University of Illinois Press, 1987.

Kornbluth, Joyce L., and Fredericksen, Mary, eds. *Sisterhood and Solidarity: Workers Education for Women, 1919–1984.* Philadelphia: Temple University Press, 1984.

Kovel-Jarboe, Patricia. "Empowering the Rural Adult Learner:Problems and Strategies." Paper presented at the Annual Meeting of the American Association for Adult and Continuing Education, Washington, D.C., October 1987. ERIC Document ED 287 015.

Kroupa, Eugene A. "Wisconsin Farmers' Use and Understanding of Broadcast Market Information: A Survey of Wisconsin Farmers and Radio and Television Stations." Doctoral dissertation. University of Wisconsin, 1970.

Lane, David A. "An Army Project in the Duty-Time General Education of Negro Troops in Europe, 1947–1951." *Journal of Negro Education, 33* (Spring 1964): 117–124.

Leith, Donald M. "Implementing Democracy: The Des Moines Forum." *Religious Education, 29* (April 1934): 113–119.

Levitan, Sar A., Johnston, William B., and Taggert, Robert. *Still A Dream: The Changing Status of Blacks Since 1960.* Cambridge: Harvard University Press, 1975.

Levitan, Sar A., Mangrum, Garth L., and Marshall, Ray. *Human Resources and Labor Markets: Employment and Training in the American Economy.* 3rd ed. New York: Harper and Row, 1981.

Long, Huey. *New Perspectives in the Education of Adults in the United States.* London: Croom Helm, 1987.

Loomis, Charles, et al. *Rural Systems and Adult Education.* East Lansing: Michigan State College Press, 1953.

MacLellan, Malcolm. *The Catholic Church and Adult Education.* Educational Research Monographs, Volume 8, Number 5. Washington, D.C: The Catholic University of America, May 1935.

Mangrum, Garth L., and John Walsh. *A Decade of Manpower and Development and Training.* Salt Lake City: Olympus Publishing Co., 1973.

Marshall, Ray. "Manpower Policies and Rural America." *Manpower, 14* (April 1972): 15–19.

Marshall, Ray. *Rural Workers in Rural Labor Markets.* Salt Lake City: Olympus Publishing Co., 1974.

Maxey, Spencer J. "Progressivism and Rural Education in the Deep South, 1900–1950." In *Education and the Rise of the New South.* 47–71. Edited by Ronald Goodenow and Arthur White. Boston: G. K. Hall, 1981.

McAlister, Jane E., and McAlister, Dorothy M. "Adult Education for Negroes in Rural Areas: The Work of the Jeanes Teachers and Home Farm Demonstration Agents." *Journal of Negro Education, 14* (Summer 1945): 331–340.

McCannon, Roger S. *Serving the Rural Adult: A Demographic Portrait of Rural Adult Learners.* 1981. ERIC Document ED 256 529.

McCorkle, James L. "Agricultural Experiment Stations and Southern Truck Farming." *Agricultural History, 60* (Spring 1988): 234–243.

McDaniel, Robert H., et al. "Barriers to Rural Education: A Survey of Seven Northwest States." *Report of the Northwest Action Agenda Project, Washington State University.* 1986. ERIC Document ED 275 462.

McGee, Leo. "Decline of Black Owned Rural Land: Implications for Adult Education." *Adult Leadership, 55* (March 1977): 207–209.

McGee, Leo. "Booker T. Washington and George Washington Carver: A Tandem of Adult Educators at Tuskegee." *Lifelong Learning, 8* (October 1984): 16–18, 31.

McLaurin, Sylvia, and Coker, Robert. "Notes Towards The Establishment of Educational Partnerships in Rural Communities." 1986. ERIC Document ED 296 853.

McMurray, Linda. *George Washington Carver: Scientist and Symbol.* New York: Oxford University Press, 1981.

Mirengoff, William, and Rindler, Lester. *The Comprehensive Employment and Training Act: Impact on People, Places, and Programs: An Interim Report.* Washington, D.C.: National Academy of Sciences, 1976.

Mitchell, Theodore R. *Political Education in the Southern Farmers' Alliance, 1887–1900.* Madison: University of Wisconsin Press, 1987.

Montgomery, Mabel. *South Carolina's Wil Lou Gray.* Columbia, S.C.: Vogue Press, 1963.

Moorland, J. E. "The Young Men's Christian Association Among Negroes." *Journal of Negro History, 9* (January 1924): 127–138.

Moss, Jefferey, and Loss, Cynthia B. "A History of Farmers' Institutes." *Agricultural History, 62* (Spring 1988): 150–163.

Muraskin, William. "The Hidden Role of Fraternal Organizations in the Education of Black Adults: Prince Hall Freemasonry as a Case Study." *Adult Education, 26* (1976): 235–252.

Murray, Stanley N. *The Valley Comes of Age: A History of Agriculture in the Valley of the Red River of the North, 1812–1920.* Fargo, N.D.: North Dakota Institute for Regional Studies, 1967.

National Symposium on Home Demonstration Work: Report of Proceedings, March 23–28, 1958. East Lansing: Kellogg Center, Michigan State University.

Neufeldt, Harvey G. "Southern Educational Reform and the Revitalization of the Rural Community." Paper presented at the annual meeting of the American Educational Studies Association. San Francisco, California, November 1984.

Neufeldt, Harvey G., and Akenson, James E. "The Southern Illiteracy Campaign, 1911–1930: A Study in Ideology, Southern Progressivism and Victorian Attitudes." Paper presented at the

History of Education Society Meeting, Atlanta, Georgia. November 1985.

Neufeldt, Harvey G., and McGee, Leo, eds. *The Education of the African American Adult: An Historical Overview.* Westport, Conn.: Greenwood Press, forthcoming.

Neverden-Morton, Cynthia. "Self Help Programs as Educative Activities of Black Women of the South, 1895–1915: Focus on Four Key Areas." *Journal of Negro Education, 51* (Summer 1982): 207–221.

Neverden-Morton, Cynthia. *Afro-American Women of the South and the Advance of the Race, 1895–1925.* Knoxville: University of Tennessee Press, 1989.

Neverden-Morton, Cynthia. "African American Women and Adult Education in the South, 1895–1925." In *Education of the African American Adult: An Historical Overview.* Edited by Harvey Neufeldt and Leo McGee. Westport, Conn.: Greenwood Press, forthcoming.

Oldendorf, Sandra B. *Highlander Folk School and the South Carolina Sea Island Citizenship Schools: Implications for the Social Studies.* Doctoral dissertation. University of Kentucky, 1987.

Oldendorf, Sandra B. "Vocabularies, Knowledge and Social Action in Citizenship Education: The Highlander Example." *Theory and Research in Social Education, 16* (Spring 1989): 107–120.

Omer, Mahmoud H. *Analysis of Selected Factors Associated With Participation of Iowa Young Farmers in Argicultural Extension Programs.* Doctoral dissertation. Iowa State University, 1987.

Osborne, George. "The Southern Agricultural Press and Some Significant Rural Problems, 1900–1940." *Agricultural History 29* (July 1955): 15–22.

Parman, Donald L. *The Navajo and the New Deal.* New Haven: Yale University Press, 1976.

Punke, Harold H. "Literacy, Relief and Adult Education in Georgia." *School and Society, 42* (October 12, 1935): 514–517.

Punke, Harold H. "Membership and Interests of Adult Education Classes." *School Review, 47* (February 1939): 110–120.

Rasmussen, Wayne D. *Agriculture in the United States: A Documentary History.* 4 vols. New York: Random House, 1975.

Rasmussen, Wayne D. *Taking the University to the People: Seventy-Five Years of Cooperative Extension.* Ames, Iowa: Iowa State University, 1989.

Reddick, L. D. "Adult Education and the Improvement of Race Relations." *Journal of Negro Education, 14* (Summer 1945): 488–493.

Reddick, L. D. "The Negro in the United States Navy During World War II." *Journal of Negro Education, 32* (January 1947): 201–219.

Reeves, Floyd W. "Adult Education as Related to TVA." *School and Society, 44* (August 29, 1936): 257–266.

Reid, Ira. *Adult Education Among Negroes.* Washington, D.C.: Associates in Negro Folk Education, 1936.

Reid, Ira. "The Development of Adult Education for Negroes in the United States." *Journal of Negro Education, 14* (Summer 1945): 299–306.

Robbins, Gerald. "Rossa B. Cooley and Penn Schools: Social Dynamo in Negro Rural Subculture, 1909–1930." *Journal of Negro Education, 33* (Winter 1964): 43–51.

Roberts, Albert, and Israel, Henry. "Rural Work of the Young Men's Christian Association." American Academy of Political and Social Science Annals 40 (March 1912): 140–148.

Rural Adult Education FORUM. "Empowerment Through Education," 1 (April–May 1989): 6.

Sachs, Carolyn E. *The Invisible Farmers: Women in Agricultural Production.* Totowa, N.J.: Rowman and Allanheld, 1983.

Salmond, John A. "The Civilian Conservation Corps and the Negro." *Journal of American History, 52* (January 1965): 75–88.

Saloutos, Theodore. *Farmer Movements in the South, 1865–1933.* Berkeley: University of California Press, 1960.

Schor, Joel. "The Black Presence in the U.S. Cooperative Extension Service Since 1945: The American Quest for Service and Equity." *Agricultural History, 60* (Spring 1986): 137–153.

Schwieder, Dorothy. "Education and Change in the Lives of Iowa Farm Women, 1900–1940. *Agricultural History, 60* (Spring 1986): 200–215.

Scott, Ray. *The Reluctant Farmer: The Rise of Agricultural Extension to 1914.* Urbana: University of Illinois Press, 1970.

Scruggs, C. G., and Smith, Mosely W. "The Role of Agricultural Journalism in Rebuilding the Rural South." *Agricultural History, 53* (January 1979): 22–79.

Shimkin, Demetri B. "Black Problems in Rural Development." In *Rural Community and Regional Development: Perspectives and Prospects: A Seminar Series, Spring Semester, 1972–73.* 53–73. Urbana: Department of Agricultural Economics. University of Illinois, 1974:

Sitkoff, Harvard. "The New Deal and Race Relations." In *Fifty Years Later: The New Deal Evaluated.* 98–12. Edited by Harvard Sitkoff. Philadelphia: Temple University Press, 1985.

Sitkoff, Harvard, editor. *Fifty Years Later: The New Deal Evaluated.* Philadelphia: Temple University Press, 1985.

Smith, Clarence B., and Wilson, Meredeth C. *The Agricultural Extension System of the United States.* New York: John Wiley and Sons, 1930.

Smith, Eldon D., and Anschel, Kurt. "Education in the Strategy of Regional Development: A Retrospective View and an Alternative Perspective." In *Education in Appalachia: Proceedings from the 1987 Conference on Appalachia.* Edited by Alan J. DeYoung: 51–58. Lexington, Ky.: The Appalachian Center, University of Kentucky, 1987.

Smith, Hilda W., and Donald, Barbara. "Federal Training for Household Employment." *Journal of Home Economics, 27* (April 1935): 215–217.

Smith, Ralph. "The Contributions of Grangers to Education in Texas." *Southwestern Social Science Quarterly, 21* (March 1941): 312–324.

Socolofsky, Homer E. "The Development of the Copper Farm Press." *Agricultural History, 31* (October 1957): 34–43.

Southern Rural Education Association. Fifth Annual Conference, April 18–20, 1990. Unpublished Program Announcement and Call for Proposals. n.d.

Spears, Jacqueline. "Educational Response to the Rural Crisis: Model Programs in the Midwest." 1987. ERIC Document ED 296 821.

Spears, Jacqueline, and Maes, Sue C. "Postsecondary and Adult Education in Rural Communities." Paper presented at the National Rural Education Forum, Kansas City, Missouri, August 1985.

Stewart, Cora W. *Country Life Readers. Third Book.* Richmond, Va.: B. E. Johnson Publishing Company, 1917.

Stewart, Cora W. *Moonlight Schools for the Emancipation of Adult Illiterates.* New York: E. P. Dutton, 1922.

Stubblefield, Harold W. *Adult Education for Civic Participation: A Historical Analysis.* Doctoral dissertation. Indiana University, 1973.

Stubblefield, Harold W. *Towards a History of Adult Education in America: In Search for a Unifying Principle.* London: Croom Helm, 1988.

Sturgis, Cynthia. "How're You Gonna Keep 'Em Down on the Farm? Rural Women and the Urban Model in Utah." *Agricultural History, 60* (Spring 1986): 182–199.

Thompson, Charles H. "The Federal Program of Vocational Education in Negro Schools of Less Than College Grade." *Journal of Negro Education, 76* (July 1938): 303–318.

True, Alfred C. *A History of Agricultural Extension Work in the United States, 1785–1923.* Miscellaneous Publication No. 15. Washington, D.C.: U.S. Government Printing Office, 1928.

Ware, Susan. "Women and the New Deal." In *Fifty Years Later: The New Deal Evaluated.* 113–132. Edited by Harvard Sitkoff. Philadelphia: Temple University Press, 1985.

Washington, Booker T. *Working With Hands: Being a Sequel to 'Up From Slavery' Covering the Author's Experiences in Industrial Training at Tuskegee.* New York: Doubleday, Page and Company, 1904.

Weiss, Nancy. *Farewell to the Party of Lincoln.* Princeton: Princeton University Press, 1983.

Wessel, Thomas R. "Agent of Acculturation: Farming in the Northern Plains Reservation, 1880–1910." *Agricultural History, 60* (Spring 1986): 233–245.

White, G. Gary, and Rose, Cyndy. "Empowering the Older Adult Learner: Community Education as a Delivery System." *Lifelong Learning, 11* (May 1988): 20–22, 30.

Wik, Reynold M. "The USDA and the Development of Radio in Rural America." *Agricultural History, 62* (Spring 1988): 177–188.

Wilkening, Eugene A. "Joint Decision Making in Farm Families as a Function of Status and Role." *American Sociological Review, 23* (April 1958): 187–192.

Wilkerson, Doxey A. "The Participation of Negroes in the Federally-Aided Program of Agricultural and Home Economics Extension." *Journal of Negro Education, 7* (July 1938): 331–334.

Wilkerson, Doxey A. *Special Problems of Negro Education.* Washington, D.C.: Government Printing Office, 1939.

Wilkerson, Doxey A. "Section E: The Vocational Education and Guidance of Negroes: The Negro and the Battle of Production." *Journal of Negro Education, 11* (April 1942): 228–239.

Wilkerson, Doxey A., and Penn, Lemuel A. "The Participation of Negroes in the Federally-Aided Program of Civilian Vocational Rehabilitation." *Journal of Negro Education,* 7 (July 1938): 319–330.

Williams, Lillian. "Black Communities and Adult Education: YMCA, YWCA, Fraternal Organizations." In *The Education of the African American Adult: An Historical Overview.* Edited by Harvey Neufeldt and Leo McGee. Westport, Conn.: Greenwood Press, forthcoming.

Woodward, Ellen S. "W.P.A.'s Program of Training for Housework." *Journal of Home Economics,* 31 (February 1939): 86–88.

Wright, Marion T. "Negro Youth and the Federal Emergency Programs: CCC and NYA." *Journal of Negro Education,* 9 (July 1940).

The Rural Education Dilemma as Part of the Rural Dilemma: Rural Education and Economics

Craig Howley

Educators and economists, with few exceptions (e.g., Carnoy and Levin, 1985; DeYoung, 1989), do not understand each other's work very well. After all, supply and demand (for economics) and teaching and learning (for education) are very different phenomena. Most educators are concerned with the means to encourage learning, with the effectiveness of instruction. Most economists are concerned with the aim of increased productivity, with the efficiency of education. The differing assumptions and methods of economic and educational research also contribute to the lack of mutual understanding (Coleman, 1988).

Although this chapter deals with the possible connections between rural education and economics, it will not lose sight of the fundamental differences that *do* exist between, say, learning and investment. One important fact, however, is not stressed in this chapter: nearly everyone—educators, economists, and ordinary citizens—believes in the value of schooling.[1]

The Problematic Relationship of Education and Economics

While most economists agree that greater educational attainment contributes to improved national economic performance, studies have not generally confirmed a similar conclusion with respect to rural areas (Deaton and McNamara, 1984). The problematic relationship of education and economics entails a number of themes. Two are critical: the first empirical, and the second theoretical. The empirical theme entails the *direction of causality*: does the economy determine educational experience, or does education determine economic growth? The theoretical theme is perhaps more important: what is the proper *aim of education*?

The typical answers shape public debate and action. One of the goals of the discussion that follows is to show the true scope of the theoretical debate, so that readers can better evaluate proposals for the development of rural schools and rural economies.

Direction of Causality

Is education a stronger cause of economic development, or is economics (especially *political economy*) a stronger cause of educational development?[2] Both points have been argued well, but the contemporary public debate has not considered the second line of evidence at any length as it has proceeded with school reform in America (DeYoung, 1989; cf. Sher, 1988a).

What are the reasons for this oversight? First, the so-called school-effectiveness movement has waged a successful campaign to repudiate James Coleman's work, carried out in the midst of the fervor for educational equity of the 1960s. Coleman and his colleagues (Coleman, 1966) found that schools—in the aggregate—tended not to be the vehicle for social mobility that Americans had up to that time thought they were (Jencks et al., 1972, 1979).

Second, following the Vietnam War, America experienced a period of intense economic insecurity: high inflation, high unemployment, sluggish GNP growth, instability of financial institutions, and strong economic challenge from abroad (Heilbroner and Thurow, 1985). Some of these threats persist today, despite reduced inflation and higher employment rates.

The reaction to Coleman. Coleman's study (Coleman, 1966) influenced many thinkers who agreed with his major conclusion. The study provided further evidence that the *political economy* has determined educational development both in contemporary and historical American society (Aronowitz and Giroux, 1985; Bowles and Gintis, 1976; Carnoy, 1982; Carnoy and Levin, 1985; Jencks et al., 1972; Jencks et al., 1979; Katz, 1968; Mosteller and Moynihan, 1972; Oakes, 1985; Spring, 1976; Wright, 1979). Among educators and citizens in general, however, the work of these thinkers probably represents a minority viewpoint.

The school-effectiveness movement, which reflects the dominant character of schooling in America, has interpreted Coleman's work differently from the observers cited in the previous paragraph. Representatives of that movement interpreted Coleman's finding to mean that schools *could not* make a difference in students' lives (e.g., Bennett, 1986; Mace-Matluck, 1987). This interpretation is simplistic (DeYoung, 1989; cf. Coleman and Hoffer, 1987).

School effects and causality. The origins of the school-effectiveness movement are rooted in the classic study Pygmalion in the Classroom (Rosenthal and Jacobsen, 1968). Rosenthal and Jacobsen suggested how—at the classroom level—schools worked systematically in accord with students' backgrounds. The study inaugurated a new line of research, the school effects literature. The school effects literature documents the effects schools *do* have, positive or negative. The school effects literature allows educators to target improvement efforts within schools and classrooms.[3]

Since 1968 some findings of the school effects literature have been appropriated by the school-effectiveness movement, largely with the support of state and federal education agencies, to build an optimistic—and professedly neutral—view of school improvement (e.g., Joyce, Hersh, and McKibbin, 1983). Many educators now believe that a sound technology of school improvement exists and that it can be applied to achieve whatever national or regional priorities policymakers may set (e.g., Mace-Matluck, 1987).

Educators are less secure about applying this neutral improvement technology to rural schools or districts, which differ substantially from the metropolitan schools in which most effectiveness studies were conducted (e.g., Buttram and Carlson, 1983; Coburn and Nelson, 1987; Development Associates Incorporated, 1988; Gailey and Lipka, 1987; Phelps, 1989; Stephens, Perry and Sanders, 1988). These writers agree that school effectiveness must be carefully interpreted within local contexts.

Whereas much of the educational rhetoric surrounding effectiveness regards the causes of school improvement as a settled matter, leading school effects researchers frankly admit that the issue of causality is moot (e.g., Cooper and Good, 1983; Hanushek, 1989). Others have been disappointed with alleged causes that produce no effect (e.g., Marzano, 1984).

Rural Schools and Economic Development
as a National Aim

The new aim of education (restoration of national "economic competitiveness") has emerged with little debate. Alternative aims have become less and less considered.

Earlier in the century, the aims of education were still vigorously debated and discussed, but, following the traumas of the Great Depression and World War II, "life adjustment"[4] was the commonly accepted aim of education (Cremin, 1961). The student activism of the 1960s only prompted calls for *more effective* life adjustment: greater attention to values "clarification" and to "relevance" (e.g., Raths, Harmin, and Simon, 1966; Postman and Weingartner, 1969). In a compelling critique, Michael Katz, then a young radical himself, explained how all such aims were well beyond the practicable mission of the schools (Katz, 1971, p. 142).

The aim of forming *predetermined* values (e.g., compliance, punctuality) *is* consistent, however, with the legacy of life adjustment and the production of an orderly workforce (e.g., Committee for Economic Development, 1985; Edelstein and Schoeffe, 1989). Such instruction, however, never deals with unexamined assumptions underlying such values, and might better be termed inculcation. Economists concerned with efficiency recognize the place of such inculcation:

> At the national level, education is viewed as a means of developing good citizens who are politically responsible and in whom particular values can be inculcated in the educational process. In strictly economic terms, education provides skills and abilities that contribute to national economic growth and which enable individuals to be responsive to changing macroeconomic forces. This may entail such phenomena as spatial resettlement and occupational adjustments to structural changes in the economy. (Deaton and McNamara, 1984, p. 23)

Deaton and McNamara's statement rationalizes education as a unified process of life adjustment. It states a neutral ideology of efficient schooling, and subsequent discussion presents learning and teaching as technical matters (Deaton and McNamara, 1984). It links values, skill training, and national economic development. The seamless quality of the rationale (the need to restore economic competitiveness) and its implementation (e.g., minimum competency testing, school improvement plans, increases in required courses), however, obscures the unexamined assumptions on which the economic aim of education is based.

Alternative aims—the place of education in cultivating the life of the mind, in helping students examine the ethical life, or in achieving collective and individual identity—have been overshadowed by the insistent calls to enlist the schools in economic development. The alternative aims are, however, of enduring importance, and Bell (1973, 1976) considers them to be more important than ever in the emerging post-industrial world.

School improvement and the logic of human capital theory. National economic development as the primary aim of education is based on neoclassical economic theory and research. Its logic rests on the construct of "human capital," which began to be elaborated in detail during the 1950s and 1960s (DeYoung, 1989).

Human capital is an analogy comparing human beings with the physical capital used in the production process.[5] The theory hypothesizes that investments in human skills and knowledge contribute to future production much as investments in equipment and labor costs do. The construct of human capital is empirically attractive because it has explained part of the variance in GNP not accounted for by physical capital and labor inputs.[6]

In studies of human capital, educational attainment is used as a general measure of skills and knowledge, and income serves as a general measure of the market value of workers' skills and knowledge as assessed by employers.[7] The logic of human capital theory might be summarized as follows:

- The free market values certain skills and knowledge more highly than other skills and knowledge.

- Individual students are free to invest their time (principally in schools) in pursuit of the skills and knowledge that provide the chief route of access to highly valued skills and knowledge.

- Since employers tend to act rationally to maximize profit (cf. Coleman, 1988; Heilbroner and Thurow, 1985), the market rewards skills and knowledge according to the differential benefits employers derive from such skills and knowledge.

- Acquired skills and knowledge are responsible for the association of attainment and income.

- The association of educational attainment and income explains the residual variance in GNP not explained by fixed capital and labor costs alone.

The conclusion follows that wise investments in this resource will strengthen the economy. The educational reforms proposed in the 1980s are natural extensions of human capital theory: The knowledge and skills of the workforce—learned largely in school—are held to be a significant influence on the quality of America's international economic competitiveness, and the mediocrity of the American school experience is held to be a significant factor in the erosion of the nation's global economic standing (cf. DeYoung, 1989).

Excellence as efficiency in rural schools. With a reform mission grounded in human capital theory (a national interest based on economic dominance), a presumed technical base in school-effectiveness research and development, and a rhetorical base in national reports (the educational "excellence" required by such a mission), state legislatures have framed policy intended to cultivate better-trained workers.

Available evidence, however, suggests that rural schools are expected to carry out this mission ("excellence") with only meager financial support (e.g., Brizius et al., 1988; Lyson, 1989; Stephens, 1988). Without additional funding, then, the rhetoric of excellence is actually a call for increased *efficiency* in rural schools (cf. Deaton and McNamara, 1984, p. 20).

Rural schools, however, are not likely to increase efficiency short of deferring needed maintenance and construction, curtailing bus service, or terminating the administratively expensive categorical aid programs on which they rely (Deaton and McNamara, 1984; Honeyman, Thompson, and Wood, 1989; Howley, 1989a, 1989b; Meyer, Scott, and Strang, 1986; Sher, 1983; Silver and DeYoung, 1986; Thompson and Stewart, 1989). Given the constraints of terrain, poverty, and small scale, rural schools *already* operate with great efficiently (e.g., Talbert, Fletcher, and Phelps, 1987).

Finally, research indicates that, given adequate working conditions, teachers make the difference in student achievement (Goodlad, 1984; Hanushek, 1989; Sizer, 1985). Though there is some debate, ample research also suggests that the quality of the teaching force has declined (Schlechty and Vance, 1983; Vance and Schlechty, 1982; Weaver, 1983). If projections of supply and demand are correct, the problems of teacher quality will be compounded by a teacher shortage (Weaver, 1983). For rural schools, both problems are *already* acute (Regional Laboratory for the Northeast and Islands, 1988).

Restoring Global Dominance

The new aim of education—underwriting America's economic competitiveness—contains three unexamined assumptions worth a closer look. The first assumption is that the phrase refers to a self-evident meaning. The second assumption is that the restoration is feasible, and the third is that it is worthy to be a major aim of education.

First assumption. "Competitiveness" is a term *never* examined in any of the reports that features it as rationale. Although arguably in a period of change, the national economy is nonetheless still quite competitive; American international economic dominance is what has been lost (Heilbroner and Thurow, 1985). The role of international corporations in the quest for international economic domination is potentially greater, however, than the role of nation states (cf. Barnet and Muller, 1974; Carnoy and Levin, 1985; Heilbroner and Thurow, 1985; Melman, 1985).

Second assumption. The comparative international position of the United States economy has *not* improved since the crisis of the early 1980s, and the economies of other nations (e.g., Japan, Germany) continue to record substantially higher GNP growth rates than the United States. South Korea, Indonesia, Chile, and other Pacific nations exercise a degree of economic power unimagined for them even 15 years ago. Third-world debt—amassed during the 1950s and 1960s to finance purchases from American businesses—continually threatens to destabilize the Western economic system (Heilbroner and Thurow, 1985; Jacobs, 1984; Kubo, 1986; Nolan and Lenski, 1985; Weede, 1987). In fact, international economic forces of such magnitude are sufficient to undo whatever economic benefits might accrue from improved schooling (cf. Carnoy and Levin, 1985; Stephens, 1988). An improved American schooling may not contribute much to restoration of America's dominance of the world economy.

Third assumption. Whereas vigorous economic development can be a celebration of life (Jacobs, 1984), it can also entail relations of domination and exploitation (Marcuse, 1955). None of the reports asked if the goal of restoring "competitiveness" were a worthy goal of education. A number of writers suspect restored "competitiveness" will perpetuate a world economic order based on domination, exploitation, and the misery that such relationships entail (e.g., Bowles, Gordon, and Weisskopf, 1984; Coleman, 1988; DeYoung, 1989; Keizer, 1988; Schumacher, 1979; Wigginton, 1985).

Many critics of human capital theory believe that American domination of the world economy has created additional hardships among people in the developing world rather than ameliorating preexisting hardships (Amin, 1976; Carnoy, 1982; Zachariah, 1985).[8] The hardships include increased dependency on the developed world, unbalanced economic growth, and, more recently, austerity measures to stem third-world default on development loans (e.g., Bornischer and Chase-Dunn, 1985; Delacroix, 1977; Jacobs, 1984; Kubo, 1986; London and Smith, 1988; Sica and Prechel, 1981; Weede, 1987).

The Dilemma of Life and Learning in Rural Areas

The notion of dependency in analyzing the dilemma of life and learning in rural areas is important because it has the potential to explain why many rural areas have failed to achieve relative improvements in quality of life, despite many decades of concern for such improvements.

Rural Dependency and National Priority

Some observers find that the features that characterize third-world dependency also characterize the relationship of rural areas to national (or urban) economies *within developed countries* (e.g., Dunaway, 1989; Jacobs, 1984; Nelson and Lorence, 1988; McSwain, 1986; Page, 1985; Pottinger, 1985; Prattis, 1979). Empirical data support the presence of such features in rural America. For example, rural areas are becoming more tightly bound to the national economy (e.g., Kitchen and Zahn, 1986; Quan and Beck, 1987; Stephens, 1988); most rural areas have "specialized" economies (e.g., Bender et al., 1985; Brown and Deavers, 1987b; Deavers and Brown, 1985; Lyson, 1989; McCormick and Turque, 1989); and since 1980 the nonmetropolitan share of federal spending has diminished sharply (Dubin, 1989; Lyson, 1989; Stephens, 1988). Finally, federal spending in nonmetropolitan areas does not promote economic development (Dubin and Reid, 1988; Jacobs, 1984; Lyson, 1989).

Empire in a new land. Since its beginning, the United States has been a nation organized for empire. Empire-building entails economic and political integration on a grand scale, and rural America seems always to have served that end (Cubberley, 1922), even in its most remote locations (Dunaway, 1989; Silver and DeYoung, 1986). Initially, colonists were the instruments of another nation's empire-building schemes, but after the American revolution the new nation managed its own "manifest destiny" (Williams, 1966, 1969). The process entailed systematic exploitation of natural resources, genocide against the native population, and maintenance of a substantial slave population. These actions were also taken by contemporary European powers in Africa and Asia.

Conquest and development rested as much on speculation and finance as on productive labor. Historians (e.g., Williams, 1969) have shown how first European, and then, Eastern capital, invested in railroads, dominated the land markets of the nineteenth century, and in rapid order (Dunaway, 1989) integrated American agricultural production into the world economy. By the close of the nineteenth century America was becoming an international industrial empire with expanding economic influence. The Republican party—which represented manufacturing, business, and financial interests—became the voice of progress, political liberalism, and international empire (Bell, 1973; Meyer et al., 1979; Williams, 1969).

The rural experience as part of empire-building. In the nineteenth century, American citizens, both foreign-born and native, were constructing an exemplary nation as a conscious act (Crewin, 1980; Meyer, Tyack, Nagel, and Gordon, 1979). They were repudiating the values and structures of life in rural Europe, including the traditional values that still bound rural Europe together in the nineteenth century. Progress was the contemporary watchword (Hobsbawm, 1962), and Americans sought to create the most progressive of nations. Progress meant improvement in the quality of life—better transportation, mechanization of field and household labor, electrification, and—notably—access to education and learning as the route to personal advancement (cf. Cubberley, 1922).

The course of empire was legitimated by a national consensus about the American political, economic, and social experiment (Cremin, 1980; Spring, 1986; Meyer et al., 1979; Silver and DeYoung, 1986). Williams (1969) believes the drive to empire was a cultural ethos developed and propagated by American business, but subscribed to by virtually all citizens—most of whom were rural residents. The Republican party played an important role, as Meyer and colleagues' empirical work suggests (Meyer et al., 1979).

Most white settlers of the American continent in the nineteenth century were hardly attached to the places they settled, as the record of their vigorous geographic mobility suggests (Theobald, 1989; Williams, 1966). The historical commitment of Americans has not been to traditional rural values or principles but to progress through a back-breaking phase of empire-building. Rural life was, throughout the nineteenth century, a temporary site of progress from which most people fled to the cities—soon, if they could (Cubberley, 1922). Since the end of the nineteenth century, however, Americans have become increasingly more concerned with the ethical alternative that the rural experience seems to entail (e.g., Borsodi, 1933; Cubberley, 1922; Mumford, 1944; Nearing and Nearing, 1970).[9]

Developing nations around the world are repeating the American experience, in terms of urbanization, if not in terms of progress and well-being. Ledent (1982), for example, estimates

that India, Egypt, and Honduras (all now with less than 50%
urban population) will each have populations that are 75%–
90% urban by the year 2050.

Rural schooling and nation-building. In an original
analysis, Meyer and colleagues (1979) demonstrate the role
played by the rural school in building the American empire,
during as late a period as 1870 to 1930. Their regression
analyses show that, throughout this period, both urbanization
and manufacturing had a consistently *negative* relationship to
school enrollment, whereas Republican party dominance had a
consistently *positive* relationship to school enrollment in this
period. This study corrects the misperception that the
increased access to public education was caused by
urbanization, industrialization, and the concomitant growth of
bureaucracy in American education. According to Meyer and
colleagues (1979, p. 592),

> the spread of schooling in the rural North and West
> can best be understood as a social movement
> implementing a commonly held ideology of nation-
> building. It combined the outlook and interests of
> small entrepreneurs in a world market, evangelical
> Protestantism, and an individualistic conception of the
> polity.

While rural schools doubtless served as a site for local
community events, it is clear that they also played an important
role in integrating remote areas into a national political economy
(Boli, Ramirez, and Meyer, 1985; Cremin, 1961; Elson, 1964;
Grubb, 1985; Silver and DeYoung, 1986; Theobald, 1989;
Zachariah, 1985).

National and Local Economic Structures

Once the continental empire was firmly established, the
opportunity of the frontier quickly became the "rural problem"
(Silver and DeYoung, 1986; cf. Cubberley, 1922). According to
Cubberley (1922, p. 4), the rural problem was that "rural
people and rural institutions have not changed rapidly enough
to keep pace with the demands of the new civilization."

Cubberley believed "the main single remedy which must be applied to the rural life problem is educational, and consists largely in a redirection of rural education itself" (Cubberley, 1922, p. 105).

Like Cubberley, contemporary observers conclude that rural people are too poor, illiterate, inflexible, and too lacking in leadership to confront "modern" reality (cf. Hobbs, 1987; Knutson and Fisher, 1988; Porter, 1989; Ross and Rosenfeld, 1987). They promote education as the key to "revitalizing" rural life (e.g., Bloomquist, 1988; Brown and Deavers, 1987b; Hobbs, 1987, 1989; Knutson and Fisher, 1988; Rosenfeld, 1989; cf. Cubberley, 1922). Education, reconceived as information and training, will empower rural communities to become more competitive.

Although all writers understand that education is part of a larger social and economic context, many analyses lack a critical assessment of the influence of economic structures on rural education. Recent work both by neoclassical and political economists suggests the scope of the influence of economic structures. Political economists stress the role of economic structures, in general, whereas neoclassical economists stress the role of individual characteristics (Zachariah, 1985).

Individual Characteristics or Economic Structures?

Some researchers understand that individual characteristics such as poverty and unemployment (or poor school achievement and adult illiteracy) may serve an economically functional purpose, despite their deplorable nature. According to Tomaskovic-Devey (1987, p. 59), for example, personal "characteristics—age, gender, race, and education—do not cause poverty. Rather, these are the characteristics used in the United States to *allocate poverty*" [original emphasis]. This view is neither new nor radical. Duncan (1968) made a similar point about discrimination against blacks.

According to this view, such characteristics as race are used in our culture to determine who must, as a result of the economy's *need* for poverty, actually live in poverty. These characteristics do not *cause* poverty, and there is nothing inherent in the attributes of white males that make them more valuable human beings than black women. A (hypothetically) different sort of social organization might, with as slender a claim to reason, allocate poverty to white males.

Both neoclassical economists and political economists have operationalized the concepts of core and periphery (e.g., Bloomquist and Summers, 1988; Reif, 1985; Tomaskovic-Devey, 1987). Some of their studies examine, not the effects of individual characteristics, but the effects of economic structures. According to Kalleberg (1989, p. 587) dual labor market studies[10] are "particularly useful for linking phenomena at macro and micro levels of analysis."

Illustrative studies. Stevens (1983), in an analysis of dual labor market employment in the Northwest timber industry, found that the 25,000 "peripheral" workers—those most likely to be affected by market volatility—did not behave rationally by the standards of macroeconomic theory. Staying with a job—which would help them accumulate human capital (Mincer, 1989)—was *not* economically productive for these workers. In fact, changing jobs frequently helped these workers maximize income. At the level of the workers' lived experience, economic structures elicited behavior that, though rational in the local context (where the dual labor market operates), appeared at the same time to be irrational from the perspective of human capital (a macroeconomic perspective that minimizes local conditions).

More broadly based empirical research, predicated on the premise that economic structures affect issues relevant to quality of life issues (poverty, unemployment, equality of income distribution, educational attainment), indicates that the presence in a county of industries that represent the "core" (monopoly manufacturing industries for the most part: national firms with a local branch plant or division) and large family farms (as opposed to corporate and commercial farms) produce cumulative *positive economic effects* over time (Reif, 1987; cf. Bloomquist and Summers, 1988). The problem with core industries, as Lyson (1989) notes, is that they often do not stay long enough to produce cumulative benefits.

By contrast, the prevalence in rural counties of extractive industries (mining, agriculture in general, forestry, and fishing), state employment (education, social service, government), peripheral manufacturing[11] and both large corporate and very small, part-time farming seem to have a *negative* effect on socioeconomic conditions over time (see, for example, Reif, 1987; Bloomquist and Summers, 1982; 1988; Tomaskovic-Devey, 1985, 1987).

Other research indicates that extractive industries and routine manufacturing (i.e., "peripheral" rather than "core" manufacturing) predominate in rural areas (Bender et al., 1985; Brown and Deavers, 1987a; Deavers and Brown, 1985; DeYoung, 1985; Rosenfeld et al., 1985, 1989). If the analyses of researchers like Lyson (1989), Reif (1987), and Tomaskovic-Devey (1985) are correct, then the comparatively poor quality of rural life is an effect of the economic structures that operate in rural areas. Lyson (1989) calls for reform of the haphazard de facto economic development policies that destroy rural communities.

Macroeconomics as fiction. One of the most original economic critiques of recent decades has been made by Jane Jacobs (Hill, 1988). Jacobs' critique incorporates features of dependency theory and dual labor market theory (e.g., the cities as locations of core activities and structures, and rural areas as locations of peripheral activities and structures), of capitalist ideology (e.g., the value of innovation in development, the importance of wise investment), and of politicized environmentalism (e.g., the importance of small-scale, mixed-use city planning and neighborhood preservation). As a result, Jacobs cannot be neatly classified as a radical, liberal, or conservative (Hill, 1988).

Jacobs (1984) is most sharply critical of what she considers to be the *economic fiction* of the nation state. Macroeconomics—upon which national policy decisions largely rest—treats the nation as the unit of analysis, but according to Jacobs, national and international data obscure the much greater variety of economic relations that exist *within each nation*. The larger the nation, the more it functions as an empire, and the greater the variety of contradictory economic conditions within it (Jacobs, 1984).

According to Jacobs, macroeconomic analysis—especially in large nations or empires—actually obscures the structures and processes that create economic vigor. She believes that urban economies, not national economies, are the sources of economic growth. Macroeconomics is thus built on false premises. Instead of analyzing national economic data, economists should investigate economic relations among cities and among cities and the rural areas that they dominate (Jacobs, 1984).

Jacobs cautions that empire (she uses both the United States and the Soviet Union as examples) *impedes* economic development in the long run. Periods of growth and geographic expansion incorporate vast areas that have different economic needs and different roles to play in the economic development of the empire. Later, such differences invite comparisons and pleas for equal treatment to the central government, which typically responds in two ways. First, it seeks to maintain its empire by force (often how it was constructed in the first place). Second, it seeks to stem social unrest by transfer payments of various sorts intended to ameliorate the worst inequalities (cf. Dubin and Reid, 1988; Lyson 1989).

Jacobs (1984) calls both responses "transactions of decline." Transactions of decline are nonproductive economic expenses, since neither programs of transfer payments nor militarism promote economic development (cf. Dubin and Reid, 1988; Melman, 1985). Transactions of decline bring about economic stagnation as the empire becomes consumed in an attempt to ensure its continued existence. According to Jacobs, it is ultimately a hopeless struggle.

Rural, national, and urban analyses. Rural areas in general seem to stand in relation to the urban or the national economy as "peripheral" areas. Macroeconomic analysis, because it concentrates on the generality of the national economy, tends to overlook the status of rural areas. Perhaps, as Jacobs (1984) suggests, the reason for this seeming oversight lies in the nature of the macroeconomic fiction. If Jacobs is correct, then rural areas depend for a marginal prosperity on their trade with urban areas, where economic development occurs.

Wallerstein (1984), however, suggests that the balance of trade between rural and urban areas will be so constructed as to impoverish rural areas. Ultimately, as Tomaskovic-Devey (1987) suggests, the personal characteristics of rural residents (illiteracy, race, low educational attainment) may in this case be used to "explain" the impoverished condition of rural areas. Indeed, this "explanation" *is* accepted at least in part by many economists and educators (Bender et al., 1985; Bloomquist, 1988; Bloomquist and Summers, 1988; Brown and Deavers, 1987a; Deaton and McNamara, 1984; Hobbs, 1987; Lyson, 1989; Rosenfeld et al., 1985, 1989). Rural educators and others who believe that developing the human capital of rural areas will lay the groundwork for local economic development may, if the critics are right, be disappointed. At best, "effective" education will allow those who receive it the opportunity to migrate to core employment opportunities.

The Economic Marginality of Rural America

Economic structures appear to influence the quality of life in rural areas. Economic marginality is, with respect to the economy as a whole, the structural analog of poverty with respect to the experience of individuals. Economic marginality entails the questionable profitability of an occupation or enterprise, and is usually associated with routine production that is no longer the site of major new economic development (e.g., Barkley, Keith, and Smith, 1989; Jacobs, 1984; Lyson, 1989). Individual poverty, however, is one indication of economic marginality, since marginal enterprises often yield low wages for those employed in them (Lyson, 1989; cf. Weber, Castle, and Shriver, 1987). In rural America, the poor are often employed, though they often do not have as much employment as they would like (O'Hare, 1988).

Poverty. In rural America, the experience of poverty is clearly a persistent problem (Porter, 1989) and possibly a growing one (Lyson, 1989; O'Hare, 1988). A brief review of current poverty data suggests the extent of the problem.[12] In

1987 poverty rates in nonmetropolitan America (that is, areas outside cities and their surrounding suburbs) were not only higher than metropolitan poverty rates, but they equaled the poverty rates in central cities. For whites (including Hispanics), the nonmetro and central city poverty rates are identical. For blacks, the nonmetro poverty rate substantially *exceeds* the central city rate. The intensity of rural poverty varies by region: In the South and the West (regions that together contain more than 2/3 of the nation's poor people), nonmetro poverty rates *exceed* central city poverty rates. (According to Lyson [1989] the disparities between the rural and urban South are growing *worse*.) In the Northeast, the nonmetro poverty rate is substantially lower than the central city poverty rate, and in the Midwest it is somewhat lower.

According to Reif (1987), the extractive industries over time contribute to a worsening of economic conditions. The work of others strongly suggests that the peripheral labor market attached to those industries is the origin of the most intense poverty associated with extractive enterprises (Stevens, 1983; Tomaskovic-Devey, 1982, 1987). Some observers believe that the relationship between poverty and employment in extractive industries is weakening (Bloomquist, 1988). Duncan and Duncan (1983), however, show that high incomes in coal-mining do not usually translate to improved socioeconomic conditions (i.e., investment in the local community, increased public revenues, improved human services, or equalized income distribution).

More generally, the available evidence suggests that socioeconomic conditions in rural counties where peripheral manufacturing dominates is usually associated with relatively poor socioeconomic conditions (Bloomquist, 1988; Bloomquist and Summers, 1988; Lyson, 1989; Pottinger, 1985; Reif, 1987; Rosenfeld et al., 1985, 1989; Summers et al., 1988; Tomaskovic-Devey, 1987). In addition, there is some evidence that in rural counties where government employment predominates (including employment in education), socioeconomic conditions are also relatively poor (Pottinger, 1987; Reif, 1987). Bloomquist and Summers (1988) believe, however, that government employment—via increases in the number of clerical jobs—tends to equalize income distribution in counties with economic growth, at least in the period 1960–1970.

Marginality, nonhuman capital, and the obsolescence of labor. As Bell (1973) notes, a key feature of post-industrial society is the continuing obsolescence of labor, particularly "labor" construed as the sale of the time of proletarian workers of undifferentiated—and increasingly devalued—skills. The obsolescence of labor is the *progressive* replacement of labor by nonhuman capital (plant, machinery, and other fixed assets). In the process of obsolescence, each remaining worker in the enterprise becomes responsible for a greater amount of capital and for a greater amount of output. As an enterprise matures, then, capitalization increases, worker productivity increases, costs (and prices) per unit of output drop, and eventually profitability falls to a marginal level, all things being equal (Wright, 1979). This is the process by which marginal economic enterprises come into being—those in which workers are few and profits are comparatively low (cf. Lyson, 1989).[13]

When such a technological change affects the occupational structure of rural areas, Jacobs (1984) refers to it as a clearance. Workers are "cleared" from the process of production, to their detriment unless they can find another occupation. Rural workers are also cleared in the sense that if other occupations are not available, they abandon the rural area for the city.[14]

It may seem that marginal enterprises serve no productive purpose, but this impression ignores the significance of economic structure and function. As an enterprise becomes progressively more marginal, it can be integrated into more profitable enterprises, either by the corporation that owns it (perhaps as part of planned diversification), or by another corporation interested in diversifying its operations (to which the owning corporation can sell the enterprise). It can also be relocated to areas (e.g., in the third world) where labor costs are much less than they are in rural America.

In practice, corporations exercise various alternatives to avoid the negative effects of operating a marginal enterprise. For example, they may seek favorable government policies; they may practice innovative financial manipulations; they may engage in aggressive labor practices; they may seek a monopoly in the markets in which they operate; or they may invest in continued technological improvements (Heilbroner and Thurow, 1985).

In this way marginal enterprises, though in themselves not necessarily very profitable, are nonetheless *productive*. They are incorporated into a larger unit, to which they contribute stability. Stability might take the form of guaranteed supply or demand; possible advantages in the firm's end market; or access to transfer payments associated with the marginal enterprise (e.g., depletion allowances and other deductions, subsidies, and investment tax-credits).

As an economic base of routine production, marginal enterprises contribute to overall economic production and development. Corporate accounting departments, for example, generate no profit, but firms do not therefore eliminate them. Marginal enterprises—if they cannot be eliminated—become, like accounting departments, part of the cost of doing business. Not only need they not be profitable, they may necessarily be operated at a loss, and, depending on the corporation's overall structure, it may even be to a corporation's advantage to operate the enterprise at a loss.[15]

Specialization and rural enterprises. In general, industries best suited to rural America are those "with routine technology and established markets" (Lyson, 1989; McGranahan, 1987, p. 3; cf. Barkley et al., 1989). These are precisely the sorts of industries described here as marginal enterprises.[16]

Recent empirical descriptions demonstrate how much life in rural America has changed even since 1950 or 1960 (Bender et al., 1985; Brown and Deavers, 1987a; McGranahan, Hession, Hines, and Jordon, 1986; Rosenfeld et al., 1985, 1989; Stephens, 1988). Agricultural production can no longer be taken to be the characteristic rural enterprise, as it was in the past (e.g., Cubberley, 1922). Other industries are now equally important to the economic life of rural areas.

Behind this emerging diversity, however, lies increased *specialization*, as the work of Bender et al. (1985) particularly suggests. These researchers (employed by the Department of Agriculture) developed an 8-part typology of nonmetropolitan counties: farming-dependent, mining-dependent, manufacturing-dependent, retirement-dependent, government services, federal lands, persistent poverty, and unclassified.[17]

Perhaps half of all rural counties have an economic base in natural resource "extraction."[18] Making a liberal estimate of duplicated counties, perhaps 1460 counties (or fully 70% of classified nonmetropolitan counties) depend either on extractive industries or manufacturing.[19]

If mining-, farming-, and timber-dependent counties[20] are considered to be the extractive sector of rural economies, then rural specialization can be seen as a trend even within a single sector. Since 1969 the number of counties in these categories has increased by 156%. Of this increase, 20% is attributable to mining, 2% to timber, and 77% to farming (cf. Weber et al., 1987). This specialization has developed even as services have become the fastest-growing sector of the economy generally.

Clearances as labor obsolescence in rural enterprises. The extractive industries, in general, have become, and continue to become, less labor-intensive and more capital-intensive (Brown and Deavers, 1987b). For example, even since 1960 the amount of labor required to harvest 100 bushels of corn has diminished by 85% (from 20 to 3 hours) and simultaneously the average corn yield has increased 115% (from 55 to 118 bushels per acre). In the same (quite recent) period, the number of farms has declined by 75% (from 20 to 5 million). The farm population continued to decline at a rate of 2.5% per year during the 1980s, and appears to have decreased by 5% in 1986-1987 (U.S. Bureau of the Census, 1988).

Data reported by Kendrick and Grossman (1980) also suggest that productivity growth in the extraction industries exceeds productivity growth in the private domestic economy as a whole. Furthermore, while labor input to the economy as whole *increased* at an annual rate of +0.5% during the postwar period, labor inputs in farming, mining, and lumber industries *decreased* steadily (–3.9%, –0.3%, and –1.2%, respectively) during the same period.[21] Throughout the extractive industries reports like that of a planned $30 million wood-processing plant employing only 120 workers (Stevens, 1983), will become increasingly more common as robotics are applied to routine production.

Manufacturing is another industry now common in rural America, and Bender and colleagues (1985) classified 678 counties as manufacturing-dependent. Rural manufacturing differs from extractive industries in its closer location to urban areas (Bloomquist, 1987). Jacobs (1984) calls such areas "transplant" regions. Rural manufacturing counties tend to be nearer urban centers than are counties specialized in extraction, and, if adjacent to growing metropolitan areas, will become urbanized (Jacobs, 1984). This analysis indicates that even the rural growth of the 1960s and 1970s—which was associated largely with growth in manufacturing (McGranahan, 1987)—may have reflected urbanization more than rural development.

The marginal nature of rural manufacturing is documented in recent reports (e.g., Bender et al., 1985; Barkley et al., 1988; Lyson, 1989; McGranahan, 1987). Both Lyson (1989) and McGranahan (1987) note that firms—whether small or large corporations—tend to locate their routine manufacturing jobs in rural areas. Labor obsolescence also seems to be the norm in such enterprises. Even after the national "recovery" from the severe recession of the early 1980s, these rural enterprises offered 12% fewer jobs in 1986 than in 1979 (McGranahan, 1987, p. 7).[22]

Summary: Rural economic marginality. The empirical studies cited above suggest the extent to which rural areas are part of the national economy, and they suggest the functions such a role entails. The rural life problem is no longer the farm problem (cf. Cubberley, 1922). Fewer than 8% of *rural* people live on farms; and half of those farms have gross sales less than $1000 per year (U.S. Bureau of the Census, 1988).[23] Rural areas seem to render specialized service to the national economy by serving as a site for specialized production by marginal enterprises that provision the nation with energy, minerals, food and fiber, and simple manufactured goods. Productivity in such industries is rising, and labor inputs are falling. Rural residents have a long history of underemployment and low participation in the labor market (McGranahan, 1987). To an unmeasured degree, this history contributes to their acceptance of low wages and periods of unemployment and underemployment as a condition of life (Cobb, 1982).

Analysts agree that a number of problems must be confronted in the future. The strategy most frequently endorsed by educators and rural development experts (e.g., Bender et al., 1985; Brown and Deavers, 1987a; Hobbs, 1987, 1989; Lyson, 1989; Nachtigal, 1988; Sher, 1987) is to improve human capital (or human resources) in rural areas. Most observers appear to believe that more education and training will improve rural socioeconomic conditions, an issue of causality examined in the first section of this chapter. Observers like Zachariah (1985, p. 21), however, warn that available evidence indicates that:

> it is not possible, ever again, to portray formal education as Atlas shouldering the burden of transforming individuals in order to accelerate development. It is now doubtful whether formal education is two-faced Janus, with the ability to learn from the mistakes of corporate capitalism as well as state socialism and wisely create a new society of the future.

The limits of neoclassical analysis. The recommendation to improve human capital can, however, be understood in light of popular critiques of neoclassical economics.[24] Bowles et al. (1984, p. 5) note the essential assumption: Whereas the economy is a creation of people, and its basic relationships are social relationships, neoclassical economics "has adopted the view that the economy runs like a machine, a clockwork mechanism in perpetual synchrony." In neoclassical economics, social relations are not an object of inquiry. As a result, human beings—creatures of culture and ideology that they are—have a questionable place in neoclassical economics.

Human capital theory, however, integrates human beings into the neoclassical analysis as the location of economically productive skills and knowledge. Its interpretation of the knowledge, skills, and experience of human beings as *capital* is significant because the free movement of private capital is perhaps the key feature of capitalism (cf. Smith, 1960/1776).[25]

In the neoclassical analysis, rural areas are *geographic sites* that provide for the development of certain utilities that should ultimately benefit the national economy. Likewise, people are merely sites of the skills, knowledge, and experience that apparently contribute to economic growth.[26] The values and culture of a people who chance to occupy a particular territory are immaterial to development, in this view. If economic development does not occur (or, as in the case of the national economy, is perceived to lag) neoclassical economics may recommend the improvement of human capital as one possibility.

Because neoclassical economics does not inquire about the role of social relations, and because with human capital it separates skills and knowledge as a factor of production separate from individual human beings, it can view particular human beings as *impediments* to economic development. The quickest remedy to economic stagnation or decline, therefore, is not education but *replacement* of the existing capital stock. Displaced rural citizens can be "retooled" to serve the aims of the national economy. By treating human beings as a capital stock, neoclassical economics can "free" workers of the places to which they are irrationally attached.[27]

The neoclassical clockwork comes apart, however, when economics seeks to investigate regional, ethnic, and gender issues (Bowles et al., 1984; Kalleberg, 1989; Williams, 1988). Pottinger (1987) showed how a Reagan-era Presidential Commission, asked to identify barriers to economic development, overlooked the relevant skills and knowledge immediately available in a depressed American Indian economy and reported that deficient human capital was the chief barrier to development. Pottinger demonstrated that there were already too few jobs to make use of the *available* skills of local people.

A study by Snipp and Sandefur (1988) confirms this analysis—Indians who migrate and remain long enough in urban areas benefit principally from the availability of more and better quality work. Duncan (1986) makes a similar point about the limited employment prospects in central Appalachia and the attraction of cities: lack of jobs, not a deficient workforce keep people in poverty. Both Lyson (1989) and Sher (1988a) believe that the creation of good jobs must be given a priority that defacto rural development policies have never acknowledged. Both these observers note that economic justice is the foundation of economic development.

Without a view of economic structures and social relations, neoclassical analysis, if honest, can report only great "diversity" (Zachariah, 1985; cf. Bender et al., 1985). The findings of such research, however, tend to support the inference that the socially created structures that govern the macroeconomic clockwork *require* the economic marginality of rural areas (cf. Bender et al., 1985; Brown and Deavers, 1987a; Weber et al., 1987).

The Relationship Between Rural Education and Economic Marginality

Mounting evidence shows that marginal rural enterprises—and the local economies they structure—are tied more and more closely to national and international economic life (Brown and Deavers, 1987b; Stephens, 1988). This trend, which is a long-term historical development (Dunaway, 1989), has important implications for schools in rural areas (Meyer et al., 1979; Silver and DeYoung, 1986; Stephens, 1988).

Although neoclassical economics may link marginal rural enterprise to deficient human capital, other evidence indicates that rural economic marginality derives, not from the deficient skills and knowledge of rural people but from the culture and ideology that rationalize national economic structures (Bell, 1973; Grubb, 1985; Silver and DeYoung, 1986; Zachariah, 1985).

Ideological principles of national schooling. When schools were first imagined for this country, the type of education proposed was an education in the practical arts of mechanics and farming (Cremin, 1980). Americans are persistently and unfailingly practical in their approach to education (Bell, 1973; Counts, 1930; Cremin, 1980; Cuban, 1983; Hofstadter, 1963).

The complex of ideas associated with this trait—for example, acquisitiveness, instrumentality, efficiency, novelty, and individuality—characterize the ideology of capitalism, according to Bell (1976). These values pervade American education and structure perpetual school "reform" in this country (Cremin, 1961; Cuban, 1983; Silver and DeYoung, 1986).

The construction of standardized schooling. Nationally instrumental schools required a systematic administration, and business management served as the model (Callahan, 1962). Shortly after the turn of the twentieth century, school administrators adopted the principles of scientific management directly from business (Callahan, 1962; Cremin, 1961; DeYoung, 1989; Katz, 1971; Spring, 1986).

The result has been the standardization of schooling, so that schools generally resemble each other more than they differ (cf. Goodlad, 1986; Schmuck and Schmuck, 1989). Existing differences are continuously scrutinized so that the positive differences can be identified, understood, and replicated elsewhere. The successful replication of effective practices, of course, may well cause schools to resemble one another still more closely (see, e.g., Navarro, Berkey, and Minnick, 1986).

Standardized schools exhibit the ideological themes mentioned above—acquisitiveness, instrumentality, efficiency, novelty, and individuality. These themes are now embedded features of all American schools (cf. Cremin, 1961, 1980; DeYoung, 1989; Katz, 1971; Spring, 1976; Tyack, 1974).

Acquisitiveness in education, as in economics, is a driving force in America.[28] It refers especially to the accumulation of capital (Bell, 1976), and school administrators have been dramatically successful in acquiring control of fixed and labor capital, as the history of school district consolidation suggests.[29] Consolidation brought more capital under the control of centralized administration—land, buildings, equipment, and labor. In the process teachers have lost autonomy (Katz, 1971; McNeil, 1985; Samuels, 1970; Smith and DeYoung, 1988; Wigginton, 1985) and communities have lost the control of these resources (Dunne, 1983; Sher, 1977, 1986).[30]

Instrumentality, as noted above, pertains to the aims of American education. When social science (as in studies of human capital) validates an instrumental purpose, it establishes a rationale for increased vocationalism and careerism as aims of education. Although the American common education, as Cremin notes, was imagined as practical even at the time of the Revolution, the orientation of higher education in America has, until recently, been less instrumental (Barzun, 1968; Stephens and Roderick, 1975). Increasingly, however, careerism has displaced study of the liberal arts even at the most elite institutions (see e.g., Katchadourian and Boli, 1985). In rural schools, located in economies dominated by marginal enterprises and in presumed need of economic development, educational improvements are tied to instrumental aims even more firmly than they are elsewhere (Carnoy, 1982; Grubb, 1985).

Efficiency encompasses the consensus about operations. Efficiency refers, at base, to completion of a required function for the least possible cost. In industrial operations, quality control is able to determine when increased efficiency interferes with quality. No such standards exist in education. The influential Rand Corporation summed up contemporary educational attitudes about efficiency in 1974:

> Increasing expenditure on traditional educational practices is not likely to improve educational outcomes substantially. There seem to be opportunities for significant reduction or redirection of educational expenditures without deterioration in educational outcomes. (Averch et al., 1974, pp. 171–175)

In rural areas, where sparsity and transportation costs increase expenditures, schools are often accused of being inefficient (DeYoung, 1987). Talbert and colleagues (1987) report evidence, however, that demonstrates that rural schools in a persistently poor region are typically very efficient. Howley (1989a) suggests that rural schools, as a group, may be *too* efficient.

Novelty relates to the American tradition of innovation in education and business. In business, novelty is associated with the development and marketing of new products. In education, novelty is reflected in the enduring preoccupation of educators with the reform of schooling (Cuban, 1982; Katz, 1968, 1971; Spring, 1986).[31] Educational innovations translate directly into new products, which are usually produced by private enterprise. When public funds support the development of new educational products, private enterprise benefits twice. The most successful innovations in American education have arisen during the most conservative political eras: the beginnings of consolidation and the common school (1840–1860); scientific management (1890–1920); new math and science curricula (late 1950s); and school effectiveness (1980s) (Callahan, 1962; Cremin, 1961; Cuban, 1983; Katz, 1968; Spring, 1986).

Rhetorical respect of individuality permeates American education, and educators universally claim an interest in educating the "whole child." Schools, at least in rhetoric, seek to "individualize" their instruction so as to meet the "educational needs" of particular students. During the twentieth century, much innovation and differentiation (a handmaiden of efficiency) have taken place in an attempt to accomplish this end: age-grade placement, vocational education, homogeneous grouping by ability levels, the comprehensive (and consolidated) high school, compensatory education, career education, and special education. Some of these programs are additions outside the regular program, a tacit admission of the difficulty of changing routine practice, according to some observers (e.g., Cuban, 1982; Spring, 1986).

The continuity of proposals for reform. In the early decades of the century, reformers in education and government believed that the quality of rural life in general was deteriorating (e.g., Cubberley, 1922). They saw education as the tool to revitalize and integrate rural areas into the emerging national political economy.[32] The rhetoric of the early part of the century is, however, not much different from the rhetoric of the last decades of the century:

> We should act at once because of the stress of
> foreign competition. We are twenty-five years behind
> most of the nations that we recognize as competitors.
> We must come nearer to the level of international
> competition. As every establishment must have a first-
> class mechanical equipment and management, so
> must it have in its workmen skill equal to that of
> competitors, domestic and foreign. . . . It is their
> misfortune that [American workers] have not been
> given by this country that measure of technical
> instruction that is their due. (National Association of
> Manufacturers, 1905; cited by Cuban, 1983, p. 187)

Now, as then, rural schools are viewed as targets for
"restructuring" (Silver and DeYoung, 1986; e.g., Committee of
Twelve, 1898; Mid-Continent Regional Educational Laboratory,
1988); now, as then, rural schools are encouraged to provide
more practical training to rural youth (DeYoung, 1989; Grubb,
1985; e.g., Hobbs, 1989; Sher, 1987, 1988b; Ross and
Rosenfeld, 1987).

Their concern for local conditions is as genuine, for
example, as those of previous rural reformers (e.g., Cubberley,
1922). Unlike their predecessors, however, contemporary
reformers call for training entrepreneurs instead of employees,
and they recommend training relevant to services instead of
farming and manufacturing. The practical intent of
contemporary reformers, however, is nonetheless identical to
that of earlier reformers (DeYoung, 1989; Grubb, 1985):
improved economic performance through improved education,
especially better occupational or technical training (e.g., Hobbs,
1989).

Vocationalism and economic marginality. In educational
practice, human capital theory is implemented as vocationalism
(Stronach, 1988). Grubb (1985) defines vocationalism broadly,
as occupationally related educational differentiation that occurs
at every level of schooling. He notes:

> In fact, the basic purpose of schooling for individual
> students has come to be defined in vocational terms.
> In most countries, the ethic of staying in school to
> improve one's occupational standing—rather than for

moral or political development, for example—has
become dominant during the twentieth century.
(Grubb, 1985, p. 538)

Grubb describes a number of specific problems
associated with using education (in secondary, postsecondary,
and higher education) to achieve economic goals. The first is
educational inflation. As enrollment expands, returns to the
lowest levels of educational attainment (for example, completing
high school) lose their value. The recent analysis by Murphy
and Welch (1989) confirms this fact: Part of the dramatic
increase in returns to a college degree in the 1980s is
accounted for by a 10%–16% decline in real wages for high
school graduates.

Second, rates of return to education tend to fall for
students who pursue advanced degrees. Many studies (for
example, Gordon, 1979; Murphy and Welch, 1989;
Psacharopoulos, 1981) confirm this fact, which neoclassical
economics explains as the phenomenon of diminishing marginal
returns. Grubb notes an alternative explanation, however:
education serves to allocate jobs. This explanation implies that
higher levels of educational attainment may not increase
productivity, even though they offer a modest return on the
investment in human capital (Collins, 1979).

Third, vocationalism does not, contrary to popular belief,
serve to increase economic equality (e.g., Levin, 1984). It fails
to do so because it parallels workplace differentiation, which,
through associated wage and salary differentials, necessarily
creates greater income variability (Shackett and Slottje, 1986).
Jobs become more specialized; in the process, both higher-
wage and lower-wage jobs are created; as training efforts, both
in and out of school, reinforce the workplace differentiation,
income variability (and hence, income inequality) increases.
Shackett and Slottje (1986) discovered that the increase in
educational attainment in their longitudinal study was
significantly related to growing income inequality.[33]

Stronach (1988, p. 67) is puzzled by the "unreason" that
characterizes vocationalism as a continuing proposal to address
economic woes (cf. Grubb, 1985; Zachariah, 1985). He posits

a ritual role for the propaganda that accompanies vocationalism.[34] According to Stronach (1988, p. 68), "ritual addresses crisis, its means are rhetorics . . . and its end is reassurance." He concludes:

> This kind of unreason is not based on rational error or simply ideological duplicity. It centers on a need to reassure the powerful as much as it seeks to mystify the powerless—and indeed the evidence seems to be that it succeeds better at the former.

Stronach's assessment brings the discussion full circle to the beginning of this chapter and the reactions to Coleman's findings. Human capital theory and the school-effectiveness movement form a tight ideology of schooling, with the technology of school improvement the means and the development of human capital the ends. The cultural values upon which the ideology is based entail acquisitiveness, efficiency, instrumentality, and novelty.

The Ideological Roots of Rural Educational Marginality

Marginal enterprises do not exist at the center of technical development; instead, they provide essential goods or services on the basis of routine production (Bloomquist, 1987). Unless protected by special arrangements, marginal economic enterprises produce low rates of profit (cf. Duncan and Duncan, 1983).

In the context of economic marginality, standardized (and nationally instrumental) schools create the norms and expectations that establish rural educational as a marginal enterprise. All the features of capitalist ideology described previously apply here as well. The following analysis will, however, concentrate on efficiency, novelty, and instrumentality as these characteristics most directly reflect the marginality of rural education.

The norm of efficiency—in the context of the other norms of standardized schooling—has the greatest effect in structuring rural schools as marginal enterprises. Because rural schools have expenses that—due to remoteness and small scale—are

necessarily higher than urban schools (Bagby et al., 1985;
Deaton and McNamara, 1984; Honeyman et al., 1989),
normative comparisons force rural schools to economize more
than other schools (Augenblick and Nachtigal, 1985; Howley,
1989a; Meehan, 1987).

Second, standardized operations (for example,
administration of state- and federally-funded categorical aid
programs) require greater expenditures in rural than in urban
schools, possibly because the required oversight effort
imposes a diseconomy of scale on districts with low student
enrollment (Meyer et al., 1986). Meyer and colleagues, using a
national data set, discovered that dependence on categorical
federal funding (e.g., Chapter I, P.L. 94–142) generates more
administrative positions and additional expenditures than other
kinds of funding. Rural districts rely more on state and federal
revenue than other districts (Honeyman et al., 1989), and, with
smaller enrollments, their administrative costs per student are
necessarily higher (cf. Meyer et al., 1986).

Third, novelty—or, in educational terms, the ideals of
innovation, improvement, and progress—imposes additional
expectations on rural schools. Rural schools that are already
strapped to meet ordinary operating expenses have difficulty
acquiring the goods and services necessary to support the
perpetual innovation and improvement that are normatively
expected of all districts. Acquiring computers, for example, has
become a pressing concern of rural districts (Honeyman et al.,
1989). Recently adopted reforms impose additional burdens,
and the available appropriations are not usually sufficient for
rural districts to meet the mandated reforms (Brizius et al.,
1988; Lyson, 1989; Stephens, 1988).

Indeed, most rural districts encountered problems
meeting the standards in place prior to the reforms of the
1980s (Dunne, 1983). In his analysis of the plight of schools in
the rural South, Lyson (1989) attributes the cause to previous
rural development efforts, particularly the competitiveness
among rural communities to attract industry. These
communities offered tax breaks, low-interest loans, and funded
construction projects to attract manufacturing plants. In so
doing they denied themselves the benefits of an increased tax-

base and assumed new debts. When these subsidized industries left the area, as many did in the 1980s, some of the communities were in worse financial shape—due to debts incurred—than they were before. Coupled with the decline in federal funding for rural areas, the result is disaster for these communities and their schools.

The ultimate utility of an economic enterprise is profit. The ultimate utility of the educational enterprise, at least since the late 1940s, has come more and more to be economic development, both for individuals and for society as a whole. In metropolitan areas the economic development that tends to occur naturally (Jacobs, 1984) serves to justify economic development as the overriding aim of education. In rural areas, however, despite rising educational levels, substantial development has not taken place (DeYoung, 1989; Grubb, 1985; Lyson, 1989; Prattis, 1979; Pottinger, 1987; Stronach, 1988; Zachariah, 1985).

Finally, the rhetoric that dominates discussions about the aims of schooling is a minimal expectation of the possible benefits of education. The desperate concentration on economic development as the aim of education handicaps thinking about the educational mission. The recent concern for students' "higher-order thinking" illustrates the problem well, and that concern is disturbing because higher-order thinking is conceived to be the most important deficiency in the competitiveness of the American workforce (Committee for Economic Development, 1985; Edelstein and Schoeffe, 1989). Surely the nurture of students' thinking is among the most worthy of educational aims; yet, in the context of vocationalism, thinking, too, becomes a thing—a set of skills, a kit of practical tools for economic development—rather than the habits of intellect that characterize skepticism, inquiry, and critique. Because the relationship between specific educational practices and economic development is so tenuous with respect to individuals (DeYoung, 1989; Grubb, 1985; Williams, 1988), educational planning based on the premises of economic development may be, as Stronach (1988) alleges, a kind of witchcraft that serves a purpose other than education.

Vocationalism and Entrepreneurship in Rural Education

Nations in the modern world have universally cherished the hope that education would provide the engine of economic development and the means of achieving more equal societies. Twenty years of phenomenal growth in education, both in developing and developed nations, has provided virtually no empirical data that justifies the hope (Carnoy, 1982; DeYoung, 1989; Grubb, 1985; Levin, 1984; Williams, 1988; Zachariah, 1985). If human capital theory cannot explain the economic plight of rural areas, if vocationalism has not provided the economic development it has promised to rural areas, and if the technology of school improvement is problematic for rural schools, then what concepts might be educationally relevant to the dilemma of learning in rural areas?

There are two alternative views. The first view accepts the instrumental strategy of improving rural economies through rural education as valid. It criticizes the kind of vocational training provided in the past to rural students, and proposes a different kind of training (cf. Sher, 1987). The second view, however, rejects vocationalism as a valid strategy. It bases its rejection on evidence that suggests schools are weak tools for reshaping the economic context in which they exist (cf. Jencks et al., 1972; 1979).

The New Vocationalism: Entrepreneurship

Neoclassical economics exercises an increasingly more powerful influence on rural education, despite the lack of evidence that local investments in human capital contribute much to rural economic development (Carnoy, 1982; Deaton and McNamara, 1984; Grubb, 1985; Hobbs, 1987; McNamara, 1987; Knutson and Fisher, 1988; Stronach, 1988; Zachariah, 1985). Because neoclassical economists regard the value of human capital in macroeconomic development as firmly established (e.g., Deaton and McNamara, 1984), the challenge has become how to devise strategies of investment in human capital that *do* contribute to rural economic development.

Retooling vocationalism. According to many observers (e.g., Friedman, 1987; Hobbs, 1989; Knutson and Fisher, 1988; Ross and Rosenfeld, 1987; Sher, 1989) the evidence indicates that the vocational strategies of the past were in error because they did not take into account predictions about the emerging post-industrial order (cf. Bell, 1973; Toffler, 1970).

In this view, the means of education, not its aims, were at fault. This lack of foresight had a two-fold result. First, it resulted in the training of *employees* in a set of limited skills: conformity, punctuality, the willingness to accept the direction of others, and rudimentary academics (Sher, 1989). Second, it tied the content of training to an economic sector that would in the future produce fewer jobs, while other sectors would (unexpectedly) produce more jobs (Hobbs, 1989).

These results are two sides of the same problem. Managers in the goods-producing industries have not required most employees to think; rather they have required them to follow procedures established by others (Hobbs, 1987; 1989). In the context of the conventional organization of an American goods-producing industry, this low academic expectation is a requirement of industrial efficiency. Lately, however, American business has come to understand that this approach to training workers is short-sighted (Committee for Economic Development, 1985; Edelstein and Schoeffe, 1989).

The historical changes discussed previously also provide evidence of a need for a changed educational method, given the dominant vocational aims of education. During the 1970s and 1980s, while the metropolitan economy presumably retooled to accommodate the emerging service sector, rural economies continued to specialize in extraction and manufacturing. Technological innovations in extractive industries put some residents out of work. Footloose manufacturing firms departed for the third world, putting other residents out of work. During the economic recovery of the 1980s, rural areas did not recover to the same extent as urban areas (McGranahan, 1987).

The way in which rural education should be changed seems clear on the basis of this critique: the aim of education as occupational training remains, but the content and methods need to be aligned with the requirements of post-industrial occupational prospects. Hence, schools should change the kind of occupational training given to rural students.

Three principles guide these changes. First, the post-industrial era is thought to require more highly-trained workers; second, the service industry is predicted to provide most new jobs; and third, rural areas have special service "niches" that no one but local residents are likely to fill (Hobbs, 1987).

Although many rural residents now earn their living in specialized enterprises, they spend that income outside their communities, in larger towns or in urban areas, since local services are not available. Schools can contribute to local economic growth by producing local entrepreneurs to fill those local service niches (Hobbs, 1987; Sher, 1988b).

In this view of vocationalism, entrepreneurs are thought to represent a type of emerging post-industrial citizen, and all students are potential entrepreneurs (Friedman, 1987). Existing entrepreneurs, of course, embody the cultural values of capitalism we cited above. They are task-oriented (they are instrumental); they work hard to achieve success (they are acquisitive); they are innovators (they are concerned with novelty); and they know how to maximize their resources (they are efficient) (Friedman, 1987; Hoy, 1987; Pulver, 1987).

Programs that use rural schools as centers of entrepreneurship and business incubation[35] have been started in scattered places around the nation. Jonathan Sher, who heads North Carolina's Rural School-Based Enterprise Program, is perhaps the conceptual leader in school programs that aim to develop rural entrepreneurs. Sher (1988) presents such training as a variety of cultural resistance and school reform. His knowledge of the rural context is substantial: He is skeptical of the contribution of schooling to economic development;[36] he understands how schools train impoverished students for compliance; and he understands the economic constraints under which rural schools operate. According to Sher (1987), rural enterprise programs will, however, accomplish several purposes. They will help keep students in school by making the schools more relevant, they will improve students' self-esteem, and they will revitalize local communities.

The value and limits of entrepreneurship. The justification for both the old and new vocationalism depends on the success of their application rather than on the significance (meaningfulness) of their teachings. Vocationalism has always aimed to develop new attitudes to work, provide relevant skills, and keep rural students in local communities (Grubb, 1985). On these points, rural enterprise training is no different from the vocationalism put forward in earlier eras. It differs principally in the kind of attitudes and skills it proposes to develop in students.

The proponents of entrepreneurship training, however, can differ substantially among themselves about which attitudes and skills to teach students. Some proponents appear to have in view the cultivation of a kind of Jeffersonian society of independent business people who will apply post-industrial technology to the stewardship of society in much the way Jefferson had originally hoped independent small-scale farmers would apply pre-industrial technology to stewardship of the earth.[37] The traditional appeal of this vision is strong among Americans. To the extent that it guides programs of entrepreneurship, it could help students consider the larger issues of meaning that *should* be the chief concern of education (Arendt, 1978; Bell, 1973, 1976; Keizer, 1988; Wigginton, 1985).

While it is true that learning how to design and manage a successful business is more meaningful than learning punctuality and compliance, it is also true that the realities of the economic structure impose a limit on how many rural students can become successful entrepreneurs (Lyson, 1989). Some observers believe that the hope of self-employment is a distracting delusion that serves to legitimate wide inequalities among the sexes, races, classes, and geographic regions (e.g., Wright, 1979). To the extent that this analysis is correct, entrepreneurship training is misguided.

A Theoretical Interlude: Learning Versus the Development of Human Capital

Some principles to focus the concluding discussion are in order. First, *learning* (as noted in the introduction) is a process that is fundamentally different from investment. Second (a principle arising from the first), however important material conditions may be in shaping the experiences of the workplace, the role of *culture and ideology* in the classroom is paramount. Third (a principle arising from the first two), the *value of education* is not limited to, or even best conceived as, its relationship to earnings. Fourth, the institutional role of schooling is contested ground, so that an alternative view of rural education need not resolve whether or not the ultimate institutional role of schooling is to legitimate the existing inequity of the social order or to contribute to the construction of a new one. It will inevitably do both. Finally, to focus the concluding discussion, the terms "culture" and "ideology" need definition.

Culture. A narrow definition restricts culture to "the . . . symbolic forms . . . which seek to explore and express the meanings of human existence in some imaginative form" (Bell, 1976, p. 12). The advantage of this definition is that it relates the notions of equality, justice, and—more generally—culture and ideology to the economic changes that are overtaking society.

Culture in this sense is not so the subject of anthropology but is rather the imaginative realm of the mind, with the specific habits of intellect (including aesthetic and scientific perception) used by artists and scholars to address the enduring questions of life (Bell, 1976). The role of the schools, in this view, is to strive to make that realm accessible to all students. Learning is a cultural act, and if such an act is to take place, teachers must develop a shared discourse with which they can encounter questions of enduring significance with their students (cf. Giroux, 1983).

Ideology. Ideologies are codes of values that function to organize and legitimate a polity (Bell, 1976). As mere political tools, however, ideologies become dogmatic and contradictory, and they can advance whatever interests those who control the political agenda wish to pursue. Another sense of the term applies to learning, however, because

> it is in the character of ideologies not only to reflect or justify an underlying reality but, once launched, to take on a life of their own. A truly powerful ideology opens up a new vision of life to the imagination; once formulated, it remains part of the moral repertoire to be drawn upon by intellectuals, theologians, or moralists as part of the range of possibilities open to mankind. (Bell, 1976, pp. 60–61)

It is in the nature of the human mind, as it applies reason and judgment, to construct coherent ideologies from knowledge, values, and experience (Arendt, 1978). Though it uses knowledge, such construction is not knowledge; rather it is "understanding," the making of meaning (cf. Arendt, 1978).

The debasement of knowledge as information. A serious cultural problem of the emerging post-industrial world is that it blurs the distinction between information, knowledge, and understanding (Bell, 1973; Wiener, 1950). Facts are thought to "speak for themselves," and the possession of facts (information) is equated with knowledge. When learning becomes the acquisition of information (as in a curriculum and instructional routine that teaches only basic skills for a vocational purpose), education is debased.

The debasement draws education into a wider cycle of cultural devolution: Science devolves to technology; culture devolves to consumption; and education devolves to mere experience (Bell, 1973, 1976). As a cultural phenomenon, this process resembles the physical phenomenon of entropy, the tendency of organized systems to become disorganized (cf. Bell, 1976; McLuhan, 1964; Toffler, 1974; Wiener, 1950).

In the reductionist modality of knowledge-as-information, even the distinction between knowledge and information has vanished. Learning becomes a kind of *unmediated* transfer of information, unmediated not only in its directness, but in the absence of an instructional authority. The construction of meaning disappears as an aim of education, since it is neither information nor skill.[38]

Cultural and ideological critique of entrepreneurship training. In addition to its material limits as retooled vocationalism, rural enterprise training has cultural and ideological limits. Whereas good rural academic instruction makes a commitment to a progressive ideology and to the preservation of culture and the construction of meaning (Keizer, 1988; Wigginton, 1985), the *new* vocationalism continues the *old* vocationalism's commitment to the ideology of capitalism.

Bell (1976) points out that the cultural weakness of capitalism lies in the way it separates culture and technical skill. Culture is debased and becomes a realm in which the meaning of literature, history, or art is a matter of subjective taste and private pleasure. Complex considerations of taste, judgment, and meaning are not simply viewed as too difficult for ordinary students, they are seen to be inappropriate topics of classroom discourse, a potential violation of an individual's privacy. This trend trivializes the humanities, which are the source of the values that not only sustain society but that permit social progress (Bell, 1976; cf. Wigginton, 1985). The humanities are problematic in the context of vocationalism because—unlike enterprise training—they do not imply some immediate course of action (cf. Hobbs, 1989, p. 11). Technical skill, which does imply an immediate practical effect, becomes the focus of training and economic advancement, however weak or questionable the empirical connection between it and economic development below the macroeconomic level (e.g., for blacks, women, or rural residents).

Finally, most entrepreneurship training resembles the vocationalism of earlier eras in its conception of the aims of education: it assumes that knowledge, learning, and understanding have value only in so far as they serve hypothetical practical ends in the world. In the most debased form, education becomes *mere* training intended to serve particular, predetermined ends. Entrepreneurship training is as prone to this error as any sort of vocational training.

Culture and Ideology in the Rural Classroom

The sorts of pedagogical issues considered next are invisible to the neoclassical economists who elaborate human capital theory, which treats a given level of educational attainment as a utility of equal significance to both the national economy and individual consumptive ability.[39] As the following discussion illustrates, however, the conditions of instruction in schools do contribute to students' subsequent fate in the employment market. But in the classroom, culture and ideology inevitably come to the fore, and economic structures seem more distant (cf. Aronowitz and Giroux, 1985; Giroux, 1983).

Curriculum and instruction: The higher- and lower-orders. The issues of equality and justice are major problems in any society, whether capitalist, socialist, or communist (Bell, 1973; Carnoy, 1982). They can be dealt with only briefly here, in the context of a discussion of curriculum and instruction pertinent to the second kind of education, proposed next, for rural schools.[40]

The schools are segregated by class and race according to residential patterns (Jencks et al., 1979). The children of workers (the lower orders) get essentialism—basic skills stripped of context and meaning—and the children of elites (the higher orders) get perennialism (Anyon, 1987; Bowles and Gintis, 1976; Giroux, 1983; Jackson, 1981; Wilcox, 1982; Wilcox and Moriarity, 1977). Most educators, therefore, denounce perennialism (treatment of the "high culture") as an instrument of oppression or as an increasingly irrelevant body of knowledge (e.g., Carnoy, 1982; Giroux, 1983; McLuhan, 1964; Toffler, 1970).

Liberal and radical objections to the perennialist curriculum are founded on the misperception that the perennialist curriculum, and not the basic skills curriculum, is elitist. In fact, both perennialism (the higher-order curriculum) and essentialism (the lower-order curriculum) *together* reproduce the social divisions of American society as an artifact of the way contemporary American schools are organized (Bowles and Gintis, 1976; Grubb, 1985; Oakes, 1985).

Instructional methods commonly associated with *both* perennialism and essentialism (impersonal, decontextualized instruction), however, are deservedly condemned by many observers. Oxendine (1989) and Wigginton (1985) demonstrate how teaching to promote the life of the mind might be organized at the elementary and secondary levels.

The distinction between curriculum and instruction is essential, however. Good instruction cannot take place without good curriculum. Bell (1973) contends that certain bodies of knowledge are of enduring importance, and experiential instructional methods (e.g., Oxendine, 1989; Wigginton, 1985), while powerful motivators of learning, have, as instructional methods, a limited scope.[41]

For example, although Wigginton's teaching is guided by a coherent ideology that underwrites an imaginative view of life (Wigginton, 1985), the experiential method of itself does not define the curriculum, nor can it be the *principal* instructional strategy with which to consider all of history, great literature, higher mathematics, foreign languages, or science. At the same time, experiential methods could be much more widely used to improve instruction in more traditional academic subjects such as these.[42]

Good higher-order instruction of this sort is probably more difficult to achieve widely than effective instruction in basic (or thinking) skills, for which specific formulas exist (e.g., Joyce et al., 1983). Adler (1983), however, describes the general features of such instruction, and rural teachers like Keizer (1988) and Wigginton (1985) typically (perhaps intuitively) practice the instructional routines commended by Adler.

Meaning Versus Instrumentalism: The Dilemma of Rural Education

First vocational training, and now enterprise training, have been extolled as a means of keeping the rural way of life from disappearing altogether. The history of the American empire and the present economic status of rural America, however, suggest that the material tradition is exploitation, of rural resources and rural people. Whether this tradition *can* be ended may be moot. Wigginton (1980) claimed it was too late for his county.

Rural life and learning, however, may have another role than the instrumental one actually accorded them in the economic structure. The features of rural life—solitude, the imminence of the natural world, and kinship with neighbors, for the most part—may have an enduring intellectual and ethical significance for the American culture as a whole, which is rooted in a rural experience.

The isolation and imminence of the natural world in rural areas provide a context for the life of the mind, which has little scope beyond professionalism in the urban context. Intellectuals have historically looked to rural life as the inspiration for the development of a strong pastoral theme in American thought (Jacobs, 1984; Sample, 1989; Theobald, 1989). More generally, the search for virtue is in America bound up with stewardship of the earth (e.g., Berry, 1978, 1984, 1986; Nearing and Nearing, 1970). The rural tradition embodies an ethical ideal (an ideology) that encompasses individual, community, and nature. Schooling in rural America might embody such an ethic—which relates to concern for the social and natural environment as well as for the intellect— better than it has.

This alternative entails the preservation and construction of meaning and reflection in a developed culture that is notable for its anti-intellectualism (Hofstadter, 1963; Howley, 1987; cf. Storr, 1988). Rural schools, which have been instruments of empire-building, have done little to look at their mission in this way, and it might be argued that rural schools as they are cannot begin to carry out such a mission. The material conditions of rural and economic marginality seem almost insurmountable.

Is it, however, coincidental that a *rural teacher* has written one of the most eloquent statements of why the creation of meanings, not vocationalism or the development of human capital, warrants the work of the schools? Perhaps not. Keizer (1988, p. 68) writes,

> For consider, if the real world is as full of injustice,
> waste, and woe as it appears to be, and school has no
> other purpose than to prepare young people to man
> and woman the machinery of the real world, then
> schools are pernicious institutions. They serve to
> perpetuate rather than remedy evils. We would do as
> well to burn as to maintain a school that does no
> more than mirror and foreshadow the real world.

This view pits rural education as cultural act (the preservation and extension of culture) against education as an economic end (global domination and integration). The life of the mind works on the appreciation and making of fine distinctions and on the examination of contradictions (cf. Bell's "discordant knowledge").

If Bell's (1973, 1976) analyses of post-industrial society and the cultural contradictions of capitalism are correct, an education that fails to equip most students with an intimate knowledge of their culture and with the tools of judgment and reason—so they can confront the significant questions of human existence—will surely fail them and their various communities badly. Rural schools can and should contribute to the most essential mission of education: the nurture of minds that construct meaning.

There is little doubt that students thus prepared *will* contribute substantially to the well-being of their communities. The chief impediment to this alternative, however, is our continuing devotion to the idea of efficiency, which, ironically, grounds the aims of education in a practicality that remains merely hypothetical (Carnoy, 1982; Grubb, 1985). As Stronach (1988) points out, it has not even mattered that the promises of vocationalism are hollow. It is past time to reconsider the aims of rural education: Educators should learn that schools cannot *directly* change the social and economic structures in which they are embedded. Their mission, instead, should be to help students encounter the enduring human questions and to construct the valid meanings that are the only route to the creation of a more just society and a more productive world.

NOTES

1. For a time during the 1970s the alleged need to "deschool society" was debated (Illich, 1970), but the proposal was never taken very seriously. In the 1980s, however, the need to "restructure" rural schools has continued, in a very different theoretical context, some of the themes raised by Illich.

2. See Carnoy (1985) for a brief discussion of the political economy of education. "Political economy" considers the interplay of economic and social forces; "economics" generally refers to *neoclassical* economics, the technical discipline used to study monetary relationships. Economics is based on the assumption that human beings act to maximize economic benefits (or "utilities" in the jargon of economics). The principal utilities analyzed by economics are income (for labor) and profits (for capital). The scope of political economy is wider than the scope of economics because it views the economy as a set of social relationships. Political economy combines qualitative and quantitative methods; the neoclassical method is purely quantitative and its mathematics are comparatively more sophisticated than the mathematics of quantitative research in education.

3. Much school improvement effort, however, is targeted at management and administrative leadership rather than instruction.

4. The life adjustment curriculum may embody the quest for stability undertaken by those who lived through the Depression and the war that followed. The world is no longer viewed as inherently stable, and the life adjustment curriculum is no longer in vogue (cf. Hofstadter, 1963; DeYoung, 1989). It has, however, left among educators a legacy of excessive concern for the happiness contingent on conformity (Howley, 1987).

5. The analogy between physical and human capital raises many troubling and interesting questions: What distinguishes human capital from labor capital? What are the components of human capital? To what extent is uncredentialed human capital competitive with credentialed human capital? How is human capital formed? How is profit from human capital realized? Who

controls the accumulation of human capital—the individual, corporations, or the government? Why do blacks and women and working-class individuals accumulate less human capital for equal investments? Can the nonmarket effects of human capital be measured? How does human capital contribute to increased productivity? Will increasing the quality of human capital reduce income inequality? Evidence is accumulating on many of these questions.

6. Regression studies rarely account for all the variance in a dependent variable. Unexplained variance might be the result of omitted variables, or it may result from (multiplicative) interaction effects omitted in the design of the research. Variables not taken into account in the human capital model include class structure, the effect of different types of fixed capital investment (e.g., investment in capital goods versus investment in financial assets), and interaction effects of race, gender, and class background (cf. Wright, 1979, 1985). A recent study of the effects of operational scale on student achievement demonstrates how important interaction effects can be. Previous studies had yielded mixed results (Friedkin and Necochea, 1988). Friedkin and Necochea, however, using a term that accounted for the interaction of size and community socioeconomic status, showed that large schools in poor communities produced strong negative results, whereas in affluent communities large schools produced moderate positive results.

7. Goodman (1979) evaluated five human capital models, with various combinations of educational attainment the independent variables and income the dependent variable. The equation that explained the greatest amount of variance included 8 educational and 3 demographic variables (but not race, gender, or class background). It accounted for approximately 17% of the variation in individuals' earnings. One may conclude, therefore, that other factors shape human capital (discounted lifetime earnings) more strongly than education.

8. Wallerstein, for example (1984, pp. 31–32), explains the mechanism of exploitation as the ancient practice of unequal exchange: "What was remarkable about capitalism as a historical system was the way in which this unequal exchange could be hidden. . . . The . . . key lay in the very structure of the capitalist world-economy, the seeming separation . . . of the economic

arena . . . and the political arena (consisting ostensibly of separate sovereign states). . . . How did this unequal exchange work? . . . Commodities moved between zones in such a way that the area with the less 'scarce' item 'sold' its items to the other area at a price that incarnated more real input (cost) than an equally-priced item moving in the opposite direction. What really happened is that there was a transfer of part of the total profit being produced from one zone to another. Such a relationship is that of coreness-peripherality. By extension, we can call the losing zone a 'periphery' and the gaining zone a 'core.'"

9. A chief concern of these critics has been the notion of industrial efficiency. Industrial efficiency is a strong theme in American education, and it will be considered in a subsequent discussion.

10. Studies of the dual labor market examine market segmentation at a microeconomic (regional or sector) level. Dual labor market theory entails comparison of the primary versus secondary labor market, in which the primary market pays higher wages, offers greater job security and is dominated by larger ("core" or "monopolistic") enterprises. The secondary market offers lower wages, less security, and is dominated by smaller ("peripheral" or "competitive") enterprises. Whereas dependency theory implies a certain critical perspective on the international political economy, dual labor market theory has been applied to advantage by both neoclassical economists (e.g., Bloomquist and Summers, 1988) and political economists (e.g., Williams, 1988).

11. Peripheral firms are also known as "second-sector" enterprises (Wright, 1979) or "competitive-sector" enterprises (Bloomquist and Summers, 1982). Such concepts derive from the dual-labor market theory. This use of the terms "core" and "periphery" in studies of the dual-labor market illustrates the fact that dependency theorists refer more to *economic* structures than to the associated geographic locations of those structures (e.g., rural vs. urban; third- vs. first-world).

12. The data reported here can be found in *Poverty in Rural America: A National Overview* (Porter, 1989).

13. Compare Bell (1976, pp. xiv and xiv[n]) on the distinction between a labor theory of value and a knowledge (or human

capital) theory of value. The two views may reflect workers' positions as rural residents, on the one hand, and as national citizens on the other. In an age when human knowledge becomes embodied in fixed capital (i.e., machines controlled by computers), labor obsolescence may well include the replacement of labor (or human capital) by the knowledge codified in machines (cf. Weiner, 1950). The wages of the remaining workers need not decline, since overall labor costs will have been minimized, and wages tend to be relatively good in highly capitalized industries (Heilbroner and Thurow, 1985; McGranahan, 1987; Williams, 1988).

14. Jacobs notes that clearances, which result from technological innovation (in agriculture or mining, for example), and abandonment need not occur simultaneously. Abandonment can occur without a technological incentive, as among peasants who abandon subsistence farming because they mistakenly believe a better life is available in urban areas, or as among extractive workers who move to the city during market "busts."

15. In fact, public policy usually provides help—often substantial—to marginal enterprises (e.g., Duncan and Duncan, 1983; Stevens, 1983). This impression is confirmed empirically by Turner and Starnes (1976), who report that transfer payments to corporations and to the wealthy in general far exceed those to individuals and the poor.

16. The term "established market" is better understood as referring to the fundamental necessity of the product of the industry—for example, coal, timber, or food and fiber—than to an orderly market. Energy, timber, and agricultural markets are, when unregulated, notoriously "volatile." Indeed, Duncan and Duncan (1983) believe that coal operators favor perpetuating volatile markets as a means of rationalizing public expenditures that support private profit-taking and reduce opportunities for local development.

17. The categories of the typology (with the exception of the unclassified counties), however, are not mutually exclusive. Nonetheless, 67% of classified counties belong to one type only; 26% belong to two types; and only 7% belong to three or more

types. Unclassified counties account for 15% of the universe of 2,443 nonmetropolitan counties.

18.   Contrast the terms "extraction" as used by economists with "husbandry" as used by farmers. Extraction accords a utilitarian priority to local resources as sources of exports, whereas husbandry accords an ethical priority to the maintenance of local resources as sources of future well-being.

19.   Data in Bender et al. (1987) cannot be disaggregated to account for duplicates among types; moreover "timber-dependency" is not a category in the typology. I estimated the number of unduplicated counties by summing the number of mining-, farming-, timber-, and manufacturing-dependent counties, accepting 67% as unduplicated, and estimating (conservatively) that half of the remaining counties (i.e., 289) would be duplicates within the total group.

20.   The latter are not separately typed by Bender and colleagues, but they are by Weber, Castle, and Shriver (1987). The discussion here combines data from both reports, so that figures reported may include duplicated counts. The term "mining," as used here, includes energy and non-energy mining as well as drilling for oil and gas.

21.   The period is 1948–1976, which ends during the energy crisis of the 1970s as "stagflation" became a puzzling phenomenon. See Kendrick and Grossman (1980), Tables 3–2, 3–4, and 3–5. The figures for mining are probably underestimates of the long term rate of decline (Duncan, 1986; Weber et al., 1987).

22.   Kendrick and Grossman (1980) do not provide a dual labor market analysis that would confirm labor obsolescence in rural manufacturing. Nonetheless their evidence suggests that labor input in the manufacturing of many basic goods has declined—as opposed to the general labor input increase in manufacturing as a whole. On the basis of the analyses of Bender and colleagues (1985) and McGranahan (1987), one might hypothesize that such industries tend to be located in nonmetropolitan areas.

23.   Beaulieu and Mulkey (1986) report that farm families that operate farms producing between $2,500 and $20,000 in gross sales

derive *over* 100% of their net income from off-farm work (i.e., on paper these farms tend to show small losses). In conventional terms, these farms are not profitable, though they are obviously productive. Perhaps they provide quality of life benefits (subsistence benefits, scope for independent productive labor, closeness to the natural world) that cannot be reckoned as profit.

24. Most of the analyses of the economic plight of rural areas are conducted by *neoclassical* economists (see note 2 in the first section of this chapter).

25. The free movement of labor is also a feature of capitalism. Capital moves as a powerful mass, however, whereas labor moves as comparatively powerless individuals.

26. This is a process of reification (turning humans into things). That is, people become things (sites) in which development, directed from outside the people themselves, takes place. Skills, too, are viewed as things that are transplanted to people-as-things, rather than being presented as the legacy of culture that they really are. Instead of being actors (subjects of culture), people are, in this view, passive recipients (objects of development) and skills, too, tend to be viewed as static objects of strictly utilitarian value.

27. Compare Stevens'(1983) discussion of timber workers who in maximizing wages (by changing jobs frequently) also diminish their human capital. From the viewpoint of neoclassical economics—based on the assumption of maximizing income and profit—the workers seem to act as if they are *irrationally* attached to the place in which they live. In fact, however, they strike a good local compromise, but one that will harm them if they must relocate to an urban area (with their emancipated human capital) in the future.

28. I use the term descriptively to indicate aggressively sought increases in magnitude or scale, not pejoratively to indicate greed.

29. Consolidation has reduced the number of school districts by 90% since 1900. The drive toward centralization has prompted some critics (for example, Everhard, 1982) to characterize American public schooling as a "monopoly."

30.   There are, of course, benefits to rational organization and bureaucracy as compared to more primitive forms of organization (Weber, 1947), and few would argue that a return to older forms—such as patronage—would improve schools. Most contemporary educators, however, argue that schools should involve communities in school governance and that more teachers should organize their classrooms to fit their images of what good instruction should be.

31.   Many observers refer to educational fads. See Mitchell (1979) for a literate and amusing view of educational fads.

32.   Historical data suggest that rural areas were already well integrated into the national economy (Dunaway, 1989; Meyer et al., 1979). Revitalization in 1920 probably had more to do with a romantic view of rural freeholders, who were abandoning the land. Cubberley (1922) was understandably dismayed by a large increase in tenant farming. He correctly understood tenant farming to be bad for the land as well as for a democratic social order.

33.   Such findings reverse initial hypotheses that more education would decrease inequality (cf. Mincer, 1980).

34.   Vocationalism, in this analysis, is the instrumental aim of education as a strategy for economic development (at the macroeconomic level) and job-training or career-building (at the individual level). Since it is known that vocationalism does not provide the economic benefits imagined for it, its continuing popularity must serve some purpose. Stronach identifies this purpose as ritualistic rather than ideological, since it lacks coherence.

35.   In schools, business incubation is a program in which teachers guide students in identifying a business niche, developing a business plan, locating financial backing, planning for operation startup, and managing the fledgling business. Business incubation, which is a tactic of small business development agencies, need not, of course, occur in schools.

36.   "The rhetoric about strengthening the economy by strengthening education is flowing hot and heavy across our nation. . . . To the

extent that corporate leaders can blame the education sector for our nation's economic woes, they can divert attention away from their own short-sightedness, greed, and poor management" (Sher, 1989, p. 40).

37.   See Sher's *North Carolina Today: A State of Emergency, a State of Grace, a State of Anticipation* (1988) for such a vision of society.

38.   Compare the ideas of thinking as skills and thinking as the construction of meaning. The construction of meaning entails, among other activities, an analysis of values and the synthesis of experience and knowledge. Thinking skills, for the most part, are the value-free procedures of mathematics and the natural sciences. The representation of thought as a skill debases not only the educational mission but the richness of the human intellect as well (Bell, 1973, 1976), where philosophic, aesthetic, and social values adhere even to so "pure" a discipline as mathematics (Weiner, 1950).

39.   Levin (1984), Williams (1988), and Wright (1979) demonstrate, however, that the returns to similar levels of education vary greatly according to gender,race, and class. Wright's empirical work is significant because it investigates the effects of class using a dichotomously organized class structure.

40.   Carnoy (1982) summarizes the equalization potential of education in an excellent article. Levin (1984) illustrates that even the effect of equalizing educational attainment at a high level would effect earnings inequality only slightly. Bell (1973, 1976) presents several extended and insightful discussions of the issues of equality and justice as they pertain to both education and economics in post-industrial America. Grubb's (1985) excellent review demonstrates how vocationalism contributes both to educational and economic inequality.

41.   According to Puckett (1989), Wigginton and his colleagues recognize this problem and are taking steps in address it.

42.   The innovative math and science curricula of the 1950s and 1960s did incorporate the notion of "inquiry." Bruner's inquiry-based social studies unit (Bruner, 1966) earned a great deal of

notoriety when it was criticized as un-American on the floor of the U.S. Congress.

REFERENCES

Adler, M. *The Paidea Proposal: An Educational Manifesto.* New York: Macmillan, 1982.

Amin, S. *Unequal Development: An Essay on the Social Formations of Peripheral Capitalism.* New York: Monthly Review Press, 1976.

Anyon, J. "Social Class and the Hidden Curriculum of Work." In *Justice, Ideology, and Education: An Introduction to the Social Foundations of Education.* 210–226. Edited by E. Stevens and G. Woods. New York: Random House, 1987.

Arendt, H. *The Life of the Mind.* New York: Harcourt Brace Jovanovich, 1981.

Aronowitz, S., and Giroux, H. *Education Under Siege: The Conservative, Liberal, and Radical Debate Over Schooling.* South Hadley, Mass.: Bergin & Garvey, 1985.

Augenblick, J., and Nachtigal, P. "Equity in Rural School Finance." Paper presented at the National Rural Education Forum, Kansas City, Missouri, August 1985. ERIC Document Reproduction Service No. ED 258 788.

Averch, H. *How Effective is Schooling? A Critical Review of Research.* Englewood Cliffs, N.J.: Educational Technology Publications, 1974.

Bagby, J., Carpenter, C., Crew, K., DeYoung, A., Eller, R., Hougland, R., Jones, J., Nash, F., and Tickamyer, C. *Education and Financial Resources in Appalachian Kentucky* (Appalachian Data Bank Report No. 2). Lexington, Ky: University of Kentucky,

Appalachian Center, 1985. ERIC Document Reproduction Service No. ED 266 902.

Barkley, D., Keith, J., and Smith, S. *The Potential for High Technology Manufacturing in Nonmetropolitan Areas.* Corvallis, Ore.: Western Rural Development Center, Oregon State University, 1989.

Barnet, R., and Muller, R. *Global Reach: The Power of the Multinational Corporations.* New York: Simon and Schuster, 1974.

Barzun, J. *The American University: How It Runs, Where It Is Going.* New York: Harper & Row, 1968.

Bell, D. *The Coming of Post-Industrial Society: A Venture in Social Forecasting.* New York: Basic Books, 1973.

Bell, D. *The Cultural Contradictions of Capitalism.* New York: Basic Books, 1976.

Bender, L., Green, B., Hady, T., Kuehn, J., Nelson, M., Perkinson, L., and Ross, P. *The Diverse Social and Economic Structure of Nonmetropolitan America.* Rural Development Research Report Number 49, United States Department of Agriculture, Economic Research Service. Washington, D.C.: United States Government Printing Office, 1985. ERIC Document Reproduction Service No. ED 262 939.

Bennett, W., ed. *What Works: Research About Teaching and Learning.* Pueblo, Colo: Office of Educational Research and Improvement, 1986. ERIC Document Reproduction Service No. ED 263 299.

Berry, W. *The Unsettling of America: Culture and Agriculture.* New York: Avon, 1978.

Berry, W. *Meeting the Expectations of the Land: Essays in Sustainable Agriculture and Stewardship.* San Francisco: North Point Press, 1984.

Berry, W. "Does Community Have a Value?" In *Proceedings of the 1986 Conference on Appalachia.* 3–8. Edited by R. Eller. Lexington, Ky.: Appalachia Center, University of Kentucky, 1986.

Bloomquist, L. "Change and Persistence in Poverty Rates." In *Community Economic Vitality: Major Trends and Selected Issues.* 61–68. Edited by G. Summers, L. Bloomquist, T. Hirschl, and R. Shaffer. Ames, Iowa: North Central Regional Center for Rural Development, 1986. ERIC/CRESS Accession No. RC 017 053.

Bloomquist, L. "Performance of the Rural Manufacturing Sector." In *Rural Economic Development in the 1980s* (ERS Staff Report No. AGES870724). Edited by D. Brown and K. Deavers. Washington, D.C.: Economic Research Service, U.S. Department of Agriculture, 1987.

Bloomquist, L., and Summers, G. "Organization of Production and Community Income Distribution." *American Sociological Review,* 47 (1982): 329–337.

Bloomquist, L., and Summers, G. "Employment Growth and Income Inequality." In *Community Economic Vitality: Major Trends and Selected Issues.* 69–74. Edited by G. Summers, L. Bloomquist, T. Hirschl, and R. Shaffer. Ames, Iowa: North Central Regional Center for Rural Development, 1988. ERIC/CRESS Accession No. RC 017 053.

Boli, J., Ramirez, F., and Meyer, J. "Explaining the Origins and Expansion of Mass Education." *Comparative Education Review,* 29 (1985): 145–170.

Bornischer, V., and Chase-Dunn, C. *Transnational Corporations and Underdevelopment.* New York: Praeger, 1985.

Borsodi, R. *This Ugly Civilization.* New York: Harper & Brothers, 1933.

Bowles, S., and Gintis H. *Schooling in Capitalist America.* New York: Basic Books, 1976.

Bowles, S., Gordon, D., and Weisskopf, T. *Beyond the Waste Land: A Democratic Alternative to Economic Decline.* Garden City, N.Y.: Anchor Press/Doubleday, 1984.

Brizius, J., Foster, S., and Patton, H. *Education Reform in Rural Appalachia, 1982–1987.* Washington, D.C.: Appalachian Regional

Commission, 1988. ERIC Document Reproduction Service No. ED 303 287.

Brown, D., and Deavers, K., eds. *Rural Economic Development in the 1980s* (ERS Staff Report No. AGES870724). Washington, D.C.: Economic Research Service, U.S. Department of Agriculture, 1987a.

Brown, D., and Deavers, K. "Rural Change and the Rural Economic Policy Agenda for the 1980s." In *Rural Economic Development in the 1980s* (ERS Staff Report No. AGES870724, chapter 1). Edited by D. Brown and K. Deavers. Washington, D.C.: Economic Research Service, U.S. Department of Agriculture, 1987b.

Brown, D., and Deavers, K. "Economic Dimensions of Rural America." Paper presented at the Rural Development Policy Options Workshop, Birmingham, Alabama, October 1988. ERIC/CRESS Accession No. RC 016 970.

Buttram, J., and Carlson, R. "Effective School Research: Will It Play in the Country?" *Research in Rural Education,* 2 (1983): 73–78.

Callahan, R. *Education and the Cult of Efficiency.* Chicago: University of Chicago Press, 1962.

Carnoy, M. "Education for Alternative Development." *Comparative Education Review, 26* (1982): 160–177.

Carnoy, M. "The Political Economy of Education." *International Social Science Journal, 37* (1985): 157–173.

Carnoy, M., and Levin, H. *Schooling and Work in the Democratic State.* Stanford, Calif.: Stanford University Press, 1985.

Cobb, J. *The Selling of the South: The Southern Crusade for Industrial Development 1936–1980.* Baton Rouge, La.: Louisiana State University Press, 1982.

Coburn, J., and Nelson, S. *Characteristics of Successful Indian Students.* Portland, Oregon: Northwest Regional Educational Laboratory, 1987. ERIC/CRESS Accession No. RC 016 698.

Coleman, J. *Equality of Educational Opportunity* (Summary Report). Washington, D.C.: U.S. Office of Education, Department of Health, Education, and Welfare, 1966. ERIC Document Reproduction Service No. ED 012 275.

Coleman, J. "Social Capital in the Creation of Human Capital." *American Journal of Sociology, 94* (supplement, 1988): S95-S120.

Coleman, J., and Hoffer, T. *Public and Private High Schools: The Impact of Communities.* New York: Basic Books, 1987.

Collins, R. *The Credential Society: A Historical Sociology of Education and Stratification.* New York: Academic Press, 1979.

Committee for Economic Development. *Investing in Our Children: Business and the Public Schools.* New York: Committee for Economic Development, 1985. ERIC Document Reproduction Service No. ED 261 117.

Committee of Twelve. *Report of the Committee of Twelve on Rural Schools.* Washington, D.C.: U.S. Government Printing Office, 1898.

Cooper, H., and Good, T. *Pygmalion Grows Up: Studies in the Expectation Communication Process.* New York: Longman, 1983.

Counts, G. *The American Road to Culture: A Social Interpretation of Education in the United States.* New York: John Day, 1930. Facsimile reprint edition by Arno Press-New York Times, 1971.

Cremin, L. *The Transformation of the School.* New York: Vintage Books, 1961.

Cremin, L. *American Education: The National Experience.* New York: Harper & Row, 1980.

Cuban, L. "Persistence of the Inevitable: The Teacher-Centered Classroom." *Education and Urban Society, 15* (1982): 26–41.

Cuban, L. "Corporate Involvement in Public Schools: A Practitioner-Academic's Perspective." *Teachers College Record, 5* (1985): 183–203.

Cubberley, E. *Rural Life and Education: A Study of the Rural-School Problem as a Phase of the Rural-Life Problem.* Boston: Houghton Mifflin, 1922.

Deaton, B., and McNamara, K. *Education in a Changing Rural Environment: The Impact of Population and Economic Change on the Demand for and Costs of Public Education in Rural America.* Mississippi State, Mississippi: Southern Rural Development Center, 1984. ERIC Document Reproduction Service No. ED 241 210.

Deavers, K., and Brown, D. *Natural Resource Dependence, Rural Development, and Rural Poverty.* (Rural Development Research Report No. 48). Washington, D.C.: Economic Research Service, U.S. Department of Agriculture, 1985. ERIC Document Reproduction Service No. ED 258 775.

Delacroix, J. "The Export of Raw Materials and Economic Growth: A Cross-National Study." *American Sociological Review, 42* (1977): 795–808.

Development Associates, Inc. *Academic Performance of Limited-English-Proficient Indian Students in Reservation Schools.* Arlington, Va.: Development Associates, Inc, 1988. ERIC/CRESS Accession No. RC 016 746.

DeYoung, A. "Economic Development and Educational Status in Appalachian Kentucky." *Comparative Education Review, 29* (1985): 47–67.

DeYoung, A. "The Status of American Rural Education Research: An Integrated Review and Commentary." *Review of Educational Research, 57* (1987): 123–148.

DeYoung, A. *Economics and American Education: A Historical and Critical Overview of the Impact of Economic Theories on Schooling in the United States.* New York: Longman, 1989.

Dubin, E. *Geographic Distribution of Federal Funds in 1985* (ERS Staff Report AGES89–7). Washington, D.C.: Economic Research Service, U. S. Department of Agriculture, 1989. ERIC/CRESS Accession No. RC 017 245.

Dubin, E., and Reid, N. "Do Federal Funds Help Spur Rural Development?" *Rural Development Perspectives, 5* (1988): 2–7.

Dunaway, W. *The Incorporation of Southern Appalachia into the World-Economy, 1700–1900.* Work in progress. University of Tennessee, Knoxville, Tennessee, 1989.

Duncan, C. "Myths and Realities of Appalachian Poverty: Public Policy for Good People Surrounded by a Bad Economy and Bad Politics." In *Proceedings of the 1986 Conference on Appalachia.* 25–32. Edited by R. Eller. Lexington, Ky.: Appalachia Center, University of Kentucky, 1986.

Duncan, C., and Duncan, W. "Coal, Poverty, and Development Policy in Eastern Kentucky." In *Rural Development, Poverty, and Natural Resources Workshop Paper Series, Part V.* 25–46. Washington, D.C.: National Center for Food and Agricultural Policy, Resources for the Future, 1983. ERIC Document Reproduction Service No. ED 258 753.

Duncan, O. "Inheritance of Poverty or Inheritance of Race?" In *On Understanding Poverty.* Edited by D. Moynihan. New York: Basic Books, 1968.

Dunne, F. "Good Government vs. Self-Government: Educational Control in Rural America." *Phi Delta Kappan, 65* (1983): 252–256.

Edelstein, F., and Schoeffe, E. *A Blueprint for Business on Restructuring Education.* Washington, D.C.: National Alliance of Business, 1989.

Elson, R. *Guardians of Tradition: American Schoolbooks of the Nineteenth Century.* Lincoln, Neb.: University of Nebraska Press, 1964.

Everhard, R. *The Public School Monopoly: A Critical Analysis of Education and the State in American Society.* Edited by R. Everhard. Cambridge, Mass.: Ballinger, 1982.

Friedkin, N., and Necochea, J. "School System Size and Performance: A Contingency Perspective." *Educational Evaluation and Policy Analysis, 10* (1988): 237–249.

Friedman, R. "The Role of Entrepreneurship in Rural Development." In *Proceedings of the National Rural Entrepreneurship Symposium.* 1–6. Edited by B. Teater. Mississippi State, Miss.: Southern Rural Development Center, 1987.

Gailey, H., and Lipka, R. "Cooperative Curriculum Planning in a Small Rural School System." *Illinois Schools Journal, 24* (1987): 34–40.

Giroux, H. *Theory and Resistance: A Pedagogy for the Opposition.* South Hadley, Mass.: Bergin & Garvey, 1983.

Goodlad, J. *A Place Called School: Prospects for the Future.* New York: McGraw-Hill, 1984.

Goodman, J. "The Economic Returns of Education: An Assessment of Alternative Models." *Social Science Quarterly, 60* (1979): 269–283.

Grubb, W. "The Convergence of Educational Systems and the Role of Vocationalism." *Comparative Education Review, 29* (1985): 526–548.

Hanushek, E. "The Impact of Differential Expenditures on School Performance." *Educational Researcher, 18* (1989): 45–62.

Heilbroner, R., and Thurow, L. *Understanding Macroeconomics.* 8th ed. Englewood Cliffs, N.J.: Prentice-Hall, 1985.

Hill, D. "Jane Jacobs' Ideas on Big, Diverse Cities: A Review and Commentary." *Journal of the American Planning Association, 49* (1988): 367–381.

Hobbs, D. "Learning to Find the 'Niches': Rural Education and Vitalizing Rural Communities." Paper presented at the Annual Meeting of the National Rural Education Association (Research Forum), Lake Placid, New York, October 1987. ERIC/CRESS Accession No. RC 016 625.

Hobbs, D. *Education Reform and Rural Economic Health: Policy Implications.* Charleston, W.V.: Appalachia Educational Laboratory, 1989.

Hobsbawm, J. *The Age of Revolution, 1789–1848.* New York: Mentor Books, 1962.

Hofstadter, R. *Anti-Intellectualism in American Life.* New York: Knopf, 1963.

Honeyman, D., Thompson, D., and Wood, R. *Financing Rural and Small Schools: Issues of Adequacy and Equity.* Charleston, W.V.: ERIC Clearinghouse on Rural Education and Small Schools, 1989. ERIC/CRESS Accession No. RC 017 315.

Howley, C. "Anti-Intellectualism in Programs for Able Students (Beware of Gifts: An Application)." *Social Epistemology, 1* (1987): 175–181.

Howley, C. "Efficiency and the Characteristics of School Districts: A Study of 178 Kentucky Districts." *Research in Rural Education, 6* (1989a): 43–55.

Howley, C. "Synthesis of the Effects of School and District Size: What Research Says About Achievement in Small Schools and School Districts." *Journal of Rural and Small Schools, 4* (1989b): 2–12.

Hoy, F. "Who Are the Rural Entrepreneurs?" In *Proceedings of the National Rural Entrepreneurship Symposium.* 7–14. Edited by B. Teater. Mississippi State, Miss.: Southern Rural Development Center, 1987.

Illich, I. *Deschooling Society.* New York: Harper & Row, 1970.

Jackson, P. "Secondary Schooling for the Privileged Few: A Report on a Visit to a New England Boarding School." *Daedelus, 110* (1981): 117–130.

Jacobs, J. *Cities and the Wealth of Nations: Principles of Economic Life.* New York: Random House.

Jencks, C., Smith, M., Acland, H., Bane, M., Cohen, D., Gintis, H., Heyns, B., and Michelson, S. *Inequality: A Reassessment of the Effect of Family and Schooling in America.* New York: Harper & Row, 1972.

Jencks, C., Bartlett, S., Corcoran, M., Crouse, J., Eaglesfield, D., Jackson, G., McClelland, K., Mueser, P., Olneck, M., Schwarz, J., Ward, S., and Williams, J. *Who Gets Ahead? The Determinants of Economic Success in America.* New York: Basic Books, 1979.

Joyce, B., Hersh, R., and McKibbin, M. *The Structure of School Improvement.* New York: Longman, 1983.

Kalleberg, A. "Linking Macro and Micro Levels: Bringing the Workers Back into the Sociology of Work." *Social Forces, 67* (1989): 582–592.

Katchadourian, H., and Boli, J. *Careerism and Intellectualism Among College Students.* San Francisco: Jossey-Bass, 1985.

Katz, M. *The Irony of Early School Reform.* Cambridge, Mass.: Harvard University Press, 1968.

Katz, M. *Class, Bureaucracy, and Schools.* New York: Praeger, 1972.

Keizer, G. *No Place But Here.* New York: Viking, 1988.

Kendrick, J., and Grossman, E. *Productivity in the United States.* Baltimore, Md.: Johns Hopkins University Press, 1980.

Kerr, C. *The Uses of the University.* New York: Harper & Row, 1963.

Kitchen, J., and Zahn, F. "Interest Rates, Farm Prices, and the U.S. Farm Sector." *Rural Development Perspectives, 3* (1986): 21–24.

Knutson, R., and Fisher, D. *Focus on the Future: Options in Developing a New National Rural Policy.* College Station, Tex.: Department of Agricultural Economics, Texas A&M University, 1988.

Knutson, R., Pulver, G., and Wilkinson, K. "Toward a Comprehensive Rural Development Policy." Paper presented at the Rural Development Policy Options Workshop, Birmingham, Alabama, October 1988. ERIC/CRESS Accession No. RC 016 971.

Kubo, Y. "Urban Concentration and Rural Growth: A Two-Sector Analysis." *Journal of Regional Science, 26* (1986): 579–593.

Ledent, J. "Rural-Urban Migration, Urbanization, and Economic Development." *Economic Development and Cultural Change, 30* (1982): 507–538.

Levin, H. "Assessing the Equalization Potential of Education." *Comparative Education Review, 28* (1984): 11- 27.

Levin, H. "Accelerating Elementary Education for Disadvantaged Students." Paper presented at the Summer Institute of the Council of Chief State School Officers (CCSSO), Whitefish, Montana, 1987.

London, B., and Smith, D. "Urban Bias, Dependence, and Economic Stagnation in Noncore Nations." *American Sociological Review, 53* (1988): 454–463.

Luloff, A., and Chittenden, W. "Rural Industrialization: A Logit Analysis." *Rural Sociology, 49* (1984): 67–88.

Lyson, T. *Two Sides to the Sunbelt.* New York: Praeger, 1989.

Mace-Matluck, B. *The Effective Schools Movement: Its History and Context.* Austin, Tex.: Southwest Educational Development Laboratory, 1987.

Marcuse, H. *Eros and Civilization.* New York: Vintage, 1955.

Marzano, R. *A Study of Selected School Effectiveness Variables: Some Correlates That Are Not Causes.* Aurora, Colo.: Mid-Continent Educational Laboratory, 1984. ERIC Document Reproduction Service No. ED 253 328.

McCormick, J., and Turque, B. "America's Outback." *Newsweek* (October 9): 78–80.

McGranahan, D. "The Role of Rural Workers in the National Economy." In *Rural Economic Development in the 1980s.* (ERS Staff Report No. AGES870724, chapter 2). Edited by D. Brown and K. Deavers. Washington, D.C.: Economic Research Service, U.S. Department of Agriculture, 1987.

McLuhan, M. *Understanding Media: The Extensions of Man.* New York: McGraw-Hill, 1964.

McGranahan, D., Hession, J., Hines, F., and Jordan, M. *Social and Economic Characteristics of the Population in Metro and Nonmetro Counties, 1970–1980* (Rural Development Research Report No. 58). Washington, D.C.: Economic Research Service, 1986. ERIC Document Reproduction Service No. ED 274 486.

McNeil, L. "Teacher Culture and the Irony of School Reform." In *Excellence in Education: Perspectives on Policy and Practice.* 183–202. Edited by P. Altbach, G. Kelly, and L. Weis. Buffalo, N.Y.: Prometheus Books, 1985.

McSwain, H. *Appalachia: Similarities to the Third World.* Columbus, Ohio: Rural Resources, 1985.

Meehan, M. *A Demographic Study of Rural, Small School Districts in Four Appalachian States* (Occasional Paper No. 25). Charleston, W.Va.: Appalachia Educational Laboratory, 1987.

Melman, S. *Profits Without Production.* New York: Knopf, 1985.

Meyer, J., Scott, W., and Strang, D. *Centralization, Fragmentation, and School District Complexity.* Stanford, Calif.: Stanford Education Policy Institute, Stanford University, 1986. ERIC Document Reproduction Service No. ED 271 838.

Meyer, J., Tyack, D., Nagel, J., and Gordon, A. "Public Education as Nation-Building in America: Enrollments and Bureaucratization in the American States, 1870–1930." *American Journal of Sociology, 85* (1979): 591–613.

Mid-Continent Regional Educational Laboratory. *Redesigning Rural Education.* Aurora, Colo.: Mid-Continent Regional Educational

Laboratory, 1988. ERIC Document Reproduction Service No. ED 297 897.

Mincer, J. "Human Capital and the Labor Market: A Review of Current Research." *Educational Researcher, 18* (1989): 27–34.

Mitchell, R. *Less Than Words Can Say.* Boston: Little, Brown, 1979.

Mosteller, F., and Moynihan, D., eds. *On Equality of Educational Opportunity.* New York: Random House, 1972.

Mumford, L. *The Condition of Man.* New York: Harcourt Brace, 1944.

Murphy, K., and Finis, W. "Wage Premiums for College Graduates: Recent Growth and Possible Explanations." *Educational Researcher, 18* (1989): 17–26.

Navarro, R., Berkey, R., and Minnick, F. "The Art of Becoming an Instructional Leader." Paper presented at the Annual Meeting of the American Educational Research Association, San Francisco, California, April 1986. ERIC Document Reproduction Service No. ED 281 314.

Nearing, S., and Nearing, H. *Living the Good Life.* New York: Schocken, 1970.

Nelson, J., and Lorence, J. "Metropolitan Earnings Inequality and Service Sector Employment." *Social Forces, 67* (1988): 492–511.

Nolan, P., and Lenski, G. "Technoeconomic Heritage, Patterns of Development, and the Advantage of Backwardness." *Social Forces, 64* (1985): 341–335.

Oakes, J. *Keeping Track: How Schools Structure Inequality.* New Haven, Conn.: Yale University Press, 1985.

O'Hare, W. *The Rise of Poverty in Rural America.* Washington, D.C.: Population Reference Bureau, 1988.

Oxendine, L. *Dick and Jane are Dead: Basal Reader Takes a Back Seat to Student Writings.* Charleston, W.Va.: Appalachia Educational Laboratory, 1989. ERIC/CRESS Accession No. RC 017 200.

Page, V. "Reservation Development in the United States: Peripherality in the Core." *American Indian Culture and Research Journal, 9* (1985): 21–35.

Phelps, M. *Access: The Role of an Outside Agency in Facilitating Rural School Change in Southern Appalachia.* Unpublished manuscript. Cookeville, Tenn.: Tennessee Technological University, 1989.

Porter, K. *Poverty in Rural America: A National Overview.* Washington, D.C.: Center on Budget and Policy Priorities, 1989. ERIC/CRESS Accession No. RC 017 182.

Postman, N., and Weingartner, C. *Teaching as a Subversive Activity.* New York: Delacorte Press, 1969.

Pottinger, R. "Indian Reservation Labor Markets: A Navajo Assessment and Challenge." *American Indian Culture and Research Journal, 9* (1985): 1–20.

Powell, A., Farrar, E., and Cohen, D. *The Shopping Mall High School: Winners and Losers in the Educational Marketplace.* Boston: Houghton Mifflin, 1985.

Prattis, I. "The Survival of Communities: A Theoretical Perspective." *Current Anthropology, 20* (1979): 361–375.

Psacharopoulos, G. "Returns to Education: An Updated International Comparison." *Comparative Education, 17* (1981): 321–341.

Puckett, J. *Foxfire Reconsidered: A Twenty-Year Experiment in Progressive Education.* Chicago: University of Illinois Press, 1989.

Pulver, G. "Education Implications." In *Proceedings of the National Rural Entrepreneurship Symposium.* 134–136. Edited by B. Teater. Mississippi State, Miss.: Southern Rural Development Center, 1987.

Quan, N., and Beck, J. "Public Education Expenditures and State Economic Growth: Northeast and Sunbelt Regions." *Southern Economic Journal, 54* (1987): 361–376.

Raths, L., Harmin, M., and Simon, S. *Values and Teaching.* Columbus, Ohio: Merrill, 1966.

Regional Laboratory for the Northeast and Islands. *Attracting, Retaining, and Developing Quality Teachers in Small Schools.* Andover, Massachusetts: Regional Laboratory for the Northeast and Islands, 1988. ERIC/CRESS Accession No. RC 016 824.

Reif, L. "Farm Structure, Industry Structure, and Socioeconomic Conditions in the United States." *Rural Sociology, 52* (1987): 462– 482.

Rosenbaum, J. "The Stratification of the Socialization Process." *American Sociological Review, 40* (1981): 48- 54.

Rosenfeld, S., Bergman, E., and Rubin, S. *After the Factories.* Research Triangle Park, North Carolina: Southern Growth Policies Board, 1985. ERIC/CRESS Accession No. RC 017 084.

Rosenfeld, S., Bergman, E., and Rubin, S. *Making Connections: "After the Factories" Revisited.* Research Triangle Park, North Carolina: Southern Growth Policies Board, 1989. ERIC/CRESS Accession No. RC 017 125.

Rosenthal, R., and Jacobsen, L. *Pygmalion in the Classroom: Teacher Expectation and Pupil's Intellectual Development.* New York: Holt, Rinehart & Winston, 1968.

Ross, P., and Rosenfeld, S. "Human Resource Policies and Economic Development." In *Rural Economic Development in the 1980s* (ERS Staff Report No. AGES870724, chapter 15). Edited by D. Brown and K. Deavers. Washington, D.C.: Economic Research Service, U.S. Department of Agriculture.

Sample, T. "Why Save Rural America: A Theological/Ethical Perspective." *The Rural Sociologist* (Winter 1989): 19–26.

Samuels, J. "Impingements on Teacher Autonomy." *Urban Education, 5* (1970): 152–171.

Schlechty, P., and Vance, V. "Institutional Responses to the Quality/Quantity Issue in Teacher Training." *Phi Delta Kappan, 65* (1983): 94–101.

Schmuck, P., and Schmuck, R. "Democratic Participation in Small-Town Schools." Unpublished manuscript, Lewis and Clark College, Department of Educational Administration, 1989. ERIC/CRESS Accession Number RC 017 410.

Schumacher, E. *Good Work.* New York: Harper & Row, 1979.

Shackett, J., and Slottje, D. "Labor Supply Decisions, Human Capital Attributes, and Inequality in the Size Distribution of Earnings in the U.S., 1952–1981." *The Journal of Human Resources, 23* (1986): 82–100.

Sher, J. "Bringing Home the Bacon: The Politics of Rural School Reform." *Phi Delta Kappan, 65* (1983): 279–283.

Sher, J. *Heavy Meddle: A Critique of the North Carolina Department of Public Instruction's Plan to Mandate School District Mergers Throughout the State.* Raleigh, North Carolina: N.C. School Boards Association, 1986. ERIC Document Reproduction Service No. ED 270 245.

Sher, J. "Making Dollars by Making Sense: Linking Rural Education and Development in Appalachia." Paper presented at the Annual Conference on Appalachia, University of Kentucky, Lexington, Kentucky, October 1987. ERIC/CRESS Accession No. RC 017 011.

Sher, J. *North Carolina Today: A State of Emergency, a State of Grace, a State of Anticipation.* Chapel Hill, N.C.: North Carolina Association of Educators, 1988a. ERIC/CRESS Accession No. RC 016 944.

Sher, J. *Overview of North Carolina's Rural School-Based Enterprise Program.* Chapel Hill, N.C.: University of North Carolina, Small Business and Technology Development Center, 1988b.

Sher, J. *Challenging the Comfortable Stereotypes: Rural Education and Rural Development.* Charleston, W.V.: Appalachia Educational Laboratory, 1989. ERIC/CRESS Accession No. RC 017 195.

Sher, J., ed. *Education in Rural America: A Reassessment of the Conventional Wisdom.* Boulder, Colo.: Westview, 1977.

Sica, A., and Prechel, H. "National Political-Economic Dependency in the Global Economy and Educational Development." *Comparative Education Review, 25* (1981): 384–402.

Silver, R., and DeYoung, A. J. "The Ideology of Rural/Appalachian Education, 1885–1935: The Appalachian Education Problem as Part of the Appalachian Life Problem." *Educational Theory, 36* (1986): 51–65.

Sizer, T. *Horace's Compromise: The Dilemma of the American High School.* Boston: Houghton Mifflin, 1985.

Smith, A. *Inquiry Into the Wealth of Nations (excerpts).* In *Introduction to Contemporary Civilization in the West.* 1314–1333. Edited by M. Harris, S. Morgenbesser, J. Rothschild, and B. Wishy. New York: Columbia University Press, 1960. (Original work published 1776.)

Smith, D., and DeYoung, A. "Big School vs. Small School: Conceptual, Empirical and Political Perspectives on the Re-emerging Debate." *Journal of Rural and Small Schools, 2* (1988): 2–11.

Snipp, M., and Sandefur, G. "Small Gains for Rural Indians Who Move to Cities." *Rural Development Perspectives, 5* (1988): 22–25.

Spring, J. *The Sorting Machine: National Educational Policy Since 1945.* New York: Longman, 1976.

Spring, J. *The American School 1642–1985.* New York: Longman, 1986.

Stephens, E. *The Changing Context of Education in a Rural Setting.* Charleston, W.Va.: Appalachia Educational Laboratory, 1988. ERIC/CRESS Accession No. RC 017 110.

Stephens, E., Perry, W., and Sanders, J. "Designing Organizational Effectiveness Studies of Rural and Small Schools." Paper presented at the Annual Meeting of the National Rural Education Association, Bismarck, North Dakota, October 1988. ERIC/CRESS Accession No. RC 017 070.

Stephens, M., and Roderick, G. *Universities for a Changing World: The Role of the University in the Later Twentieth Century*. New York: Wiley, 1975.

Stevens, J. "Development and Management of Forest Resources for Rural Development in the Pacific Northwest." In *Rural Development, Poverty, and Natural Resources Workshop Paper Series, Part V*. 47–83. Washington, D.C.: National Center for Food and Agricultural Policy, Resources for the Future, 1983. ERIC Document Reproduction Service No. ED 258 75.

Storr, A. *Solitude: A Return to the Self*. New York: The Free Press, 1988.

Stronach, I. "Vocationalism and Economic Recovery: The Case Against Witchcraft." In *Education in Transition: What Role for Research*. 55–70. Edited by S. Brown and R. Wake. Edinburgh, Scotland: Scottish Council for Research in Education, 1988.

Talbert, E., Fletcher, R., and Phelps, M. "Forty Rural Schools: A Study of Effectiveness." Paper presented at the Annual Meeting of the American Educational Research Association, Washington, D.C., April, 1987. ERIC Document Reproduction Service No. ED 289 639.

Theobald, P. "The Ideological Foundations of Midwest Rural Education." Unpublished manuscript, University of Illinois, Champaign, Illinois, 1989. ERIC/CRESS Accession No. RC 017 081.

Thompson, D., and Stewart, G. *Achieving Equity in Capital Outlay Financing: A Policy Analysis for the States*. Charleston, W.V.: ERIC Clearinghouse on Rural Education and Small Schools, 1989. ERIC/CRESS Accession No. RC 017 314.

Toffler, A. "The Psychology of the Future." In *Learning for Tomorrow: The Role of the Future in Education*. 3–18. Edited by A. Toffler. New York: Vintage, 1974.

Tomaskovic-Devey, D. "Industrial Structure, Relative Labor Power, and Poverty Rates." Paper presented at the Annual Meeting of the American Sociological Association, Washington, D.C., 1985.

Tomaskovic-Devey, D. "Labor Markets, Industrial Structure, and Poverty: A Theoretical Discussion and Empirical Example." *Rural Sociology, 52* (1987): 56–74.

Tyack, D. *The One Best System: A History of American Urban Education.* Cambridge, Massachusetts: Harvard University Press, 1974.

U.S. Bureau of the Census. *Rural and Rural Farm Population: 1987* (Current Population Reports, Series P–27, No. 61). Washington, D.C.: United States Government Printing Office, 1988. ERIC/CRESS Accession No. RC 016 857.

Vance, V., and Schlechty, P. "The Distribution of Academic Ability in the Teaching Force: Policy Implications." *Phi Delta Kappan, 64* (1982): 22–27.

Wallerstein, I. *Historical Capitalism.* London: Verso, 1984.

Weaver, W. *America's Teacher Quality Problem: Alternatives for Reform.* New York: Praeger, 1983.

Weber, B., Castle, E., and Shriver, A. "The Performance of Natural Resource Industries." In *Rural Economic Development in the 1980s* (ERS Staff Report No. AGES870724, chapter 5). Edited by D. Brown and K. Deavers. Washington, D.C.: Economic Research Service, U.S. Department of Agriculture, 1987.

Weber, M. *The Theory of Social and Economic Organizations.* Edited by T. Parsons. Translated by A. Henderson and T. Parsons. New York: Free Press, 1947.

Weede, E. "Urban Bias and Economic Growth in Cross-National Perspective." *International Journal of Comparative Sociology, 28* (1987): 30–42.

Wiener, N. *The Human Uses of Human Beings: Cybernetics and Society.* Rev. ed. Boston: Houghton Mifflin, 1950.

Wigginton, E. "Empowerment Through Education." *Hands On, 3* (1980):
57–61. Special titled *National Workshop for Cultural Journalism:
Workshop Report.* Edited by S. Reynolds. ERIC/CRESS Accession
No. RC 017 201.

Wigginton, E. *Sometimes a Shining Moment.* Garden City, N.Y.: Anchor
Press/Doubleday, 1985.

Wilcox, K. "Differential Socialization in the Classroom: Implications for
Equal Opportunity." In *Doing the Ethnography of Schooling.*
268–309. Edited by G. Spindler. New York: CBS College Books,
1982.

Wilcox, K., and Moriarity, P. "Schooling and Work: Social Constraints on
Equal Educational Opportunity." *Social Problems, 24* (1977): 204–
213.

Williams, R. *Beyond Human Capital: Black Women, Work, and Wages.*
Wellesley, Mass.: Center for Research on Women, Wellesley
College, 1989.

Williams, W. *The Contours of American History.* Chicago: Quadrangle,
1966.

Williams, W. *The Roots of the Modern American Empire: A Study of the
Growth and Shaping of Social Consciousness in a Marketplace
Society.* New York: Vintage, 1969.

Wimberley, R. "Dimensions of U.S. Agristructure: 1969-1982." *Rural
Sociology, 52* (1987): 445–461.

Woods, F., Ross, P., and Fisher, D. "Rural Poverty Policy." Paper
presented at the Rural Development Policy Options Workshop,
Birmingham, Alabama, October 1988. ERIC/CRESS Accession
No. RC 016 972.

Wright, E. *Class Structure and Income Determination.* New York:
Academic Press, 1979.

Wright, E. *Classes.* London: Verso, 1985.

Zachariah, M. "Lumps of Clay and Growing Plants: Dominant Metaphors of the Role of Education in the Third World, 1950–1980." *Comparative Education Review, 29* (1985): 1–21.

PART II
RURAL EDUCATION IN
THE FIELD: SOURCES
FOR PRACTITIONERS

Identifying, Recruiting, Selecting, Inducting, and Supervising Rural Teachers

Dwight Hare

There are two essential variables of the teacher labor market in rural and small schools: distance from a college with a teacher education program and distance from an urban area. To fully understand staffing and teacher training in rural and small schools, one must understand the role these two play in teachers' deciding where they will teach.

Barnett Berry (1984), in his study of the teacher labormarket in the southeast, describes these variables well. Berry interviewed school administrators, teachers, college students, and college administrators from urban and rural areas; the responses of those interviewed provide interesting insights into the workings of the teacher labor market.

> Generally, education students in universities (and teachers in school systems) want to teach in a place that is "familiar." However, definitions of "familiar" appear to differ according to the background of the student or teacher. For urban students, familiar tends to mean teaching "back home," in their university town, or in a place like their university town. (Berry, pp. 45–46)

Rural students reported in the Berry study, however, either that they became "familiar" with their university town and wanted to stay, or that they

> [tend] to come to the University from a particular rural town, having been taught by "Mrs. K", then [want to go] back to [their old school] to take over for "Mrs. K" when she retires. (Berry, p. 46)

The impact of university location and community size is easily understood through the supply and demand of teachers, which was the particular focus of this work. According to Berry:

> The process of recruiting and selecting teachers in school systems emerges from the characteristics of the locale itself. School systems within "highly mobile" metropolitan areas . . . and those in close proximity to universities take on a particular characteristic—a plethora of "applicants on file . . ." In metropolitan and university communities, school system officials "assume the right people will walk in the door . . . as people are leaving, people are coming.". . . In university communities and in metropolitan areas, professional schools (medicine, law) attract "able spouses," and industry brings in "certified wives." (Berry, pp. 45–46)

Larger metropolitan systems do little recruiting, but what little they do is to

> travel to a few select universities to increase the "reservoir" in such "critical areas" as math and science. As one (large metropolitan) administrator noted, "We may hire 30 to 40 math and science [per year] and our reservoir is 50." (Berry, p. 50)

Larger systems

> "can court and sign outstanding people" early in the recruiting season and later place them in the most

appropriate vacancy. As one central office administrator noted, "we can justify signing a '3.5' (GPA) any time." Hiring is a year-round process. . . . (Berry, p. 54)

These are not, of course, the typical conditions in small and rural school systems. Because of the effects of distances from urban areas and universities, rural schools face differing problems with teacher supply and demand. As an administrator in a large metropolitan area noted regarding contrasting city-country practices in hiring teachers, "Ours is like an employment agency, and theirs is like an executive search" (Berry, 1984, p. 54).

Small rural schools and school systems, which have traditionally struggled to ensure an adequate supply of teachers, now find themselves also forced to face issues of quality. Those systems which have never achieved equity in either financial resources or availability of personnel are now expected to demonstrate excellence in facilities and curriculum (Hare, 1986).

Traditional literature on the function of personnel directors and their departments presents an urban bias familiar to other aspects of educational research and policy (DeYoung, 1987). Small, rural school systems often do not have a personnel director: the personnel responsibility is that of the superintendent or is an additional responsibility of a supervisor (elementary, secondary) or a director (e.g., of child welfare or school based federal programs).

The personnel function is perhaps most properly considered as part of the teacher labor market. This use allows us to see the initial and continual employment of teachers within a market concept and to understand this market in economic terms: supply, demand, accessibility, fluctuations, mobility, local conditions, etc. The purpose of this chapter is to present the aspects or characteristics of the teacher labor market as they exist (and can be understood) in rural schools.

It is important to understand that a basic tenet of this chapter is that the teacher labor market is actually a series of related teacher labor markets. That is, the availability of teachers for employment is (often) a function of: state salary schedules, local supplements, availability of other employment, location of teacher training institutions, etc. A related tenet is that only school systems themselves can successfully address their teacher labor market, and then only when they understand how their teacher labor market works.

This chapter breaks the teacher labor market into six distinct, though quite interrelated, aspects, applicable to the employment of teachers in rural and small schools. Links are made between each market aspect and system policy necessary to correct for, or adjust to, local market conditions.

Identification

Before schools (urban or rural, large or small) can find teachers, they must know where to look. A necessary first step in finding new teachers is to determine where our present teachers come from and why they stay, and why teachers who leave do so. To understand their teacher labor market (TLM), schools will need to understand their teachers and why they do what they do. The best way to understand teachers is to talk with them. This is not a new concept; it is a major element of personnel evaluation. The exit interview is just as important, if not more so, than the employment interview. Berry (1984) began his study of the TLM with a number of questions regarding the identification of teacher characteristics important in employment. Among these were the following:

> Where do teachers come from?
>
> What characteristics do school systems look for in teachers?
>
> How do students and teachers engage in their placement in teaching positions? (p. 5)

Mathews (1989), in his case study of the TLM in a rural school system in Louisiana, began with:

Where do teachers come from who teach in Concordia Parish?

Why do they come to Concordia to teach?

The questions to be asked are: Where do our teachers live; where did they go to college; and how is it that they came to teach in our school(s) at this time? Once we begin to identify our existing teachers and their motivations, we may more effectively recruit those teachers we want and need. When we understand, for example, that many of our teachers were also our students and we understand why they now teach for us, we can begin to identify those students we want teaching for us in the future.

By asking such questions we also begin to see where our teachers do *not* come from. This allows rural systems to identify pools of perspective teachers not presently utilized. This does not guarantee, of course, that once pools are identified they can become sources of teachers; neither does it guarantee that there is an unutilized pool of teachers.

When we begin to examine where our teachers come from and why they teach for us, we can also begin to understand why they leave. Though this is properly considered under the *retention* of teachers, an understanding of a local TLM requires an understanding of why teachers leave.

Like understanding where teachers come from, understanding why teachers leave is no guarantee we can keep them. Often, when teachers who are in the metropolitan pool are not selected by the local system, they seek employment in surrounding systems until a position opens up "back-home." This is not to suggest that these teachers should not be hired; rather, it emphasizes the necessity of schools and systems researching their own TLM. Identification, then, requires schools and school systems to conduct research to understand who their teachers are, why they teach in our schools, and why they leave. This research procedure, like its findings, will be based in local context and on local variables. As contexts and variables differ, so will teacher labor markets.

It is important to note that much of what follows will be
reports of the efforts of rural schools and universities as they
attempt to recruit, select, induct, supervise, and retain teachers;
what makes these programs successful is *not* just the program,
but the variables of local systems. That is, before you try a
teacher recruitment program in your system, determine the
variables that make this program work where it did and
compare them to your variables. To know what will work in our
schools requires us to first know our schools, what works,
what doesn't, and why. As Miller and Sidebottom (1985a) note:

> In order to gain a competitive edge in hiring the best
> and most qualified teachers, rural and small school
> officials must discover what would motivate a
> prospective teacher to seek employment in their
> districts. (p. 15)

Recruitment

The recruitment of teachers is typically considered as
attending teacher job fairs and attempting to interest those in
attendance that your school system is where they will find
fame, fortune, challenge, and happiness as teachers. While this
is an important aspect of the teacher labor market, typical rural
and small schools which wait for a position to become vacant
can never successfully address staffing needs. The first
consideration of teacher recruitment is to interest those
students presently attending our rural and small schools not
only in teaching but in teaching in our rural and small schools.
The majority, or at least a sizeable percentage, of those
presently teaching in our rural and small schools are from rural
areas and attended rural and small schools. In researching the
local TLM, the first questions asked are where do our teachers
come from and how is it that they are teaching in our system
now. Once we understand that our present students are our
future teachers, we understand that problems associated with
long-term teacher shortages in rural areas may be more

effectively addressed in our rural and small schools than in colleges and universities. This is not to ignore the importance or necessity of state and federal resources, but problem identification and solution is often situation specific.

It is important to note that considering teacher recruitment for future needs is a recognition that in rural and small schools the TLM is (and always has been) problematic. That is, we have never had (nor will we have) too many great teachers of every subject or grade. Successful schools will be those that recruit now for the future.

William Castetter (1981), in his classic text on personnel, notes the necessity of recruiting for short-term and long-term needs.

> . . . the recruitment facet of the personnel function has both short- and long-range implications. The short-range plan involves those activities carried on to meet the current demands for personnel that continually exist in every organization. . . . The long-term plan includes those activities designed to assure continuous supply of qualified professional and service personnel. (p. 126)

Miller and Sidebottom (1985a) present three basic assumptions of a successful recruitment plan.

> First, recruiting is a year-long, ongoing activity. Every public appearance, trip, and school event are opportunities to create a good name for the district and publicize its virtues.

> Second, recruiting requires help from everyone in the school and community. There is a role for students, parents, concerned citizens, college students, alumni and staff.

> Third, quality attracts quality. A school district must have a visible commitment to excellence in all areas if it expects to draw outstanding applicants. (p. 19)

Assumption three, quality attracts quality, combines the necessity of short-term and long-term recruitment plans, and brings to the forefront the question all recruiters must eventually ask: "What is it that we have to attract teachers to?" As Wise, Darling-Hammond, and Berry (1987) note, "successful recruitment depends upon the attractiveness of teaching" (p. 81). To attract (recruit) teachers, then, requires teaching to be attractive. This returns us to the questions we asked in the previous section: where do our teachers come from? Why do they teach for us? As Horn (1985) states:

> Attracting the "right" person and the "best" person for a teaching position is certainly not a science and likely not an art. Intuition, luck, and common sense are probably as often used as any objective measures on recommended recruiting procedures. . . . (p. 14)

Horn presents suggestions from Seifert and Simone (1980–81) for the development of a recruiting plan. In summary, these are as follows:

1. The easiest and most efficient plan for teacher recruitment involves a competitive salary and extra duty pay schedule.

2. The district can subsidize the cost of teacher retraining to fit the needs of the school district.

3. The district may offer to pay the costs of a teacher earning a master's degree, and, in turn, the teacher makes a commitment to teach in the district for three years after receiving the degree.

4. The district may identify outstanding junior level education majors in the various colleges and universities, select those students that meet the district's needs, and offer financial assistance in the form of scholarships.

5. The district may identify and actively recruit outstanding teachers in larger districts and prospective teachers that were raised and educated in smaller schools by reminding these individuals of the many benefits they received while growing up in a small town atmosphere.

6. The district may emphasize teacher autonomy and direct access to administration.

7. The school district could provide less expensive housing for teachers.

8. The school district could encourage the business community to help by providing employment for teachers.

9. In order to attract effective teachers, it may be necessary to provide employment opportunities for the teacher's spouse. (p. 15)

Matthes and Carlson (1985) offer ten approaches to teacher recruitment.

1. Pay expenses of candidate to visit school district and moving expenses.

2. Show willingness to hire husband and wife teams.

3. Provide assistance in locating housing and employment for spouse.

4. Emphasize local school autonomy.

5. Involve local community patrons and civic groups in recruitment efforts.

6. Provide an aggressive fringe benefit package that includes health benefit plan, supplemental

retirement plan, dental plan, personal leave, life insurance, financial support for graduate studies.

7. Stress special features—geography, climate, historical sites, cuisine, and isolation.

8. Emphasize the inherent advantages of small schools but be honest about their limitations as well.

9. Seek individuals who resided in rural areas before and who are most likely to return.

10. Emphasize the quality of rural life and the availability of leisure time activities. (pp. 3–4)

A major recruiting device is the student teaching experience. Teacher training institutions typically insist on placing students in schools near their institution. While this is understandable financially from the college/university standpoint, it is also true that the student teaching experience is a major recruitment tool for those good urban/suburban schools utilized for student teaching. Rural systems not utilized have neither the opportunity to present their good schools to student teachers (or to the university supervisors of student teachers) nor the opportunity to observe student teachers teaching. The better student teachers, then, are knowledgeable of and experience (only) good urban/suburban schools. Additionally, these schools get first choice based on insider knowledge. To change this system, rural and small schools will need to develop policies and programs to get student teachers into their schools. If these are to work at all, rural and small schools will need to provide teacher training institutions with acceptable options. Associated costs may be more easily justifiable when they are considered as a necessary recruitment expense.

Horn (1985) mentions a number of universities with rural education programs; these include Western Montana College, Brigham Young University, Berea College (Kentucky), Western

Michigan University, and the University of North Dakota. Miller and Sidebottom (1985a) expand this list to 18 universities. Yet, Horn (1985) also found that teacher training programs with an on-going rural focus had:

> . . . the interest and commitment of possibly only one individual to develop and conduct a program for rural/small school teachers in these institutions. . . .
>
> . . . institutional support and commitment seem to be relatively weak. (p. 29)

Long-term commitment for teacher education programs which utilize rural and small schools for the student teaching experience, then, would seem to belong only with rural and small schools themselves. The impact of the student teaching experience as a factor in the TLM, however, cannot be minimized.

Miller and Sidebottom (1985a) report that the recruitment efforts of the Carrizozo (New Mexico) Municipal Schools include encouraging their teachers to use their professional leave to teach in colleges of education.

> These practitioners are able to convey the realities of rural life and education and encourage prospective graduates to consider starting their careers in Carrizozo. (p. 22)

The same authors also report the following programs have been found effective in teacher recruitment:

> —arranging interest free loans to help with moving expenses.
>
> —picking up travel and other costs for employment interviews.
>
> —stating any attractive benefits.

They also note the practice of forgiveness loans which originate in the district.

> One incentive that has special appeal to local residents is a practice whereby a local community member is sent to college on a district-paid scholarship in return for several years service to the school district. (p. 23)

Such an approach has been reported as successful in nursing, an occupation quite similar to teaching (Hare, 1985). Tennessee has also considered a program in which doctors would have their medical school loans repaid if they agree to practice in "underserved" areas (*Nashville Banner Editorial*, April 19, 1989).

Caddo Parish (Louisiana) Schools have combined efforts with local businesses and offer an incentives package for certified minority teachers who will sign a teaching contract with Caddo Schools. This package includes rent paid on apartments and other incentives.

Recruitment materials are increasing in frequency of use and in message. Hare (1988) reports the development of VCR tapes for use at teacher job fairs to dispel myths about rural systems. One system, for example, included shots of the local McDonald's, Wal-Mart, Catholic Church, swimming pool, and tennis courts to let prospective teachers see for themselves that just because the system was rural, it was not without social amenities. Another system developed brochures with maps to show students just how close they were to area universities and graduate programs.

In this author's judgment, all recruitment efforts depend in important ways upon initial identification questions of where our teachers come from and how they came to teach for us. Once we can identify our present sources, we can enhance our recruitment efforts toward these sources. We can also initiate efforts to tap those sources we are not presently utilizing or are underutilizing. Recruitment is a year-round process and involves continually selling the community as well as the school. Effective recruitment plans are for both the short- and long-term. Most importantly, however, "quality attracts quality" (Miller and Sidebottom, 1985a, p. 19).

Selection

It is easy to think of personnel selection in typical terms of position availability, job description, candidate screening, specific certification, and choice among those qualified. In rural and small schools, however, it is rarely this simple. While a large urban/suburban high school may have a position for a person certified in chemistry, a rural, small school may need a person to teach chemistry, physics, biology, and earth science, to sponsor the science club, and to coach softball, etc.

Because of small student enrollment and often single sections of an individual course, the selection of a person to teach in a small, rural school generally occurs from a smaller pool of applicants. The urban/suburban criteria of specialization are replaced by a demand for multiple teaching certifications, the necessity of flexibility in teaching multi-aged students, and a willingness to become involved in extra-curricular activities.

Castetter (1981) believes that "the thrust of the personnel selection process is to achieve congruency between people and positions" (p. 159). The decision of which candidate to employ in rural and small schools is often complicated by concerns beyond the teaching abilities of the individual candidates. For example, it is not unusual to find a rural school system sufficiently close to an urban area to employ teachers who live in the urban area. Neither is it unusual for these teachers to seek positions in the urban area.

Such teachers, then, might teach in the rural area only until a position opens up in a school nearer where they live. Thus, some rural systems seemingly have a high teacher turnover rate because of their location and not because of the quality of their system. It seems reasonable for a principal in a rural system to choose a local person to fill a position and not a person from the urban area, regardless of who is the "better" teacher, because, if the urban teacher is hired, the position may well be vacant again in a year or so. It is important to note that this question, "why do we hire the people we do?" is to be addressed in our initial research into the identification of the variables affecting our TLM.

It may seem at first that a selection process for teachers involving other than academic considerations is the antithesis of professionalism. To those who know and understand rural areas and their schools, however, it is only rational to consider teachers as people outside the classroom as well as teachers within.

Seifert and Simone (1980–81) identified numerous characteristics needed by teachers in rural and small schools, including being:

> —Certified and able to teach in more than one subject area or grade level.
>
> —Prepared to supervise several extra-curricular activities.
>
> —Able to teach a wide range of abilities in a single classroom.
>
> —Able to adjust to the uniqueness of the community in terms of social opportunities, life styles, shopping areas, and constant scrutiny.
>
> —Able to overcome the students' cultural differences and add to his/her understanding of the larger society. (cited in Horn, 1985, p. 14)

It is, of course, advantageous to recruit only those who could be selected, but this is often not possible. Because "curriculum designs and content of teacher education departments and colleges have focused primarily, if not exclusively on the needs of urban and suburban communities" (Campbell, 1986, p. 1), teachers who consider rural schools often are not certified in multiple areas, have not had multicultural experiences, and are not prepared for the many nonteaching requirements expected in rural and small schools.

    Rural schools which select such teachers are making an investment and taking a risk. They risk that these teachers will not earn the additional certification needed, will not participate (willingly) in nonteaching requirements, and will not "fit in" with the community. Only if such employed teachers stay and learn to "fit in" will the investment pay off.

    In these times of teacher shortages, it may be necessary to recruit and select those willing to become certified, effective teachers in rural and small schools. This investment is part of the long-range planning Castetter (1981) considered so vital in recruitment. Also vital in long-range planning to recruit and retain teachers is the necessity for an effective induction program.

Induction

    William Castetter, in his classic work *The Personnel Function in Educational Administration* (1981), presents the necessity of viewing induction in an organizational context and as a continual process.

> Induction may be defined as a systematic organizational effort to assist personnel to adjust readily and effectively to new assignments so that they can contribute maximally to the work of the system while realizing personal and position satisfaction. This definition . . . goes beyond the conventional view that induction is concerned only with personnel assuming new assignments . . ., those reassigned . . ., or those assuming new roles. . . . A school system can recruit, select, assign, and transfer personnel, but until these individuals become fully adjusted to the work to be performed and the colleagues with whom it is performed, they cannot be expected to give their best effort to attaining the goals of the institution. (pp. 189–190)

    From this perspective, induction in rural and small school systems is not only to the system and school but also to the rural area itself; not only to the school but to each course (and its position in and among all other courses); not only to the courses but to the students, etc. This is a constant process made obvious by effective rural and small school administrators. To Castetter, induction is the "one way" in the "employment cycle" to move "between the day of the new assignment and the time when one becomes a self-motivated, self-directed, fully effective member of the enterprise" (p. 190).

This process is not to be confused with some form of brainwashing. Rather, it is a systematic, conscious effort to ensure organizational goals and increase organizational effectiveness. Induction, as an element of the TLM, returns to the assumption that our rural and small schools have goals and objectives, make plans, attempt change, and evaluate.

Wise et al. (1987) call *induction* an "initial transition period . . . of assistance and assessment of new hires" (p. 71). They further note:

> Effective support requires systematic training and support to help new teachers achieve higher levels of competence, and formal designation of the provider of assistance and expertise—principal, department chair or other senior teacher, or Central Office supervisor. "Induction programs" suggest something more formal than . . . "new teacher programs. . . ."(p. 71)

Wise et al. (1987), in their description of schools in East Williston, New York, emphasize the importance of induction:

> In East Williston, the tight coupling among selection processes (from recruitment to evaluation) impacts favorably upon new hires. Curriculum associates, who are involved in the entire selection process, communicate the district's expectations to new teachers, tailor staff development to meet their specific needs, and evaluate them upon the extent to which they meet these expectations. This close articulation among selection processes may not be possible in large school districts. (p. 71)

Miller and Sidebottom (1985a) agree such "activities are interactive and work with an advantage in rural and small schools, which have a closeness and warmth said to be lacking in many large schools" (p. 27). They also describe the induction activities of a California school.

> Many rural and small schools have developed ideas to help teachers find their place within the school and community. Van Sweet of the Dos Palos Joint Union Elementary School District in California suggests a one-day orientation program of preservice education for new faculty prior to the arrival of returning staff for the start of school. The information activities help to establish an early sense of employment security, he says. The day-long session should be followed by a social gathering for faculty, spouses, members of the board of education and administrators. During the next 30 days, the building principal and superintendent should have a short follow-up session to answer and resolve problems that have arisen. (pp. 25–26)

Horn (1985) expresses well the interrelationship between effective recruitment and retention:

> As a final note about recruitment, there are noticeable exceptions to the generalizations expressed about ineffective recruiters from small districts. In a personal communication with Otto Bufe (personal communication, June 25–26, 1985), Superintendent of the school in Grand Marais, Michigan, he described what I perceived to be a very effective practice. First, one must understand that Grand Marais is located on the southern shore of Lake Superior in the Upper Peninsula of Michigan. It is geographically isolated, and although beautiful during the short summer, winters are harsh with an annual snow fall of over 200 inches and subzero temperatures. The area is battered by extremely cold winds that seem to never cease. In addition, unemployment exceeds 50 percent in a town of 350, and the K–12 school has a total enrollment of 85 students. The school operates one bus, and the threat of consolidation lingers.

> Consolidation with the nearest district would require students to ride up to four hours per day in a bus. Teacher salaries are low, about $13,000 for a beginning teacher, and all teachers have multiple grade levels, and/or several (5–6) areas of preparation. At first consideration, one would question why any one would want to teach there. However, Mr. Bufe describes his teachers as absolutely top quality. Each teaching candidate visits with the teachers and students in the school, parents in their homes, and other townspeople in their workplaces. They are given very thorough orientation to the town and surrounding area. Strengths of the school and opportunities to make significant decisions and provide leadership in the school are emphasized. In essence, the school *and* community are "sold" to the candidate, in a positive, realistic sense. By the end of the intensive interview/orientation, one would expect mutual interest or mutual disinterest between the candidate and the school's representative, but clearly a teacher in this school would be well aware of this situation. (pp. 17–18)

Induction is not only to schools and communities, but, as Castetter (1981) states, is the period of time "between the day of the new assignment and the time when one becomes a self-motivated, self-directed, fully effective member of the enterprise" (p. 190).

Supervision (Evaluation and Improvement)

Directly related to the continual induction process is the need for effective, meaningful supervision of teachers. Unfortunately, supervision is not a field of study in which there is a great deal of consensus. It should be done, of course, but just how and by whom, just when and to what end, are debatable issues. Our purpose here is neither to offer the definitive statement on supervision nor a prescription for a successful supervision program. But it does seem reasonable to suggest that the basic assumption of supervision should be the improvement of instruction. Successful rural and small schools, then, design a program to induct new teachers into the instructional expectations of the school and supervise teachers in achieving instructional success. But in all cases, the emphasis is on improved instruction.

With the emphasis of supervision on instructional improvement, evaluation is no longer an attempt at a ranking of teacher performance. It assumes the larger role of assessing growth, determining change, and considering goals. Evaluation is a continual process of finding out how well we are doing and if we are doing what we should. It involves organizational goals and expectations as well as the teacher within the school.

Evaluation is also a time for teachers to examine their role and position. We too often think of teacher evaluation as a time when we decide whether we want to retain specific teachers and how to fix the marginal ones and forget that teachers must also decide if they want to stay with us.

When we employ teachers, we make promises, either actual or implied—courses to teach, class size, support—and when teachers face the choice of going to another school or staying with us, they evaluate us, too—promises kept, teaching conditions, prospects for improvement, etc. Given such a perspective, the purpose of supervision and evaluation by a school system ought to primarily focus on improvement. Such a view of improvement assumes the creation of reasonable, attainable goals and objectives, and the creation of a consensus necessary to achieve them.

If schools want to employ teachers who continue to improve, then it seems reasonable that teachers would want to work in schools which continually improve. If we expect teachers to improve their instruction, teachers will expect improvement in the conditions of and resources for instruction. Improvement becomes the benchmark by which teachers decide to retain us.

Supervision, evaluation and improvement are not simple procedures and each has a different role to play in staffing rural and small schools. Harris, McIntyre, Littleton, and Long (1985) describe well both the interrelationship of these three and the bad reputation which precedes them.

Some of the information that is collected to serve formative evaluation purposes can be used to serve other processes as well; however, the instruments and process that are appropriate for various purposes tend to be quite different. . . . For example, relatively formal and infrequent summative evaluations are quite appropriate for the purpose of determining whether to renew the contracts of most teachers, assuming that continuous formative evaluation has occurred in the meantime; on the other hand, to fill out a rating scale on a teacher once a year on the assumption that it will help the teacher improve is an exercise in futility. The point is that school administrators . . . should approach the task one purpose at a time and avoid the usual to seek one simple, easy, all-purpose "solution." This type of oversimplification has contributed much to the bad reputation that the whole evaluation process now has; supposedly aimed mostly at the improvement of performance, in practice the process tends to be negative and punitive, feared and rejected by evaluatees, and not helpful to anybody. (pp. 227–229)

The University of Wyoming's Department of Vocational Education (Reynolds, 1985) has a traveling seminar and support program for first-year teachers. Their program is based on assumptions of first-year teachers which effective local supervision (evaluation and improvement) programs would address.

—Teachers in rural schools have a unique need for inservice during their first year of teaching. They often find themselves in a department of one, floundering through problems of budgets, curriculum revisions, and management of laboratories with very few local sources of assistance.

—Beginning teachers in rural schools often find themselves too far away from a . . . university. . . .

—Beginning teachers in rural areas, especially, need
the opportunity to share the problems and successes
with colleagues. (p. 1)

Just offering "inservice" for first-year teachers has as little
opportunity for success as does present inservice programs.
As the Southeast Educational Development Lab found,

among rural, small schools . . . staff development
efforts in the five-state region tended to be episodic in
nature, rather than being systematic, needs-based,
participant-owned, and long-term, which are
characteristics of more effective systems. (*SEDL
Newsletter*, p. 4)

Flannagan and Trueblood (1986) believe rural teachers
are "wary of evaluation from 'outsiders'"(p. 3). This supports
O'Connel and Hagan's (1985) contention that rural "systems
must 'match' teacher improvement to the needs of adult rural
learners" (p. 4). Citing the work of Wilsey and Killion (1982),
they report the importance of providing

follow up support so that on-site supervision can give
participants assistance in adapting ideas and making
necessary changes in order to implement the
knowledge, skills, and attitudes acquired in training.
Just as staff development leaders must consider the
match of learning environment and the stages of adult
development, so also must supervisors adjust their
orientation to supervision. (p. 7)

As Reynolds (1985) notes, it is the first year which is
most important for teachers and the supervision (evaluation
and improvement) during this year takes on added importance.

The experiences that beginning teachers encounter
during that first, formative year, whether successful or
unfortunate, have a major effect of the habits and
pedagogical practices maintained during their
professional lifetime. By providing assistance to these
teachers, helping them with curriculum decisions,

student motivation problems, classroom teaching
techniques, budgeting, facility management, youth
organizations, community resource utilization, and
budgeting of time, opportunities for more success and
less failure are enhanced. (p. 2)

Retention

Salmon, Sava, and Thompson (1988) note that: "The
problem of poor retention of quality teachers stems in part from
some of the same factors responsible for the low attraction (to
teaching) in the first place." (p. 4) In rural and small schools,
then, we can probably say that many teachers leave for the
same reasons we had trouble recruiting them in the first place.
If we were to consider these six elements of the TLM as a loop,
retention is the point where we return to Identification and the
answers to our questions: Why do our teachers stay? Why do
our teachers leave? Only by understanding these can we
Recruit and Select the teachers we want, and only by offering
meaningful, effective Induction and Supervision (Evaluation and
Improvement) can we hope to Retain the teachers we wish.

The decision by a rural or small school to Retain a teacher
is vital in the life of that school. There are few if any positions in
which to hide the ineffective teacher and never a sufficient
surplus of funds to create such a position. The decision to
tenure or to continue to employ is crucial.

Too often, however, teachers are retained because there
is no sufficient reason not to. The personnel decision of
whether to retain is not an isolated decision but is part of the
other aspects of the TLM. That is, when individuals are hired
according to organizational needs and expectations, decisions
to retain these individuals are also based on organizational
needs and expectations.

But of greater concern in the TLM is the ability of rural
and small schools to retain those teachers they wish to retain.
While it will probably never be possible to keep all their good
teachers—some move with his or her spouse, have children,

return to school—it does seem reasonable that once systems understand why teachers leave, and they take those steps possible to address these problems, then more teachers will stay.

The retention of good teachers is vital for rural and small schools to maximize their position in the teacher labor market. Retaining good teachers provides the models necessary to recruit our students to teaching, form the nucleus of a staff concerned with the improvement of instruction, and is vital to retain other good teachers. The retention of good faculty, however, follows directly from the original identification of why our teachers stay and why they leave.

Matthes and Carlson (1985) note in their research the emphasis teachers who stayed in specific schools placed on "school administrators. . . creating professional conditions in which teachers can find rewards and a professional identity" (p. 9). Lewis and Edington (1983), in their study of why teachers left small schools in New Mexico, believe administrators can begin to determine teachers "at risk to turnover" (p. 7). They describe teachers as stayers or leavers and conclude:

> —Teachers intent upon staying in a given small district were motivated to come to that district most often by its proximity to home and family.
>
> —Teachers intent upon leaving are more likely to be single than married.
>
> —Teachers hired in a small district are more likely to leave within the first five years.
>
> —Stayers like small towns and villages more than did leavers though both prefer rural setting to the city.
>
> —Leavers were more ambitious for administrative positions.
>
> —Stayers were more satisfied with job and community. (p. 6)

Seyfarth and Bost (1986) surveyed school superintendents and concluded that salary and work settings are correlated with teacher turnover levels.

> Districts with higher pay and more fringe benefits had lower levels of turnover, while districts with large numbers of employees who commute 25 miles to their jobs and in which many buildings were old and out of date had higher levels of turnover. (p. 1)

Chapman and Green (1986) tested Chapman's model of the influences on teacher retention. They state that while:

> [T]he roots of attrition reach back to differences in initial career commitment and early work experiences. . . . [The] results from this study underscore the importance (to retention) of current work conditions, which can be influenced by school administrators. . . . [T]he results suggest that the attention administrators give to assuring the quality of professional life that new teachers experience can have long-term impacts on the career development of those teachers. This finding challenges a considerable amount of current practice, in which the newest teachers often receive the least desirable assignments and may have little contact with administrators during their first year. (p. 277)

This is not to mitigate the effect that such programs as child care (preschool and after school), community volunteers (to reduce paper work and nonteaching assignments), and reduced costs for housing could have on teacher retention. Indeed, it points directly to our original questions of identification.

Conclusion

> Two decades of federal programs, experimental teacher training programs, and occasional foundation

> efforts directed at the problems (of teacher staffing)
> have yielded mixed results. The more educators learn
> about recruitment and retention in rural and small
> schools, the more complex the topic is. (Miller and
> Sidebottom, 1985b, p. 5)

Personnel considerations for rural and small schools are much more complex than just deciding to hire and fire. Personnel decisions are more properly considered as interrelated aspects of a teacher labor market. The creation and continual improvement of effective schools require quality and effective teachers willing to improve.

Because there are numerous teacher labor markets, it is especially necessary for rural and small schools to research this labor market to determine where their teachers come from, why they stay, and why they leave. Only then can rural and small schools begin the process to attract, employ, and retain teachers of high quality.

REFERENCES

Berry, Barnett. *A Case Study of the Teacher Labor Market in the Southeast.* Southeastern Regional Council for Educational Improvement, Research Triangle Park, North Carolina, November 1984.

Campbell, Milo K. "Preparing Rural Elementary Teachers." U.S. Department of Education, Washington, D.C., March 1986.

Castetter, William B. *The Personnel Function in Educational Administration.* New York: The Macmillan Company, Inc., 1981.

Chapman, David W., and Green, Michael S. "Teacher Retention: A Further Examination." *Journal of Education Research, 79* (May–June 1986): 273–279.

DeYoung, A. J. "The Status of American Rural Education Research: An Integrated Review and Commentary." *Review of Education Research 57,* no. 2 (1987): 123–148.

Flannagan, K., and Trueblood, C. "Designing Effective Rural School Staff Development Programs." Paper presented at the National Rural Education Association Conference, Little Rock, Arkansas, October 1986. ERIC Document Reproduction Service No. ED 275467.

Hare, Dwight. "Local School Finances in Louisiana: Disparities, Discrepancies, and Disgrace." Paper presented at Midsouth Education Research Association Annual Meeting, 1986.

Harris, Ben M., McIntyre, Kenneth E., Littleton, Vance C., Jr., and Long, Daniel F. *Personnel Administration in Education.* Boston: Allyn and Bacon, Inc., 1985.

Horn, Jerry G. *Recruitment and Preparation of Quality Teachers for Rural Schools.* Department of Education, Washington, D. C., August 1985.

Lewis, Ted, and Edington, Everett D. *Small District Teacher Study, Executive Summary.* New Mexico State University, June 1983.

Matthes, William A., and Carlson, Robert V. *Recruitment and Staff Development of Teachers: A Rural Perspective.* U.S. Department of Education, October 1985.

Mathews, Jerry. "Teachers: Finding and Keeping the Best in Rural and Small Schools." Unpublished manuscript, Northeast Louisiana University, Graduate School of Education, 1989.

Miller, James, and Sidebottom, Dennis. *Teachers: Finding and Keeping the Best in Small and Rural Districts.* Arlington, Va.: American Association of School Administrators, March 1985.

O'Connell, Carleen, and Hagans, Rex. *Staff Development in Rural Schools.* Northwest Regional Educational Laboratory, Portland, Oregon, November 1985.

Reynolds, Carl L. *Young Teacher Seminar: A Model for Rural Teacher Education In-service.* Laramie: University of Wyoming-Laramie, October 1985.

Salmon, Paul, Sava, Samuel, and Thompson, Scott. *Teacher Incentives: A Tool for Effective Management.* A joint publication of NASSP, NAESP, and AASA.

Seifert, E. H., and Simone, P. "Personnel Practices for Recruiting and Keeping Effective Teachers in Smaller Schools." *The Small School Forum 2,* no. 2 (1980–1981): 12–13.

Seyfarth, John T., and Bost, William A. "Teacher Turnover and the Quality of Worklife in Schools: An Empirical Study." *Journal of Research and Development in Education, 20,* no. 1 (Fall 1986): 1–6.

Wise, Arthur E., Darling-Hammond, Linda, and Berry, Barnett. *Effective Teacher Selection: From Recruitment To Retention.* Santa Monica, Calif.: The Rand Corporation, January 1987.

The Organization and Reorganization of Small Rural Schools

David H. Monk

Introduction

Organizational solutions to problems facing small rural schools have a long history and are popular among policy makers. The thinking seems to be that there is some heretofore elusive organizational structure that once found will resolve these problems once and for all time. This faith in organizational solutions is testified to by the numerous structures that have been proposed and experimented with and belied by the persistence of problems and the recurring, almost circular, nature of the debate.

In light of this it makes sense to take stock of the various organizational solutions that have currency in this debate and examine how they differ and what their respective strong and weak points are. This is the central task of the present essay. It builds upon an earlier effort (Monk, 1988) and attempts to make further progress toward understanding the compatibilities that exist among the numerous organizational solutions. This ought to be useful since the idea is not to choose only one organizational form to the exclusion of all others but rather to choose an appropriate combination of forms and respond imaginatively to whatever inconsistencies and tensions arise.

The essay is structured around a distinction between comprehensive and partial forms of organization remedies. Each is examined in light of its fundamental theoretical orientation and the existing empirical research. The term organization is used broadly to include relatively informal instances of cooperation across separate organizational entities as well as more institutionalized and formal means of organizing productive activities.

Comprehensive Reorganization Remedies

Comprehensive reorganization entails the merger or consolidation of two or more organizationally distinct schooling units into a single organizational entity. This can be accomplished in various ways including the annexation of one unit by another and the dissolution of two units into a new previously nonexistent schooling unit. Various terms are used to describe these reorganizations including: merger, union, consolidation, and centralization, to name only a few. Schools as well as school districts can be the focus of these comprehensive reorganization efforts.

There is a well developed body of theory drawn largely from economics that serves as the basis for the comprehensive reorganization approach. Economists have developed a theory of scale which holds that within limits when scale (i.e., size) is small, unit operating costs tend to be higher than when scale is large. (For discussion, see Stigler, 1966; Hirshleifer, 1980; Nicholson, 1985.) This theory has been applied to education and on the basis of several well-known studies (perhaps the best known and most widely cited is Cohn, 1968, but there are others: Hind, 1977; Illinois State Board of Education, 1985; North Carolina Board, 1986; Riew, 1966, 1986; Ratcliff, Riddle, and Yinger, 1988), it has been concluded by some that it costs more to achieve the same educational outcomes in small compared to large organizational settings.

There is also ample precedent for the formation of larger schooling units out of smaller constituent units. Between 1930 and 1972, the number of school districts declined almost eightfold from approximately 128,000 to fewer than 17,000. During the same period, the number of schools declined from approximately 262,000 to 91,000. These declines occurred at a time when K–12 enrollments were increasing dramatically, and the net result was significant growth in the average size of schooling units. Specifically the average district was fifteen times larger in 1972 than in 1930; the average school was five times larger in 1972 than in 1930 (Guthrie, 1979). This rapid growth in the average size of school districts and schools and the concomitant decline in the number of separately organized local educational agencies are eloquent testimony to the enthusiasm with which this policy has been pursued (Haller and Monk, 1988).

There are, however, serious problems with the comprehensive approach to reorganization. The problems stem not so much from flaws in the underlying theory as from the application of the theory to the particular instances of production represented by classrooms, schools, and school districts. Several of these problems are reviewed below.

Optimal Size

The unit cost of producing an educational outcome can vary with the size of the schooling unit. To the degree that a unit cost curve has a U-shape, it costs more to produce the outcome in a very small as well as in a very large organizational setting, and it becomes meaningful to think of an optimal (mid-range) size for schooling organizations.

However, it is important to realize that education is characterized by numerous outcomes. Each outcome can have its own production features, and these will be reflected in a series of outcome specific unit cost curves. The key point is that these unit cost curves, one for each outcome produced, need not coincide. To the extent that this is the case, it becomes quite problematic to believe that there is any such thing as an optimal size for an educational activity. The irony here is that even if there are scale economies that apply to each educational outcome looked at separately, it does not necessarily follow that there is such a thing as an optimal or even a preferred school or school district size.

For example, social and affective outcomes seem to be more efficiently produced in small size settings. For a review, see Hamilton (1983). In contrast, some evidence suggests that cognitive outcomes as measured by standardized test scores can be more efficiently produced in larger size settings. Studies calling for larger school or school district size tend to be focused on cognitive test score outcomes. For reviews see Fox (1981) and Bilow (1986).

Magnitude and Range of Scale Economies

Empirical research has thrown light on the magnitude and range of scale economies associated with one of the more typically studied educational outcomes—cognitive achievement test score gains. There seems to be a trend toward reducing the wideness of the range over which scale economies are believed to exist. Some of the earliest studies on the subject suggested that this range is quite wide. For example, in Hanson's 1964 study the optimal size for New York State districts was 160,000 students. Cohn's 1968 study, which included a better control for qualitative differences, recommended a high school size in the neighborhood of 1,500.[1]

More recently attention has been given to even smaller numbers. For example, Walberg and Fowler's 1987 New Jersey study is consistent with the claim that economies of scale in the production of cognitive test score gains are real and perhaps substantial but are exhausted by the time a district reaches 120 per grade level. This is ironic since the Walberg and Fowler study is currently being trumpeted by those seeking to preserve schools and school districts with much lower enrollments. The reason for the irony is that most of the Walberg and Fowler study is focused on the negative relationship they found between learning outcomes and size for those schooling units with more than 120 pupils per grade level.

Friedkin and Necochea (1987) also reported results that are inconsistent with conventional thinking about scale economies. Their California data reveal negative relationships between district size and pupil achievement among low SES populations. These results are more consistent with the view that large size occasions diseconomies which manifest themselves in the form of lower student performance.

It is interesting that this trend toward smaller numbers arises even without paying attention to the social outcomes of schooling. Once these outcomes are added, the trade-off problem discussed in the previous section applies. In this regard it is noteworthy that little mention of size was made in the national reports on education issued during the 1980s. When size was mentioned (for examples see Boyer (1983) and Goodlad (1984) it was usually in reference to schools having grown too large. For more on the implications of the national reports issued during the 1980s on the future of small rural schools, see Haller and Monk (1988).

The Realization of Scale Economies

Tapping primary sources. Economic theory holds that there are two major sources of scale economies: savings from making more efficient use of indivisible (i.e., lumpy) inputs and savings from returns to specialization. Monk (1987) found that once a high school reaches an enrollment of 100 per grade level, there was little evidence of efforts to tap these two major sources of economies. Specifically, he found that beyond the 100 pupil per grade level there was neither an increase in average class size nor evidence of additional specialization on the part of teachers.

Findings such as these raise more questions than they answer. For example, why is it that high school teachers do not take advantage of the increased opportunity to specialize in larger (beyond 100 pupil per grade level) high schools? Is it because the returns to such specialization are nil, or because administrators or parents or union officials prevent it for other reasons? Or is it a by-product of recently declining enrollments and reflective of a tactic employed by teachers to avoid being vulnerable to lay-offs?

And why are not class sizes allowed to increase to take advantage of the alleged "over-supply" of teacher resources in the small class settings found within small high schools? Is it because in fact there is no oversupply and a teacher in a class with 26 students is fully employed?[2] If this is the case, it would appear that economies of scale in fact are exhausted by the time a high school reaches 100 pupils per grade level. Or is it that efforts to reduce class size are making it impossible to realize what may be in fact significant scale economies?

Levels of decision making. Scale economies, to the extent that they are real and realized, can manifest themselves in a wide variety of ways. Examples include taxpayer savings and improved educational programs. The final mix of benefits is the outcome of a complex interaction among decision makers at a variety of levels in schooling systems. For example, scale economies might be "spent" on diversifying a curriculum, but how can it be ensured that the curriculum grows in a coherent and sensible way? Teacher decision making plays a key role here and interacts with administrator and lay-person decision making. In his New York sample, Monk found evidence of apparently frivolous courses in the larger high schools' curriculums.[3] He also found that specialized courses like calculus and advanced placement courses were not necessarily present within large high schools' curriculums. On the basis of these results, he concluded that large high school size in itself is no guarantee of a coherent comprehensive curriculum.

Student decision making also needs to be considered. A high school might offer a coherent comprehensive curriculum only to have students refuse to take advantage of what is offered. Again, Monk's New York data address this issue. He reported that surprisingly small percentages (on the order of 10%) of students in high schools with 3,000 pupils enroll in those courses that are unavailable within high schools where the enrollment is 100 pupils. He raised questions about the wisdom of reorganizing entire school districts if the chief beneficiaries are such small percentages of students. This question takes on added significance once it is recognized that reorganization can occasion significant community unrest, the topic of the following section. This question also prompts a search for other less disruptive and perhaps more cost effective means of meeting the needs of students who seek the courses that are available only in larger high schools. Finally, it raises questions about why such small percentages of students are taking these courses. What may be most appropriate is a change in the interface between the decision making of students and school officials in the selection of courses.

Hidden costs. It is important to recognize that the means by which scale economies are realized can themselves generate costs. For example, it is well established in the research literature that transportation costs need to be included in assessments of reorganization possibilities (Sher and Tompkins, 1977, White and Tweeten, 1973, Guthrie, 1979). A full accounting of these costs has the effect of making consolidations in sparsely settled areas less attractive than in otherwise similar settings where increased transportation costs play a smaller role.

Some of the costs associated with comprehensive reorganization are less easily quantified than the impact on transportation. Several case studies now exist (DeYoung and Boyd, 1986; Monk and Haller, 1986; and Peshkin, 1982) which document the turmoil some communities have experienced as part of reorganization efforts. The divisiveness which arose in these cases can be very costly and seriously interfere with the production of educational, not to mention other socially desirable outcomes.

The potential for these costs to arise leads to questions about whether they can be avoided. This amounts to asking whether there exists a body of technical knowledge that can be drawn upon to minimize and perhaps eliminate community unrest as a byproduct of reorganization. In New York a cottage industry has grown up around the efforts of the state to encourage comprehensive reorganization. Consultants, usually retired state education department officials, are hired by school districts (using state provided funds) to provide advice regarding the wisdom of reorganization options. Monk and Haller (1986) reviewed the reports of these consultants during the early 1980s and were highly critical on the grounds that the reports failed to provide balanced treatments of the advantages and disadvantages of reorganization. According to Monk and Haller, these consultants demonstrated their ignorance of the underlying research base dealing with reorganization and scale economies and provided one-sided treatments that without exception recommended reorganization.

If Monk and Haller are correct in their assessment of these reports and if the reports are representative of the kind of technical expertise available elsewhere to schools and districts considering reorganization, there is good reason to question the adequacy of the existing knowledge base regarding the implementation of comprehensive reorganizations. And if the existing base is inadequate, an even more difficult and important question arises: Is it even possible for such technical knowledge to exist? No attempt will be made here to answer this question definitively, but there are reasons for being skeptical of an affirmative answer.

First, it is important to recognize that the remaining small schools and districts in this nation have maintained themselves in the face of a remarkably successful reorganization reform movement. These schools are not small accidentally. Each is in some significant respect a "hard-case" from the reorganizers' perspective. They may be situated in remote areas where the geography makes reorganization inadvisable or there may be man-made barriers such as wide differences across units in debt and deferred maintenance.

Second, in addition to being "hard-cases" many of the remaining small schooling units are highly unique. Their uniqueness stems in part from the long-term interaction between past efforts to encourage and/or impose comprehensive reorganization solutions with the unique constellation of personalities and structural features found within the affected communities. Reorganization is not something dealt with at the surface of communities. It is deeply personal and can only be understood by delving into the internal complexity of communities. A significant experience with a reorganization attempt has fundamental and longstanding effects on communities. These communities are transformed and the transformation contributes to their uniqueness. A series of reorganization experiences only adds to the uniqueness of the community.

To the degree that uniqueness characterizes the remaining cases, it will be difficult if not impossible to generate transferable information about how to facilitate comprehensive reorganization even when a compelling case can be made in terms of available and realizable scale economies.

It seems prudent to doubt whether some set of insights are readily available which once achieved will somehow overcome what has become decades of successful resistance to comprehensive reorganization efforts. The hardness and uniqueness of the remaining cases make faith in the arrival of such knowledge a bit pollyannish.

However, it most certainly does not follow that the presence of real and unavoidable costs in the form of community unrest is sufficient in itself to dismiss comprehensive reorganization as a solution to the problems of small rural schools. The benefits of reorganization may be sufficiently large in the net that the costs, real and substantial though they may be, are worth bearing.

New Developments

One potentially promising development involves pursuing comprehensive reorganization on a gradual and more individually tailored basis. This turns the technical knowledge issue on its head and essentially concedes that there are no universal approaches or designs that generalize across the remaining small schooling units. Rather than view this as an obstacle, it can be viewed as an engine to drive the subsequent reorganization. The idea is to let the communities involved develop a reorganization design that is consonate with local conditions and history. It could very well provide for a gradual reorganization with built in check points and options for changing direction. It might also provide for a partial reorganization in the sense discussed in the next section.

Such an approach presumes that the state is less concerned about the details of how schooling units are organized than it is with the ultimate production of educational outcomes. In effect the state would say to the districts: We have little interest in how you organize yourselves so long as your students achieve the agreed upon learning outcomes. As testing and measurement become more sophisticated, such outcome oriented accountability systems are likely to gain in importance. A reduction in state specification of organizational alternatives is a logical byproduct of such a shift toward outcome based accountability systems.

Partial Reorganization Remedies

Interest in the partial reorganization of schools or school districts grows from the same conceptual base as does interest in the comprehensive approach discussed in the previous section. The goal is to increase enrollment levels as a means of capturing economies of scale. What makes the approach partial is a greater degree of deference paid to the autonomy of the pre-existing organizational units. A partial reorganization may even involve the creation of a new organization to oversee a partial union of participating units. Thus, in stark contrast to comprehensive reorganization where there is a reduction in the number of organizations, the partial reorganization remedy can add to the number of education organizations within a state.

This greater deference to the autonomy of pre-existing organizational units has advantages as well as drawbacks. The advantages include a hoped-for reduction in the level of community resistance on the grounds that the reorganization does not eliminate any community's school.[4] The drawbacks take various forms but can all be viewed as additional barriers on the ability of school officials to realize scale economies. Critics of the partial approach lament the scale economies that are lost because of the continued deference to separately organized schools and districts; proponents celebrate the economies that are realized and argue that even these would be unavailable if states insisted on treating reorganization as an "all-or-nothing" matter.

The following discussion assesses past efforts to pursue the partial reorganization approach. The focus is on the difficulties that have been encountered on the grounds that these are instructive to those interested in pursuing the approach more successfully in the future. Attention then turns more briefly to some new forms of partial reorganization that are beginning to attract attention and appear to have promise.

The Level of Formality and its Implications for Stability

Perhaps the most common form of partial reorganization involves the regional delivery of selected instructional services, most typically those involving vocational and/or special education services. The rationale is that these services are the most costly to deliver by small schooling units and that significant economies can be realized if constituent units can find a means to cooperate in their delivery.

The means found for this cooperation to occur vary dramatically across the states. It can be highly formalized such as the Boards of Cooperative Education Services (BOCES) in New York or quite informal such as the cluster approach developed by Paul Nachtigal (1984) working in conjunction with the Mid-Continent Regional Education Laboratory.

Such large variability in the formalness of the new organizational structures which achieve partial reorganization invites questions about the conditions under which formal as opposed to informal sharing is preferable. Galvin (1986) examined this question and identified five conditions which contribute to the ease with which sharing takes place. According to Galvin: stability, consensus, evenness in the distribution of benefits, low levels of competition, and low levels of additional expense all contribute to ease of sharing.

Galvin next linked ease of sharing with organizational structure and posited the thesis that the easier the sharing, the less formal needs be the organizational structure. To illustrate his thesis he distinguished between the "dumptruck" type of sharing and the sharing of specific instructional programs such as a foreign language offering. In their synthesis of Galvin's work Monk and Haller (1986, p. 89) put it this way:

> It is easier to share a dump truck than a foreign
> language course. In the case of the dump truck, the
> number of actors involved is small, there is
> widespread consensus about what dump trucks can
> and should accomplish, competition is minimal, and
> there is mutual advantage. In contrast, the foreign
> language exchange involves a large number of actors
> (students, teachers, parents, administrators, bus
> drivers, etc.), consensus need not exist about what
> language to teach, the selection of the instructor and
> instructional methods may be problematic, and there
> can be an implied message—derived from the
> competition between the schools—that the sending
> school is in some ways inferior to the receiving
> school.

Galvin concluded that the organizational mechanisms
used to facilitate the dump truck kind of sharing need to be
different from those used to facilitate the sharing of courses and
other services that are less easily shared. The former lend
themselves to informal arrangements. The latter do not.

However, it is not as if making the arrangement formal
somehow eliminates the barriers that exist. In his follow-up
research, Galvin (1989) identified the conditions within highly
formalized administrative structures that either facilitate or
impede successful and long term sharing. On the basis of an
empirical analysis of sharing within New York's BOCES units,
he concluded that structural characteristics such as variability
of wealth and size among component members is directly
related to the level and mix of services shared. He found less
evidence supporting the commonly held view that larger size of
the formal cooperative contributes unambiguously to higher
levels of sharing (Stephens, 1979; Cates, 1981; Campbell et al.,
1975).

The Potential for Inconsistency

The willingness of a state to tolerate or encourage partial
reorganization as a means of realizing scale economies reflects
an admission, grudging or otherwise, that comprehensive
reorganization in itself is not an all-purpose remedy for the

problems of small rural schooling units. In making this admission the state runs the risk of undermining whatever efforts it is making elsewhere to promote comprehensive reorganization as the preferred remedy. Local schooling officials are likely to reason: Why reorganize comprehensively if we can cooperate with neighbors and offer on a regional basis the programs we find most difficult (costly) to provide individually? If the state provides financial incentives to encourage the delivery of services at a regional level, the reluctance of individual units to reorganize comprehensively is further enhanced.

One response to this inconsistency is for the state to restrict the kinds of services that can be offered cooperatively. For example, restrictions can be imposed so that only vocational and special education services are eligible for regional delivery on a cooperative basis. Such restrictions have been justified by the claim that even in relatively large districts, these courses frequently fail to attract sufficient enrollments for cost-effective operation. The exclusion of "core academic" courses can reflect an underlying belief that if a district is so small that it cannot cost-effectively offer core academic courses, the preferred solution is comprehensive district consolidation. A serious drawback to this approach is that it places the state in the position of having to decide what does and does not count as an acceptable non-core academic course offering. Defensible criteria for making this judgment are difficult to develop.

The Impact on Administrative Complexity

A serious pursuit of partial reorganization remedies can add significantly to the administrative complexity of a state's schooling system. To the degree that organizational features of cooperatives need to be tailored to the nature of the services being shared, states committed to the partial reorganization approach could find themselves operating with any number of different types of sharing units scattered across the landscape. Moreover, individual schooling units could find themselves belonging to any number of different cooperatives or clusters, each focusing on the delivery of a particular service or combination of services. Minnesota is an example of a state where a wide range of different kinds of cooperative arrangements are available to individual schooling units.

The resulting complexity needs to be reckoned with and fully considered since it can significantly interfere with the provision of educational opportunities in a cost-effective fashion. A state might seek to contain the adverse effects of this complexity by restricting the nature and range of cooperative administrative units that it permits. But such restrictions have their own drawbacks if the net effect of forcing all sharing into a single or small number of administrative structures is a reduction in the range and/or level of sharing that takes place.

The Role Played By Instructional Technology

While the impact of instructional technology in small rural schools is too large a topic to be done justice here,[5] there is a dimension of the topic that is highly relevant and worth exploring. Many of the new technologies require sharing across separately organized schooling units, and this need to share can prompt the formation of new organizational structures designed to facilitate such sharing. These new organizational structures are properly viewed as instances of partial reorganization.

What has become known as "distance education" is a good example of how new technologies give rise to increased need for sharing across separately organized schooling units. If a lesson is being telecast as part of an inter-active, two-way instructional program that involves multiple sites, the receiving schools must coordinate with the sending school. This coordination goes far beyond relatively minor details such as agreeing on a time during which the lesson will be transmitted. Potentially sensitive matters need to be decided such as the selection of the course(s), the identity of the instructor(s), the content of the lesson(s), the nature of the student evaluation(s), the evaluation(s) of the instructor(s), and the composition of the class(es), to name only a few. In addition, there are internal effects that need to be considered including jealousies and rivalries that can arise between those faculty who are and who are not participating.

This kind of sharing is not straightforward and has many of the characteristics which Galvin (1986) asserts require a formal organizational structure for success. One of the current problems seems to be that more attention is being devoted to technical aspects of the innovations (e.g., the advantages of microwave transmission over cable) than have been devoted to the implicit and sometimes less than obvious demands for sharing. It is at least conceivable that the organizational features of a cooperative devoted to taking advantage of distance education technologies needs to be quite different from that designed to facilitate the more conventional kind of sharing that involves the transportation of either students or teachers.

It is also worth noting that even if the technology develops impressively and the sharing difficulties are resolved, there is no guarantee that differences in educational opportunities associated with size and ruralness will disappear or be significantly reduced. The new technologies may also make it possible for large, non-rural schools to take greater advantage of returns to specialization and to avoid indivisibilities. It is a mistake to think that small rural schools are the only places where courses cannot be offered because there are too few students to fill a class (Monk, 1987). Distance education technologies will also make it possible for larger, non-rural schools to expand their curricular offerings so that the net effect may be more of a parallel increase in the incidence of small, specialized courses than a catching up of small rural schools to what is offered elsewhere.

New Directions

Just as was the case for the comprehensive reorganization remedy, there are new directions in which partial reorganization seems to be moving. The two that will be mentioned here are both potentially quite controversial and have not been tested in practice to any great extent. They are, nevertheless, quite instructive and worthy of consideration.

Shared administrative services. It is not uncommon for schooling units in rural areas to share administrative officers such as superintendents or business managers (Sederberg, 1985). Nor is it uncommon for schooling units to join in a collective for specific administrative services such as payroll or purchasing.

But there is an additional way in which administrative services could be shared that has received much less attention. This kind of sharing de-emphasizes the uniqueness of educational administration and stresses the similarities or compatibilities associated with the administration of a wide range of social services. It involves sharing the administration of schools with the administration of other social services provided publicly within small and rural communities. It involves joining units of government that heretofore have been quite distinct. Rather than hire a team of administrators to administrate several different schools or school districts over what might be a formidable geographic area, a single administrative team would be hired by the rural community to oversee the provision of the complete range of services ordinarily provided by school districts, towns, villages, and perhaps counties. This kind of reorganization might be called "cross-function reorganization."

A partial reorganization along these lines offers the advantage of preserving local autonomy in the administration of education as well as other social services. A duly constituted school board could function, as could the relevant local town and/or village boards. These boards would jointly employ the administrative team. Such an administrative assignment would undoubtedly be challenging, but the same can be said of the shared superintendencies studied by Sederberg (1985). Such administrative assignments can also be looked at as attractive opportunities.

It is not stupid to argue that the specialization and compartmentalization of different units of local government (schools, health and social services, corrections, transportation, and so forth) is highly inefficient even in relatively densely settled regions. Educational administrators routinely deal with transportation, food preparation, and health-related services. Indeed, experimental programs such as the one currently underway in Rochester, New York, are designed to broaden the schools' mandate so that schools play larger roles in the day-to-day lives of students. Moreover, administrators of local governments also deal routinely with the provision of educational services. For example, educational programs offered by Cooperative Extension units are based at the county level.

There are, nevertheless, drawback associated with this conception of partial reorganization. There may be a uniqueness to school administration that makes it difficult or impossible for non-school administrators to perform well. For example, it could be difficult for a county administrator who was untrained as an educator to evaluate teachers. But, such functions could be contracted for, perhaps on a state level. The state might make available at cost the services of professional teacher evaluators. The local administration would simply contract to have this service performed.

There is also the danger of interjecting partisan politics into the schools. Reformers have worked hard to limit the role played by partisan politics in the schools, and the conception of partial reorganization described here could be viewed as a step backwards. But this ought not to suggest that schools operate in some sort of political vacuum. There surely is a politics of education with schools organized in their current form. The central question that needs to be answered is: What would happen to the politics of education were such a mingling of education and other types of local government services to occur?

Residential Schools

A state might establish residential schools as a means of overcoming the problems facing small rural schools. The goal would be to join individual schooling units on a state (or sub-state) level to provide a range of educational services. It is a logical extension of the delivery of selected services regionally on a cooperative basis. The residential feature has the advantage of making possible more indepth programming. It also offers a potentially powerful means of breaking down the isolation and lack of diversity that can be found in certain small rural schools.

Proposals for residential schools are highly controversial, in part because local schooling units are reluctant to lose students. One response to the controversy could be to limit the residential character of the schools. For example, a residential school could be structured, not so much as a four-year substitute high school, but as a school students would attend for relatively short blocks of time, such as a single semester. A student from a rural high school might attend the state residential school for one semester in the sophomore year to take a block of advanced science, humanities, and social science courses and then return to the home school for the balance of the sophomore year as well as for the junior and senior years. A more ambitious program could provide for a return to the residential school for a follow-up semester, perhaps during the senior year. Participating students would benefit not only form the opportunity to study an advanced and specialized curriculum not offered in their home school but also from the opportunity to meet and interact with students from all around the state. A program restricted to summers only would be even less controversial.

While such restrictions on how residential the program is may reassure communities over the loss of their youngsters, several potentially serious problems remain. For example, not all subjects lend themselves to relatively short, intensive periods of study. Moreover, the local schooling unit is likely to face difficulties re-introducing into the home school curriculum students who have attended the residential schools. Finally, there are questions to ask about how to best select students to attend residential schools. States would want to guard against these schools turning into either elite institutions or "dumping grounds" that detract from equality of educational opportunity.

Clearly, these are important questions and problems. But, it should be equally clear that these questions and problems are neither unanswerable nor insolvable. For example, time spent in the residential school could be supplemented with longer term contact through the mail, electronic media, or perhaps through periodic meetings during summers or vacations. By expanding the contact beyond a one semester in-residence block of time, problems stemming from the shortness and intensiveness of the contact can be addressed. Concerns about elitism and articulation could be dealt with by broadening the opportunity and making it available to all students. If, for example, one-half of a school's sophomore class were to attend the residential school during the first semester and the second half were to attend during the second semester, all students could emerge with a common experience on which the home school could build. Moreover, the teaching resources freed in the home districts, due to the absence of half the sophomore class, could be devoted to curriculum development at the local level.

Policy Implications

What are the policy implications regarding the organization and reorganization of small rural schools that follow from this review of the accumulated research? There are at least the following six:

1. Recognize that larger school or district enrollment is not sufficient in itself to achieve desirable results. The data, not to mention common sense, seem clear on this point.

2. Recognize that the recommended optimal sizes have been declining over time and that the idea of an optimal school or district size does not stand up to close scrutiny.

3. Be more attentive to the unique nature of each instance of possible reorganization and be respectfully skeptical about expert advice based on experiences elsewhere.

4. Recognize that as better measures of educational outcomes are obtained and serve as the basis for accountability systems, it will become less and

not more important to specify district and school organizational structures.

5. Be more attentive to what inhibits the long-term sharing of substantive educational programs across separately organized schooling units. It is probably a mistake to think that there exists an all-purpose cooperative administrative structure that will succeed at fostering cooperation in the delivery of a wide range of substantive educational services. Just as there is no optimal school or district size, there likely is no single optimal structuring for educational cooperatives.

6. Remain receptive to novel approaches to reorganization, keeping in mind that the schooling districts which remain small constitute "hard-cases" that probably do not lend themselves to conventional comprehensive reorganization. Be especially attentive to means by which reorganizations can be accomplished gradually or partially. Some of the new directions discussed previously (including locally designed comprehensive reorganizations, cross-function reorganizations, and part-year residential schools) warrant further attention and perhaps experimentation.

This essay has reviewed what reorganization, both in its comprehensive and partial forms, has to offer educational policy makers. The underlying research is complex and seems at times to point in inconsistent directions. If there is a single theme that emerges it is that there is no single straightforward reorganization remedy for the problems facing small rural schools. Indeed, reorganization as it has been practiced in the past is seriously tainted and difficult to defend as a remedy for the nations remaining small rural schools. It is nevertheless an option which if correctly and sensitively pursued offers considerable promise. This essay has explored some of the insights such sensitivity presupposes and thereby aspires to contribute to the policy making debate.

NOTES

1. Strictly speaking these numbers are not comparable since Hanson's study dealt with school districts and Cohn's study dealt with high schools. For more on the importance of distinguishing among the organizational level at which scale economies exist, see the review by Fox (1981), Coleman and LaRoque (1986), as well as the volume of *Education and Urban Society* devoted to size in education (Cienkus and Berlin, 1989).

2. Monk found that the average class size in his sample of New York State high schools reached a ceiling of 26 pupils among high schools with more than 100 per grade level.

3. Courses with titles like Sports in Literature and Mystery within the English Curriculum prompted this concern. Analyses of national data from the High School and Beyond data base are prompting similar concerns. These data indicate that a course with the title Rock Poetry is to be found within American high schools with sufficient frequency to warrant a separate code. For more on this work, see Haller et al., in press.

4. To the extent that partial reorganizations are viewed as a prelude to comprehensive reorganization the hoped for reduction in turmoil can fail to materialize.

5. For perceptive treatments that include a healthy degree of skepticism about the likely impact of recent technological developments on education, see Cuban (1986) and Levin and Meister (1985). For a treatment in the context of a production model with discussion of the implications for small rural schools, see Monk (1990).

REFERENCES

Bilow, Scott. "The Size of School Districts: Economic and Psychological Perspectives." Ithaca, N.Y.: Department of Education, Cornell University, 1986.

Boyer, E. L. *High School: A Report on Secondary Education in America.* New York: Harper and Row, 1983.

Campbell, Roald F., et al. *The Organization and Control of American Schools.* 2d ed. Columbus, Ohio: Charles E. Merrill Publishing Company, 1975.

Cates, Carolyn. "Collaborative Arrangements That Support School Improvement: A Synthesis of Recent Studies." 1981. ERIC no. ED 264653.

Cienkus, Robert T., and Berlin, Barney M. "Size: The Ultimate Issue." *Education and Urban Society, 21,* no. 2 (1989).

Cohn, E. "Economies of Scale in Iowa High School Operations." *Journal of Human Resources, 3,* 4 (Fall 1968): 422–434.

Coleman, P., and LaRoque, L. "The Small School District in British Columbia: The Myths, the Reality, and Some Policy Implications." *Alberta Journal of Educational Research, 32,* no. 4 (1986): 323–335.

Cuban, L. *Teachers and Machines: The Classroom Use of Technology Since 1920.* New York: Teachers College Press, 1986.

DeYoung, Alan J., and Boyd, Tom. "Urban School Reforms for a Rural District: A Case Study of School/Community Relations in Jackson County, Kentucky, 1899–1986." *Journal of Thought, 21,* 4 (1986): 25–42.

Fox, W. "Reviewing Economies of Size in Education." *Journal of Education Finance, 6,* 3 (Winter 1981): 273–296.

Friedkin, N., and Necochea, J. "School System Size and Performance: A Contingency Perspective. *Educational Evaluation and Policy Analysis, 10,* 3 (1988): 237–249.

Galvin, Patrick. "Sharing Among Separately Organized Administrative Units: Promise and Pitfall." Department of Education, Cornell University, 1986. ERIC Document #016355.

Galvin, Patrick. "Determinants of School District Participation in Regional Cooperative Services: The Case of New York State's BOCES." Ph.D. dissertation in progress, Department of Education. Cornell University, 1989.

Goodlad, J. I. *A Place Called School.* New York: McGraw-Hill, 1984.

Guthrie, J. W. "Organizational Scale and School Success." *Educational Evaluation and Policy Analysis, 1,* 1 (1979): 17–27.

Haller, Emil J., and Monk, David H. "New Reforms, Old Reforms, and the Consolidation of Small Rural Schools." *Educational Administration Quarterly 24,* 4 (1988): 470–483.

Haller, Emil J., Monk, David, Spotted-Bear, Alyce, Griffith, Julie, and Moss, Pamela. "School Size and Curricular Offerings: Evidence from High School and Beyond." *Educational Evaluation and Policy Analysis,* in press.

Hamilton, S. F. "The Social Side of Schooling: Ecological Studies of Classrooms and Schools." *Elementary School Journal, 83* (1983): 313–334.

Hanson, Nels W. "Economy of Scale as a Cost Factor in Financing Public Schools." *National Tax Journal, 17* (1964): 92–95.

Helge, Doris. "Problems and Strategies Regarding Regionalizing Service Delivery: Educational Collaboratives in Rural America." 1984. ERIC no. ED 242449.

Hind, Ian W. "Estimates of Cost Functions for Primary Schools in Rural Areas." *Australian Journal of Agricultural Economics, 21,* 1 (April 1977): 13–25.

Hirshleifer, Jack. *Price Theory and Application.* 2d ed. Englewood Cliffs, N.J.: Prentice-Hall, 1980.

Illinois State Board of Education. *Student Achievement in Illinois: An Analysis of Student Progress.* Springfield: Author, 1985.

Levin, H. M., and Meister, G. R. *Educational Technology and Computers: Promises, Promises, Always Promises.* Stanford, Calif.: Institute for Research on Educational Finance and Governance, School of Education, Stanford University, 1985.

Monk, David H. "Secondary School Size and Curriculum Comprehensiveness." *Economics of Education Review, 6, 2* (1987): 137–150.

Monk, David H. "Disparities in Curricular Offerings: Issues and Policy Alternatives for Small Rural Schools." Charleston, W.Va.: Policy and Planning Center, Appalachia Educational Laboratory, 1988.

Monk, David H. *Educational Finance: An Economic Approach.* New York: McGraw-Hill, 1990.

Monk, David H., and Haller, Emil J. *Organizational Alternatives for Small Rural Schools: Final Report to the New York State Legislature.* Ithaca, N.Y.: Department of Education, Cornell University, 1986.

Nachtigal, Paul. "Clustering for Rural School Improvement." Aurora, Colo.: Mid-Continent Regional Educational Laboratory, 1984.

Nicholson, W. *Microeconomic Theory.* Chicago: The Dryden Press, 1985.

North Carolina Department of Public Instruction. *Report of the State Superintendent on Schools and School Districts in North Carolina.* Raleigh: State Department of Public Instruction, 1986.

Peshkin, A. *The Imperfect Union: School Consolidation and Community Conflict.* Chicago: University of Chicago Press, 1982.

Ratcliff, Kerri, Riddle, Bruce, and Yinger, John. "The Fiscal Condition of School Districts in Nebraska: Is Small Beautiful?" In *Nebraska Comprehensive Study.* Edited by Michael Wasylenko and John

Yinger, Directors. Final Report to the Nebraska Legislature. Syracuse, N.Y.: Metropolitan Studies Program, The Maxwell School, Syracuse University, 1988.

Riew, J. "Scale Economies, Capacity Utilization, and School Costs: A Comparative Analysis of Secondary and Elementary Schools." *Journal of Education Finance 11,* 4 (1986): 433–446.

Riew, J. "Economies of Scale in High School Operations." *Review of Economics and Statistics, 48* (August 1966): 280–287.

Sederberg, Charles H. "Multiple District Administration for Small-Rural Schools." *The Rural Educator* (Fall 1985): 19–24.

Sher, J. P., and Tompkins, R. B. "Economy, Efficiency, and Equality: The Myths of Rural School and District Consolidation." In *Education in Rural America.* Edited by J. P. Sher. Boulder, Colo.: Westview, 1977.

Stephens, E. Robert. "The Establishment and Abolishment of a Statewide System of Education Service Agents: The Kentucky Experience." 1979. ERIC no. ED 207206.

Stigler, G. J. *The Theory of Price.* 3d ed. New York: Macmillan Company, 1966.

White, Fred, and Tweeten, Luther. "Optimal School District Size Emphasizing Rural Areas." *American Journal of Agriculture Economics, 55,* 1 (1973): 45–53.

Technological Delivery Systems and Applications for K-12 Instruction in Rural Schools

Bruce O. Barker

As administrators in rural and small schools strive to deliver quality education to their students, the obstacles of teacher availability, low student enrollment in selected courses, and geographical isolation beg for solutions. In the past, approaches to solve these problems have included pairing agreements, traveling teachers, correspondence study courses, and/or school district consolidation. Some of these practices still have value; however, new—and in many cases better approaches—are now available through technology.

The Growing Interest in Distance Education

Today's technologies have given rise to increased interest in the concept of *telecommunicated distance education*—the live, simultaneous transmission of a teacher's lessons from a host classroom or studio to multiple receive site classrooms in distance locations. Two-way live communication in real time, whether audio and/or video between the teacher and students permits the instruction to be interactive. Students at any one site are not only provided two-way audio and/or video communication with their instructor but are also able to

203

communicate directly with students at other sites during the instructional process.

State-sponsored curriculum reforms, reduced state fiscal revenues, impending teacher shortages, and advances in telecommunications technology have spawned great interest in distance education technologies as an alternative delivery methodology. The opportunity for live, teacher/student interaction through telecommunications technologies has caught the attention of many state and national education and policy decision makers. Congressional passage of $100 million for five years of Star Schools funding which began in 1988 is a prime example of national interest to provide rural schools with increased educational opportunity by use of new and emerging technologies.

With limited fanfare, many rural schools across the United States have been using distance learning technologies to help them offer elective or required courses for which a certified teacher is not available or to deliver quality teacher inservice training which otherwise might not be provided.

Types of Technologies Used for Distance Learning

Several different types of audio and/or video technologies are available which are being used by many rural and small schools as alternatives to face-to-face education, making it possible to provide instruction over long distances. These technologies permit the delivery of televised courses via low power television, Instructional Television Fixed Services (ITFS), cable, fiber optics, satellite, or slow scan TV. Courses can be delivered in either a one-way or two-way TV format depending on the hardware equipment available at both the origination site and the receive (distant) site locations. Courses are also being delivered via microcomputers networked via regular telephone lines, fiber optics, or microwave telephone signal.

Of the popular distance education technologies currently in use, televised satellite transmissions are receiving the greatest attention, followed by microcomputer based teleteaching, generally referred to as audiographics. Two-way TV courses delivered either via fiber optics, microwave, or cable are also receiving a great deal of interest from informed educators in rural areas.

Satellite Telecommunications

Satellite communication systems employ microwave terminals on the satellite transponder (a combination of receiver, converter, and transmitter) as well as on ground or earth stations commonly referred to as down-link or up-link dishes. The result is a highly reliable and high capacity communications circuit. The satellite itself is positioned in geosynchronous orbit over the equator about 22,300 miles above the earth. The rotation of the satellite thereby matches the rotation of the earth causing it to appear motionless above earth stations. Three equally spaced satellites could send and receive signals over the entire world. The satellite's transponder acts as both a receiver for up-link transmissions and a transmitter for down-link transmissions. Earth stations can be fixed or mobile. A positive characteristic of satellite communications is that the cost of transmission is insensitive to distance. This is not true in the case of telephone or other land line communications systems. In other words, the cost of satellite transmission between Los Angeles and New York is no higher than that between Los Angeles and San Diego.

Televised classes are nothing new in education. What is new, however, is live, two-way communication made possible by linking satellite technology with regular telephone service. Live TV broadcasts are beamed from the host site classroom or studio via an up-link dish to the satellite transponder. The signal is then beamed back to down-link dishes at the various receive site locations. In this configuration, satellite technology permits one-way transmission of voice, data, and full-motion video. Audio talk-back by participants at the receive site locations is over regular telephone lines. On the basis of one-way video, two-way audio communication, the instruction is deemed to be interactive. By picking up a telephone, students at subscribing schools can call in questions, usually on a toll-free telephone line, and hear their instructors' answers on the air. Students can both see and hear their instructor over the classroom television but are unable to either see or talk directly to students located at different sites. The teacher cannot see students but is able to respond to questions or comments whenever students call in on the telephone line. The technology is also capable of electronic copy distribution to create hard copy handouts, exams, and course administration materials sent via satellite directly to the receive sites. In each of the systems now in operation, a classroom facilitator who may be either an aid, volunteer, or another teacher usually sits in with the students to operate the equipment, distribute materials, and provide assistance as appropriate. In most cases, student homework assignments are sent via the postal service to their TV teacher(s) for evaluation.

Microcomputer Audiographics Teleteaching

Audiographics is a PC-based system which incorporates computer-generated graphics that function much like an electronic chalkboard. The system requires specially designed telecommunications software that is available for Apple and MS-DOS microcomputers. The telecommunications software allows the user to create computer graphics and multi-sized text known as slides which can then be transmitted from one computer to another. Once on-line with other compatible PCs, the system operates on a "common screen" basis; that is, whatever graphic or textual material (slide) is executed from the host screen/monitor (location) automatically shows up on all the other screens (distant locations) simultaneously. Visual exchange of slides is in a still-frame mode. Motion is not possible except in a limited sense when using a graphics tablet. The distance between the computers may be only two yards or 12,000 miles. It does not matter. Computers are linked over regular telephone lines for two-way visual exchange of text and/or graphics. Two-way audio interaction between the teacher and students at distance sites is via a speaker telephone, also over regular telephone lines. Students at distance sites may speak with their teacher or with other students at different sites at any time to ask questions or make comments. Among the major strengths of this approach to telecommunicated distance education are: (a) Local districts maintain control of the master teacher, programming, and scheduling; (b) small class size is guaranteed; (c) the system supports student-to-student interaction between sites in addition to teacher/student interaction; and (d) low costs.

The model for audiographic teleteaching is usually a collaborative arrangement between two to three school districts to form a cooperative. The "network" co-ops human, financial, and equipment resources. Each member has an equal voice in determining curriculum content, scheduling, hiring of the teleteacher, etc. Cooperatives can be formed and dissolved on an as needed basis from a larger consortium of telecommunication partners, but the focus remains one of local control. Inasmuch as cooperatives are typically limited to networks of two to three districts, small class size is guaranteed. In present on-going audiographic teleteaching cooperative networks, the average class size ranges between 4–15 students with class size seldom exceeding 30 students (Wydra, 1987). This guarantee of small class size ensures greater opportunity for both teacher/student interaction and student-to-student interaction. Use of an audio bridge allows students an opportunity to interact not only with their teacher but also with other students at different sites. Along with teacher/student interaction, the opportunity for student-to-student interpersonal communication between all sites—albeit electronically—is a major advantage of this approach to distance education in contrast to some other telecommunications delivery systems. The prospect of student-to-student exchanges not only increases the likelihood of socialization between students but also fosters the potential for peer tutoring and small group study.

The telecommunications software required to operate the audiographics network runs on either Apple II or MS-DOS microcomputers. The software lets the user create computer text/graphics known as "slides" which are transmitted from one computer to another.

Slides created with the graphics software are saved on floppy disks as "slide shows." The disk for each slide show must be at both the host site and at the receive site in order to be displayed simultaneously. The slides are made on the "host" computer, saved to disk, then a copy of the disk must be made and is either mailed or downloaded to the receive site school. Slide shows must be prepared in sufficient time to allow for delivery from host to receive site classroom. As a result, teleteacher lessons must be pre-planned and prepared. The visuals exchanged between computers are still-frame. Motion is not possible.

Several factors are inherent in an audiographics delivery approach: (1) students in separate schools and do not see each other or the teacher; (2) the teacher does not see the students; and (3) all participants in the learning process (teacher and students) are looking at computer screens to share a common visual reference and communicating by voice over speaker telephones. According to Martin (1986),

> Since the teacher cannot see the students he must get oral and/or visual feedback [via the computer and/or speaker telephone] from them to make sure they understand the material. This system-based necessity also gives telelearning its most potentially positive feature: the necessity for interaction. For this system to work, the students must be involved in the learning process. They must be participants, not recipients. (p. 2)

Two-way TV Systems

In most two-way, full-motion interactive TV systems, each participating school has a fully equipped classroom which allows a teacher in one location and students at one or more distant schools to both see and hear each other during instruction. Transmission is typically over cable, fiber optics, or microwave. The typical model is similar to that described for audiographics. A cooperative arrangement between two to five school districts is established to form a telecommunications cooperative that co-ops human, financial, and equipment resources in order to provide fully interactive television programming over several channels between member schools.

Not only are students able to interact with their TV teacher, but they are also able to see, hear, and communicate freely with their TV classmates at different schools. Establishment of a two-way TV system is usually very expensive requiring the installation of either a microwave tower or laying fiber optics or cable between participating schools. In addition, each participating school must equip a classroom/studio with TV monitors, cameras, microphones, and other related equipment items. Costs to schools, however, can often be reduced when partnership arrangements are formed between telephone or cable TV companies.

In addition to full-motion video and full audio interaction between all participants, the advantages of two-way TV cooperatives are similar to those mentioned for audiographics. Class size is usually kept small; and the TV teachers and the curriculum are controlled by local cooperative members.

Selected Distance Education Programs in Rural Schools

Interest in telecommunicated distance education has grown so rapidly in recent years that it is impossible to accurately document the many projects presently underway in the United States or being considered. Partly as a result of Federal Star Schools funding, and certainly as a result of the growing interest in distance learning, the growth of satellite TV networks for K–12 instruction has been phenomenal. In fact, interactive satellite broadcasts for K–12 instruction are now received by over 1000 schools in more than 40 states. This is somewhat breathtaking when one considers that interactive satellite TV broadcasts for K–12 instruction first began among a smattering of schools in 1985.

Yet the current interest in distance learning is not confined to satellite technology alone. Successful interactive TV projects delivered via microwave, fiber optics, or cable are operating between cooperating high schools in a multitude of states. And, microcomputer based teleteaching which links personal computers and speaker telephones over regular telephone lines are being used in Utah, Pennsylvania, New York, Alaska, Nevada, North Dakota, South Dakota, Louisiana, and Texas to name just a few states.

Although a large number of successful distance learning programs and projects are now operative in many rural schools in the United States, only a few are highlighted in this chapter. Nevertheless, these reflect the growth and interest in this innovative approach to enhance curricular opportunities for students in small schools and in geographically isolated communities.

The TI-IN Network, San Antonio, Texas

The TI-IN Network Incorporated is a privately supported and managed, for-profit vendor of satellite programming to schools. TI-IN is the largest interactive satellite systems for K–12 credit programming, teacher inservice training staff development, and student enrichment viewing in the United States. In the Fall of 1985, TI-IN became the first private vendor in the United States to broadcast live, one-way TV courses via satellite to subscribing high schools. At the end of its first year of operation, TI-IN was broadcasting 14 accredited high school courses to over 50 high schools scattered throughout Texas, California, and Arkansas (Barker, 1987). One year later, 17 different high school courses were being received by over 150 downlink sites in 25 different states (Rash, 1988). At the close of the 1989 school year, TI-IN broadcasts were received by over 750 subscribing schools in 29 states and enrolled over 4000 students (Babic, 1989). In 1988 TI-IN was one of four successful applicants for funds from the Federal Star Schools' program. The amount awarded for 1988–89 was $5.6 million. With federal funding for Star Schools, TI-IN has entered into a multi-state, nine partner educational network that has significantly expanded program options to subscribing schools.

Live TV broadcasts are beamed nationwide from TI-IN studios located at San Antonio via a Ku up-link antenna to the Spacenet II satellite. TI-IN broadcasts four channels of programming on two transponders. Ku band transmissions have a higher range of frequencies than C band transmissions and this results in clearer reception with less terrestrial interference (Batson, 1987).

The TI-IN uplink antenna and broadcast studios are located at the Texas Education Agency Region 20 Education Service Center in San Antonio. TI-IN leases office space and studio time from Region 20. High school classes originate from three teaching studios simultaneously, with broadcasts aired over three separate channels. All cameras and equipment in the high school teaching studios are controlled by the instructor. Each instructor has the capability to preload slides, videotapes, and superimpose printing across the bottom of the TV screen.

High school credit classes are broadcast a total of 175 instructional days per school year. Class instruction is 50 minutes in length per class. Instructional broadcasts are scheduled according to the Central time zone. TI-IN has established a ceiling of 200 students in any one class. High school classes begin the first of September and end the last full week in May. To all its subscribing schools, TI-IN offers over 20 high school credit offerings, more than 400 hours of yearly staff development programming, more than 40 student enrichment courses, and a variety of special programs.

Satellite Telecommunications Educational Programming, Spokane, Washington

The Satellite Telecommunications Educational Programming (STEP) network is an interactive TV instructional delivery system that telecasts live instruction via satellite uplink from broadcast studios contracted by Education Service District 101 in Spokane, Washington to downlink dishes at subscribing school districts in an eight state area. Broadcast signals, both video and audio, are carried from the classroom studios by means of satellite technology to receive site locations. Audio talk-back from the students is over standard telephone lines.

In 1986, STEP began broadcasts of five high school courses to 13 school districts in Washington state. This increased to 41 the second year. In early 1989, the network had grown to over 80 downlink sites in eight states, and ranks as one of the larger K–12 distance learning programs in the country. The network has the capability of broadcasting throughout North America and Hawaii. Most districts that belong to the network are small and rural.

Education Service District 101 is one of nine education service units in Washington. Like their counterparts in other states, the role of the education service districts in Washington is to act as a liaison between local school districts and the Office of the State Superintendent of Public Instruction. ESDs also conduct programs in response to the needs of local districts and assist in equalizing educational opportunities for students. ESD 101 services a seven county area that includes 59 public school districts and 55 state approved private schools. Because of its satellite uplink capabilities, ESD 101 has received permission from the state legislature to deliver its TV courses beyond its customary service area to the entire state and outside state boundaries. The impetus to form the STEP network came from superintendents of small, rural school districts in ESD 101's service area. In late summer of 1985, ESD 101 administrators were approached by a number of school superintendents in the service area asking for help in delivering high school credit courses in curricular areas where it was difficult to either locate or recruit certified teaching personnel, primarily in the foreign languages and mathematics.

ESD 101 officials had previously considered distance education as an alternative to provide smaller schools with added course offerings. Numerous options including TV courses delivered via microwave, fiber optics, cable, and satellite were considered. ESD administrators wanted the capability to broadcast to the entire state of Washington, and for that reason selected satellite.

STEP offices are located in the same building as RXL Communications, a 12,000 square foot, privately owned broadcast center in downtown Spokane. STEP uses a Ku uplink which is capable of transmitting in either a half or full transponder format. The RXL Communications center has a state-of-the-art broadcast studio from which all programming originates. One-way video and audio signals are transmitted from the studio to a G-STAR III satellite over a full transponder (transponder 3). Talk-back from students is possible over four separate telephone lines which feed into the studio. Phone calls during broadcasts are received by an engineer in the studio, who screens all calls, then prints the name of the student and site location on the teleprompter in the studio to alert the teacher. The call is then entered into the studio for audio broadcast to all sites.

At the local sites, students gather around a 25" television monitor to watch the TV lesson. Receive site classrooms are equipped with one or two telephones, shared among students, for use in calling the STEP studio. STEP broadcasts high school classes Monday through Thursday, four days each week, 144 calendar days during the academic year. Classes begin the first week in September and run through the end of May. An open day with no broadcasts (Friday) gives local schools the freedom to let students catch up on homework assignments, take tests that have previously been sent from STEP, or allows for review of content presented earlier in the week.

Five high school classes are offered: Pre-calculus, Japanese I, Advanced Senior English, Spanish I and Spanish II. All classes meet Washington state curriculum standards. Each high school credit class offered can be taken in a dual credit format (both high school and college credit). Students who elect to enroll for the college credit option pay the college tuition fee. The network also offers some 20 staff development programs and a limited number of student enrichment classes at the elementary and junior high level.

All STEP high school teachers hold Washington State teaching certificates. Reciprocity agreements for teacher certification exist in the states receiving STEP high school courses. Each teacher also holds adjunct faculty status with one of the area's local community colleges (Gibson, 1989). This relationship allows classes to be offered on the basis of dual credit.

The Panhandle Share-ED Fiber Optics Video Network in Beaver County Oklahoma

The panhandle of western Oklahoma is the least populated and most geographically isolated portion of the state.

Three counties make up the panhandle—Cimarron, Texas, and Beaver. The panhandle is that area of Oklahoma that is due north of the Texas panhandle and due south of western Kansas, approximately 160 miles long by 35 miles wide. In the 1920's this area was known as the "dust bowl" and inspired Steinbeck's famous novel *The Grapes of Wrath*.

Beginning in the Fall of 1988, four small school districts in Beaver County began supplementing their high school curriculum via a two-way, full-motion, state-of-the-art fiber optics television network. The system links a designated TV classroom in each of the districts four high schools. The two-way TV system has enabled the four districts to share teachers electronically for an expansion of high school credit courses. In addition, administrators have used the system to offer in-service training to teachers, provide community education programs for local residents, and for conference meetings of administrators and teachers between schools.

Establishment of the system is the culmination of several years of investigation into alternative technologies by school administrators in Beaver, Balko, Forgan, and Turpin school districts. The technology permits both audio and video interaction between the host teacher and students at each of the receiving site locations. Students can both see and hear their teacher as well as see and hear their "classmates" at the different sites. Likewise, the teacher is able to both see and hear each student at the remote site(s).

Beaver County is the most eastern of the three counties which comprise the panhandle area of extreme western Oklahoma. The area is some 300 miles northwest of Oklahoma City. The county consists of 1,817 square miles with a total population of approximately 7,500 residents. The county's economic base is chiefly wheat and cattle production. Several small oil fields are also present in the area. The terrain is rolling prairie.

The county's four school districts each serve a large land area. Yet, the K–12 student population in each district is small: Beaver, about 500 students; Forgan, about 200; Balko, about 150; and Turpin, about 400. The districts are remote and isolated. Teacher housing is provided for many of the teachers in the area.

In the past, many of the advanced and special courses, if offered at all, were provided on an alternative year basis. Due to the low student enrollment in select or special courses, it had been cost prohibitive to employ a full-time certified instructor. Based on past experience—even if funds were available—it has often been difficult to secure the services of a qualified instructor willing to move and remain in the panhandle area for a long period of time.

Since the early 1960s the four districts had cooperated in sharing "circuit riding" or traveling teachers for selected courses. As instructional demands increased and the pool of qualified teachers decreased, however, the option of traveling teachers became less viable. The four superintendents and their respective school boards had frequently met to discuss alternatives that could be adopted that would ensure quality instruction in low incident courses to students and at the same time avoid loss of local control over the curriculum and individual school identity. Several of the superintendents had read about successful two-way TV systems that were operative in Wisconsin and Minnesota. It was decided that district administrators would pursue the possibility of implementing a two-way, full-motion interactive instructional television system.

Installation of the fiber optics video network was three and one-half years in the making. In the Fall of 1985, five administrators from the four Beaver County schools and the Oklahoma State Department of Education's Director of Rural Education traveled to Trempealeau County, Wisconsin to observe a two-way instructional TV system delivered via cable that had been frequently cited in the literature on interactive television instruction. Following that visit, it was mutually agreed that the four districts would seek external funding to enter into a four school cooperative to initiate their own two-way TV interactive instructional system. The four superintendents organized an effort to contact each of the private foundations in Oklahoma as well as public agencies to seek grant monies to support the establishment of a fiber optics TV network between the four schools. Approximately $350,000 required to fund the project was provided by the Robert S. and Gracye B. Kerr Foundation of Oklahoma City, the McCasland Foundation of Duncan, Oklahoma, the Oklahoma State Board of Education, the State Legislature and the Office of Rural Education in the Oklahoma State Department of Education.

The network consists of 51 miles of four strand and eight strand fiber optic cable that connects Balko, Turpin, Forgan, and Beaver school districts to each other. TV cameras and television monitors are located at each school. Also, each school is equipped with a studio/classroom for broadcasting and receiving classes. The system is completely interactive, allowing for total audio and visual communication between the teacher and students at each school.

When designing the studio/classrooms, administrators were aware that the uniqueness of their system would attract numerous visitors. Accordingly, each classroom has a glass partition observation area that is outside camera range and which has been designed to suppress noise from discussions or comments among observers. The intent has been to minimize any disruption from interested outsiders that might affect student learning.

The studio/classrooms are essentially identical at each school and were designed to accommodate TV instruction. Each site is able to either transmit or receive instruction. There are eight 25 inch color TV monitors or screens at each studio/classroom. Four monitors are mounted from the ceiling or the back wall and face the area where the teacher stands to present instruction. In this manner the teacher at the "host" site is able to see classrooms for students at each of the three receiving schools as well as the image at the host site where the camera is focused. Four TV screens also face the students seated in each classroom. This allows them to see the TV teacher on one screen and their peers at each of the three sites on the remaining screens. At the respective host classroom, students can elect to watch their teacher "in person" or on the TV. Each classroom is also equipped with a videotape recorder that can be used to display a video, or to record a class for a student who might be absent.

Teacher-student interaction and student-to-student interaction over the network is perhaps the closest to a traditional classroom setting that present day telecommunications technologies permit. The microphones are on an open line; therefore full audio communication is possible between all sites. The open audio line also negates the need for any telephone dialing. Consequently, audio communication is immediate. There is no delay when asking a question, making a comment, or talking to either the teacher or another student at a distant site. The use of fiber optics has also helped to ensure that the audio transmission quality is probably the best possible with today's technologies. Overall class size has intentionally been kept small with no classes exceeding 20 students total (between all four sites). Teachers know each student personally and are able to involve all pupils in the learning process.

The teacher station can best be described as a lectern or podium that faces the student seating area. An overhead camera can zoom in, much like an overhead projector, on materials the teacher might want to display on the TV screen. A second camera can focus directly on the teacher for lecture or discussion. A third camera focuses on the students. At each site, the teacher is able to easily switch from one camera to another. At the host site, if the teacher wishes to step down from the lecture area to work individually with students, she can simply switch to the camera that focuses on the students then walk down among her "live" class. Students at the remote sites would see and hear their TV teacher walking among and talking with their class mates at that site.

Exchange of written materials (homework, tests, assignments, etc.) is generally by means of facsimile machines located next to the teacher station in each studio/classroom. Classroom materials have also been exchanged between schools by counselors who travel from one school to another or occasionally by teachers who may live in one district but teach in another. The local highway patrol has even delivered written materials between schools.

For the 1988–89 school year, most programming has been for high school credit courses. Four high school courses have been offered—Art History, Spanish, Advanced Placement

English, and Accounting II. In each case of "distance delivery," administrators at receiving schools have not allowed students to enroll in TV courses unless (1) the class was not offered locally or (2) if offered locally, a conflict in the student's schedule did not permit enrolling in the more traditional course when offered at the school. During its first year of operation, over 60 students (approximately 15 percent of the total high school student body in the four districts) enrolled in TV courses. These have generally been higher achieving, college bound students. Overall class size, for all sites, at any one time has ranged from five to 20 students.

Numerous community education classes have been offered over the system involving topics such as aerobics, self-image improvement, world travel, gardening, landscaping, financial aid for college bound students, farm aid, etc. Because the TV network is cooperatively managed by the four schools, superintendents and building principals have direct control over matters related to programming, selection of teachers, scheduling of classes, criterion for students taking TV courses, control of overall class size, etc.

The Northeastern Utah Telelearning Project, Roosevelt, Utah

The Northeastern Utah Telelearning Project began in 1985 on a one-year pilot basis between the Unitah Basin Area Vocational Center (UBAVC) located some 150 miles east of Salt Lake City and three local schools (Tabiona, 75 miles to the west; Rich, 206 miles to the north, and Manila, 70 miles to the northeast). The pilot project was endorsed by the Utah State Office of Education and the Northeastern Utah Educational Services Center. All classes originated from the UBAVC at Roosevelt. The three schools were linked with the UBAVC by means of a microcomputer audiographics network over dedicated telephone lines. Three classes were taught the first year.

The project was expanded the second year (1986–87) to include four more schools (Altamont, 18 miles to the northwest; Duchesne, 30 miles to the southwest; Thompson, five miles west; and Union High School, directly across the street from the vocational center). Each of the schools served are small and rural. The grade levels and approximate total student enrollments at the schools are: Altamont, grades 7–12, 300 students; Duchesne, 7–12, 300; Manila, 7–12, 70; Rich, 9–12, 130; Tabiona, 7–12, 100; Thompson, an ungraded alternative school which serves only behavioral disordered children, 25 students; Union, 10–12, 575. Seven classes were taught during the second year and duplex television (two-way TV) capabilities were also added to one school site. In its third year of operation (1987–88) a UHF (ultra high frequency) channel permitting simplex television (one-way TV) was added to four sites on the network. In 1988–89, facsimile machines were added at each site.

Factors which led to UBAVC's development of the Northeastern Utah Telelearning Project included (Miller, 1988):

1. Geographical isolation of schools within the service area of the UBAVC.

2. Decreased funding from state and local sources, but increased graduation requirements with stricter graduation guidelines.

3. Availability of appropriate technologies and people interested in learning how to utilize the technologies within the constraints of limited funding and existing school systems.

4. Desire and support of local school district administrators to promote a telelearning system to their schools.

5. A declared need to provide increased educational opportunity to rural school students in the area.

As noted a combination of technologies are used by the UBAVC to deliver distance education offerings to the seven area schools presently served. Use of these technologies by the UBAVC evolved over a four year period. Each developed individually and can be independent of one another, yet they are also compatible and can also be used together.

The first was a microcomputer audiographics system hookup that uses dedicated telephone lines. Audiographics software produced by Wasatch Backboard System of Salt Lake City linked microcomputers for visual exchange of graphics and textual information between a host microcomputer at UBAVC and microcomputers at the three schools linked to UBAVC. Audio interaction between teachers and students was over a second set of dedicated phone lines.

In the second year of operation (1986–1987), UBAVC expanded the audiographics network to three more area schools and began using a portion of the state's broad-band microwave telecommunications system known as EDNET. EDNET is an interactive (two-way, full-motion) video and audio, closed-circuit microwave television system that presently reaches 15 key population centers throughout the state. Three EDNET sites—Roosevelt, Manila, and Vernal—are in the UBAVC's service area. EDNET's main purpose is to distribute university and K–12 courses, vocational education and medical care instruction to communities who might not otherwise have access to quality instruction. EDNET is also used for administrative meetings and statewide inservice training sponsored by the Utah State Office of Education. Hence, as configured during the second year, distance learning courses were delivered from UBAVC in an audiographics format via dedicated telephone lines to Rich, Altamont, Tabiona, Duchesne, and Thompson schools. Union High School students at Roosevelt walked across the street from the high school and attended courses in the classroom/studio. The students at Manila High School were connected with all of the other schools via the audio hookup and with UBAVC via duplex television delivered between Roosevelt and Manila over EDNET. During that same year, Manila and Roosevelt discontinued use of dedicated telephone lines and took advantage of multiplex sideband frequencies and codec devices to transmit, via microwave, audiographics instruction between the two schools.

In the third year, Northeastern Utah Telelearning Project administrators learned through contact with officials at KUTV-Channel 2 (the NBC affiliate) in Salt Lake City that an Ultra High Frequency (UHF) translator located on Tabby mountain, 60 miles northwest of Roosevelt was not being used. Administrators at the Northeastern Utah Educational Service Center negotiated with KUTV to purchase the translator and necessary broadcast equipment for $5000. Consequently, simplex television (one-way TV) is now broadcast from Channel 61 originating at the UBAVC in Roosevelt to Altamont, Tabiona, Duchesne, and Thompson schools. In fact, the signal actually covers several hundred square miles and is received in over 5000 homes in northeastern Utah. In addition to audiographics via microcomputers, distance education students at these five schools are now permitted a one-way, full-motion video presentation of classes broadcast from UBAVC. Audio interaction is via an audio bridge, operated by U.S. West, over the dedicated telephone lines.

In the fourth year of operation (1988–89), facsimile machines were added at each of the sites. The UBAVC at Roosevelt serves as the broadcast center for all classes delivered over the network. All sites are connected with the UBAVC by means of either dedicated telephone lines, UHF signals, and/or microwave signals. A Darome audio bridge at UBAVC links all sites together for audio communication.

Six and one-half hours of high school and/or college programming (concurrent enrollment) is generated each weekday from the Center. Since its inception, a variety of credit courses for students have been offered over the network. Advanced Placement English, Advanced Placement History, and Chemistry/Physics were taught during the network's pilot year of operation. During the second year, offerings were expanded to a three quarter hour mathematics sequence taught through Utah State University Extension Services and offered for concurrent enrollment (both high school credit and college credit), a three-quarter hour English/history sequence from USU Extension Services offered for concurrent enrollment, a one-semester junior high art class (during one semester the class was provided to 7th graders and during the second semester it was offered to 8th graders), a one-year Physics class, a one year Principles of Technology class, a one-year Technical Writing class, and a one-year German language class. For the third and fourth years, program offerings have included German I, Chemistry, and Physics, and concurrent enrollment college credit courses from the Utah State University Extension Services in Algebra, Calculus, English, Art History and Criticism, Computer Applications in Business.

Of the approximately 1500 high school students in the UBAVC's service area, program administrators estimate that over 100 students will benefit from telelearning classes each year. During the program's first four years of operation, over 400 students have taken distance learning courses. Many high school students have completed anywhere from three to 15 quarter hours of college credit course by means of the concurrent enrollment option. These credits are fully accepted by Utah State University or can be transferred to any of the other state sponsored institutions of higher education in Utah.

The Pennsylvania Audiographics Teleteaching Project

The Pennsylvania Teleteaching Project (PTP) is a statewide audiographics network, using microcomputers and speaker telephones connected over standard telephone lines. The project was formally established in the Commonwealth of Pennsylvania in 1986 to provide increased educational opportunities for students attending small high schools with limited curriculum offerings.

The search for alternatives to better educate students denied access to a full range of curriculum offerings motivated the Pennsylvania Department of Education (PDE) to look to telecommunications as a possible solution. According to officials of the Pennsylvania Department of Education:

> The problem was (and is) that many students in the State do not have the opportunity to take courses necessary for the completion of their educational program by the traditional method, i.e., students and teachers in the same classroom at the same time, in the same place. For a variety of reasons, this is not

always possible and the result is the
disenfranchisement of the child so denied.
(Pennsylvania Teleteaching Project, p. 15)

The use of telecommunications technologies was seen as
a promising instructional technique that could be used to
broaden curriculum opportunities for students. Actual
development of the PTP goes back to 1985 when professors at
Mansfield University in the northeast portion of the state
operated a successful audiographics pilot project between the
university and five high schools in the Southern Tioga School
District. In 1986, the Pennsylvania Department of Education
provided $526,000 to establish the Pennsylvania Teleteaching
Project which was managed by professors at Mansfield
University during its first year of operation. Funds from the
PDE provided 29 school districts with audiographics
teleteaching equipment and software. By the end of the year,
the schools had shared 19 different courses and served over
200 students. For 1987–1988, 32 schools comprised the
network, and in 1988–1989 it had grown to 48 schools. In its
first three years of operation, approximately 1,600 students
have taken teleteaching courses.

Since 1987, the PTP has been managed by administrators
at the Riverview Intermediate Unit in Shippenville, Pennsylvania.
The project is the largest state sponsored PC based
audiographics system in the United States. Of the projects 48
members in 1989, most are rural school districts, but
participating members also include several intermediate units
(education service centers) and two juvenile detention facilities.

The PTP's model for audiographic teleteaching is usually a
joint arrangement between two to three school districts to form
a partnership to share teachers and courses. Of the 48 schools
participating in the Project, no partnership for course sharing
exceeds three member schools at one time. According to
program administrators, this is one of the Project's strengths.
Due to the collaborative arrangements of two or three schools
linked together the local districts maintain control of the
teleteacher, programming, and scheduling. Class size is also
kept small. State guidelines allow classes to be no larger than 30

students, regardless of the number of sites joined together. Classes in the Project average around 15 students. In most cases, this is between two schools (Hajdu, 1989).

Furthermore, it is not unusual for a school to be a member of more than one partnership. And, for mergers between schools to be formed on an ad-hoc basis to meet curriculum needs between schools, then dissolve once those needs have been met. Because the network is linked by regular telephone lines for both the speaker telephones and the microcomputers, different schools can join together to teach a specific course, then dissolve their relationship after the course has been taught. Connecting both video and audio lines between schools is simply completed by dialing each schools' telephone number. The ease of linking together has promoted a great deal of cooperation between schools.

The Delaware-Chenango Board of Cooperative Educational Services (BOCES) Audiographics Network and Program for Electronic Field Trips, Norwich, New York

The Delaware-Chenango BOCES Telelearning Project uses an audiographics teleconferencing system similar to that used by the Pennsylvania Teleteaching Project. Participating schools are connected via telephone lines into the BOCES' Instructional Support Services office in Norwich. A MicroLinx bridge at the BOCES central office is able to connect any configuration of six sites together at one time. With upgrading, the bridge has the capacity to link a total of any 14 sites at one time.

The audiographic system permits two-way audio interaction and two-way microcomputer networking between all the sites that are connected to each other over the bridge. Visuals on the computers can be created using multiple colors with special audiographics software and these can be "telecommunicated" in real-time via modem from one microcomputer to another. Since on-line transmission of graphics is relatively slow, visuals prepared in advance of class are stored on floppy disks and the disks sent via BOCES courier to the student sites.

Voice communication between sites is via speaker telephones, leaving the hands free to work with the computer keyboard or to use the graphics tablet. Students can speak with their teacher or peers as graphics or text are being conveyed via computer. Each site is also equipped with a facsimile machine for exchange of written materials, homework, and tests. In some instances, materials between the teacher and students are mailed. Instruction can originate from any of the sites. The teleteacher is typically a teacher in one of the schools who has accepted the added task, with overload pay, of teaching a teleclass. Classes are taught with or without students at the originating school.

The BOCES's Telelearning Project has been operational since 1985. The first pilot class offered was a mini-course (non-credit) in astronomy. The class originated from New Berlin High School and was received by 25 students at six other high schools. The course was taught after school (in order to accommodate variance in bell schedules) two days per week for 45 minutes over an eight week period, or 16 times. All but three students completed the course. Several reported in a survey at the end of the class that they actually preferred not seeing the teacher (even though they didn't know him) because it was less distracting.

Following the successful pilot class, a high school credit Advanced Placement (AP) Calculus course was offered to 13 students divided among four different schools. In 1986–87, three high school classes were offered: AP Calculus, AP English, and Spanish III. For the 1987–88 school year, five high school courses were offered: AP Calculus, AP Chemistry, AP English, AP European History, and Music Theory. The number of schools linked together for courses typically ranged between three to five. For the 1988–89 school year, two high school credit courses were offered, AP English and AP Calculus. Both courses were offered for dual credit in area colleges. Students who elect to enroll for the college credit option are responsible to pay the tuition fee. High school classes are delivered five days per week. Each runs about 45 minutes.

Two schools in the BOCES service area have used audiographics to teach homebound students. At one school, an eighth grade student was given audiographics equipment to use at home while recuperating from back surgery. The computer, graphics tablet, and speaker phone made it possible to provide classroom instruction to the student at home, allowing him to participate in class discussion and not fall behind his peers.

A unique feature is the telelearning project is the "electronic field trip." Over 50 electronic field trips are conducted by schools in the BOCES region each year. An electronic field trip is a voice, telephone conference call from one of the schools in the region to an outside authority or classroom (computers and audiographics are not used). In the past, calls have been made to Alaska, Hawaii, Georgia, Texas and many other states. Calls outside the United States have been made to England, South Africa, Australia, etc. Some of the types of individuals/groups contacted have included classrooms, city mayors, rock musicians, a computer software designer, children's book authors, university professors, etc. Telelearning project administrators believe that one of my major interests in distance learning among BOCES schools has been the electronic field trip. Rural students are frequently quite isolated and have little, if any, cross-cultural contact. One of the major needs of such rural students is the need to come in contact with other people in other areas. The electronic field trip is a very simple and inexpensive way to give students contact with experts in a variety of areas. Electronic field trips have been and continue to be popular among BOCES schools (Wickler, 1989).

Advantages and Disadvantages of Distance Education Technologies

As the distance education technologies become more accepted by local and state educational leaders, rural educators must also recognize that distance education technologies are not an educational panacea. There are definite advantages and there are disadvantages to each technology as well as differences between program providers. Some of the advantages and disadvantages of three of the more popular technologies—satellite delivery, audiographics delivery, and two-way full-motion TV delivery are listed below. The lists are presented to provoke thought and are by no means exhaustive.

Advantages of Satellite TV Teaching

1. Students can see the teacher.

2. Full-motion video is possible.

3. Teacher/student audio interaction is possible.

4. Real-time print distribution of handout material is possible with most systems.

5. Satellite technology can be merged with other media (e.g., fax, videotapes, etc.)

6. Satellite signals are distance insensitive—large geographical areas and many remote sites can be covered simultaneously helping to reduce costs by sharing them among a large number of users.

7. Most satellite systems are a "turn-key" operation. Programming, instruction, grading of students, distribution of materials, etc., are provided by the satellite vendor.

Disadvantages of Satellite TV Teaching

1. Program offerings are centralized limiting local control by local districts. This may result in loss of local control of teaching and interpretation of the curriculum by local education units.

2. The TV teacher cannot see the students.

3. An audio "echo" is often inherent in student talk-back through the TV system when telephoning to interact with the TV teacher.

4. Some receive dishes (Ku band) are weather sensitive—during heavy rains or snows, the signal can be lost.

5. The potential exists for large class size.

6. There is very limited student-to-student interaction at different sites. The technology seems to chiefly promote teacher-student interaction and not student-to-student interaction.

7. Large satellite systems that broadcast throughout the United States can promote the creation of a "national curriculum."

8. Bell scheduling conflicts, time zone differences, differences in dates for scheduling spring breaks, holidays, etc., often conflict with local school schedules and are not easily resolved.

Strengths of Audiographic Teleteaching (Microcomputer Networking)

1. Low cost is terms of hardware, software, and maintenance.

2. Relatively simple to learn and to operate.

3. Perpetuates rural school traditions of (a) small class size, and (b) local control of the teacher and the curriculum.

4. Permits not only teacher-student interaction but also allows for student-to-student audio interaction as well as computer graphic interaction.

5. Any participating site can serve in either a "receive" or a "transmit" mode.

6. Presentation of instruction emphasizes content and organization of material rather than the personality of the teacher, because students do not see the teacher.

7. Students at all sites and the teacher share the same visual reference on the computer screen.

8. Operates over regular dial-up telephone lines making it possible for virtually any school in the United States to link up with another school if both are supplied with necessary equipment and software.

Weaknesses of Audiographic Teleteaching (Microcomputer Networking)

1. Motion of video images is not possible.

2. The instructor cannot see the students, nor can students see the instructor or other students at distance sites.

3. Extraneous "noise" or interference on the telephone lines can cause voice transmission on the speaker telephones to occasionally "break up."

4. Transmission costs for telephone toll charges can become excessive.

5. The video graphics/image displayed between computer monitors is limited to the size of the computer screen unless additional hardware costs are incurred.

6. Lesson planning (creation of computer visuals) can be considerably time consuming for the teacher, and floppy disks must be distributed to all remote sites prior to instruction.

7. Requires a commitment by school administrators in terms of human resource time to recruit teleteachers and classroom facilitators, train teachers and facilitators, manage the system, etc.

Advantages of Two-way TV Instruction (Fiber Optics, Some Microwave Systems, Cable, etc.)

1. Two-way, full-motion video is possible between all sites; students can see the teacher as well as other students at different sites, and the teacher can see all students at all sites.

2. Most systems presently in operation are small networks that promote local control of the teacher and curriculum and maintain an overall small class size.

3. Open-line microphones allow for full teacher-student and student-to-student audio interaction. That is students can interact audibly not only with the TV teacher but also with students at other sites.

4. Most TV signals are usually unaffected by weather.

Disadvantages of Two-way TV Instruction (Fiber Optics, Microwave, Cable, etc.)

1. Cable (to be used as an extra broadcast channel) in many rural areas is still not available.

2. Fiber optics, although becoming more available, is still not accessible in many rural communities; also it is very expensive to lay if it has not already been installed.

3. Virtually all successful two-way TV systems are based around a partnership arrangement between the local school and business or industry officials in the area; some rural

communities may not have the "required" pool of human resources available.

4. Most systems require a large amount of capital investment to get started.

Even though there are some disadvantages associated with each technology, the advantages seem to far out weigh the disadvantages. Furthermore, some of the stated disadvantages may in the future be eliminated as professionals in the field find solutions around some of the concerns identified.

Selected Issues in Using Distance Education Technologies

It is expected that distance education technologies in rural schools will become more widespread, more sophisticated, and less costly. Successful use of technologies demands that certain issues be considered by administrators who are thinking of adding a distance education program to their school. The issues listed below seem to be common among most projects. The manner in which each is addressed, however, often varies between vendors and/or type of system used.

Materials Transfer

Each distance education project must establish an efficient and reliable system to exchange materials between participating schools. Tests, quizzes, assignments, textbooks, and other materials may be transported by postal service, teachers who live in one district but teach in another, fax machines, etc.

Classroom Management

A single policy for dealing with students in distance education courses should be established and enforced. A consistent procedure for dealing with student discipline problems is vital to the success of a distance education program.

Remote Site Visits by Teachers

Students at remote classrooms should have the opportunity to periodically meet their teacher "in the flesh" and become personally acquainted. The same is true for getting acquainted with other students at different sites.

Levels of Interaction

Are students able to interact only with their distance education teacher or can they also interact freely during the class with other students at remote sites? Technologies that permit interaction only between teacher/student are much more limiting instructionally than those that permit both teacher/student and student/student interaction.

Extent of Course Offerings

Programs that offer a wide variety of courses or a broad curriculum are generally more favorably received than those that offer only a few courses.

Selection of Teachers for Distance Education Delivery

Distance education teachers of necessity must be "master" teachers. This implies not only that they understand and model principles from the literature on "effective teaching," but that they also know how to best use the respective telecommunications medium to convey their teaching. For example, we can learn much from the field of mass communications (e.g., commercial radio and television) in regards to how to present information via the airwaves. Furthermore, teaching pedagogy—as related to distance education—requires forced interaction between teacher and students, a slower pace of instruction, clear logical presentations with good structure, etc.

Technical Breakdown

There will be "down time" with any system. Anyone who drives a car knows that technology doesn't always work. Who's going to fix things when they break down. Maintenance agreements with vendors and contractors are important factors for policy makers to consider when forming a cooperative or entering into an agreement with a large distance education vendor.

Teacher Training

Some training of teachers is essential. Regardless of how exotic or exciting the technology may be, it will never be a substitute for poor instruction. Ultimately, the significance of the content presented and the quality of the presentation delivery will be much more important than the technology used to convey the message. Effective training of teachers and classroom facilitators is vital for program success.

The "Personal Touch"

There must be a personal touch between both the students and the teacher regardless of the distances involved. The students at the remote sites must feel a sense of belonging to the host site classroom. The teacher should call the students by name, look directly into the camera (if the instruction involves TV delivery) as though he/she is looking at them. The telephone adage to "reach out and touch someone" definitely has meaning when delivering distance education course work.

Scheduling

One of the biggest problems with large distance education programs is the matter of bell scheduling. This becomes compounded when programs are broadcast over different time zones. The matter is not easily resolved because a school district's bell schedule is dependent upon bus routes, lunch schedules, elementary and middle school schedules, etc. A related problem is the scheduling of local school start and ending dates, parent teacher conferences, state mandated teacher inservice or preparation days that close classes, variation in Spring breaks and Christmas vacations, etc. Another concern is the issuance of grades. Some schools operate on a 9-week grading period while others are on 6, 12, and 18-week student evaluation periods. The need to satisfy the requests of individual schools cannot be taken too lightly.

Local Control

Many rural school districts fiercely protect local control of their curricula and scheduling. Most often, they do not want outside "experts" dictating what classes will be taught and when. Local educators should have a choice of options when selecting a distance education alternative. For example, if a school selects one of the present satellite vendors, a steerable dish with a dual Ku and C band feedhorn should be the standard downlink dish. This would allow the school an opportunity to take classes from a selection of satellite vendors and not be "locked in" to just one provider. The school, thereby, has control in terms of selecting programs and offerings, and to some extent scheduling.

Class Size

Overall class size will have a direct impact on opportunities for student interaction. Small, locally controlled cooperatives usually limit class size and thereby enhance opportunities for interaction between the teacher and students. Systems that have a national focus (e.g., satellite vendors) may have 200+ students enrolled (in some cases over 1000 students) resulting in very limited opportunities for interaction. In such cases, the program provider should have in place a student support system which assures that individual students do not "get lost in the cracks" when they call in for help or need assistance.

Summary

There seems to be a real energy and interest about what in happening in the area of telecommunicated distance learning and its potential benefit to rural schools. Without question, the success of any telecommunicated distance education delivery system will ultimately depend more upon the quality of instruction delivered than upon the type of technology used.

The cost of establishing and maintaining interactive telecommunication networks for instructional purposes is high and varies significantly between types of technology used and the size of the network desired. In many cases, the monetary cost for schools to use telecommunicated distance education alternatives is still considered prohibitively high. As with the entire telecommunications industry, however, costs have been and are continuing to drop. Although pricing is definitely important, the potential for interactive teaching/learning and the fact that geographically dispersed student bodies can be served simultaneously are appealing factors that have sparked state and national interest in telecommunicated distance education. As individual networks grow, costs will continue to drop as expenses are distributed among more users.

The research base, though scant at present, suggests that students who study via telecommunicated distance education approaches perform as well as their counterparts in traditional classroom settings (Barker and Patrick, 1989; Ellertson, 1987; Galvin, 1987; Moorehouse, Hoaglund, and Schmidt, 1987; Whittington, 1987). Without question, telecommunicated teaching is an effective means to reach out to new, and vast, audiences in geographically isolated setting who otherwise would not be afforded educational equity. In fact, in terms of their potential to benefit students in small and geographically isolated schools, telecommunicated distance learning technologies and their applications may be the biggest education breakthrough since the microcomputer.

REFERENCES

Babic, J. *Personal Communication*, April 1989.

Barker, B. O. "Interactive Learning by Satellite." *The Clearing House*, *61*, no. 1 (Fall 1987): 13–16.

Barker, B. O., and Patrick, K. R. "Instruction Via Satellite Television: An Exploratory Analysis of Teacher Effectiveness." *Research in Rural Education, 5*, no. 3 (1989): 31–36.

Batson, B. H. "Technically Speaking in Plain English." *TI-IN Network News, 2* (November 1987): 2, 7.

Ellertson, K. *Report on Distance Learning: A National Effectiveness Survey*. Unpublished report prepared under with the Pennsylvania Teleteaching Project. Mansfield University, Mansfield, Pennsylvania, 1987.

Galvin, P. *Telelearning and Audiographics: Four Case Studies*. Unpublished report. Norwich, New York: Delaware-Chenango Board of Cooperative Educational Services, 1987.

Gibson, R. "Closing the Gap: Distance Learning by Satellite Keeps Rural Schools Competitive and Open." *Rural Electrification* (January 1989): 26–30.

Hajdu, D. *Personal Communication.*, May 1989.

Martin, D. J. *Audiographics Conferencing in Small Rural Schools in New York State: A Model for Developing Shared Teleconferenced Services Between Rural School Districts*. Unpublished report, Delaware-Chenango Board of Educational Services, Norwich, New York, May 1986.

Miller, G. T. W. "Distance Learning in Northeastern Utah: A Summary of the Distance Learning Technology and the Northeastern Utah Telelearning Project." Paper presented at the annual conference of the National Rural Education Association, Bismarck, North Dakota, September 24–28, 1988.

Moorehouse, D. L., Hoaglund, M. L., and Schmidt, R. H. "Interactive Television: Findings, Issues, and Recommendations." Paper presented at the Vision for Rural and Small Schools Conference sponsored by the Illinois State Board of Education, Springfield, Illinois, September 17, 1987.

"The Pennsylvania Teleteaching Project." Booklet published by the Pennsylvania Teleteaching Project Demonstration Center, available from Riverview Intermediate Unit, R.D. 2, Greencrest Drive, Shippenville, Pa. 16254 (no date).

Rash, P. "What Factors Affect a Successful Partnership?" Presentation at the Learning by Satellite III Conference, Oklahoma City, Oklahoma, March 7–9, 1988.

Wickler, F. V. *Personal Communication*, March 1989.

Whittington, N. "Is Instructional Television Educationally Effective? A Research Review." *The American Journal of Distance Education,* *1*, no. 1 (1987): 47–57.

Wydra, D. *Secrets of Teleteaching.* Mansfield, Pa.: Wydra Teleteaching Associates, 1987.

Meeting the Needs of Special Student Populations in Rural Locales

Terry R. Berkeley
and
Barbara L. Ludlow

The rural character, the rural contributions, and the rural state-of-affairs in education seem to be absent from national discussions about education in general, and special education in particular. This is especially true in terms of policy requirements where distinctions in favor of rural locales are rarely made, and where the impact on education of the sociology and traditions of country life are usually ignored. This is not a trivial matter! The current absence of focus on "things rural" in education is indicative of a prevailing national attitude about smallness and difference which one might suppose are presumed to be less important and, thus, less worthwhile. One only has to review the early and mid-1980s reports on the status of American education (DeYoung, 1987) to realize that two-thirds of the nation's school districts and one-third of the nation's children (Helge, 1984a) are typically omitted from consideration. Yet, the richness of rural heritage and rural culture in education has been documented in those locales, and, certainly, beyond those places. People who live and work in rural areas know, understand and value rural perspectives, even if at first glance people who are "from away" think those views and/or concerns are parochial.

This situation is exacerbated in the consideration of rural education programs that have been specifically designed to benefit the individual members of "special students populations," i.e., individuals with special needs. In preparing to write this chapter, for example, we discovered that during the five-year period since the publication of the special edition of *Exceptional Children* (January 1984) focusing on rural special education, not a single article in either that journal or the *Journal of Special Education* had a title that connoted the notion of rural. Moreover, we had to go to an 1981 edition of *Exceptional Children* to find the next previous article about rural special education (e.g., Helge, 1981), and in our review of the past ten-years of the *Journal of Special Education* not a single title appeared featuring the rural perspective. Only sporadically is any reference to special education in rural settings to be found; and typically such work appears in journals of comparatively limited circulation (e.g., Joyce and Wienke, 1989, *Teacher Education and Special Education*).

This situation is tempered by an understanding that educational programs for "special student populations" as a concerted national priority are in the midst of their early adolescence. The implementation of school programs to meet the needs of students with special needs only began to be designed and implemented on a wide scale in the mid- to late–1960s. These programs were initiated as a result of far-reaching legislative reforms requiring that considerable, specific effort be made on behalf of those students in this society who were in the greatest need of assistance. In turn, personnel issues and service issues evolved as a result of these reforms; thus, some of the needs of these students continue to be unmet, some of these students are still unknown, and new conditions that affect these students in negative ways continue to be identified. We believe that this should not be unexpected, especially when national legislative reform (for example, the Elementary and Secondary Education Act of 1965; Public Law 89–313, State Operated Programs; and Public Law 94–142, the Education for All Handicapped Children Act of 1975) is used to direct the resolution of concerns that force one group of people in need to be dependent upon another, more powerful group of people, no matter how much the reform is needed to resolve essential inequities, or loss of freedoms, in a democratic society (Dimond, 1973; Weintraub et al., 1976).

It is not surprising that the expectations and promises inherent in the landmark reforms enacted from the mid–1960's to the mid–1970's to equalize the educational opportunities of poor, disadvantaged, and handicapped children have not been universally embraced. Since schools mirror what occurs in the rest of society (Featherstone, 1971), programs designed for students with special needs, the focus of this chapter, are often viewed negatively due to societal attitudes. These negative attitudes reflect a general lack of understanding of the abilities of the people who find themselves isolated into these groups (Wolfensberger, 1988), as well as from the resulting continuing debate as to whether the allocation of resources to these citizens is cost effective (Wolfensberger, 1972; Castellani, 1987).

Public Law (P.L.) 94–142, the Education for All Handicapped Children Act of 1975 [a.k.a., the Education of the Handicapped Act (EHA)], is the broad-based civil rights and regulatory reform that was enacted to assure that all students with handicaps, regardless of the severity of their disability, would receive a free appropriate public education designed to meet their unique educational needs, usually, within the context of special education programs. We view the present status of services for children with special needs in rural areas as reflecting, generally, the problems associated with special education in all areas of the nation with, of course, a provocative focus on things rural.

A number of seminal studies have been published by the Harvard University Collaborative Study of Children with Special Needs (e.g., Raphael, Singer and Walker, 1987; Singer et al., 1986; and Walker et al., 1988). In a particularly useful article from this group on schools as agents of social reform, Singer & Butler (1987) found significantly different results in their review of the quality of local school district implementation of services supported by and adhering to the provisions of P.L. 94–142.

These differences were found to be in terms of personnel (p. 134), parent participation (p. 141), per child resource allocations (p. 146), and the performance gains (outcomes) of students enrolled in special education (p. 147). Two of the five districts examined in this study had a somewhat rural flavor, though they each included a medium-sized urban center and several suburban towns. The authors concluded:

> EHA has not succeeded . . . in providing a uniform entitlement for all handicapped children. Instead, the law has had differential results depending upon where the child happens to live and his individual family circumstances. . . .
>
> Likewise, poverty, family disorganization, and stress are such powerful influences when compared to whatever transpires at school that one wonders whether a social reform based solely in the schools can countervail against formidable societal forces . . . . Notwithstanding variations in programs across states, districts, and children, it is (an) overall transformation of attitudes and practices that best reflects EHA's enduring impact at the local level. (pp. 151–152)

Singer & Butler's understanding should not be thought of as alarming, even though many local and state officials opposed the new law (Pittinger and Kuriloff, 1982). Yet, Singer & Butler seem to reflect the current, national cross-section of thinking about EHA's implementation, including those individuals and groups whose interest is essentially rural special education. More specifically, we divide the major areas of concern about the implementation of EHA into four categories: personnel supply and demand; personnel quality; service delivery; and, service quality.

Personnel Issues

The availability of an adequate supply of qualified and appropriately trained personnel is one key component of the rural special education dilemma. Rural school administrators have reported difficulties in both recruitment and retention of teachers and other specialists as major barriers to effective educational programming for students with special needs (Helge, 1979; Kirmer, Lockwood, Mickler, and Sweeney, 1984; Smith-Davis, Burke and Noel, 1984; Latham and Burnham, 1985; Ludlow, 1985; Will, 1985; Ludlow, Bloom, and Wienke, in press). These problems are especially critical for low-incidence handicapping conditions, such as severe/profound/multiply handicaps, emotional disturbance, and sensory impairments, as well as for related services including speech and language therapy, and occupational and physical therapy.

Personnel Supply and Demand

Personnel supply and demand in special education is a growing concern for state education agencies, institutions of higher education, and local school systems in rural states. Three facets of the supply/demand issue have been identified:

1. there is a critical shortage of teachers and other specialists to staff rural special education programs for students with special needs;

2. administrators are experiencing difficulty in recruiting qualified teachers to fill special education positions in rural schools; and,

3. rural school district are unable to retain qualified and experienced special educators.

These problems jeopardize the quality of educational programming for students with special needs in the nation's rural schools in a number of ways. The lack of available personnel means that some rural students may be unserved (e.g., no program is available) or underserved (e.g., the program is provided by staff without sufficient experience, or the program is offered on a limited basis). The inability to recruit teachers and other specialists permits untrained staff with limited skills and experience to design and implement programs that may not adequately meet the needs of students with special needs. And, the failure to retain qualified personnel in professional positions results in program inconsistency and instability that may hamper the attainment of student learning outcomes.

Yet, the supply and demand crisis in special education in rural areas will not be solved merely by expanding the number of personnel preparation programs, or by increasing the number of professionals they produce. As Sontag & Button (1980) noted nearly a decade ago,

> The difficulty posed by such areas is not the problem
> of preparing quantities or sheer numbers of teachers,
> but of preparing teachers who are willing and capable
> of teaching in areas which impose disincentives. (p. 6)

The ultimate solution to the personnel supply and demand crisis lies in insuring a sufficient pool of qualified candidates who are prepared and willing to fill special education positions in rural areas and who are adequately supported in continuing employment by rural schools and communities.

Personnel Shortage

Rural schools require an adequate supply of trained and certified professionals to meet the demand for teachers and other specialists to staff special education programs. Recently, a coalition of professional organizations warned of an impending crisis in special education personnel supply and demand ("Personnel Shortage," 1989). A statement by Marrs (1984) expresses this concern succinctly: "We are simply not preparing a sufficient number of qualified personnel for rural special education programs in rural areas" (p. 335). A series of studies spanning the past 10 years have pointed to a long-standing shortage of qualified special educators to fill these positions (Sontag and Button, 1980; Smith-Davis, Burke and Noel, 1984; Lauritzen, 1988; "Shortage of Qualified Special Education Personnel," 1989), a shortage that is especially severe in rural areas (Helge and Marrs, 1982; McLaughlin, Smith-Davis, and Burke, 1986).

Efforts to alleviate the personnel shortage have been undertaken at all organizational levels of the education hierarchy. The federal government has allotted additional funds to improve the availability and accessibility of special education degree and certification programs by providing stipends for full-time students, salaries for additional faculty, and resources for program development and/or expansion (Noel, Burke, and Valdivieso, 1985; Marozas and May, 1988).

Institutions of higher education have created and implemented a variety of innovative program models to deliver instruction and supervision to rural special education students (Johnson and Amundsen, 1987; Egan, McCleary, Sebastian, and Lacy, 1988; Joyce and Wienke, 1988; Ludlow, Faieta, and Wienke, 1988; McIntosh & Raymond, 1988). State education agencies have reduced or simplified requirements for teaching certification, or instituted emergency teaching certificates (Helge, 1984a; O'Connor and Rotatori, 1987). Rural school administrators have resorted to employing untrained personnel on temporary out-of-field permits (Pipho, 1986; Smith-Davis, 1986) and a growing number of paraprofessionals in place of certified professionals (Putnam and Bruininks, 1986; Ludlow, Bloom and Wienke, in press).

While these practices have resulted in many effective and innovative solutions to the supply/demand crisis in special education, they are not without problems. The limited pool of applicants for rural special education positions places constraints on administrator employment decisions. Federal and state regulations may dictate employment of an individual with recognized "paper credentials" rather than an individual with less formal training, but suitable temperament, experience, and interest to succeed in a rural setting. Hiring practices may also be affected by the availability of financial aid to school systems for special education programs which, in many states, is linked to the certification status of personnel.

Personnel Recruitment

Rural schools frequently experience difficulty recruiting people to fill new or vacant professional positions because: (1) they must compete for the limited pool of personnel preparation program graduates with urban and suburban districts that offer better salaries and fringe benefits, more varied social opportunities, and greater possibilities for professional advancement (Helge, 1983; O'Connor & Rotatori, 1987); and, (2) many otherwise qualified graduates are unwilling to locate in rural areas (Marrs, 1984).

A variety of innovative recruitment strategies have been designed to address this situation. The federal government has funded two national centers to stimulate interest in special education careers through the American Council on Rural Special Education's Rural Job Referral Service and the National Clearinghouse for Professions in Special Education. Institutions of higher education have initiated more aggressive efforts to recruit students for special education training programs, particularly by targeting nontraditional groups such as liberal arts program graduates, unemployed or retired workers, and housewives returning to the workforce who reside in rural areas (National Information Center for Handicapped Children and Youth, 1983). State education agencies and school districts have developed attractive marketing materials to announce available positions through advertisements and job fairs, as well as special incentive systems to lure professionals to rural areas ("Special Education Personnel Recruitment Practices," 1987).

Personnel Retention

The retention of special education professionals has also been a persistent problem in rural school systems. Various studies have estimated that the average attrition rate in rural schools may be as high as one-third to one-half of all special education positions each year (Helge, 1979, 1984; Ludlow, 1985). This attrition occurs for several reasons: (1) untrained personnel employed on temporary permits lack the skills to deal effectively with students with special needs (Smith-Davis, 1985;

Pipho, 1986); (2) inappropriately trained personnel are unsuccessful in coping with the unique, stressful aspects of rural education, and experience job dissatisfaction that leads to burnout (Bina, 1981; Marrs, 1983); and, (3) beginning professionals with no prior experience in rural areas frequently have difficulty adjusting to learning conditions, social relationships, and cultural values more typical of rural settings (Mallory & Berkeley, 1987).

To date, few successful efforts directed at improving the retention of special education professionals in rural areas have been reported in the literature. Yet, the urgency of the problem demands the consideration of strategies such as financial incentives, improved working conditions, and adequate administrative support. As Ludlow (1985) noted,

> teacher recruitment and retention problems are ultimately interrelated. Decreasing the turnover rate by encouraging teachers to remain in special education will necessarily also relieve needs for hiring new personnel. (p. 25)

Addressing the retention problem promises to result in a reduction in the overall personnel shortage, and to significantly influence the supply and demand cycle in rural special education.

Personnel Quality

Insuring and maintaining the quality of special education personnel represents another challenge for the nation's rural schools. Considerable controversy surrounds three questions related to personnel quality:

1. what constitutes appropriate preservice preparation for rural special educators?

2. how can the effectiveness of professional personnel who are providing programming for students with special needs be evaluated?

3. what are the inservice training needs of rural special
   educators to insure adequate professional
   development?

Preservice Preparation

The nature of preservice preparation for special
education professionals in rural areas has been the subject of
much debate. Rural special educators confront unique
constraints in meeting the requirements of students with special
needs. Limited access to specialized curriculum models,
instructional materials, and adaptive equipment often requires
professionals to improvise, create, or do without needed
resources (Barker and Beckner, 1987). The unavailability of
related service personnel often forces special education
teachers to assume the roles of practitioners of specialized
disciplines, such as providing language training, administering
therapeutic interventions, and devising functional adaptations
(Helge, 1982). And, special educators in rural areas typically
are asked to address a range of student needs in cross- or
multi-categorical settings (Helge, 1984a).

Most existing personnel preparation programs do not
address the development of knowledge and skill competencies
needed for effective professional work in rural areas (Sher,
1977; Helge, 1983). Graduates are trained to work with
categorical groups (e.g., students with specific learning
disabilities), or with a limited range of disabilities (e.g., speaking
populations with articulation and syntax disorders). And, few
training programs provide instruction in rural culture or provide
field experiences in rural settings to acclimate students to the
demands of rural special education programs.

The prevalent practice of employing untrained personnel
on emergency certificates also raises the issue of how to
provide preservice training to practicing, but as yet uncertified,
teachers. With employment in the schools, these individuals are
unable to pursue full-time studies in traditional preparation
programs (Spencer, Noel, and Boyer-Schick, 1985).
Nevertheless, these special educators represent the group most

urgently in need of appropriate training in special education content knowledge and instructional skill.

Efforts to address these preservice preparation issues have focused on the design of training programs specifically aimed at the preparation of personnel to work effectively in rural schools, as well as on the expansion of training program accessibility to rural areas. Institutions of higher education have used state and federal funds to implement a variety of on-the-job personnel preparation delivery models. Preservice instruction has been delivered to rural special educators via video and satellite broadcasts (Egan et al., 1988), computer-assisted instruction (Johnson and Amundsen, 1987), and off-campus courses and adjunct field trainers (McIntosh and Raymond, 1988), while practicum supervision is frequently provided in on-the-job settings by means of university and/or school district personnel (Joyce & Wienke, 1988; Ludlow, Faieta & Wienke, 1988).

Helge (1984a) has called for collaboration across the education hierarchy in the development of preservice preparation programs with a rural flavor. She said,

> Federal and state governments should provide support for innovative teacher training programs and address critical personnel shortages in rural special education.
>
> Federal support should encourage collaborative efforts between state education agencies and universities designed to determine positions and types of personnel needed, and devise appropriate personnel preparation programs. (p. 304)

Staff Evaluation

Systematic and meaningful staff evaluation is essential to the promotion of personnel quality, but it is often neglected by special education administrators in rural schools. The findings in several studies have suggested that failure to evaluate personnel results in doubts about personnel effectiveness, which, in turn, contributes to rural professional burnout (Helge, 1984a). Yet, a search of the literature identified no reports of evaluation systems or strategies designed to assess the effectiveness of special education professionals serving students with special needs in rural areas. The lack of attention to evaluation concerns may be due to the following reasons: (1) rural school administrators are so overwhelmed by the pressing need to locate and hire personnel for new and vacant positions that they are unable to direct sufficient time and attention to employed personnel; (2) the turnover of personnel in professional positions is so rapid that there is insufficient time to initiate meaningful evaluation processes; and (3) many special education administrators in rural areas (who often have no expertise in special education or their training is limited to a single area of specialization) feel unqualified to determine what and how to evaluate personnel.

Evaluation also is a critical component of and solution to the problem of personnel retention. Evaluation data that document the characteristics of professional effectiveness is needed if local school districts are to develop and justify incentive systems aimed at encouraging effective personnel to continue in rural special education positions. Evaluation data is also necessary for the successful implementation of professional development activities to prevent the attrition of personnel because of burnout. In Helge's (1987) words,

> there probably will be no one available to evaluate the effectiveness of the program. A year or more may pass before the new teacher is able to visit a similar classroom and to compare its quality to his or her own program. This unintentionally nonsupportive situation can contribute not only to the insecurity of the teacher, but to staff attrition. (p. 54)

Staff Development

The quality of special education personnel in rural areas can only be promoted through the provision of meaningful and systematically implemented staff development activities.

Adequate inservice training is important in maintaining and refining the skills of effective teachers and other specialists, but it is especially critical in promoting the acquisition of competencies by untrained or inappropriately trained individuals who have proven to be ineffective in meeting the needs of students with special needs. Yet, the design and delivery of inservice training for special educators in rural areas is complicated by three factors: (1) generally, rural schools have limited access to advanced training programs offered by colleges and universities; (2) rural educators have few financial resources for travel to workshops, conferences, and other professional development activities; and (3) attrition hampers on-going staff development efforts. The small number of special educators in rural school systems, coupled with their diverse needs for specialized information and skills, and their high turnover rate makes it difficult for administrators to offer appropriate and adequate inservice training programs.

State education agency and local school system personnel have initiated numerous creative alternatives to the provision of staff development for rural special educators. Combining new instructional technologies and existing community personnel resources, school districts provide inservice training in special education via distance learning, video tapes and disks, computer networks, and through peer observation and consultation (Helge, 1979; Educating Handicapped Students, 1983; Scott, 1984; O'Connor and Rotatori, 1987). Staff development may be a key component in any effective solution to the teacher supply and demand issue. Inadequate staff development has been cited as a major cause of personnel retention problems (Helge, 1981). Ludlow (1985) stressed the pivotal role of staff development in addressing the reciprocal problems of recruitment and retention,

> Only when teacher trainers offer inservice programs on a regular and continuing basis designed to meet the teacher's immediate needs and local administrators follow-up with consistent and supportive supervisory contacts, retention problems (and with them recruitment problems) can be alleviated. (pp. 25–26)

Service Delivery Issues

We have found that the delivery of services often vexes parents, teachers, specialists, and educational administrators. These are not new concerns, and they reflect, to an extent, on the personnel issues discussed previously. The problems are even more complex, however, than finding and retaining qualified teachers and specialists. Rather, these are management issues. Managing rural special education is a complex task due to the great variability of rural locales. Thus, the challenge is to manage service delivery in such a way as to maximize service quality. These are the major topics in the area of service issues.

Service Delivery

Helge (1984a) talked about the differences in the geographic culture of rural schools. She noted,

> Rural subcultures vary tremendously. They range geographically from remote islands and deserts to clustered communities, and economically from stable classic farm communities to depressed lower socioeconomic settings and high growth 'boom or bust' communities. The array of rural schools ranges from isolated schools serving as few as 1 to 10 children in a location 350 miles from the nearest school district, to schools located in small clustered towns or surrounded by other smaller districts. (p. 294)

As a result, management and logistical concerns usually have been major considerations in the implementation of a comprehensive special education program designed to meet the free appropriate public education requirements of EHA.

Beane (1983) viewed the educational administrator's role in managing special education services as the resolution of a series of dilemmas. Some of these dilemmas are:

1. What would you do if the Board of Education insisted on refusing flow-through funds in order to avoid federal monitoring?

2. What would you do if several children lived in areas that often become inaccessible during the winter months?

3. What would you do if parents of a minority group would not participate in the school system's parent-teacher organization?

4. What would you do if several children needed home-bound services and your school system could not afford a home-bound teacher?

5. What would you do if your school system lacked the funds to meet the need for an occupational therapist and adequate facilities to provide therapy? (pp. 22, 26, 33, 42–43).

The resolution of these dilemmas (or the inability of local school district officials to recognize the existence of these dilemmas) will have an impact upon the delivery special education services *and* the quality of the special education services designed to meet the requirements of students with special needs. Specifically, service delivery concerns are focused on related services, transportation, and programming to meet the requirements of students with low incidence special needs.

Related Services

In 1981, Helge reported, "Increasingly scarce resources combined with additional education service requirements (e.g., related services) have emphasized the need for interorganizational relationships in rural schools" (p. 6). The lack of available related services personnel previously discussed in this chapter coupled with increased service requirements on the part of students with special needs in rural locales creates a considerable challenge for school personnel to overcome, especially when this has to be done in a cost-effective manner (Helge, 1979).

But, what is the scope of the related services problem? There is little doubt that the enactment and implementation of EHA has stimulated a tremendous growth in the delivery of related services. Helge (1980) stated, "Related Services, previously existent in less than 10% of all rural districts/cooperatives sampled, increased approximately 50% after the implementation (of EHA)" (p. 24). No comparable data for any time after the 1980 report, though, exists. Given the data associated with the difficulty in finding related service professional to work in rural areas, the problem, no doubt, is still significant.

Helge (1984), McIntosh and Raymond (1987), and Silver (1987) have suggested that a range of interagency collaborative agreements to resolve the related services dilemma is needed. Customarily, these agreements are between several rural school districts or between the schools and other human service agencies. Sometimes, a school district will employ a related service professional on a contract basis as a consultant to the system (Dunn and Grey, 1988). In this case, the individual conducts evaluations of students suspected of having special needs, develops goals and objectives to assist in the remediation of needs, and consults with special education teachers about the implementation of those goals and objectives.

Transportation

Helge (1984a) pointed out that transportation costs and logistics as well as weather conditions and great distances make it difficult to deliver the great array of services needed by students residing in many rural locales. In fact, Helge (1980) reported that geographic distance, inadequate transportation services, weather, and poor roads were major concerns of state and local special education personnel in her study of special education service delivery before and after the 1975 enactment of EHA.

While transportation problems are frequently mentioned by rural special educators, no data is available about the extent to which transportation inadequacies actually impact upon the special education services delivered to students with special needs in rural locales. Therefore, it might be assumed that: (1) local school district personnel cope with these issues and deliver services in spite of the problems which exist; and, these issues are mentioned only to point out the difficulties which must be overcome in rural areas; (2) local school district personnel devise methods of "reaching" those students with special needs who are enrolled in special education when transportation is halted by weather or poor roads, and educators and parents do not think that problems exist; or (3) local school district personnel are not interested in revealing to state and federal officials or researchers about the methods they use to manage transportation dilemmas.

It is likely, though, that (1) and (2) above are the options of choice selected by rural special educators to cope with transportation problems which arise on a daily basis. Helge (1984b) said,

> This . . . partly reflects the rural norm of "taking care one's own" . . . It is also partially attributable to the practical nature of rural educators. They tend to "make do" when given inadequate resources. . . . (p. 313)

Children with Low-Incidence Special Needs

In terms of program delivery for students with low incidence disabilities, the lack of specialized related service personnel and adequately trained and appropriately skilled teachers has been discussed previously. Yet, another issue for local school district administrators is the cost of providing services to these students because there are not enough of these children. Helge (1984b) pointed out that since there are so few children who make-up a particular disability category, developing a program for one or two students is neither practical or cost effective.

Related to cost and logistics, the broadest spectrum of service delivery models for children with low-incidence disabilities do not exist in rural locales. In addition, Helge (1984b) reported that other barriers for providing services to students with low-incidence disabilities exist, and these include: (1) population sparsity; (2) distance from where services are provided to where a student lives; (3) weather; (4) language; (5) cultural differences; (6) family lifestyle and economics; and (7) history of special education services delivery (pp. 315–317).

Each of these factors often makes it difficult to find ways to marshall the resources necessary to provide all of the specialized services that should be available to students with low-incidence special needs. However, recent changes such as technological innovations, more focused rural personnel preparation programs, and increased attention to providing services to children with special needs earlier in their lives seem to be trends which may assist in bringing about an improved service delivery system for these students.

Service Quality

The issue of the quality of special education services is significant in rural areas when considered from the multiple perspectives of parent participation, the availability of technical resources, per child resource allocation, and program evaluation. In terms of the range of these concerns, the quality of services reflects prevailing negative attitudes toward students with handicaps to a pronounced need for a commitment by educational leaders to determine, to tell, and to share the complete story of the costs, outcomes, and processes of special education programs in local school districts.

Parent Participation

Helge (1979, 1980, 1984a, 1984b), Marrs (1984), and Abdo & Milizia (1987) discussed the critical importance of including parents in special education programming for their children. The message of these authors has been quite similar. Abdo & Milizia (1987) summed it up best by noting "The idea is a simple one: Children do better in school when parents and educators work together" (p. 1). Increasing the level of meaningful parental involvement is quite challenging for local school district personnel given their negative professional perceptions of parent-educator partnerships in the public educational enterprise.

Helge (1980) found that parent participation was essential to high quality special education programs, and that "staff development regarding skills in working with parents of the handicapped" (p. 62) might resolve those factors that inhibit participation. In her study of the implementation of special education in rural areas, conducted just after the implementation of EHA, she identified staff attitudes that hindered meaningful parent participation: (1) "some staff felt that parents should passively approve school decisions" (p. 62); (2) "considerable misunderstanding exists on the part of rural parents regarding special education" (p. 62); (3) an attitude that "school experts know what is best for students" (p. 62); (4) "parent involvement is (only) attendance at IEP meetings" (p. 62); and (5) "parents . . . should be grateful for any services provided to their children, whether they are appropriate or not" (p. 62).

On a cultural level, there are other problems which affect the likelihood that parents will participate in educational decisionmaking. For instance, Helge (1980) also found that it may be impossible to obtain "parent permission in areas (e.g., Apache Nation lands) in which no language exits" (p. 63), and understanding what usually appears to be a basic notion about special education does not occur when one is "relating terms such as learning disabilities when a particular subculture has had no concept of such a term" (p. 63).

Availability of Technical Resources

Helge (1984a, 1984c) reported that new technology is not as readily available in rural areas. She noted that students enrolled in rural special education classes are less likely to receive the benefits brought about by new technological advances. Helge's comments advise that there should be a concern toward increasing the availability of technological resources in rural schools. Yet, this is only one aspect of a technological puzzle that will assist in improving the quality of special education services in rural areas.

Hofmeister (1984) reported on the incredible advantages of using technology in rural locales. In fact, his optimism was directed in two ways: first, toward the availability of information that is not usually found in rural areas; and, second, toward the notion of excellence. His discussions focused on the ability of the teacher to use interactive and noninteractive technologies in order to obtain and use new information in such a way to foster educational excellence from the perspective of the teacher *and* the student. He commented,

> The new technological tools offer immediate and more distant promises. The realization of these promises will depend on the degree to which rural educators prepare themselves to capitalize on the advantages and avoid the problems associated with the new technologies.
>
> Because these new tools are communication oriented, rural educators have much to gain by developing their technological literacy. (p. 348)

Per-Child Resource Allocation

Per child resource allocation has been an issue of concern in rural areas for a long time. Helge reported several times (1979, 1981, 1984a) that the financing of special education services in rural areas suffers in contrast from that received in other areas. In particular, she noted, "Rural 'advocates' (are) fewer in number and therefore less vocal; sparse populations facilitate policies ignoring rural problems" (1984a, p. 299).

In a comprehensive study of per pupil expenditures of special education in three metropolitan school districts, Singer & Raphael (1988) found significant differences in the costs associated with providing special education services. Given

Helge's notion of fewer 'advocates' speaking up for special education in rural areas (thereby implying fewer resources for planning and implementing programs), the differences in per child resource allocation in rural areas, perhaps, is more varied.

What did Singer & Raphael find? The differences in costs of special education in the districts they studied resulted primarily from the student's placement. In turn, "where a child is placed determines, in large part, the services he will receive" (p. 61), i.e., the type of placement determines the nature and amount of related services an individual needs and, perhaps, will receive; thus, placement factors add to the variability of per child costs. The study did not include data on the costs of transportation, although transportation costs in rural areas add to the per pupil allocation of resources. Yet, a question remains: should transportation costs be considered part of the per child cost of special education? If the answer is in the affirmative (which is probably the case), then, the direct financial support required for specialized personnel, adaptive equipment, curricular materials, instructional supplies, and program evaluation, for example, will probably be less than what is needed to adequately support the program.

In the only study we found that detailed per pupil special education expenditures in a rural area (rural Kansas), McGinley (1988) reported on data from Herbel's 1976 work that interestingly parallels the Singer & Raphael findings. Herbel noted that variations in per pupil costs of rural special education are due to students special education placement and related service needs.

Program Evaluation

The final consideration under the broad rubric of service quality is program evaluation. There is a need to focus on the processes *and* outcomes of special education. Two evaluation questions must be answered: Are we as a local school district implementing our special education program as we intended it to be implemented (process evaluation)? How well is our special education program accomplishing its goals (outcome evaluation) (Berkeley, 1988)? It is important to note, the percentage of individual education plan instructional objectives met by students enrolled in special education is *not* a valid measure of student outcomes.

EHA includes two specific requirements aimed at determining the quality of special education services through program evaluation activities. First, EHA requires local school districts to evaluate their special education programs on an annual basis and include evaluation reports in their special education plans. These plans are used by state education agency officials to obtain and distribute financial support authorized in the federal statute. Second, the federal government is charged with the responsibility of monitoring state and local compliance with EHA requirements. While the present form of EHA does not include an examination of the quality of local services, compliance reviews serve a program evaluation function since this process forces a local district to review its adherence to auditing, paperwork management, and procedural safeguard requirements.

With the exception of the work by Singer and Butler (1987) and the other studies by the Harvard group (mentioned earlier), as well as an article and subsequent book by Gartner and Lipsky (1987) and Lipsky and Gartner (1989), no other reports of individual local school district program evaluations have been published. However, Laird (1988) and Berkeley (1988, 1989) have commented on the need for and benefit of having available for review comprehensive local school district special education program evaluation reports. The issue is no longer just trying to determine the promising practices in special education which often are discussed in these reports (Meyen, Vargason and Whelan, 1983) and Marozas and May (1988). Rather, special educators and policy makers need to review these reports to determine the degree to which EHA is being effectively implemented.

Concluding Comments

The significance of the special education personnel and service issues confronting rural school systems, in our opinion, is in no way diminished by the current lack of research data and the paucity of program reports addressing the concerns of personnel supply and demand, personnel quality, service delivery, and service quality. It seems to us that these concerns, while they may be colored by the unique characteristics of rural culture and rural geography, in many respects, are the same issues which challenge the field of special education in all of the nation's schools. Many of the supposed barriers to successful implementation of educational programs for students with special needs may not be so much genuine constraints as manifestations of limiting attitudes, which might, in fact, be altered to focus on the assets of rural schools, rather than their liabilities.

The concept of rural is not a homogeneous notion; rather, rural schools reflect a multiplicity of values and conditions that represent remote Alaskan fishing settlements, tiny Midwestern farming communities, and isolated Appalachian hollows. We believe that this diversity implies that no over-arching single or general solution to the problems and concerns challenging rural special education will be found. Instead, each rural school system will need to seek its own solutions to the dilemmas of insuring the supply and quality of personnel along with the delivery and quality of services in educational programs for students with special needs. But, such diversity, we contend, reflects the best qualities of this unique pluralistic and democratic society, and offers the best hope for moving toward educational excellence and equal opportunities for *all* students in the nation's schools.

REFERENCES

Abdo, S., and Milizia, E. "Vermont Parent/Professional Partnership Workgroup: Families and Schools Do it Better Together." Paper presented at the Seventh Annual Meeting of the American Council on Rural Special Education, Asheville, N.C., 1987.

Barker, B. O., and Beckner, W. E. "Preservice Training for Special Educators: A Survey." *The Rural Educator, 8*, no. 3 (1987: 1–4.

Beane, A. *Solving Educational Dilemmas Related to Rural School Administration.* Murray, Ky., and Bellingham, Wash.: National Rural Development Institute, 1983.

Berkeley, T. R. "A Shift in Leadership Values: Services to Special Populations in Rural Locales". Paper presented at the Appalachian Educational Laboratory's Fourth Annual Rural Educational Policy Symposium, Louisville, Ky., December 1988.

Berkeley, T. R. "Testimony of the American Council on Rural Special Education on the Extension of the Education of the Handicapped Act, Parts C-G, Discretionary Programs." Presented to the U.S. House of Representatives Subcommittee on Select Education Congressional Forum, Washington, D.C., January 1989.

Bina, M. J. "Teacher Morale in Rural Areas: Implications for Administrators Regarding Teacher Burn-out and Attrition." *National Rural Project Newsletter, 3*, no. 1 (1981): 2–3.

Castellani, P. *The Political Economy of Developmental Disabilities.* Baltimore: Brookes, 1987.

Currie, P., and Rotatori, A. F. "Stressors and Reactions Experienced by Special Education Professionals." In *Issues in Special Education.* 99–112. Edited by A. Rotatori, M. M. Banbury, and R. A. Fox. Mountain View, Calif.: Mayfield, 1987.

DeYoung, A. J. "The Status of American Rural Education Research: An Integrated Review and Commentary." *Review of Educational Research, 57*, no. 2 (1987): 123–148.

Dimond, P. "The Constitutional Right to Education: The Quiet Revolution." *Hastings Law Journal, 24* (1973): 1087–1127.

Dunn, W., and Gray, B. R. "Managing Occupational Therapy in Rural Education (M.O.R.E.): Initial Findings." Paper presented at the Eighth Annual Meeting, American Council on Rural Special Education, Monterey, Calif., February 1988.

Education of the Handicapped Act, as amended, of 1975, 20 U.S.C. 1401–1468.

Egan, M. W., Sebastian, I. D., Sebastian, J. P., and Lacy, H. "Rural Preservice Teacher Preparation Using Two-Way Interactive Television." *Rural Special Education Quarterly, 9,* no. 3 (1988): 27–33.

Featherstone, J. *Schools Where Children Learn.* New York: Liveright, 1971.

Gartner, A., and Lipsky, D. K. "Beyond Special Education: Toward a Quality Education for All Students." *Harvard Educational Review, 57,* no. 4 (1987): 367–395.

Helge, D. I. *Final Project Report of the National Rural Research Project.* Murray, Ky.: Murray State University Center for Innovation and Development, 1979.

Helge, D. I. *A National Comparative Study Regarding Rural Special Education Delivery Systems Before and After Passage of PL 94–142.* Murray, Ky.: Murray State University Center for Innovation and Development, 1980.

Helge, D. I. "Problems in Implementing Comprehensive Special Education Programming in Rural Areas." *Exceptional Children, 47,* no. 7 (1981): 514–520.

Helge, D. I. "Increasing Preservice Curriculum Accountability to Rural Handicapped Populations." *Teacher Education and Special Education, 8,* no. 2 (1982): 137–142.

Helge, D. I. *Images: Issues and Trends in Rural Special Education.* Murray, Ky.: Murray State University Center for Innovation and Development, 1983.

Helge, D. I. "The State of the Art of Rural Special Education." *Exceptional Children, 50,* no. 4 (1984a): 294–305.

Helge, D. I. "Models for Serving Rural Students with Low-Incidence Handicapping Conditions." *Exceptional Children, 50,* no. 4 (1984b): 313–325.

Helge, D. I. "Technologies as Rural Special Education Problem Solvers." *Exceptional Children, 50,* no. 4 (1984c): 351–360.

Helge, D. I. "Strategies for Improving Rural Special Education Program Evaluation." *Remedial and Special Education, 8,* no. 4 (1987): 53–60.

Helge, D. I., and Marrs, L. W. "Personnel Recruitment and Retention in Rural America: A Growing Problem." *The Pointer, 26,* no. 2 (1982): 28–33.

Hofmeister, A. M. "Technological Tools for Rural Special Education." *Exceptional Children, 50,* no. 4 (1984): 344–349.

Johnson, M., and Amundsen, C. *Distancy Delivery in Alaska.* Paper presented at the Seventh Annual Meeting of the American Council on Rural Special Education, Asheville, N.C., March 1987.

Joyce, B. G., and Wienke, W. D. "Preparing Teachers in Behavior Disorders Through an Innovative Teacher Training Program." *Rural Special Education Quarterly, 9,* no. 2 (1988): 4–9.

Joyce, B. G., and Wienke, W. D. "Preservice Competencies for Teachers of Students With Behavior Disorders in a Rural Setting." *Teacher Education and Special Education, 12,* no. 1–2 (1989): 13–18.

Kirmer, L., Lockwood, L., Mickler, W., and Sweeny, P. "Regional Rural Special Education Programs." *Exceptional Children, 50,* no. 4 (1984): 306–311.

Laird, P. *Personal Communication,* October 1988.

Latham, G., and Burnham, J. "Innovative Methods for Serving Rural Handicapped Children." *School Psychology Review, 14,* no. 4 (1985): 438–443.

Lauritzen, P. "Research on Personnel Supply and Demand." *Counterpoint, 9,* no. 1 (1968): 1.

Lipsky, D. K., and Gartner, A. *Beyond Separate Education: Quality Education for All.* Baltimore: Brookes, 1989.

Ludlow, B. L. "Variables Influencing Special Education Teacher Employment in Rural Areas." *Rural Special Education Quarterly, 6,* no. 2 (1985): 24–26.

Ludlow, B. L., Bloom, L. A. and Wienke, W. D. "Rural School Services for Students With Severe Handicaps: Changes in Personnel and Programs." *Rural Special Education Quarterly, 10,* no. 3, in press.

Ludlow, B. L., Faieta, J. C., and Wienke, W. D. "Training Teachers to Supervise Their Peers: A Pilot Practicum Project." *Teacher Education and Special Education, 12,* no. 1–2 (1989): 27–32.

Mallory, B. L., and Berkeley, T. R. "The Relationship Between Rural Characteristics and the Preparation of Early Childhood Special Educators." *Rural Special Education Quarterly, 7,* no. 2 (1987): 1–5.

Marozas, D. S., and May, D. C. *Issues and Practices in Special Education.* New York: Longman, 1988.

Marrs, L. W. *Involving Citizens and Agencies in Rural Communities in Cooperative Programming for Handicapped Students.* Murray, Ky.: Murray State University Center for Innovation and Development, 1983.

Marrs, L. W. "A Bandwagon Without Music: Preparing Rural Special Educators." *Exceptional Children, 50,* no. 4 (1984): 334–342.

McGinley, K. H. *"Improving Special Education in Rural Kansas.:"* Paper presented at the Eighth Annual Meeting of the American Council on Rural Special Education, Monterey, Calif., February 1988.

McIntosh, D. K., and Raymond, G. I. *"Training Regular Education Personnel to be Special Education Consultants to Other Regular Education Personnel in Rural Settings."* Paper presented at the Annual Meeting of the American Council on Rural Special Education, Asheville, N.C., March 1987.

McIntosh, D. K., and Raymond, G. I. "Training Special Education Teachers in Rural Areas: A Viable Model." *Rural Special Education Quarterly, 9,* no. 1 (1988): 2–5.

McLaughlin, M. M., Smith-Davis, J., and Burke, P. J. *Personnel to Educate the Handicapped: A Status Report.* College Park, Md.: University of Maryland Institute for the Study of Exceptional Children and Youth, 1986.

Meyen, E. L., Vargason, G. A., and Whelan, R. J. *Promising Practices for Exceptional Children: Curriculum Implications.* Denver: Love, 1983.

Noel, M. M., Burke, P. J., and Valdivieso, C. H. "Educational Policy and Severe Mental Retardation." In *Severe Mental Retardation: From Theory to Practice.* 12–35. Edited by D. Bricker, and J. Filler. Reston, Va.: Council for Exceptional Children, 1985.

O'Connor, N. M., and Rotatori, A. F. "Providing for Rural Special Education Needs." In *Issues in Special Education.* 51–65. Edited by A. Rotatori, M. M. Banbury, and R. A. Fox. Mountain View, Calif.: Mayfield, 1987.

"Personnel Shortage Nears Crisis Proportion Field Warns." *Education of the Handicapped, 15,* no. 8 (April 12, 1989): 3–4.

Pipho, C. "Quantity vs. Quality: States Aim to Improve Teaching and Teachers." *Phi Delta Kappan, 67* (1986): 333–334.

Pittinger, J., and Kuriloff, P. "Educating the Handicapped: Reforming a Radical Law." *Public Interest, 66* (1982): 72–96.

Putnam, J. W., and Bruininks, R. H. "Future Directions in Deinstitutionalization and Education: A Delphi Investigation." *Exceptional Children, 53,* no. 1 (1986): 55–62.

Raphael, E. S., Singer, J. D., and Walker, D. K. "Per Pupil Expenditures on Special Education in Three Metropolitan School Districts." *Journal of Education Finance, 11* (1987): 69–88.

Scott, R. J. "Teaching and Learning in Remote Schools: A Dilemma Beyond Rural Education." *Information from the National Center for Handicapped Children and Youth,* September 1984.

Sher, J. P. "A Proposal to End Federal Neglect of Rural Schools." *Phi Delta Kappan, 60* (1978): 280–282.

"Shortage of Qualified Special Education Personnel Declared National Emergency." *News & Notes, AAMR, 2,* no. 3 (May 1989): 1, 5.

Silver, S. "Compliance With PL 94–142 Mandates: Policy Implications." Paper presented at the Seventh Annual Meeting of the American Council on Rural Special Education, Asheville, N.C., March 1987.

Singer, J. D., and Butler, J. A. "The Education for All Handicapped Children Act: Schools as Agents of Social Reform." *Harvard Educational Review, 57,* no. 2 (1987): 125–152.

Singer, J. D., Butler, J. A., Palfrey, J. S. and Walker, D. K. "Characteristics of Special Education Placements: Findings from Probability Samples in Five Metropolitan School Districts." *Journal of Special Education, 20* (1986): 319–337.

Singer, J. D., and Raphael, H. S. *Per Pupil Expenditures for Special Education: To Whom are Resources Provided?* Cambridge: Harvard University Collaborative Study of Children with Special Needs, 1987.

Smith-Davis, J. "Personnel Supply and Demand in Special Education." *Counterpoint 12,* (1985): p. 10.

Smith-Davis, J., Burke, P. J., and Noel, M. M. *Personnel to Educate the Handicapped in America: Supply and Demand from the Programmatic Viewpoint.* College Park, Md.: University of Maryland Institute for the Study of Exceptional Children and Youth, 1984.

Sontag, E., and Button, J. *Office of Special Education Briefing Paper.* Washington, D.C.: United States Office of Education, February 1980.

Spence, K. L., Noel, N. M., and Boyer-Schick, K. *Summary Report of a 1985 Survey of Special Education Students.* College Park, Md.: University of Maryland Institute for the Study of Exceptional Children and Youth, 1985.

Staff. "Educating Handicapped Students in Rural America." *Information from the National Center on Handicapped Children and Youth,* November 1983.

Staff. *Special Education Personnel Recruitment Practices: A Manual for Administrators.* Rosslyn, Va.: National Information Center for Children and Youth with Handicaps, June 1987.

Walker, D. K., Singer, J. D., Palfrey, J. S., Orza, M., Wenger, M. and Butler, J. A. "Who Leaves and Who Stays in Special Education: A Two-Year Follow-Up Study. *Exceptional Children, 54* (1988): 393–402.

Weintraub, F., et al., eds. *Public Policy and the Education of Exceptional Children.* Reston, Va.: Council for Exceptional Children, 1976.

Will, M. C. "Provision of Special Education Services to Rural Children and Youth with Disabilities." *Rural Special Education Quarterly, 6,* no. 4 (1985): 47–49.

Wolfensberger, W. *The Principle of Normalization in Human Services.* Toronto: National Institute on Mental Retardation, 1972.

Wolfensberger, W. "Common Assets of Mentally Retarded People that are not Commonly Acknowledged. *Mental Retardation, 26,* No. 3 (1988): 63–70.

Equality of Educational Opportunity in Rural America

Margaret S. Phelps
and
George Allen Prock

Do students in rural schools have equality of educational opportunity? The answer to this question is evasive and dependent upon the definitions and measures of educational opportunity selected. The first and perhaps the most easily addressed indicator of educational equality is fiscal equity. Plaintiffs in school fiscal equity cases have argued that while equal spending does not ensure equal education, it is a prerequisite (Colvin, 1989, p. 15). Honeyman, Thompson, and Wood (1989) distinguish between horizontal equity, equitable expenditures for similar students in similar circumstances, and vertical equity, dissimilar expenditures for special needs students in dissimilar situations such as rural schools.

Both horizontal and vertical equity are functions of fiscal neutrality which separates levels of educational funding from dependence on the local tax base and requires equal tax effort in all communities (Monk, 1984b; Thompson et al., 1989). The fiscal neutrality concept is particularly pertinent in rural communities experiencing a narrowing tax base and declining student population. According to Brown and Saks, (1983), educational expenditures are an U-shaped function of percentage of family income. Rural and town districts spend lower percentages of revenues on education but spend more per family.

Three levels of funding (local, state, and federal) contribute to educational expenditures. The fiscal neutrality theory clearly moves the focus of responsibility for funding from local communities to the states which are legally responsible for the education of their citizens (Honeyman, Thompson, and Wood, 1989). Federal funding consists of categorical grants, block grants, and general purpose grants. In the 1960's the federal government used categorical grants to provide financial assistance to students with special needs such as educationally deprived students from low-income families, handicapped children, and non-English speaking children (Bass and Berman, 1979). In the 1980s federal funding for education shifted toward block grants which disperse funds over wider constituencies, are less tied to national priorities, and require reduced accountability while providing states and/or local governments more control over the allocation or distribution of the funds (Kutner and Sherman, 1982). A study of distribution of federal funds in 1978 showed that although per capita federal support for human resources was lower in rural areas, federal spending on elementary, secondary and adult education was higher in rural areas. Federal spending for social and handicapped services in rural areas was so low as to be insignificant (Hendler and Reid, 1980).

If rural/small schools are to provide the same services as larger schools, the cost of program delivery will be higher per pupil (Bass, 1986). Honeyman, Thompson, and Wood (1989) justify this higher cost on the basis of societal investment in all individuals to the ultimate good of the society as a whole. Bilow (1986b) sees the purpose of school as being to prepare children to be able to lead "useful, happy, and productive lives" outside of school (p. 20). Thompson, Camp, Horn, and Stewart (1988) tie resource allocations to individual student needs. "The degree to which school facilities (resources) provide the greatest opportunity for individuals to fulfill their intellectual, emotional, and social capabilities is the measure of their suitability and usefulness and is the ultimate expression of equality" (p. 38). Thus, rural education should be all things to all people and provide academic, vocational and traditional agricultural studies within the confines of a shrinking rural economy, tax base, and student cohort. No student should be denied access to educational opportunities to acquire necessary skills and knowledge to secure gainful employment and become a productive citizen ("Elementary, Secondary and Higher Education in Rural N.Y. State: An Action Strategy," 1985).

Another approach to equality of educational opportunity derives from a process or input approach and places the focus on student access to enhanced curricula, equipment, and other program components. Not only are dollars per student a factor, but also the use of those dollars (Colvin, 1989). The distribution of educational resources to different students becomes the basis for determining equality within and between schools (Rossmiller, 1987). However, Colvin (1989) cited the New Jersey ruling in *Abbott* v. *Burke* which held that cost-benefit was inadequate to resolve questions of equity in the complex social organization of schools. The judge criticized accepted measures of process and outcomes for their failure to account for correlations among the multiple variables present in schools.

Efforts are underway to develop a set of generally agreed upon indicators which may be used within and across states to compare educational quality. Kaagen and Smith (1985) are working with chief state officers to develop such effectiveness indicators. In their reviews of attempts to establish national indicators, they postulated that a fundamental assumption underlying the movement to identify indicators is that educators are responsible for assessing their own successes and failures while being accountable to the public, the source of support for public education. They believe that as educational indicators provide information about the health of the educational system, the statistics should measure something that relates to that health and have meaningful policy implications. Improved educational indicators could help state and local agencies to monitor changes in program and faculty quality and student performance while alerting them to impending problems.

Indicators should also focus attention on program areas such as vocational handicapped, and gifted education which need improvement.

In addition, regional standards of educational quality may be found in the accreditation standards of regional accreditation agencies. In a study of accredited schools in one Southern state, it was found that non-rural schools were more likely to have achieved regional accreditation than were rural schools. The differences were even greater for elementary schools than for secondary schools (Phelps and White, 1988).

Although inputs have been the basis of state funding, attempts should be made to quantify educational output. The determination of input-output relationships will require longitudinal studies. McNamera, Johnson, and Deaton (1986) further charge that acceptable measures of the multiple outputs have not yet been developed and caution that the relationships between student achievement and various inputs are unknown. Variables used as output measures should be broadened to include student follow-up data in addition to standardized test scores (Colvin, 1989). Berne (1982) and MacPhail-Wilcox (1985) cited the need for equity studies to focus on the educational outcomes for individual students, particularly those who are low-achieving and/or high risk. Such an approach would require the integration of macro/microeconomic analysis in determining outcomes. Thompson, Camp, Horn, and Stewart (1988) argue that most research has not shown clear relationships between student achievement and measurable inputs such as expenditures and facilities.

Outcome measurement is further complicated by the unique community development role of rural schools. Robert J. Maurer, Executive Deputy Commissioner, New York State Education Department ("Elementary, Secondary, and Higher Education in Rural N.Y. State: An Action Strategy," 1985), observed that rural schools serve a dual purpose. In addition to meeting the educational needs of their pupils, they also must assume a key role in the life and vitality of the communities they serve.

Student Populations and Outcomes

It is not usually recognized that rural students are highly heterogeneous in ethnicity, race, place of origin, socio-economic status, lifestyle, and value orientation. The rural experience for youth is no more, or perhaps less, uniform than the urban inner city experience (Edington, 1987). This diverse student population represents one-third of the national student population and is lumped together as *rural.* "Rural New England is quite different from rural Iowa, and both are quite different from rural Alaska or rural Texas" (Rios, 1987, p. 1).

The popular belief is that small and/or rural schools provide their students education inferior to that provided by urban and suburban schools. Emerging research links differences in student achievement to socioeconomic status which is generally low in the poverty cultures of rural America and to limited curricula prevalent in many small rural schools (Edington, 1987). After a decade of growth in the 70s, income, population, and overall rural economic activity have stalled. The so-called farm crisis goes beyond the price paid for agricultural goods and permeates every aspect of rural life. Rural areas are becoming less attractive to manufacturers while collection of property taxes to provide services including education is down. Rural poverty is more pervasive in family and community impact than urban poverty. This situation is further complicated by the greater number of school-age children per capita in rural areas and the national emphasis on standardizing educational expectations. Those rural areas which are least able to provide education are expected to deliver services comparable to those elsewhere (Rios, 1987). Determining the quality of educational services is a problem which must include community and sub-culture differences in rural areas (Helge, 1987). One aspect of many rural subcultures are low family expectations of rural students' career options and the limited view by the community of existing occupational roles for rural youth (Edington, 1987). Such factors substantiate the need for federal policy which recognizes the diversity of rural communities and populations and leads to provision of necessary resources without counter-productive restrictions.

Effective policy will be dependent on rural education research which provides precise information which can be used by policy makers. Education reform efforts likewise must provide direction for school improvement in a variety of organizational alternatives (Rios, 1987).

The Rural Poor

The National Committee noted that education has different meanings for the poor and nonpoor: "To the middle class it stands for the road to better things for one's children and one's self. To the poor it is an obstacle course to be surmounted until the children can go to work" (Hooshyar and Cain, 1986, p. 3). Testimony before a U.S. Congressional Committee in 1975 revealed that only 5 percent of research dollars, 11 percent of library and material funds, 13 percent of basic vocational aid, 13 percent of dropout prevention funds, and disproportionately low levels of most other federal education funds do go to nonmetropolitan areas (Hooshyar and Cain, 1986).

Ruralness derives its definition from its isolation, both geographically and demographically, labor intensive income base, and pervasive poverty. Harl (1985) states:

> Although educational systems (in Iowa) to date have been modestly affected by the economic trauma affecting much of agriculture, successive waves of adjustment are almost certain to affect—1) the scale of educational delivery systems, 2) the way education is financed in rural areas, 3) the range of educational services available, and 4) the willingness and ability of local districts to provide levels of educational services justified by overall societal benefit and cost. (p. 4)

Bagby and others (1985) concluded: In Appalachian Kentucky, existing sources of revenue are not allowing Appalachian counties to accept full responsibility for education. They further report:

The median proportion of students classified as economically deprived in Appalachian systems exceeded the median proportion of economically deprived students in non-Appalachian systems by almost 60% in 1984. As a result of the economic hard times (early 1980's), the percentage of economically deprived students in Appalachian school districts has actually risen over the past decade. (Bagby et al., 1985, p. 7)

Brown (1987) points out that a disproportionate share of the nation's poor have resided in nonmetro areas throughout this century. For example, in 1985, the nonmetro poverty rate was 18.3 as opposed to a 12.7 metro poverty rate. Ironically, the poverty level of rural areas is usually not offset by federal support. The proportionately greater need for elementary and secondary education programs in rural areas derives from the "higher proportion of children, relatively fewer young adults and middle aged persons, and larger proportion of the elderly" (Brown, 1987, p. 6).

Research conducted by McNamera, Johnson, and Deaton (1986) indicated that in rural states (including Virginia), farm families that expected children to migrate for employment opportunity demanded higher quality education. Formal education was valued less in the most rural counties and in counties having a high proportion of non-white residents. However, Bagby and others (1985) found that while rural Kentuckians ranked economic issues higher than education as the top problem in Kentucky, they were as supportive of educational reform and increased funding as other Kentuckians.

Special and Comprehensive Education

In addition to the much higher poverty levels of rural areas, rural schools serve greater percentages of handicapped children. This is due to less prenatal and postnatal care, less availability of social services and other related factors (Helge, 1983). Consequently, rural populations include a larger number of students who qualify for special and/or compensatory education. Helge (1987) found that following the enactment of

Public Law 94–142, a dramatic 47 percent increase occurred in the rate of identification and service provision for rural students with low incidence handicaps. Edington and Martellaro (1984) concluded that the percentage of students eligible for Chapter I compensatory education programs appeared to be dependent primarily on socio-economic status and secondarily on ethnicity. Blacks, Hispanics, and lower socio-economic status whites were most often found in compensatory classes. Given the severity of educational need among the general population in rural areas, the National Association for Retarded Citizens noted in 1980 that some local school districts were discouraging expenditures for handicapped students based on a feeling that these individuals would not become productive members of society (Hooshyar and Cain, 1986).

Education For Gifted and College Bound

The Marland Commission (1972) report to the U.S. Congress stated that gifted and talented children are deprived and can suffer permanent impairment to their intellectual abilities if their special needs are not met. This report focused national attention on the plight of the gifted students in the public schools. A new definition of giftedness was formulated in an attempt to encourage state and local funding of programs for the gifted. The report called for action to eliminate the widespread neglect of gifted children and noted that identification and education of the gifted was hampered by apathy and even hostility among school personnel. These attitudes are exacerbated when attempting to meet the needs of rural gifted children (Spicker, Southern, and Davis, 1987). As stated by Howley, Howley, and Pendarvis (1986), schools attempt to serve the greatest number for the least amount of money rather than prioritizing the needs of students with special needs. Furthermore, students from economically disadvantaged homes such as are prevalent in rural areas are rarely identified for their giftedness, and even where programs for the gifted exist, these students seldom are included in them (Davis and Rimm, 1985).

Special instructional programs for gifted students are lacking in the majority of rural settings and are at best fragmented and discontinuous (Cox et al., 1985). Many small rural schools find it financially impossible to support additional programs for a limited portion of the student cohort. The best that most schools can offer to gifted students is vertical or lateral accelerated learning within the existing curriculum (Diezsi and Cummings, 1985). The limited programing for gifted students is intensified for gifted females who are less likely than males to realize their full potential (Shaffer, 1986). A growing number of educational researchers are concluding that interactive distance learning technologies may offer viable and cost-effective alternatives for educating gifted and college bound students in rural and small schools (Canter, 1986a; Barker, 1987a,b; Pease and Tinsley, 1986; Hansen, 1987).

At-Risk Students

The on-going research into the problems of dropping-out presents a dire picture of our national educational efforts. While the national dropout average hovers around 20 percent, the average dropout rate for small and rural schools may be 40 to 50 percent. The Appalachian area alone has 125 counties which exceed the national dropout average. There, 31 counties have at least twice the national average dropout rate (Pizzano, 1985). This decade, trends in rural America has been reflected in the national economy through lagging production and diminished quality of manufactured goods (Mann, 1985c).

The current literature in the field identifies the recurrent themes of low socio-economic status, teenage pregnancy, and family conflict, together with peer pressure and low self-esteem as assumed variables in understanding at-risk students. The at-risk student is typified by identification with one or more of five very broad categories; (1) ranking in the bottom two-fifths of their class, (2) over-age for their grade, (3) student selection of certain targeted curricula, (4) excessive absenteeism, and (5) exhibition of behavior unacceptable in the classroom setting.

Stratification of students is inherent within the school system. McDill (1985) suggests that increased graduation requirements incorporated in school reform efforts intensifies the academic instruction of students in pre-college curricular areas, and increases the likelihood of at-risk students to drop out. Students who fail to learn may be a product of a school that failed to teach. Mann (1985a) differentiates between dropout students who fail to learn, and pushouts, students whom the school failed to teach. Bing & Wheeler (1986) point to this group as being at greater risk of dropping out due to the pervasive low socio-economic status, low family expectations, and geographic isolation within the rural school setting.

Rock (1985) using data from the High School and Beyond Program indicates the linkage of decline in test scores with students being in general or vocational curriculum rather than an academic one. Doss (1986) found that course selection by at-risk students included school curricula with the lowest level of retention such as drama, fundamentals of mathematics, field sports and electronics. However, Doss' study indicated that while participation in varsity sports provided a high retention rate, increased academic requirements were limiting at-risk student eligibility.

Absenteeism may serve as a primary indicator of the potential of an individual student to be at risk. Catterall (1986) postulates that dropping out is the result of a lengthy process and that protracted absenteeism is indicative of the problem. Cooper (1984) and Cox and Spivey (1986) recognize the necessity of change in the absentee's self-image, attitude toward school and parents, and the level of participation of all parties to manage areas of remediation. Reid (1983a), Ranbom (1986), Porter and Gilberg-Porter (1984), and Natriello (1983) question the point at which persistent absenteeism converts to a dropout statistic, but assert that concentration of resources and establishment of priorities are essential for a prevention program to work. Hebard (1986), Kandel et al. (1983), and Lines and McGuire (1984) point to the teacher as the first line of defense in stemming persistent absenteeism. Weber (1987), VanSciver (1986), Wehlage et al. (1982), and Wehlage and

Rutter (1985) advocate the use of incentives and alternative schools as a curative of persistent absenteeism.

Behavior problems in school are usually carried over into the workplace and further deter the at-risk student from having a flourishing life cycle. Studies conducted by Ruby and Law (1983) and Rock et al. (1986) showed that overt behavior of at-risk students manifested negative attitudes toward school behavior policies. Bing and Wheeler (1986) believe that schools must make changes in their policies to reduce the potential for students to drop out.

Current dropout prevention strategies within rural schools are attempting to meet the at-risk students' unmet needs within the budgetary limitations of their fiscal scope. However, there are no guarantees that current efforts will not be superceded by some other pressing need within the educational system (Colvin, 1989; Honeyman, Thompson, and Wood, 1989; Monk, 1984a,b; Deaver and Brown, 1983).

Rural Females

Decades of research indicate that active student participation in the classroom relates to higher achievement in classrooms, but in elementary through post secondary classrooms male students receive more teaching attention than female students (Sadker and Sadker, 1982). The status of programming and expectations for females in rural areas is critical particularly in the educating of women in math and science.

There is a growing support for women's work outside of the home in rural areas (Brown, 1977). As the economic structure of rural America changes and the job and pay opportunities for females expand, the economic value of females' time increases. As the percentage of rural families living on farms decreases, the traditional expectations of the rural female as the farm wife change. Inflation and its impact on family purchasing power further encourage rural females to enter the workforce in spite of the conservative attitudes toward social behavior prevalent in rural areas. Brown and O'Leary (1977, 1979) reported that non-metro females tend to become discouraged in periods of high unemployment and refrain from searching for employment. This may be indicative of low self-esteem which Shaffer et al. (1986) identified as being a barrier to female career choice and achievement.

Rural School Outcomes

Curricular and extra curricular achievement by small school students may be similar to those of their town and city school counterparts. Muse, Ho, and Smith (1985) found that a number of graduates from small elementary schools scored well above average on college entrance examinations even though they had difficulty adjusting during their first year of high school. Barker and Gump (1964) found that students in small schools derive their satisfaction and enjoyment from displaying competence and meeting challenges. Edington and Gardener (1984) reported data collected in Montana that indicated that students in small elementary and secondary schools had more positive attitudes toward their schools and themselves than did students in larger schools. Lawrence Kiley, Superintendent of the Union Springs Central School District in New York state argues that rural students from small schools tend to be highly dedicated, responsible, and self-reliant (1985).

A higher percentage of students from small schools participate in extracurricular activities (Horn, Anschulz, Davis, and Parmley, 1986; Barker and Gump, 1964). In spite of the fact that students from small/rural schools are more likely to participate in extracurricular and classroom activities and to be more involved in leadership, they are still more likely to leave school before graduation (Pizzano, 1985).

Pedagogy in Rural Schools

Goodlad's (1983) comprehensive study of schooling in the United States revealed that teachers continue to teach very much as they were taught, using materials very much like those through which they learned while students in schools. A narrow range of teaching strategies is used, particularly in secondary schools. Classrooms are unexciting places with little emotional involvement of teachers or students. Grouping practices in elementary schools and secondary tracking result in students from low socio-economic backgrounds experiencing defeat and failure in schools. Teachers' low expectations are generally realized.

Research conducted by Barnes and Defino (1983) found in student teaching programs specific differences in methodology and content relating to rural teaching practices. The result of the comparison found that potential rural teachers expressed greater satisfaction with their training and felt better prepared for their futures as teachers. However, as inequity of rural school funding continues and the number of rural students to be served declines, the resulting loss of revenues will mean small school districts will do less hiring. Rural schools will then be staffed primarily with local teachers with the greatest seniority and least exposure to the latest methodologies (O'Connell and Hagan, 1985).

Matthes and Carlson (1986) found that academically talented teachers are more likely to leave the profession than are less academically talented teachers. They agree with Boyer (1983) in laying the burden on policy and practices of universities and colleges that "call for excellence in the schools while spending several hundred million dollars every year recruiting prospective athletes and spending virtually no time or money recruiting prospective teachers" (p.3).

Matthes and Carlson (1985) found that rural teachers valued the pace of life, cost of living and school size while suburban and urban teachers were more likely to value professional autonomy, starting salary, and other professional rewards. Rural teachers viewed support from parents and community as important while urban/suburban teachers looked to support from the administration. Matthes and Carlson also reported that rural communities are already experiencing difficulties recruiting teachers for schools with small enrollments or limited school and community facilities and for schools remote from major metropolitan areas or in communities of less than 2500 inhabitants.

Rural communities isolated from societal trends or which place teachers in a "fishbowl" situation also experience recruiting difficulties. Low salaries in rural school districts contribute to problems in recruiting and retaining teachers.

Monk and Haller (1986) found that in small schools, teacher assignment and course scheduling can be factors in equality of educational opportunities. In small schools teacher assignment to multiple subjects contributes to lower teacher productivity while scheduling of limited courses forces students to choose between desired courses. It was concluded that a school needs 400 or more students to benefit from teacher specialization. Barker (1985) also noted the greater likelihood that prospective teachers choosing to teach in rural schools would be required to teach more subjects or multiple grades. Traugh (1984) in her survey of North Dakota secondary teachers found that rural teachers worked up to 18 hours a day and were sometimes at school four nights a week and on weekends.

The needs of smaller districts for teacher licensure policies which allow for generalists with multiple endorsements is not considered by certifying institutions (Swift, 1985). Yet, the effective schools research has demonstrated a need for enhancing the professional commitment and talent evident among many rural teachers (Buttram and Carlson, 1983).

Staff development in rural schools is being further impacted by demands that teachers increase their competence in science and mathematics, higher order thinking skills, and computer-related instruction. According to O'Connell and Hagan (1985) these new curricular and instructional practices are based on abstract thought incongruent with the concrete, manual applications characteristic of the rural context. They contend that these emerging instructional systems have little transfer value in rural settings and consequently rural teachers need special preparation in motivational techniques and instructional strategies. In contrast, Hofmeister (1984) points to unmistakable signs that technology is becoming a pervasive part of rural life and that rural educators have a particular responsibility to equip their students to use information age technology.

Efforts to Equalize Educational Opportunity

The popular image of rural education may be the "bucolic, serene, one-room schoolhouse set off in the countryside with a caring, nurturing, dedicated teacher administering to the needs of the students" to the few remaining children left in the countryside (Yount, 1986, p. 1). However, the realities of rural education include a significant percentage of the nation's students, frequently taught in ever larger consolidated schools (Davis, 1985; Bilow, Monk, Haller, and Bail, 1986; Helge, 1983). While as of 1985, there were still approximately 835 one-room schoolhouses in the United States including 114 in Montana (Yount, 1986), for decades the national trend has been toward consolidation justified on the basis of greater educational opportunity for the students, increased cost effectiveness and the organizational model prevalent in urban settings (Hobbs, 1985).

School Consolidation

Consolidation of rural school districts has disrupted the rural perception of community to the point that it is no longer considered as a first alternative in solving financial problems (Barker and Muse, 1986). However, consolidation continues to be viewed as the ultimate guarantee to prevent the closing of all district schools and limiting the disruption to a limited area of the district. Alternatives to consolidation are needed that will insure student access to quality education in the rural setting. Recent research has indicated that school size is not the primary determinant of school quality. Small/rural schools are not all bad and bigger schools are not always better (Bilow, Monk, Haller, and Bail, 1986).

School district size, student body population and impact of student socio-economic status appear to make a difference in terms of how school districts spend their funds:

> Some of the differences involve spending more on one category of student rather than another and may, therefore, violate basic standards of student equity.

Different aspects of size are related to internal
resources allocation practices in different ways. The
results suggest that heretofore neglected aspects of
school district size deserve additional attention as
background factors that may be related to differences
in educational opportunities (Monk, 1984a, p. 62–63).

Rural School Consortia

Small rural school districts can use resource and program
sharing to broaden and enrich the instructional services
available (Monk and Bail, 1986). Voluntary cooperative sharing
between independent school districts has been shown to
improve program delivery and versatility beyond that possible
for individual school or district (Galvin, 1986). The simplest
form of sharing may be a planned regional inservice. However,
even the simplest plans are complicated by the logistical or
political considerations involving such things as travel
distances, availability of a central meeting facility, or similar
decisions. The more complicated forms of resource sharing
usually require needs assessments, contracts, and the
leadership of a dedicated administrator capable of bringing
about acceptable compromises for the benefit of the students
and all involved in the program. Without financial incentives,
many small rural school districts will not attempt to enter into
the kinds of cooperative arrangements necessary to address
many of the problems facing them today (Monk and Haller,
1986).

One common mechanism for district sharing is Boards of
Cooperative Education Services (BOCES) in New York or
Regional Educational Service Agencies (RESA's) in West Virginia
(Galvin, 1986; Perry, Sanders, Stephens, Marockie, 1989).
These agencies typically have a superintendent accountable to
the State Department of Education who works directly with
managers in the member districts. The major criticisms are loss
of local control, catering to demands of larger member districts,
distance from the administrative center, and salary inequities
between member districts and the regional staff. These
problems have led to the establishment of informal sharing

arrangements in New York State. These informal arrangements target identified needs of the districts and often involve the sharing of unequal programs. These sharing programs are often developed in order to enhance curriculum but also districts to save money on faculty, transportation, and instructional materials without loss of local autonomy (Galvin, 1986).

The advent of such technologies as interactive television may pave the way for increased resource sharing among regional rural schools with small class enrollments. Through the use of such technology the costs of the instructor may be shared by participating schools (Galvin, 1984). Sharing programs are often developed in order to enhance curriculum but have the added benefit of allowing districts to save money on teaching staff, transportation and teaching materials with no concomitant decline in local autonomy (Galvin, 1986).

Another alternative is the establishment of rural school consortia which tap the pool of human resources available in colleges and universities to supplement the talents and resources of regional rural school districts (Crohn and Nelson, 1986). Colleges and universities can form the basis of rural educational research and provide for missing or limited expertise in grantsmanship. Formalized partnerships between schools and colleges help diminish isolation and build morale in rural schools while serving as a catalyst for change. Consortia can document local needs and communicate those to private funding organizations and governmental agencies in efforts to attract funding for rural school improvement projects (Yount, 1986). They may assume responsibility for multi-county teacher development (Gardner and Meadows, 1989).

The organizational alternatives available to rural schools are many and varied. Their success is limited only by the vision of the leadership involved and their willingness to compromise in the best interests of students. Continued success is dependent on public and private community involvement and the infusion of external funding to enhance programing in already cost efficient rural schools (Monk, 1984b; and his chapter in this volume).

Conclusion

It is obvious that rural communities are diverse and that any comprehensive strategy for rural educational improvement must recognize that educational opportunity for rural children in the United States is not currently equal (Gjelten and Dunne, 1982). To equalize opportunities in any one dimension of schooling is inadequate if one hopes to eliminate completely the effects of differences in educational opportunities nationally (Monk, 1984b). Some graduates of rural and small schools do score at national levels on academic achievement measures and many have perhaps experienced greater affective development. However, for the students with special needs the range of services available is not equitable. Whether as a result of limited educational opportunity or characteristics inherent in poor rural populations, the dropout rate in rural areas is indicative of educational programming which is not adequate to meet the needs of the rural clientele. It appears that past efforts to consolidate rural schools or form cooperative arrangements have been inadequate to equalize educational opportunity. The impact of developing technologies remains to be seen (Dubin, 1989). As long as educational opportunity and the funding of school are treated as local problems, the current situation will continue. Only when national policy makers realize the societal cost of educationally handicapping rural youth will fundamental change occur.

REFERENCES

Alexander, Karl L., et al. "For Whom the School Bell Tolls: The Impact of Dropping Out on Cognitive Performance." *American Sociological Review, 50* (June 1985): 409–420.

Alexander, Karl L., et al. "For Whom the School Bell Tolls: The Impact of Dropping Out on Cognitive Performance." Report No. 356.

Johns Hopkins University, Baltimore, Md. Center for Social Organizations in Schools. National Institute of Education, Washington, D.C., 1985. ERIC Document ED 253 842.

Alexander, Karl L., et al. "Getting Ready for First Grade: Standards of Deportment in Home and School." Report No. 8. Center for Research on Elementary and Middle Schools, Baltimore, Md. Office of Educational Research and Improvement (ED), Washington, D.C., 1987. ERIC Document ED 291 505.

Alexander, Karl L., et al. "School Performance, Status Relations, and the Structure of Sentiment: Bringing the Teacher Back In." Report No. 9. Center for Research on Elementary and Middle Schools, Baltimore, Md. Grant (W.T.) Foundation, New York, N.Y. Office of Educational Research and Improvement, Washington, D.C., 1987. 51p. ERIC Document ED 291 841.

Anderson, B. Harold, and Brouillette, Mary DeMaio. "The Effects of Increased Academic Requirements for Graduation on Secondary Vocational Enrollments in Colorado." Fort Collins, Colo., Colorado State University Department of Vocational Education, 1985. ERIC Document ED 254 628.

Anderson, B. Harold, and King, J. Wayne. "Perceptions of High Tech Industry Executives and Administrators of Public Two Year Postsecondary Institutions Regarding the Training Needs of High Tech Industries." Research Report. Fort Collins, Colo., Colorado State University Department of Vocational Education, June 1984. ERIC Document ED 250 488.

Anderson, Jack D. "Academic Preparation and Training of Speech-Language Pathologists for Positions in Rural Schools." Paper presented at the Annual Conference of the National Rural and Small Schools Consortium, Bellingham, Wash., October 7–10, 1986. ERIC Document ED 280 642.

Arbaiter, Solomon. "Enrollment of Blacks in College: Is the Supply of Black High School Graduates Adequate? Is the Demand for College by Blacks Weakening?" Research and Development Update. New York, N.Y., College Entrance Examination Board, 1987. ERIC Document ED 290 353.

Archambault, Reginald D., ed. *Sometimes a Shining Moment: The Foxfire Experience.* Garden City, N.Y.: Anchor Press/Doubleday, 1985.

Bagby, Jane, Carpenter, Claire, Crew, Keith, DeYoung, Alan, Eller, Ronald, Hougland, James, Jones, Jean, Nash, Francene, and Tickamyer, Cecil. "Education and Financial Resources in Appalachian Kentucky." Appalachian Data Bank Report no. 2, September 1985. ERIC Document ED 266 902.

Bailin, Michael A. "The California Conservation Corps: A Case Study. Working Paper No. 5. The State Youth Initiatives Project." Public/Private Ventures, Philadelphia, Pa., 1982. ERIC Document ED 227 327.

Barker, Bruce. "Research Focus on Rural Schools in Oklahoma." Paper presented at the First Annual Conference of Communities United for Rural Education, El Reno, Okla., April 27, 1985. ERIC Document ED 256 536.

Barker, Bruce O. "The Effects of Learning by Satellite on Rural Schools." Paper presented at the Learning by Satellite Conference, Tulsa, Okla., April 12–14, 1987a. ERIC Document ED 284 693.

Barker, Bruce O. "Interactive Distance Learning Technology for Rural and Small Schools: A Resource Guide." ERIC Mini-Review. Las Cruces, N.M. ERIC Clearinghouse on Rural Education and Small Schools, 1987b. ERIC Document ED 286 698.

Barker, Bruce, and Muse, Ivan. "One-Room Schools of Nebraska, South Dakota, California, and Wyoming." *Research in Rural Education, 3* (Spring 1986): 127–130. ERIC Document EJ 352 969.

Barker, Roger G., and Gump, Paul V. *Big School, Small School: High School Size and Student Behavior.* Stanford, Calif.: Stanford University Press, 1964.

Barnes, S., and Defino, M. "The Context of Student Teaching." Paper presented at the Annual Meeting of the American Educational Research Association, Montreal, Canada, April 11–15, 1983. ERIC Document ED 234 027.

Barro, Stephen M., and Kolstad, Andrew. "Who Drops Out of High School? Findings from High School and Beyond." Contractor's Report. Center of Education Statistics, (OERI/ED), Washington, D.C., 1987. ERIC Document ED 284 134.

Bass, Gail V., and Berman, Paul. *Federal Aid to Rural Schools: Current Patterns and Unmet Needs.* Santa Monica, Calif.: Rand Corporation, 1979.

Bass, Gerald R. "Enactment and Impact of Geographical Isolation Factors in Public School Revenue Legislation in Three Selected States." Unpublished dissertation. University of North Dakota, Grand Forks, N.D., 1980. ERIC Document ED 224 102.

Bass, Gerald R. "Current Legislation Regarding the Use of Geographical Isolation Factors in Public School Revenue Calculations." Paper presented at the 36th Annual Meeting of the National Conference of Professors of Educational Administration, San Marcos, Tex., August 15–20, 1982. ERIC Document ED 224 103.

Bass, Gerald R. "Financing Rural Education." Paper presented at the 78th National Conference of the Rural Education Association, Little Rock, Ark., October 12, 1986. ERIC Document ED 280 672.

Becker, Henry Jay. "The Second National Survey of Instructional Uses of School Computers: A Preliminary Report." Paper presented at the World Conference Computers in Education, Norfolk, Va., July 29–August 2, 1985. ERIC Document ED 274 307.

Becker, Henry Jay. "Our National Report Card: Preliminary Results from the New Johns Hopkins Survey." *Classroom Computer Learning,* 6 (January 1986): 30–33.

Becker, Henry Jay. "The Impact of Computer Use on Children's Learning: What Research Has Shown and What It Has Not." Johns Hopkins University, Baltimore, Md. Paper presented at the Annual Meeting of the American Educational Research Association, Washington, D.C., April 23, 1987. ERIC Document ED 287 458.

Benally, Elaine Roanhorse, Cole, Jack T., and Quezada-Aragon, Manuella. "Issues in American Indian Education, Mexican

American Education, Migrant Education, Outdoor Education, Rural Education, and Small Schools." Edited by Erwins Flaxman. ERIC Clearinghouse on Rural Education and Small Schools, Las Cruces, N.M., 1987. ERIC Document ED 281 909.

Berne, Robert, and Stiefel, Leanna. "A Methodological Assessment of Education Equality and Wealth Neutrality Measures. Washington, D.C., National Institute of Education." 1978. ERIC Document ED 228292.

Berne, Robert, and Stiefel, Leanna. "Alternative Measures of Wealth Neutrality." *Journal of Educational Evaluation and Policy Analysis, 4* (Spring 1982): 5–20.

Berne, Robert, and Stiefel, Leanna. "Changes in School Finance Equity: A National Perspective." *Journal of Education Finance, 8* (Spring 1983): 419–435.

Bilow, Scott (Investigators: Monk, David H., Haller, Emil J., and Bail, Joe P.). "Long Term Results of Centralization: A Case Study of a Large-Rural New York School District." Ithaca, N.Y., State University of New York College of Agriculture and Life Science at Cornell University, September, 1986a. ERIC Document ED 287 629.

Bilow, Scott (Investigators: Monk, David H., Haller, Emil J., and Bail, Joe P.). "The Size of School Districts: Economic and Psychological Perspectives." Ithaca, N.Y., State University of New York College of Agriculture and Life Science at Cornell University, September, 1986b. ERIC Document ED 287 634.

Bing, Stephen R., and Wheeler, Anne, comps. "Students At-Risk and the Schools They Go To: An Advocate's Bibliography." *Equity and Choices, 3* (Fall 1986): 12–13, 28.

Blackadar, Ann Riley, and Nachtigal, Paul. "Cotopaxi/Westcliffe Follow Through Project: Final Evaluation Report." Aurora, Colo. Mid-Continent Regional Educational Lab, June 30, 1986. ERIC Document ED 285 705.

A Book of Sources: Dropout Prevention. The National Committee for Citizens in Education. Columbia, Md.: 1987.

Bouchard, Yvon. "Cross-Cultural Comparative Studies of Effective Schools: A Review and Replication." Paper presented at the Annual Meeting of the American Educational Research Association, Montreal, Quebec, Canada, April 11–15, 1983. ERIC Document ED 242 073.

Bowers, J. Howard, and Burkett, Charles W. "Relationships of Student Achievement and Characteristics in Two Selected School Facility Environmental Settings." Paper presented at the Annual Conference of the Council of Educational Facility Planning (66th, Edmonton, Alberta, Canada, October 3–7, 1987). 15p. ERIC Document ED 286 278.

Boyer, E. L. *High School: A Report on Secondary Education in America.* New York: Harper and Row, 1983.

Brandt, Ron. "Defending Public Education from the Neo-Puritans." *Educational Leadership, 44* (May 1987): 3.

Brandt, Ron. "On School Improvement: A Conversation With Ronald Edmonds." *Educational Leadership, 40* (December 1982): 12–15.

Briggs, L. D. "High Morale Descriptors: Promoting a Professional Environment." *Clearing House, 59* (March 1986): 316–319.

Brown, Byron W., and Saks, Daniel H. "Spending for Local Public Education: Income Distribution and the Aggregation of Private Demand." *Public Finance Quarterly, 11* (January 1983): 21–45.

Brown, Byron W., and Saks, Daniel H. "The Revealed Influence of Class, Race, and Ethnicity on Local Public-Schools. *Sociology of Education, 58* (July 1985): 181–190.

Brown, David L. "Demographic Trends Relevant to Education in Nonmetro America." Paper presented at the Rural Education Symposium, Washington, D.C., March 30, 1987. ERIC Document ED 283 666.

Brown, David L., and O'Leary, Jeanne M. "Women's Labor Force Activity in Metropolitan and Nonmetropolitan Areas, 1960–1970." Paper presented at the Annual Meeting of the Rural Sociological

Society, Madison, Wisconsin, September 1977. ERIC Document
ED 144 731.

Brown, David L., and O'Leary, Jeanne M. "Labor Force Activity of
Women in Metropolitan and Nonmetropolitan America: Rural
Development Research Report No. 15." Washington, D.C.
Economic, Statistics, and Cooperatives Service (DOA), 1979.
ERIC Document ED 175 622.

Brown, Dennis E. "Higher Education Students from Rural Communities:
A Report on Dropping Out." Educational Document Research
Service, 1985. ERIC Document ED 258 771.

Bryk, Anthony S., et al. "Effective Catholic Schools, An Exploration. With
a Special Focus on Catholic Secondary Schools." Washington,
D.C., National Catholic Education Association, 1984.

Buttram, Joan L., and Carlson, Robert V. "Effective School Research:
Will it Play in the Country?" Research In Rural Education, 2
(November 1983): 73–78.

Campbell, Anne. "A Rural School Scoreboard." Paper presented at the
Annual Meeting of the National Rural Education Association
Conference, Cedar Rapids, Iowa, October 12–15, 1985. ERIC
Document ED 285 709.

Canter, Gary. "The Promise of Educational Technology." Ithaca, N.Y.,
State University of New York College of Agriculture and Life
Sciences at Cornell University, September 1986a. ERIC
Document ED 287 633.

Canter, Gary. "School District Reorganization: A Qualified Success."
Ithaca, N.Y., State University of New York College of Agriculture
and Life Sciences at Cornell University, September 1986b. ERIC
Document ED 287 624.

Carlson, Robert V. "School Assessment and Improvement: How Close
is the Relationship." Paper presented at the 67th American
Education Research Association Conference, San Francisco,
Calif., April 16–20, 1986. ERIC Document ED 4 067.

Catterall, James S. "On Social Costs of Dropping Out of School." Palo Alto, Calif., Publication Sales, Stanford Education Policy Institute, 1985. ERIC Document ED 271 837.

Catterall, James S. "A Process Model of Dropping Out of School: Implications for Research and Policy in an Era of Raised Academic Standards." Washington, D.C., Office of Educational Research and Improvement, 1985. ERIC Document ED 281 137.

Catterall, James S. "Dropping Out of School as a Process: Implications for Assessing the Effects of Competency Tests Required for Graduation. Effects of Testing Reforms and Standards." Working Draft. Washington, D.C., Office of Educational Research and Improvement, 1986. ERIC Document ED293 879.

Catterall, James S. "The Effects of Alternative School Programs on High School Completion and Labor Market Outcomes." *Education Evaluation and Policy Analysis, 8* (Spring 1986): 77–86.

Catterall, James S. "Toward Researching the Connections between Tests Required for High School Graduation and the Inclination to Drop Out of School. Project: Effects of Testing Reforms and Standards." Washington, D.C., Office of Educational Research and Improvement, 1987. ERIC Document ED 293 886.

Catterall, James S. "Standards and School Dropouts: A National Study of the Minimum Competency Test, 1988." ERIC Document ED 293 857.

Chan, Tak Cheung. "A Comparative Study of Pupil Attitudes Toward New and Old School Buildings, 1982." ERIC Document ED 222 981.

Chicoine, David L., and Langston, Suzanne W. "Structural Changes in Illinois Agriculture and Industry: Impact on Illinois School Finance." Paper presented at the School Policy Conference, Decatur, Illinois, September 19, 1985.

Clark, Sam, Crase, Sedahlia Jasper, and Pease, Damaris. "Child Rearing on the Farm." Paper presented at the 10th Annual Meeting of the National Symposium on Building Family Strengths, Lincoln, Neb., May 13–15, 1987.

Colvin, Richard L. "School Finance: Equity Concerns in an Age of Reforms." *Educational Researcher, 18* (January–February 1989): 11–15.

Cooper, Michael. "Self-Indentity in Adolescent School Refusers and Truants." *Educational Review, 36* (November 1984): 229–237.

Cox, J. Lamarr, and Spivey, Rita. "High School Dropouts in Appalachia: Problems and Palliatives." Research Triangle Park, N.C., Research Triangle Institute. 1986a. ERIC Document ED 272 343.

Cox, J. Lamarr, and Spivey, Rita. "Study of High School Dropouts in Appalachia." Paper presented at the Annual Meeting of the American Educational Research Association, San Francisco, Calif., April 16–20, 1986b. ERIC Document ED 264 992.

Cox, June, Daniel, Neil, and Boston, Bruce. "Educating Able Learners: Programs and Promising Practices. A National Study." *Executive Report.* Fort Worth, Tex., March 1985. ERIC Document ED 255 019.

Cox, J. L., Holley, J. A., Kite, R., and Durham, W. "Study of High School Dropouts in Appalachia." Washington, DC, Appalachian Regional Commission. Report Number RTI/3182–01/01 FR, May 22, 1985.

Crohn, Leslie, and Nelson, Steven R. "Rural Collaboratives: A Review of the Research. Washington, D.C. Department of Education." March 1986. ERIC Document ED 271 275.

Davis, Charles E. "If We Can Haul the Milk, We Can Haul the Kids. A Personalized History of a School District." Ithaca, N.Y., State University of New York College of Agriculture and Life Sciences Cornell University, September 1986.

Davis, G., and Rimm, S. *Education of the Gifted and Talented.* Englewood Cliffs, N.J.: Prentice-Hall, 1985.

Davis, L. D. "Remote Schools: A Dilemma Beyond Rural Education." Paper presented at the 77th National Conference of the Rural Education Association, Cedar Rapids, Iowa, October 13–15, 1985. ERIC Document ED 261 836.

Deaton, Brady J. and McNamara, Kevin T. "Education in a Changing Rural Environment: The Impact of Population and Economic Change on the Demand for and Costs of Public Education in Rural America. A Synthesis of Research Findings and an Identification of Important Policy Issues." Washington, D.C. Cooperative State Research Service (DOA), February 1984. ERIC Document ED 241 210.

Deavers, Kenneth L. "New Directions in Rural Policy." Paper presented at the Annual Meeting of Southern Rural Sociological Association, Nashville, Tenn., February 3, 1987. ERIC Document ED 281 685.

Deavers, Kenneth L., and Brown, David L. "Social and Economic Trends in Rural America. The White House Rural Development Background Paper." Washington, DC. White House Domestic Policy Staff, October 1979. ERIC Document ED 192 972.

Deavers, Kenneth L., and Brown, David L. "Natural Resource Dependence, Rural Development, and Rural Poverty." Rural Development Research Report Number 48. Washington, D.C., Economic Research Service (DOA), July 1983. ERIC Document ED 258 775.

Deavers, Kenneth L., et al. "Rural Development, Poverty, and Natural Resources: Workshop Paper Series. Part I. Socio-demographic and Economic Changes in Rural America; Rural Policy: An Independent View." Washington, D.C.; Resources for the Future, Inc. 1983. ERIC Document ED 258 749.

Diezsi, Cynthia P., and Cummings, William B. "An Educational Program for Gifted and Talented Students in a Rural Setting." Paper presented at the 63rd Annual Convention of the Council of Exceptional Children, Anaheim, Calif., April 15–19, 1985. ERIC Document ED 257 271.

Doss, David A. "Ninth Grade Course Enrollment and Dropping Out." Paper presented at the 67th Annual Meeting of the American Educational Research Association, San Francisco, Calif., April 16–20, 1986. ERIC Document ED 273 678.

Doss, David A. "Desegregation and Dropping Out in One School District." Paper presented at the Annual Meeting of the American

Educational Research Association, New Orleans, La., April 1984.
ERIC Document ED 247 353.

Dubin, Elliott. "Financing Rural Elementary and Secondary Education."
Charleston, W.Va. Appalachian Regional Educational Laboratory
1989.

Eberts, Paul R. "The Changing Structure of Agriculture and Its Effects on
Community Life in Northeastern U.S. Counties." Ithaca, N.Y.
State University of New York College of Agriculture and Life
Sciences Cornell University, August, 1979. ERIC Document ED
188 806.

Edington, Everett D. "ACT Scores of Incoming Freshmen to New
Mexico State University by High School Size." October 1981.
ERIC Document ED 272 354.

Edington, Everett D., and Gardener, Clark E. "The Relationship of School
Size to Scores in the Affective Domain from the Montana Testing
Service Examination." *Education, 105* (Fall 1984): 40–45.

Edington, Everett D., and Koehler, Lyle. "Rural Student Achievement:
Elements for Consideration." ERIC Digest. Washington, D.C.
Office of Educational Research and Improvement (ED),
December 1987. ERIC Document ED 289 658.

Edington, Everett D., and Martellaro, Helene C. "Variables Affecting
Academic Achievement in New Mexico Schools." Paper
presented at the Annual Meeting of the American Educational
Research Association, New Orleans, La., April 23–27, 1984. ERIC
Document ED 271 267.

"Elementary, Secondary, and Higher Education in Rural N.Y. State: An
Action Strategy 1985." Second Symposium of the New York
State Legislative Commission on Rural Resources, New Paltz,
N.Y., February 6–8, 1986.

Elliott, Judi. "Rural Students at Risk." Paper presented at the First Annual
Success for Students At-Risk Conference, Chicago, Ill., February
4–7, 1987. ERIC Document ED 285 708.

Elrod, G. Franklin. "Work Experience for the Rural, Special Needs Student: A Pipe Dream or a Possibility?" Paper presented at the Annual Conference of the National Rural and Small Schools Consortium, Bellingham, Wash., October 4–10, 1986. ERIC Document ED 280 645.

Fine, Michelle. "Dropping Out of High School: An Inside Look." *Social Policy, 16* (Fall 1985): 43–50.

Forbes, Roy H. "State Policy Trends and Impacts on Rural School Districts." Paper presented at the National Rural Education Forum, Kansas City, Mo., August 12–14, 1985. ERIC Document ED 258 787.

Galloway, D. "Research Notes: Truants and Other Absentees." *Child Psychology and Psychiatry and Allied Disciplines, 23* (October 1983): 607–611.

Galvin, Patrick. "Sharing Among Separately Organized School Districts: Promise and Pitfalls." Ithaca, N.Y. State University of New York College of Agriculture and Life Sciences Cornell University, August 1986. ERIC Document ED 287 631.

Galvin, Patrick. "School District Reorganization: A Case Study of the Community Participation Approach." Ithaca, N.Y. State University of New York College of Agriculture and Life Sciences, Cornell University, September 1986. ERIC Document ED 287 626.

Gardner, Earl, and Meadows, Mary Lou. "Staff Development for Rural School Teachers: The Regional Inservice Connection." Paper presented at the Annual Meeting of the Southern Rural Education Association, Nashville, Tenn., April 19–21, 1989.

Gaston, Suzan N. "LSYOU: The Effects of an Alternative Organizational Framework on Students at Risk for Dropping Out." Paper presented at the 71st Annual Meeting of the American Educational Research Association, Washington, D.C., April 20–24, 1987. ERIC Document ED 282 157.

Gjelten, Tom. "A Typology of Rural School Settings." Summary presentation prepared for the Rural Education Seminar, United

States Department of Education, Washington, D.C., May 3–5, 1982. ERIC Document ED 215 858.

Goodlad, John I. "Access to Knowledge." *Teachers College Record, 84* (Summer 1983): 787–800.

Griffin, Edward, et al. "Behavioral Outcomes of Alternative Programs for Junior High School Students at Risk of Dropping Out." Paper presented at the 68th Annual Meeting of the American Educational Research Association, New Orleans, La., April 23–27, 1984. ERIC Document ED 246 077.

Hannon, Bernard S., and Pullin, John E. "Building Partnerships for Quality Education in Rural America: The School Board/School Program Partnership." Paper presented at the National Conference on Building Partnerships for Quality Education in Rural America, Washington, D.C., June 28, 1984. ERIC Document ED 261 840.

Hansen, Kenneth H. "State Educational Policy and Proposition 13 Movement. An Overview of Policy Issues." Portland, Ore. Northwest Regional Educational Laboratory, Northwest Center for State Educational Policy Studies, February 1979. ERIC Document ED 225 245.

Hansen, Kenneth H. "Defining Quality Education: An Analysis of State Educational Policy Options." Portland, Ore. Northwest Regional Educational Laboratory, December 1979. ERIC Document ED 225 251.

Hansen, Kenneth H. "Strengthening Public Confidence in Education. Issues and Action Alternatives." Portland, Ore. Northwest Regional Educational Laboratory, Center for State Educational Policy Studies, June 1980. ERIC Document ED 225 255.

Hansen, Kenneth H. "Local-State-Federal Education Relationships: Issues Regarding Block Grants." Portland, Ore. Northwest Regional Educational Laboratory, Center for State Educational Policy Studies, March 1981. ERIC Document ED 225 258.

Hansen, Kenneth H. "Improving Educational Quality in a Time of Declining Resources. An Issue Analysis Paper." Portland, Ore. Northwest Regional Educational Laboratory, Center for State

Educational Policy Studies, September 1982. ERIC Document ED 226 409.

Hansen, Kenneth H. "Megatrends in American Society: Policy Issues for State Education Agencies. An Issue Analysis Paper." Portland, Ore. Northwest Regional Educational Laboratory, Center for State Educational Policy Studies, June 1983. ERIC Document ED 253 935.

Hansen, Kenneth H. "Distance Education and the Small School: Policy Issues." Portland, Ore. Northwest Regional Educational Laboratory, Center for State Educational Policy Studies, August 1987. ERIC Document ED 287 637.

Harl, Neil E. "The Changing Rural Economy: Implications for Rural America." Paper presented at the National Rural Education Forum, Kansas City, Mo., August 12–14, 1985. ERIC Document ED 258 782.

Hebard, Amy J., et al. "Final Evaluation of the 1984–85 Community School District Attendance Improvement Program." Brooklyn, N.Y., Student Progress Evaluation Unit, Office of Educational Evaluation, 1986. ERIC Document ED 285 926.

Helge, Doris. "Addressing the Report of the Commission on Excellence in Education . . . From the Rural Perspective." Murray, Ky. American Council on Rural Special Education (ACRES), August 1983. ERIC Document ED 234 939.

Helge, Doris. "Establishing an Empirically Determined National Rural Educational Research Agenda." *Research in Rural Education, 3* (Spring 1986): 99–105.

Helge, Doris. "Strategies for Improving Rural Special Education Program Evaluation." *Remedial and Special Education (RASE), 8* (July-August 1987): 53–60.

Hendler, Charles I., and Reid, J. Norman. "Federal Outlays in Fiscal 1978: A Comparison of Metropolitan and Nonmetropolitan Areas. Rural Development Research Report No. 25." Washington, D.C. Department of Agriculture, Economics,

Statistics, and Cooperative Service, September 1980. ERIC Document ED 194 294.

Hobbs, Daryl. "Bridging, Linking, Networking the Gap: Uses of Instructional Technologies in Small Rural Schools." Paper presented at the National Rural Education Forum, Kansas City, Mo., August 12–14, 1985. ERIC Document ED 258 786.

Hodgkinson, Harold. "Today's Curriculum—How Appropriate Will It Be in Year 2000?" *National Association of Secondary School Principals Bulletin, 71* (April 1987): 2–4, 6–7.

Hofmeister, Alan M. *Technological Tools for Rural Education.* Las Cruces, N.M. ERIC Clearinghouse on Rural Education and Small Schools (ERIC/CRESS). New Mexico State University, March 1984.

Holtzman, Wayne H., Jr. "The Influence of Sociocultural Factors on the Achievement and Placement of Limited English Proficient Hispanic Students." Washington, D.C. Office of Special Education and Rehabilitative Services (ED), June 1985. ERIC Document ED 261 485.

Honeyman, David S., Thompson, David C., and Wood, R. Craig. *Financing Rural and Small Schools: Issues of Adequacy and Equity.* Charleston, W.Va. ERIC Clearinghouse on Rural Education and Small Schools, 1989.

Hooshyar, Nahid T., and Cain, Alicia. "Parent Perceptions of the Support System in the Rural Area." Paper presented at the Annual Conference of the National Rural and Small Schools Consortium, Bellingham, Wash., October 7–10, 1986. ERIC Document ED 282 672.

Horn, Jerry, Anschulz, Jeffery, Davis, Patricia, and Parmley, Fran. "A Study of Rural/Small Schools and Their Graduates in a Seven State Area." Aurora, Colo. Mid-Continent Regional Educational Laboratory, November 1986. ERIC Document ED 280 657.

Howley, C. *Intellectually Gifted Students: Issues and Policy Implications.* Charleston, W.Va.: Appalachian Education Laboratory, 1986.

Howley, A., Howley, C., and Pendarvis, E. *Teaching Gifted Children.* Boston: Little, Brown and Company, 1986.

Jacobson, Stephen L. "Administrative Leadership and Effective Small-Rural Schools: A Comparative Case Study." Ithaca, N.Y. State University of New York College of Agriculture and Life Sciences Cornell University, September 1986. ERIC Document ED 276 545.

Jensen, Darrell, and Widvey, Lois. "The South Dakota Small School Cluster." *Rural Educator, 8* (Fall 1986): 7–11.

Jones, Barbara Jean. "Preservice Programs for Teaching in a Rural Environment: Survey of Selected States and Recommendations. Summary of the Results and Recommendations." Fall 1985 22p. ERIC Document ED 261 826.

Kaagan, Steve, and Smith, Marshall S. "Indicators of Educational Quality." *Educational Leadership, 43* (October 1985): 21–24.

Kaeser, Susan C. "Citizen Guide to Children Out of School: The Issues, Data, Explanations and Solutions to Absenteeism, Dropouts, and Disciplinary Exclusion. Cleveland, Ohio. Citizen's Council for Ohio Schools, 1984. ERIC Document ED 250 421.

Kaeser, Susan C., and Hooper, Paula K. "Seventh and Eighth Grade Dropouts in Ohio: Research on Who They Are, Why They Leave and How School Districts Count Them." Cleveland, Ohio. Citizen's Council for Ohio Schools, 1983. ERIC Document ED 236 488.

Kandel, Denise B., et al. "Continuity in Discontinuities: Adjustment in Young Adulthood of Former School Absentees. *Youth and Society, 15* (March 1984): 325–352.

Kaplan, George R. "Items for the Agenda. Educational Research and the Report on Excellence." Washington, D.C. National Institute of Education (ED), 1985. ERIC Document ED 273 566.

Kitchen, Will. "Education and Telecommunications: Partners in Progress." Testimony to the Senate Committee on Labor and Human Services, March 11, 1987. ERIC Document ED 282 551.

Knapp, Clifford C., Swan, Malcolm, Vogl, Sonia, and Vogl, Robert. "Using the Outdoors to Teach Social Studies: Grades 3–10." Washington, D.C. Office of Educational Research and Improvement (ED), 1986. ERIC Document ED 269 192.

Kutner, Mark A. and Sherman, Joel D. "An Intergovernmental Perspective on Federal Education Grants." *Peabody Journal of Education, 60* (Fall 1982): 67–81.

Lawless, Ken. "The Family Support System: Education in Its Broadest Context. Harvesting The Harvestors. Book 4." Washington, D.C. Department of Education, 1986. ERIC Document ED 279 469.

LeCompte, Margaret D. "The Cultural Context of Dropping Out: Why Remedial Programs Fail to Solve the Problems." *Education and Urban Society, 19* (May 1987): 232–249.

LeCompte, Margaret D., and Goebel, Stephen D. "Can Bad Data Produce Good Program Planning? An Analysis of Record-Keeping on School Dropouts." *Education and Urban Society, 19* (May 1987): 250–268.

Lines, Patricia, and McGuire, Kent. "Education Reform and Education Choices: Conflict and Accommodation. Washington, D.C. National Institute of Education (ED), 1984. ERIC Document ED 253 960.

Lowrance, Danny, and Tweeten, Luther. "Implications of Current and Proposed Funding Plans for Oklahoma Common Schools. Research Report P–748." Stillwater, Okla. Oklahoma State University Agricultural and Experiment Station, March 1977. ERIC Document ED 195 371.

MacPhail-Wilcox, Bettye. "Fiscal Equity for Public Schools in a Nonreform State: North Carolina, 1975 to 1983." *Journal of Education Finance, 10* (Spring 1985): 417–425.

Maeroff, Gene I. "Withered Hopes, Stillborn Dreams: The Dismal Panorama of Urban Schools." *Phi Delta Kappan, 69* (May 1988): 632–638.

Mann, Dale. "Report of the National Invitational Working Conference on Holding Power and Dropouts." New York, N.Y., February 13–15, 1985a. Columbia University Teachers College, 1985a. ERIC Document ED 257 927.

Mann, Dale. "Education Vital Signs: Curriculum." *Executive Educator, 7* (October 1985b): A15-A20.

Mann, Dale. "Action on Dropouts." *Educational Leadership, 43* (September 1985c): 16–17.

Mann, Dale. "Regional Workshop on Dropout: Proceedings." Washington, D.C. Appalachian Regional Commission, 1985d.

Mann, Dale. "Dropout Prevention: Getting Serious About Programs that Work." *National Association of Secondary School Principals, 70* (April 1986): 66–73.

Marland, S. *Education of the Gifted and Talented: Report to the Congress of the United States by the U.S. Commissioner of Education.* Washington, D.C.: U.S. Government Printing Office, 1972.

Matthes, William A., and Carlson, Robert V. "Recruitment and Staff Development of Teachers: A Rural Perspective." Paper presented at the 77th Annual Conference of the Rural Education Association, Cedar Rapids, Iowa, October 12–15, 1985. ERIC Document ED 270 280.

Matthes, William A., and Carlson, Robert V. "Conditions for Practice: The Reasons Teachers Selected Rural Schools." Paper presented at the 67th Annual Meeting of the American Educational Research Association, San Francisco, Calif., April 16–20, 1986. ERIC Document ED 273 409.

McAvoy, Rogers. "Home-Bound Schools: An Alternative for Rural Areas." Paper presented at the Annual Conference of the National Rural and Small School Consortium, Bellingham, Wash., October 7–10, 1986. ERIC Document ED 280 633.

McDill, Edward L., et al. "Raising Standards and Retaining Students: The Impact of the Reform Recommendations on Potential Dropouts." *Review of Educational Research, 55* (Winter 1985a): 415–433.

McDill, Edward L., et al. *Raising Standards and Retaining Students: The Impact of the Reform Recommendations on Potential Dropouts.* Washington, D.C.: National Institute of Education (ED), 1985b.

McNamara, Kevin T., Johnson, Thomas G., and Deaton, Brady J. "A Simultaneous Model of Education Supply and Demand." Virginia Polytechnic Institute and State University, Department of Agricultural Economics, February 1986. ERIC Document ED 273 424.

Mensch, Barbara S., and Kandel, Denise B. "Dropping Out of High School and Drug Involvement." *Teachers College Record, 87* (April 1988): 95–113.

Monk, David H. "The Conception of Size and the Internal Allocation of School District Resources." *Educational Administration Quarterly, 20* (Winter 1984a): 39–67.

Monk, David H. "Stalking Full Fiscal Neutrality: The Distinction Between School District Wealth and Tastes." *Educational Theory, 34* (Winter 1984b): 55–73.

Monk, David H. "Secondary School Enrollment and Curricular Comprehensiveness: Organizational Alternatives for Small Rural Schools in New York State." Ithaca, N.Y. State University of New York College of Agriculture and Life Sciences at Cornell University, August 1986. ERIC Document ED 287 628.

Monk, David H., and Bliss, James R. "Financing Rural Schools In New York State. The Facts and Issues." Cornell Information Bulletin 182. Ithaca, N.Y. State University of New York College of Agriculture and Life Sciences, Cornell University, February 1982. ERIC Document ED 238 597.

Monk, David H., and Haller, Emil J. "Organizational Alternatives for Small Rural Schools. Final Report to the Legislature of the State of New York." Ithaca, N.Y. State University of New York College of Agriculture and Life Sciences, Cornell University, December 1986. ERIC Document ED 281 694.

Morrow, George. "Standardizing Practice in the Analysis of School Dropouts. *Teachers College Record, 87* (Spring 1986): 342–55.

Mote, Leona L., Morton, Jerome H., and Marshall, Cindy. "Career Training: Strategies for Training Disadvantaged, Rural Youth." Paper presented at the Annual Conference of the National Rural and Small Schools Consortium, Bellingham, Wash., October 7–10, 1986. ERIC Document ED 279 450.

Murphy, Sheila C., and Huling-Austin, Leslie. "The Impact of Context on the Classroom Lives of Beginning Teachers." Paper presented at the Annual Meeting of the American Educational Research Association, Washington, D.C., April 20–24, 1987. ERIC Document ED 283 780.

Muse, Ivan, Ho, Kevin T., and Smith, Ralph B. "A Study of the Performance of Students from Small Country Elementary Schools When They Attend High School." Paper presented at the National Rural Education Association Conference, Cedar Rapids, Iowa, October 12–15, 1985. ERIC Document ED 261 843.

Natriello, Gary. "Organizational Evaluation Systems and Student Disengagement in Secondary Schools." Paper presented at the Annual Meeting of the American Educational Research Association, Montreal, Quebec, Canada, April 11–15, 1983. ERIC Document ED 242 077.

Natriello, Gary. "Problems in the Evaluation of Students and Student Disengagement from Secondary Schools." *Journal of Research and Development in Education, 17* (Summer 1984): 14–24.

Natriello, Gary. *School Dropouts: Patterns and Policies.* New York, NY.: Teachers College Press, 1986.

Natriello, Gary, et al. "School Reforms and Potential Dropouts. *Educational Leadership, 43* (September 1985): 10–14.

Natriello, Gary, et al. "Taking Stock: Reviewing Our Research Agenda on the Causes and Consequences of Dropping Out." *Teachers College Record, 87* (Spring 1986): 430–440.

Nelson, Kerry D. "Report on Utah's Rural Schools." Paper presented at the 77th National Rural Education Association Conference, Cedar Rapids, Iowa, October 13–15, 1985. ERIC Document ED 261 839.

Novak, Jan, and Dougherty, Barbara, eds. "Staying In: A Dropout Prevention Handbook, K–12, Workshop Edition." Madison, Wis. Wisconsin State Department of Public Instruction, Bureau for Vocational Education. ERIC Document ED 246 315.

O'Connell, Carleen, and Hagans, Rex. "Staff Development in Rural Schools." Washington, D.C. National Institute of Education (ED), November 1985. ERIC Document ED 265 009.

Odden, Allan. "School Finance in Colorado: An Update." Paper in Education Finance No. 8. Denver, Colo. Education Commission of the States, Education Finance Center, November, 1978. ERIC Document ED 226 419.

Owens, Thomas R., and Crohn, Leslie. "Designing Excellence in Secondary Vocational Education: Application of Principles From Effective Schooling and Successful Business Practice." Paper presented at the American Vocational Education Research Association Convention, New Orleans, La., December 2, 1984. ERIC Document ED 255 733.

Payne, Milton P. "Using the Outdoors to Teach Science: A Resource Guide for Elementary and Middle School Teachers." Washington, D.C. National Institute of Education (ED), 1985. ERIC Document ED 264 059.

Pease, Pamela S., and Tinsley, Patsy J. "Reaching Rural Schools Using an Interactive Satellite Based Educational Network: Evaluating TI-IN Networks First Year." Paper presented at the Annual Conference of the National Rural and Small Schools Consortium, Bellingham, Wash., October 7–10, 1986. ERIC Document ED 281 681.

Peng, Samuel S. and Takai, Ricky T. "High School Dropouts: Descriptive Information from High School and Beyond." National Center for Education Statistics Bulletin. Washington, D.C. National Center for Educational Statistics (ED), 1983. ERIC Document ED 234 366.

Perry, Bill, Sanders, Jack, Stephens, Robert, and Marockie, Henry. "Educational Services Agencies: Their Role in Southern Education." Paper presented at the Annual Meeting of the Southern Rural Education Association, Nashville, Tenn., April 19–21, 1989.

Phelps, Margaret S., and White, Joanne. "Effective Rural Schools." Paper presented at the Annual Meeting of the Southern Association of Schools and Colleges, Atlanta, Ga., December 1988.

Pizzano, W. A. "Regional Workshop on Dropouts: Proceedings." Washington, D.C. Appalachian Regional Commission, 1985.

Porter, Robert F., and Gilberg-Porter, Jody. "Survey of Attitudes of Incarcerated Felons on Dropping Out of Public School." *Journal of Correctional Education, 35* (September 1984): 80–82.

Prestholdt, Perry H., and Fisher, Jack L. "Dropping Out of High School: An Application of the Theory of Reasoned Action." Paper presented at the Annual Meeting of the Southeastern Psychological Association, Atlanta, Ga., March 23–26, 1983. ERIC Document ED 244 178.

Quinones, Nathan. "Dropout Prevention Programs, 1985–1986. Progress Report." Brooklyn, N.Y. New York City Board of Education, 1986. ERIC Document ED 279 750.

Ranbom, Sheppard. *School Dropouts: Everybody's Problem.* Washington, D.C.: Institute of Educational Leadership, Inc., 1986.

"Regional Workshop on School Dropouts: Proceedings." Papers presented at the Appalachian Regional Commission Meeting at Atlanta, Ga., June 25–27, 1985.

Reid, Ken. "Institutional Factors and Persistent School Absenteeism." *Educational Management and Administration, 11* (June 1983): 17–27.

Reid, Ken. "Retrospection and Persistent School Absenteeism." *Educational Research, 25* (June 1983): 110–115.

Reynolds, Carl L. "Enriching the Rural School Curriculum through Telecommunications." Paper presented at the 2nd Annual Meeting of the National Rural Teacher Education Conference Bellingham, Wash., October 8–10, 1986. ERIC Document ED 275 466.

Rios, Betty Rose D. "A Directory of Organizations and Programs in Rural Education." Las Cruces, N.M. ERIC Clearinghouse on Rural Education and Small Schools, March 1986. ERIC Document ED 273 423.

Rios, Betty Rose D. "Selected Trends and Issues in Rural Education and Small Schools." Las Curces, N.M. ERIC Clearinghouse on Rural Education and Small Schools, October 1987 20p. ERIC Document ED 289 669.

Rock, Donald A., et al. "Study of Excellence in High School Education: Longitudinal Study, 1980–82 Final Report." Washington, D.C. Office of Educational Research and Improvement (ED), 1986. ERIC Document ED 275 744.

Rock, Donald A., et al. "Factors Associated with Decline of Test Scores of High School Seniors, 1972 to 1980. A Study of Excellence in High School Education: Education Policies, School Quality, and Student Outcomes. Contractor Report." Washington, D.C. Office of Educational Research and Improvement (ED), 1985. ERIC Document ED 271 517.

Rosenbaum, Paul R. "Dropping Out of High School in the United States: An Observational Study." *Journal of Educational Statistics, 11* (Fall 1986): 207–224.

Ross, Elinor P., and Fletcher, R. K. "Responses to Children's Literature by Environment, Grade Level, and Sex." *The Reading Instruction Journal* (Winter 1989): 22–28.

Rossmiller, Richard A. "Achieving Equity and Effectiveness in Schooling. *Journal of Education Finance, 12* (Spring 1987): 561–577.

Ruby, Theodore, and Law, Robert. "School Dropouts—Why Does the Problem Prevail?" Paper presented at the 19th Annual Meeting of the National Association of School Psychologists, New Orleans, La., March 4–8, 1987. ERIC Document ED 289 095.

Ruby, Theodore, and Law, Robert. "Potential School Dropouts—The Attitude Factor." Paper presented at the 91st Annual Convention of the American Psychological Association, Anaheim, Calif., August 26–30, 1983. ERIC Document ED 246 347.

Rumberger, Russell W. "Dropping Out of High School: The Influence of Race, Sex, and Family Background." *American Educational Research Journal, 20* (Summer 1983): 199–220.

Sadker, M., and Sadker, D. "An Analysis of Teacher Interaction with Male and Female Students in Grades 4, 6, and 8." Paper presented at the American Educational Research Association Annual Meeting, New York, N.Y., 1982.

Silver, Sandra. "Compliance with P.L. 94–142 Mandates: Implications for Teacher Training Programs." Paper presented at the Annual Conference of the National Rural and Small Schools Consortium, Bellingham, Wash., October 7–10, 1986. ERIC Document ED 280 631.

Shaffer, Susan M. "Gifted Girls: The Disappearing Act." *The Report Card #6.* Washington, D.C.: The Mid-Atlantic Center for Sex Equity, The NETWORK, Inc., 1986.

Slawski, Carl. "Rival Hypotheses about Teaching and Facilitating Learning." Paper presented at the Annual Meeting of the Pacific Sociological Association, San Francisco, Calif., April 11, 1980. ERIC Document ED 192 650.

Spicker, H., Southern, W., and Davis, B. "The Rural Gifted Child." *Gifted Child Quarterly, 31* (1987): 155–157.

Steinberg, Laurence, et al. "Dropping Out Among Language Minority Youth: A Review of the Literature." NCBR Report. Washington, D.C. National Institute of Education (ED), 1982. ERIC Document ED 241 831.

Steinberg, Laurence, et al. "Dropping Out Among Language Minority Youths." *Review of Educational Research, 54* (Spring 1984): 113–132.

Strong, Kathryn Ringhand. "Mountain Roads, Lonely Mesas: A Career Program for Northern New Mexico." Paper presented at the Annual Conference of the National Rural and Small School Consortium, Bellingham, Wash., October 7–10, 1986. ERIC Document ED 280 632.

Strother, Deborah Burnett. "Dropping Out." *Phi Delta Kappan, 68* (December 1986): 325–328.

"A Study of Attendance Improvement/Dropout Prevention Program in the City of New York, 1986–87." New York State Education Department, Albany. Office of Elementary, Secondary, and Continuing Education, 1987. ERIC Document ED 285 934.

Stuhr, Christian. *Fear and Guilt in Adult Education: A Personal Account of Investigations into Students Dropping Out. A CKCC Research Service Publication.* Swift Current, Saskatchewan, Canada: Cypress Hills Community College, 1987. ERIC Document ED 285 093.

Swift, Doug. "Facilitating Certification and Professional Development for Small Schools." Las Cruces, N.M. ERIC Clearinghouse on Rural Education and Small Schools, March 1985. ERIC Document ED 260 884.

Talbott, Brian, and Holmes, Nancy. "Enhancing Quality Education in Rural Washington Schools." *Curriculum in Context, 13* (Spring/Summer 1985): 21–22.

Thomas, Ruth G., and Peterson, Roland L. "Access to Educational Opportunity in Rural Communities: Alternative Patterns of Delivering Vocational Education in Sparsely Populated Areas. Volume 1: Problem, Study Design and Procedures, Findings, Conclusions, and Recommendations." St. Paul, Minn. Minnesota University, Agricultural Experiment Station, 1984. ERIC Document ED 258 733.

Thompson, David C., Camp, William E., Horn, Jerry G., and Stewart, G. Kent. "State Involvement in Capital Outlay Financing: Policy Implications for the Future." Manhattan, Kans. Kansas State University, Center for Extended Studies, College of Education, 1989.

Tomlinson, J. R., Acker, N., Carter, A., and Lindborg, S. "Minority Status, Sex, and School Psychological Services. *Psychology in the Schools, 14* (1977): 456–460.

Traugh, Cecelia. "Rural High Schools: Heart of Education in North Dakota." *North Dakota Journal of Education, 63* (January 1984): 8–18.

Valdivieso, Rafael. "1980 High School Sophomores: Whites, Blacks, Hispanics—Where Are They Now?" *Research Bulletin, 1* (Fall 1986).

VanSciver, James. "Use Rewards to Boost Student Attendance (And Public Goodwill). *Executive Educator, 8* (June 1986): 22–23.

Weber, James M. *Strengthening Vocational Education's Role in Decreasing the Dropout Rate.* Columbus, Ohio. The National Center for Research in Vocational Education, Ohio State University, 1987.

Wehlage, Gary G., and Rutter, Robert A. "Dropping Out: How Much Do Schools Contribute to the Problem?" Washington, D.C. National Institute of Education (ED), 1985. ERIC Document ED 275 799.

Wehlage, Gary G., and Rutter, Robert A. "Dropping Out: How Much Do Schools Contribute to the Problem?" *Teachers College Record, 87* (Spring 1986): 374–392.

Wehlage, Gary G., et al. "Effective Programs for the Marginal High School Student: A Report to the Wisconsin Governor's Employment and Training Officer." Washington, D.C. National Institute of Education (ED). 1982. 200p. ERIC Document ED 222 452.

Wheelock, Anne. "Dropping Out: What the Research Says." *Equity and Choice, 3* (Fall 1986): 7–11.

Widvey, Lois, et al. "A Systematic Process for Developing Special Services Cooperatives in Rural School Districts." Paper presented at the Northern Rocky Mountain Educational Research Association meeting, Jackson Hole, Wy., October 11, 1985. 17p. ERIC Document ED 269 174.

Yount, Rebecca. "The Bridge to Arcadia: School/College Collaboration and the Rural Teacher." Paper presented at the Annual Conference of the National Rural and Small Schools Consortium, Bellingham, Wash., October 7–10, 1986. 25p. ERIC Document ED 279 449.

Resources in Rural Education

Teri A. Lipinski

The amount of information available to rural educators is greater than one might initially guess. Because of the sparcity of finances for rural education and the difficulty that many districts face in recruiting and retaining qualified educators, it is easy to assume that little information is available to assist individuals in rural settings.

The problem regarding resources in rural education does not seem to be the actual availability of information, but more the diversity that exists among rural settings making application of what is found difficult. What works ever so effectively in one rural school may flop beyond belief in another.

Resources can serve to provide a skeleton upon which each locale can build a program tailored to that area's unique needs. The combination of factors to consider in program planning include a clear definition of the need itself, local customs, geography, available materials, finances, skill levels of on-site staff, community support, and the availability of consultant services.

Dissemination of information to rural areas is another problem. Because rural individuals are (by definition) isolated, it

Special thanks to Bridget Karns, Student Assistant and Librarian, National Rural Development Institute.

takes intentional effort to network with other people. Getting materials that are available into the hands of concerned rural persons takes an equal intentional effort. A list such as the one offered on the following pages can provide a starting point for those seeking information, and can offer the beginnings of networking.

The lists that follow are broad and general. Unmentioned numbers of resources were left out because of space limitation. Efforts were made to include dissemination centers that could refer the information seeker to local resources and services.

One good resource for each state is the State Department of Education, known as the Office of Public Instruction in some states, located at the state capitol. The majority of these offices have a rural component or an individual who is knowledgeable about rural issues. State departments are a good place to begin an information search because they can be helpful in identifying local resources and services, and are familiar with unique regional needs.

Some information sources have headquarters located in a politically useful and large community, with regional offices, state offices, or cooperatives established to disseminate materials. These systems provide faster service for dissemination of information that is more appropriate to the specific locale. In some cases, the lists supplied in this chapter will contain the headquarters which, in turn, can supply a list of regional offices. When contacting any of the resources below, it is recommended that one ask if local offices exist.

The resources listed offer information specific to rural education and rural special education.

Clearinghouses, General Education

Clearinghouse for Rural Education and Small Schools (ERIC/CRESS)
P.O. Box 1348
Charleston, WV 25325
800/624-9120 (outside WV); 800/344-6646 (in WV)

A clearinghouse dedicated to rural and small schools education, which also specializes in information about American Indian and Alaska Native education, Mexican American education, and migrant education. ERIC/CRESS provides a database of information; completes reviews, research, and projects; and disseminates materials nationwide.

National Rural Development Institute (NRDI)
Western Washington University
Miller Hall 359
Bellingham, WA 98225
206/676–3576

A nonprofit organization dedicated to the enhancement of rural and small school education. NRDI facilitates the exchange of resources and effective strategies through national conferences, research publications, training, and related services.

Regional Educational Laboratories

The regional educational laboratories consist of nine offices. The laboratories develop or identify numerous programs, products, and processes that appear to have promise for school improvement. The goal is to help schools solve their own problems, help policymakers make sound decisions, and install proven ideas in schools and communities.

Appalachia Educational Laboratory
P.O. Box 1348
Charleston, WV 25325
304/347–0400
States served: Kentucky, Tennessee, Virginia, West Virginia

Mid-continent Regional Educational Laboratory
12500 East Iliff Avenue
Aurora, CO 80014
303/337–0990

States served: Colorado, Kansas, Missouri, Nebraska,
                North Dakota, South Dakota, Wyoming

Research for Better Schools
444 North Third Street
Philadelphia, PA 19123
215/574-9300
States served: Delaware, Maryland, New Jersey,
                Pennsylvania, Washington DC

North Central Regional Educational Laboratory
295 Emroy Avenue
Elmhurst, IL 60126
312/941-7677
States served: Illinois, Indiana, Iowa, Michigan,
                Minnesota, Ohio, Wisconsin

Regional Laboratory for Educational Improvement of the
Northeast and Islands
290 South Main Street
Andover, MA 01810
617/470-0098
States served: Connecticut, Maine, Massachusetts, New
                Hampshire, New York, Puerto Rico,
                Rhode Island, Vermont, Virgin Islands

Northwest Regional Educational Laboratory
101 S. W. Main Street, Suite 500
Portland, OR 97204
503/275-9500
States served: Alaska, Idaho, Montana, Oregon,
                Washington, American Samoa, Guam,
                Hawaii, Northern Mariana Islands,
                Trust Territory of Pacific

Southeastern Educational Improvement Laboratory
P.O. Box 12746
Research Triangle Park, NC 27709
919/549-8216

States served: Alabama, Florida, Georgia, Mississippi,
North Carolina, South Carolina

Southwest Educational Development Laboratory
211 East Seventh Street
Austin, TX 78701
512/476–6861
States served: Arkansas, Louisiana, New Mexico,
Oklahoma, Texas

Far West Laboratory
1855 Folsom Street
San Francisco, CA 94103
415/565–3000
States served: Arizona, California, Nevada, Utah

Rural Assistance Information Network (RAIN)
518/486–6631 (remote bulletin board—need modem)
RAIN is a computerized directory of financial and
technical assistance programs available in rural areas.
Maintained by New York state, this directory lists over 375
programs offered by state agencies and 1,130 federal
programs.

Special Education

Clearinghouse on Disability Information
Office of Special Education and Rehabilitative Services (OSERS)
U.S. Department of Education
Room 3132, Switzer Building
Washington, DC 20202–2524
202/732–1723
The clearinghouse responds to inquiries about disability
issues. Particular attention is given to those concerns related to
federal funding for programs serving people with disabilities,
relevant federal legislation, and federal programs benefitting
people with disabling conditions. Free publications summarizing
legislation and federal funding are available.

National Information Center for Children and Youth with
Handicaps (NICHCY)
P.O. Box 1492
Washington, DC 20013
800/999-5599
    NICHCY provides publications and directories for families
who have a child with a disability and need information about
their child's disability, about services available which can be
helpful to their child, about federal and state laws and policies
which affect their child, about support for their family when
needed, and how to live together comfortably while meeting
everyone's needs.

Organizations, General Education

National Association of School Administrators' Small Schools
Program
1801 North Moore Street
Arlington, WV 30568
703/528-0700
    The association serves small and rural schools through a
small schools committee and offers an annual conference,
inservice training, national surveys, federal legislation
monitoring, and a network linking small and rural school
districts through AASA state affiliate organizations. The Small
School District Administrator is published to keep members
informed about association activities and interests.

National Rural Education Association (NREA)
Colorado State University
Fort Collins, CO 80523
303/491-7022
    NREA consists of members from a variety of
backgrounds who are interested in rural education concerns.
The association serves to coordinate individuals and groups
who need information about rural education, and provides
advocacy, research, and development to assist in meeting this
goal.

National Rural and Small Schools Consortium (NRSSC)
Western Washington University
Miller Hall 359
Bellingham, WA 98225
206/676-3576
   Rural and small schools present special challenges and offer special contributions. The National Rural and Small Schools Consortium (NRSSC) is an action-oriented group of individuals and agencies working to enhance rural and small school education and address associated problems. Members are from across the United States, and the list of members from various countries is growing. Over 30 national professional organizations are affiliated with the Consortium.

Special Education

American Council on Rural Special Education (ACRES)
Western Washington University
Miller Hall 359
Bellingham, WA 98225
206/676-3576
   The American Council on Rural Special Education (ACRES) is a rural "community" working together to enhance services to rural individuals with disabilities. Members include special educators, direct service providers, administrators, teacher trainers, parents, and others who are vitally concerned with the enhancement of services to rural individuals with disabilities. ACRES has members throughout the United States and a growing list of countries.

Publications: General Education Journals

Journal of Rural and Small Schools (*JRSS*)
National Rural and Small Schools Consortium
Western Washington University
Miller Hall 359

Bellingham, WA 98225
206/676–3576

The *Journal of Rural and Small Schools* is a national scholarly journal devoted exclusively to rural and small school education issues. The purpose of the Journal is to provide practical, field-oriented articles relevant to rural and small school district management and instruction, federal and other events relevant to rural individuals, progressive service delivery systems, reviews of relevant publications, and resources for rural and small school educators.

Research in Rural Education
314 Shibles Hall
University of Maine
Orono, ME 04469
207/581–2493

Research in Rural Education is a journal established to publish the results of educational research conducted in rural settings or relevant to rural education. It welcomes manuscripts descriptive of such research, appropriate literature reviews, or the results of evaluation studies.

The Rural Educator
National Rural Education Association
School of Occupational and Education Studies
Humanities Building
Colorado State University
Fort Collins, CO 80523

The Rural Educator is a professional journal written for and by those involved in rural education and university faculty specializing in the area of rural development. It is intended to serve as a means of furthering communication between university faculty and rural educators in our public schools. It is also designed to provide up-to-date information in the area of rural education.

Special Education Journals

Rural Special Education Quarterly (RSEQ)
American Council on Rural Special Education
Western Washington University
Miller Hall 359
Bellingham, WA 98225
206/676–3576

The *Rural Special Education Quarterly* is the only national scholarly publication solely devoted to rural special education issues. The purpose of the Quarterly is to provide articles concerning research in rural special education, federal and other events relevant to rural individuals with disabilities, progressive service delivery systems, reviews of relevant publications, and resources for rural special educators.

Special Topics

Cultural Diversity

ERIC Clearinghouse for Rural Education and Small Schools (ERIC/CRESS)
P.O. Box 1348
Charleston, WV 25325
800/624–9120 (outside WV); 800/344–6646 (in WV)

A clearinghouse dedicated to rural and small schools education, and includes information about American Indian and Alaska Native education, Mexican American education, and migrant education. ERIC/CRESS provides a database of information; completes reviews, research, and projects; and disseminates materials nationwide.

National Advisory Council on Indian Education (NACIE)
330 "C" Street, S.W., Room 4072
Switzer Building
Washington, DC 20202-7556

The council was established to assist the Secretary of Education in carrying out responsibilities under the Indian Education Act of 1988. NACIE serves to advise Congress and the Secretary of Education regarding federal education programs beneficial for Indian children and adults. Five regional resource and evaluation centers were established to provide assistance to local programs needing educational information.

Indian Education Resource Center I
ORBIS - Suite 200
1411 K Street, N.W.
Washington, DC 20005
States served: Alabama, Connecticut, Florida, Georgia, Illinois, Indiana, Kentucky, Maine, Maryland, Michigan, Mississippi, North Carolina, Ohio, Pennsylvania, Rhode Island, South Carolina, Tennessee, Vermont, Virginia, West Virginia, Washington, DC, Wisconsin

Indian Education Resource Center II
United Tribes Technical College
3315 S. University Drive
Bismarck, ND 58504
States served: Iowa, Minnesota, Montana, Nebraska, North Dakota, South Dakota, Wyoming

Indian Education Resource Center III
School of Education
Gonzaga University
Spokane, WA 99528
States served: Alaska, Idaho, Oregon, Washington

Indian Education Resource Center IV
NITRC
2121 South Mill Avenue, Suite 204
Tempe, AZ 85282
States served: Arizona, California, Colorado, Hawaii, New Mexico, Nevada, Utah

Indian Education Resource Center V
AIRD, Inc.
Suite 200
2424 Springer Drive
Norman, OK 73069
States served: Arkansas, Kansas, Louisiana, Missouri,
       Oklahoma, Texas

National Early Childhood Technical
Assistance System (NEC*TAS)
Publications Department
CB# 8040
Suite 500 NCNB Plaza
Chapel Hill, SC 27599–8040
612/827–2966

A *Bibliography of Selected Resources on Cultural Diversity for Parents and Professionals Working with Young Children Who Have, or are At Risk for, Disabilities* was compiled to facilitate networking and collaboration among parents and professionals working with culturally diverse populations at the state and local levels. The resources listed in this bibliography cover a range from "classics" to current entries, and include printed and audiovisual materials and selected organizations.

Distance Education, General Education

Apple Global Education (AGE)
Apple Computer, Inc.
AGE Project
Mail Stop 42-C
Cupertino, CA 95014
408/974–2872

The Apple Global Education (AGE) network connects users world-wide through the use of Macintosh computers, modems, and AppleLink electronic-mail addresses. Letters between users can be exchanged along with scientific data, computer graphics, video images, and musical compositions.

Arts and Sciences Teleconferencing Service (ASTS)
College of Arts and Sciences
Oklahoma State University
Stillwater, OK 74078
405/744-7895

ASTS was created by the university and rural schools to provide equal access for students who would otherwise not have access to upper level math, science, and foreign language classes. The satellite-delivered program is interactive and provides live broadcasts on a daily basis.

TI-IN Network
1000 Central Parkway North, Suite 190
San Antonio, TX 78232

Using the power of interactive television and the communication capabilities of satellite technology, TI-IN can teach students from coast-to-coast. Academic and career aspirations that would have been difficult, if not impossible, for students to pursue because of geographical or financial barriers can now be attained.

Special Education

Educational TeleCommunications (ETC)
Department of Special Education
University of Utah
Salt Lake City, UT 84112
801/581-8121

Educational TeleCommunications (ETC) is a video-technical consortium dedicated to developing, producing, and disseminating quality state-of-the-art educational telecommunications products and services. Training and technical assistance are provided, and research is conducted to enhance instruction.

National Special Education Alliance (NSEA)
1307 Solano Avenue
Albany, CA 94706
415/528-0747

NSEA is focused on applying microcomputer technology to the needs of persons with disabilities. A list of NSEA member centers was published in the *Rural Special Education Quarterly*, Volume 9, Number 4, which was a special issue devoted to technology and rural schools. A list can also be obtained by directly contacting Apple Computer, Inc.

SpecialNet
GTE Education Services, Inc.
2021 K Street N.S., Suite 215
Washington, DC 20006
202/835-7300

SpecialNet offers a variety of electronic bulletin boards, each of which covers a single topic. The boards are maintained by an editor with expertise in the subject matter field and are updated daily as national events warrant. SpecialNet is a subscriber system, and users may print information from the boards as well as contribute items of interest. The rural education board is maintained by the American Council on Rural Special Education (ACRES) at Western Washington University, Bellingham.

Drug and Alcohol Education

Alaska Council on Prevention of Alcohol and Drug Abuse, Inc.
7521 Old Seward Highway, Suite A
Anchorage, AK 99518
907/349-6602

The Alaska Council provides information about a variety of topics, and focuses on dissemination of materials in rural and remote areas. The council offers unique education programs and technical assistance to area schools. Minority issues are an integral part of the projects, and information is adapted to the specific needs of remote peoples.

Economic and Rural Development

Center for Agriculture and Rural Development (CARD)
578 Heady Hall
Iowa State University
Ames, IA 50011
515/294-1183

CARD focuses on agricultural and rural community research. The center links with state and federal Congressional committees, agriculture commodity groups, the private sector, and academic colleagues. The goals are to understand policy, identify issues, orient modeling and data base systems, and develop results that can be used effectively in policy formation and evaluation.

Rural Development Perspectives

United States Department of Agriculture
ERS-ARED, Room 434
1301 New York Avenue, N.W.
Washington, DC 20005-4788
202/786-1547

Rural Development Perspectives is interested in reporting research on the wide range of issues that might come under the rubric of rural studies. Topics such as production, borrowing and lending, weather fluctuations, crop prices, and federal assistance are covered. The journal is published three times per year.

Elderly

Center on Rural Elderly
University of Missouri - Kansas
5245 Rockhill Road
Kansas City, MO 64110

The Center on Rural Elderly was established to serve as a resource for health and human service professionals interested in the distinctive features of programming for elders who reside in small towns and rural communities. The activities of the center are focused on the three areas of positive preventative health practices for the elderly, education and support for caregivers of elderly persons, and intergenerational relations between elderly persons and younger generations. The center has a comprehensive minority component.

Health

National Rural Health Association
301 East Armour Boulevard
Suite 420
Kansas City, MO 64111

The Rural Health Resources Directory, compiled by the National Rural Health Association, offers a comprehensive listing of federal, national, and state organizations, offices of rural health, federal and state cooperative agreements, hospital associations, medical societies, state and regional primary care associations, Rural Health Research centers, Area Health Education Centers, the American Academy of Family Physicians state chapters, the American Academy of Pediatrics rural health coordinators, and other resources. Listings are organized by state within each category.

Mental Health

National Association for Rural Mental Health
12300 Twinbrook Parkway
Suite 320
Rockville, MD 20852
301/984-6200

The National Association for Rural Mental Health (NARMN) is a cooperating organization of the National Council of Community Mental Health Centers. The association was founded to develop, enhance, and support mental health services and service providers in rural America. NARMN's purposes are to promote the unique needs and concerns of rural mental health programs, to develop educational resources, and to disseminate information.

Social Research and Development

Western Rural Development Center (WRDC)
Oregon State University
307 Ballard Extension Hall
Corvallis, OR 97331–3607
503/737–3621

WRDC stimulates research and education in the social sciences on issues faced by rural communities. Major changes are occurring in the social, economic, governmental, and demographic structure of rural areas. The center pulls people together from across the region for a comprehensive approach to particular rural problems. Each state has a community development program associated with the land grant university's Cooperative Extension Service. The easiest way to initiate contact with the development center is through a county Extension office.

Transportation

Community Transportation Office (Rural America)
721 15th Street, NW
Suite 900
Washington, DC 20005
202/628–1480

The Community Transportation Office is an independent, non-profit membership organization that assists local governments and community oriented enterprises in small towns and rural areas in meeting their service and development needs. The organization has an affiliate in each state, a national office in Washington, DC, and regional offices in Iowa, Mississippi, and Texas. A newspaper, *Rural America*, is published about six times a year and contains articles on rural education issues.

PART III
THE FUTURE OF
AMERICAN RURAL SCHOOLING?

A Proposed Federal and State Policy Agenda For Rural Education in the Decade of the 1990s

E. Robert Stephens
and
Willis J. Perry

Introduction

The end of one decade usually witnesses a flurry of predictions, projections, and conjectures about what the next decade is likely to hold. These are usually followed by a comparable number of advocacy pleas suggesting a needed federal or state policy response required to meet the new anticipated challenges.

The field of education especially seems to be the subject of many scenarios about the future as well as the focus of numerous proposals to shape the form and the direction of the governmental response. The current high interest in the field at this time, the beginning of the last decade in this millennium, is, no doubt, at least in part, merely a continuation of the intense examination of education that began early in the preceding decade, the frequently labelled "school reform movement" of the 1980s.[1]

Yet not all important facets of education have thus far been the subject of attention in the professional and policy communities in either the earlier phases of the school reform movement or in the more recent wave of pronouncements of what ought to drive education policy in the next decade. It is of course appropriate that consideration continues to be centered on a number of educational issues that are viewed by most to be of great consequence to the educational enterprise in this nation. Surely few would argue, for example, that the attention given urban education, the need to improve the instructional program and of teaching, or efforts to increase the use of technology are important in terms of their impact on the overall quality of American education.

But, as we suggest, the debate has been uneven, mainly because it has generally omitted other equally critical aspects of the educational enterprise. One of the most glaring omissions in the current policy debate underway in the nation and in most states is the framing of a policy response to the perplexing problems and issues facing rural school districts that are to be found in large numbers in most states and thus continue to be significant.

Chapter Objectives

We have been asked to establish in this chapter what in our judgment ought to be the characteristics, components, elements, and features of a federal and state policy response for the rural education "problem" in the decade of the 1990s. We clearly support the desperate need for enlightened policies at both levels of government, the implicit assumption in our charge. But we believe there is an even more compelling need that policies at both levels of government at this time especially ought not to be only comprehensive, but integrated and cohesive as well, both within each level and across the two. It is for this reason that we paused only slightly in accepting the broad assignment to address the two roles, a difficult task under any circumstances but especially so in the necessarily limited space available here. However, the challenge presented by the scope of this assignment is in part compensated for by the potential of contributing in one small way to not just the preservation but the enhancement of the ability of the nation's still large number of rural small school districts to make important contributions to the American dream, as they have in so many ways in the past.

We have approached our task in this way. We initially review two critical topics that will hopefully raise the quality of the debate about the merits of the proposals we advance for the development of comprehensive, integrated, and cohesive federal and state policies for rural education. The first of these is a discussion where we acknowledge the complexities of structuring public policy problems such as the one we are attempting here. This is followed by a (potentially equally controversial) review of the aims of education and how and in what ways these might be or should be viewed as different for rural education.

We then summarize five lines of argument that together, in our judgment, constitute a powerful rationale for bold, new policy initiatives at both levels. Our arguments of course reflect the way we have structured the rural school "problem" as well as the aims we hold for its role in this society. Together, they represent our world view of the problem.

This discussion is followed by a summary of common, yet frequently competing criteria, that ordinarily guide both the estimation and selection of public policy choices, and then establish the relative weight we would assign these selection criteria in the exercise we are engaged in here. We then move to the identification of what ought to be the overriding strategic goals for both federal and state policy development.

We do not devote major attention here to either the description or an assessment of past or existing federal and state policy and programs aimed at assisting rural schools. For the reader who is desirous of a comprehensive recent treatment of federal initiatives in rural education we recommend: Sher's (1977) edited text that is an especially rich critique, especially of the assumptions underlying past federal (and state) initiatives; Nachtigal's (1982) excellent edited text on a whole range of relevant issues associated with the federal role in improving rural education; and, the series of monographs and

books that describe and assess, using a variety of
methodologies, the (relatively) massive six-year federally funded
Rural Experimental School Program launched in 1972 (Deal and
Nutt, 1979; Nachtigal, 1980; Herriott, 1980; Firestone, 1980;
Rosenblum and Louis, 1981).

Particularly helpful recent case or comparative studies of
state policy actions concerning rural schools are provided by
Peshken (1983), Monk and Haller (1986) for the State of New
York, Sher's work in North Carolina (1986) and in Nebraska
(1988), all on the general issue of rural school district
reorganization, the primary historical state policy response to
the rural school district "problem"; Honeyman, Thompson, and
Wood's (1989) analysis of rural school financial issues;
Thompson and Stewart's (1989) study of the financing of rural
school capital improvement programs; Low's (1988) rural
school finance study in Illinois; and, Augenblick and Nachtigal's
(1985) paper on equity issues in financing rural education. A
study, conducted by the State Research Associates (1988)
provides one-of-a-kind data on the perceptions of key
stakeholders in the thirteen member states of the Appalachian
Regional Commission, the group that sponsored the study, on
the effects of state-sponsored measures enacted in the early
stages of the first wave of the school reform movement.

Structuring the Rural Education Policy Problem

If one were to ask ten different individuals to define the
"problem" of rural education, it is likely that ten different
notions would be offered. A further complication is the high
probability that each of the ten respondents' definitions of the
"problem" would make use of much of the same information,
but of course would interpret the data differently. Such is the
difficulty of framing public policy problems generally, as we
explore briefly below.

Presented first is a discussion of the nature of the
complexities present in efforts at problem definition, the most
difficult yet essential step in arriving at policy choices. We then
review the aims of education to determine whether or not there

is a consensus that there is or ought to be special aims for rural education. These two brief discussions are followed by our conceptualization of the rural school "problem."

Mann (1975) discusses the need to increase the rigor of the definition of policy problems and that doing so will subsequently contribute to improved public policy decision making. Mann suggests the use of five characteristics that aid in distinguishing what he calls its descriptive limits and that help sort these from those that are operational or administrative in nature. According to Mann, policy problems are those that: are perceived as issues that are presently or soon will be of such a magnitude that they warrant government action; are of consequence in that they are of importance and impact the lives of many individuals; are imbedded in a (frequently) interacting network of economic, political, psychological, social psychological, and moral components; have uncertain consequences concerning their ultimate effectiveness; and, finally, as one would expect in view of the preceding four other characteristics, they have differing interests for different groups in this society, all of whom are likely to have a legitimate stake in the problem (pp. 10–17).

Dunn's (1981) discussion of the nature of policy problems establishes many of these same points but adds still other difficulties in structuring policy problems that are especially germane to our attempt here to frame the essence of the rural school "problem." In his discussion of the characteristics of policy problems, Dunn asserts:

> In reality policy problems are not independent entities; they are parts of whole systems of problems best described as messes, that is, systems of external conditions that produce dissatisfaction among different segments of the community. Systems of problems (messes) are difficult or impossible to resolve by using an analytic approach—that is, one that decomposes problems into their component elements or parts— since only rarely can problems be defined and resolved independently of one another. Sometimes it is easier to solve ten interlocking problems simultaneously than to resolve one by itself. Systems

> of interdependent problems require a holistic
> approach, that is, one that views problems as
> inseparable and unmeasurable apart from the whole
> system of why they are interlocking parts. (p. 99)

Dunn's position on the interdependence of policy problems is an extremely useful caution as are his views about the subjectivity, and as a result, the problematic nature, of policy problems. So too is his further assertion that "there are as many different solutions for a given problem as there are definitions of that problem" (p. 99).

Similar views of the characteristics of policy problems outlined by Mann and Dunn, especially the importance they place on the role of values in structuring policy questions, are given equal prominence among virtually all writers in the field (Lasswell, 1971; Dror, 1971; Kerr, 1976; Etzioni, 1976; Mood, 1983; Aronowitz and Giroux, 1985; and Shore, 1986).

The importance of structuring policy problems, as opposed to identifying their complex features, is also widely recognized. For one of the most significant viewpoints on this matter, we again cite the admonitions of Dunn (1981), whose work we prize highly and draw upon regularly in this exercise:

> . . . problem structuring is the most critical phase of
> policy analysis, since policy analysts fail more often
> because they solve the wrong problem than because
> they get the wrong solution to the right problem. The
> fatal error in policy analysis is to solve the wrong
> formulation of a problem when one should have
> solved the right one. (p. 98)

Dunn refers to errors of this type as errors of the third type (Eiii, p. 109). Brewer and deLeon (1983) in their useful six-stage conceptualization of the policy process (in this sequence, initiation, estimation, selection, implementation, evaluation, and termination) also devote substantial attention to the importance of the statement of the problem that ordinarily occurs first in the initiation phase of the policy process. They view the initiation phase as itself having four components: recognition of the problem, identification of the problem context, determination of goals and objectives, and generation of alternatives. According to Brewer and deLeon, failure to structure the problem correctly during the initiation phase "can postpone, impair, or even negate the rest of the policy process" (p. 32).

We suspect it would not be difficult for most observers of public education to quickly identify examples of public policy formulation that, in their view, reflect a failure to structure the problem correctly and thus subsequently have addressed the wrong problem, Dunn's error of the third type. Nor would it be difficult for many to establish illustrations of what in their mind represent mistakes made in the Brewer and deLeon's conceptions of what takes place in the early initiation phase, only to see substantial redirection needed in later stages of the policy cycle.

Aims of Education

As a further step in structuring our definition of the rural education "problem," we review below what seem to us to be the aims of education, with particular attention given to consideration of how and in what way the aims of rural education might or should be different.

There is of course a voluminous literature on the aims of elementary-secondary education that, especially in the recent school reform or school excellence movement, seems to grow daily.[2] We of course cannot begin to provide even a brief synthesis of this rich literature here. Rather, what will be attempted below is to summarize what seems to be a consensus of what, during a number of broad time periods in our nation's history, has been advanced as the goals and objectives of public education.

In the late 1960s, a gubernatorial study commission in Texas issued a report (Goals for Public Education in Texas, 1969) that included an excellent review of approximately thirty landmark national and prominent state reports on the aims of education that were issued from the late 1890s to the mid-1960s (e.g., The Committee of Ten on Secondary Education, National Education Association, 1893; The Commission on

Reorganization of Secondary Education of the National Education Association, 1918; The American Youth Commission of the American Council on Education, 1936; The Educational Policies Commission of the National Education Association, 1938 and 1944; The Mid-Century Committee on Outcomes in Elementary Education, 1953; The White House Conference on Education, 1955; The American Association of School Administrators' Commission on Imperatives in Education, 1966). The methodology used in the review was a (relatively) sophisticated content review of these landmark reports. The conclusion drawn by the Texas study commission was that there were certain broad areas of agreement in all the reports. That is, that while the terminology and mode of expression might vary among the reports and over time, or the classification systems used might change and the emphasis given to the goals might shift, the basic goals, however, appeared to remain constant. These six universal, persistent goals were established: intellectual discipline, economic interdependence and vocational opportunity, citizenship and civic responsibility, social development and human relationships, moral and ethical character, and self-realization. We believe this report has captured the essential aims of education that shaped educational policy for much of this century.

No such claim of consensus could be made for the ensuing twenty years, however. While there appears to be a continuing allegiance to the six broad areas of previous times, it is clear that there is accelerated pressure to both redefine the objectives used to achieve the six aims, as well as add still new definitions of what, for example, is the best way to measure their attainment.

The most recent effort to frame goals of education, as well as the objectives that ought to be pursued in their attainment, is of course the national goals statement issued jointly in January, 1990 by the White House and National Governor's Association. The goals, that are also six in number, establish that by the year 2000: all children in America will start school ready to learn; that 90 percent of students will graduate from high school; that students will demonstrate competency in

English, mathematics, science, history, and geography; students will be first in the world in science and mathematics achievement; all adults will be literate and be able to compete in a global economy as well as exercise the rights and responsibilities of citizenship; and, every school will be free of drugs and offer an environment conducive to learning (National Education Goals, 1990). It seems clear that these six new national goals are likely to shape education policy formulation well into the future. It is unlikely that the key stakeholders who struggled in an unprecedented way to develop a consensus will not stay active in seeing that their agenda comes to fruition.

Two critical points need to be stressed before we leave this brief review of the aims of education. The first is that in none of the approximately thirty landmark statements reviewed in the Texas study were rural school districts singled out in any special way. This is also the case with regard to the newly released national goals statement.

The second point to be stressed is a reminder that a number of forces have historically shaped educational policy in this nation. Stroke (1959) has identified these as the promotion of religious purpose that dominated policy in the eighteenth century, the pursuit of intellectual freedom that was emphasized in the nineteenth century, and the pursuit of "national necessities," given prominence after the launching of Sputnik in 1957. An especially rich discussion of forces shaping education is provided by DeYoung (1989). One of DeYoung's major theses is that economic issues have been dominant in the framing of education aims. There seems little argument with his thesis that the goal of enhancing economic development in the states is the clear reason why education has occupied center stage for most of the past six years, an unprecedented period on the policy agendas of most state governments and most recently, the federal government. Spring's (1988) work on the politics of education focuses on the political forces impacting on education at the federal, state, and local levels in recent years.

Are the Aims for Rural Education Different?

Over the years rural school interests, especially, as well as other national commissions have prompted goal statements for rural education. Our assessment of many of these pronouncements, while frequently identified as goal statements, generally address the need to correct perceived weaknesses in rural schools operations (e.g., increase funding, add curricular offerings, recruit staff, add specialists) in order to place rural schools on a par with the educational opportunities available in urban school districts (American Association of School Administrators, 1939; The National Commission on School District Reorganization, 1948; Department of Rural Education, 1955; President's National Advisory Commission on Rural Poverty, 1967; Department of Rural Education, 1967). As meritorious as these "goals" might be, they do not represent a substantive addition to the core, universal aims of education for all Americans in the context these are being discussed here.

One notable early exception to the tendencies cited above is the work of Butterworth and Dawson (1952) who argued the need for the community-center school in rural communities and advocated the goal "of making the school in our modern complex society a more vital and functional institution rather than a mere agency for academic and formal instruction" (p. 295). The authors would achieve this goal in four principal ways: expand the use of the facility to house other community activities, making greater use of the community as a learning laboratory, the school offering community services beyond the traditional day-school program, and the school providing leadership in coordinating a community education program (pp. 298–303).

We would also view the recent emphases on the role of the rural school in rural economic development and the similar advocacy for moving rural schools into a prominent place in rural community development as efforts to have as a goal an expectation not applied to other types of school systems. At this time we are unaware of many formal adoptions by national commissions or national special interest groups of one or both of these potential new goal statements. However, support for both initiatives seems to be gaining support in the academy and other circles (Rosenfeld, 1987; Hobbs, 1988; Mulkey, 1988; Mulkey, 1989; Raferty and Mulkey, 1989; and Southern Rural Development Center, 1989).

Our Conceptualization of the Rural Education Problem

We now establish how we conceptualize the rural education problem. It seems clear that the universally accepted aims of education make no distinctions between elementary-secondary schools serving urban, suburban, or rural schools, correctly so we believe. However, many rural districts must contend with factors beyond their control in achieving these overarching goals. Clearly, few would argue that sparsity of population, isolation, and limited resources pose huge difficulties. State government in particular has the constitutional responsibility to make the playing field even. As we shall attempt to argue below, both levels of government have compelling extra-legal reasons for doing so.

Thus, we view the rural education "problem" foremostly as one of equity that is of great consequence for many states and for the nation as well. The problem is not, in our judgment, one of Dunn's (1981) ill-structured problems (p. 107), even though it is, for example, clearly interwoven and thus interdependent on the successful solution of other policy problems.

Moreover, because of the extent of inequity present in the problem as well as the critical significance of the issue to the well-being of the entire nation, we further conceptualize the problem as one that will require the long-term commitment and joint orchestration of both federal and state governments if the problem is to be successfully addressed. We develop the rationale for this particular conceptualization in the following section.

Five Lines of Argument in Support of the Conceptualization We Use

Five lines of argument are advanced here that together shape our definition of the rural school "problem," and we believe, will aid others in similarly viewing the issue. These center on the following points:

• Rural schools are significant in number and in students served and will continue to be so as far into the future as any policy analyst or public official should safely forecast.

• Many of them are in deep trouble as a result of the recent conflux of economic and social forces impacting on them that have exacerbated the historical problems caused by isolation, sparsity of population, and fiscal limitations.

• Because of their continued significance and due to their current increasingly difficult condition, the status of rural schools ought to be of paramount interest and concern to those responsible for long-term, large-scale school improvement efforts.

• Moreover, the status of rural schools appears to be inter-linked to any meaningful, long-term efforts aimed at the economic revitalization of rural America and to the larger question of ways to affect rural community development.

• Finally, but of great importance, because of this current status, concerns about one of the centerpieces of the American ethos, equity, are widespread in rural education and this too ought to be of equal paramount interest to all.

While it may be obvious, we want to stress that the themes of our five lines of argument center on our conceptualization of the rural education problem. In our judgment most, but probably not all, of the five individually would be sufficient cause for a meaningful policy response. When taken together, however, they present a compelling case why it makes good public policy sense at this time for the policy communities at all levels to earnestly address the rural education "problem" and then commit resources for finding solutions that will be effective well into the twenty-first century.

In an interesting essay, Haynes (1989) reviews four common arguments advanced for the preservation of rural America and then discusses the complexities of each. He concludes that he is skeptical that any synthesis can be achieved given the fact that the arguments do not complement each other. We believe the five lines of argument in this statement are complementary and thus would satisfy this one important test used by Haynes.

The Significance of Rural Schools

Two measures of the significance of rural schools for which there would surely be widespread consensus concern the number of such school systems, and the number of students served by such systems. There is not a universally accepted definition of a rural school district in part due to the continued use of a variety of criteria (e.g., sparsity or density of population, isolation or distance to an urban center, smallness in size, economic and social conditions, sociocultural values, primary occupation of residents). However, the vast majority of calculations we are familiar with argue that the number of rural systems in the nation ranges from approximately one-half to two-thirds of the approximately 15,500 operating school districts in the nation.[3] Surely the welfare of anywhere from approximately 7500 to 10,000 school districts is of consequence. Furthermore, most estimates of the number of students enrolled in rural schools are in the range of approximately 20 percent of the roughly 40 million public elementary-secondary students in 1988–89, also a significant percent.[4]

From an individual state perspective, the significance of the relative health of the rural school component of many state school systems takes on even more importance. This is so because a large number of local school systems in a substantial number of states are rural, even when the most conservative definitions are used to estimate their number. For example, in an interesting new line of work, Johnson (1989), on the staff of the National Center for Educational Statistics, has developed a new system that uses ZIP code numbers to classify all public schools (but not yet districts) into seven classifications by locale and state. Rural locations are defined as a place with less than 2,500 people or a place having a ZIP code designated rural by the U.S. Bureau of the Census. For the nation, 27.35 percent of the rural schools in 1987–88 were classified as rural (p. 31). The assumption made here is that all of these were also rural school districts. The number of rural schools is greater than 50 percent of all schools in three states, represent from 40 to 49 percent of all schools in still another six, and from 30 to 40 percent in seven. This is a fairly conservative estimate in that it does not include an estimated large number of additional small schools (that is, school districts) in the next locale type used in the exercise, Small Town.

Furthermore, it is reasonable to assume that there will not be major changes in the number of rural districts in the immediate years ahead, despite renewed interest in several states to reduce the number of (usually rural) small enrollment-size districts by returning to an old policy strategy, forced school district reorganization. This policy strategy has not enjoyed widespread support in either the policy or professional communities for a number of years.[5] There has not been a significant numerical change in the number of operating units in the nation during the past two decades. Moreover, the last three most recent major state initiatives to mandate reorganization, those in Illinois, Nebraska, and North Carolina in the late 1980s, enjoyed so little political feasibility that they were either defeated or withdrawn.

These recent experiences, plus the growing use of other incentives to strengthen rural schools, suggest to us that there will continue to be large numbers of rural districts in most states for the foreseeable future. This is not to say that educationally sound reorganizations will not (indeed, should not!) take place in many regions of a number of states. Rather, the point being stressed here is that there is likely to continue to be a significant number of rural systems well into the future and the needs of these systems deserve the attention of the policy communities at both the federal and state levels. Those are not just statistics but individuals with their own aspirations for the future who can become either an asset or a liability for this society who are present in the pipeline of these schools. They represent a huge resource for the nation that simply must not be squandered through neglect.

Recent Difficulties Experienced by Many Rural Systems

The second compelling argument introduced here for renewed federal and state attention to the rural school "problem" is that the 1980s were an especially difficult time for many rural districts all across the country.

The economic and social trends affecting nonmetropolitan regions have been tracked and reported on in a number of excellent reports by the Economic Research Service of the U.S. Department of Agriculture.[6]

Those developments that have had the greatest impact on rural schools center in large part on the prolonged stress in the traditional rural industries of agriculture and energy production (oil, gas, coal, and lumber) that have contributed to high unemployment rates that in turn has contributed to the out-migration of rural populations. Moreover, the continuous fiscal crisis in agriculture and the economic stress in the energy industries has and will likely continue to compound the ability of rural governmental subdivisions to provide basic public services, including education, that are important for both rural economic development and for enhancing other aspects of the quality of life for rural residents.

Nor was the school reform movement of the 1980s especially kind to rural schools in many states. For example, the early emphasis in many state legislative remedies for improving the quality of the instructional program (e.g., increased graduation requirements, more science and math and foreign language) and efforts to improve the quality of teaching (e.g., more stringent certification requirements) as well as efforts to improve the quality of the teaching profession (e.g., increased minimum salaries) were particularly difficult for many rural systems.[7] The merits of these and other legislative enactments are not being argued here. Rather, what is being stressed is that many of these enactments exacerbated a number of the traditional problems faced by large numbers of rural systems such as the problem of depth and breadth in the secondary school curriculum, the problem of attracting and retaining staff, and lack of fiscal support.

Significance for School Improvement Efforts

The third leg of our five-part argument of the importance of renewed attention to the plight of rural schools follows closely from the first two. That is, if the rural school component continues to be a significant proportion of rural state school systems, as past history suggests, and if this component continues to be faced with increased difficulty in mounting a quality program, as seems to be the case in many situations, then clearly this component will hardly be in a position to respond to the increasingly ambitious school improvement efforts underway in the nation.

This dire prediction of the fate of many promising school improvement initiatives seems obvious to us. Unless, of course, the state and federal governments are willing to pour increasingly huge sums of monies into direct fiscal support of rural education, an unlikely event. As Congress continues to wrestle with the "peace dividend," for example, the line of advocates for the use of these funds to address other domestic needs becomes longer. How education will fare in this competition is problematic at this time.

There is a significant literature that has established substantial evidence that it is at the implementation phase at the local school district or local school building sites where many promising, highly touted educational change efforts are thwarted and their potential compromised (Bailey and Mosher,

1978; Berke and Kirst, 1972; McLaughlin, 1975; Ingram and Mann, 1980).[8]

On a more positive note on the rural school-school improvement connection, Stephens (1988) argues that the state must capitalize on the strengths of rural schools in that:

> This final implication might well be the most important of all. Many observers of rural education consistently cite a number of strengths that good rural systems regularly exhibit: small class sizes that facilitate individualized attention, low dropout rates, a safe orderly environment, development of student leadership qualities, strong faculty identity and commitment to the school, strong parental interest and involvement, and strong community support (Barker, 1985; Beckner, 1983; Jess, 1985; Nachtigal, 1982; Sher, 1977). In a discussion of the rapidity of changes impacting this society, Hobbs (1983) suggests four particular strengths of rural districts that might cause them to "become the educational trendsetters of the 1990s" (p. 25). The peculiar strengths that Hobbs sees in rural systems that together increase their capacity to adapt to change include: their history of seeking solutions to problems caused by scarce resources, their small size that facilitates flexibility, their diversity that facilitates experimentation with different options, and their close working relations with their communities that promote collaboration with minimal bureaucratic red tape. . . . (pp. 1–2)

> It is important to note that many of the strengths of rural systems are strikingly similar to a number of the characteristics of effective schools identified in recent years that have also served as, however roughly, the policy goals for much of the "first round" of reform and that are proposed as the centerpieces of the next generation of reform.

> The implication for the policy communities of these similarities of strengths in rural systems and the

research literature on effective schools is both clear and sobering. That is, how can policies be designed that will retain those features of good rural districts while simultaneously accommodating the inevitable adjustments that must be made in the rural school district component of the state system of education caused by the new realities of education in a rural setting? The reconciliation of these two competing needs will challenge the creativity of the policy communities as few other policy quandaries have in recent years. (pp. 78–79)

The Education-Economic Development Link

One of the encouraging developments in recent years is the apparent growing consensus in the policy communities, especially at the federal level, that an urgent need exists for the promotion of meaningful, long-term policies that will result in the economic revitalization of nonmetropolitan America (Revitalizing Rural America, 1986; Focus on the Future: Options in Developing a New National Rural Policy, 1988; New Alliances for Rural America, 1988; Signs of Progress, 1989; A Hard Look at USDA's Rural Development Programs, 1989).[9]

The formulation of specific policies to achieve this goal is still being debated, and the shape and direction these efforts will take is unknown at this time. There is one feature, however, that is largely unchallenged in all of the discussions about alternative ways to enhance the economic vitality and competitiveness of rural regions. Indeed, the centerpiece of most proposals for affecting more balanced growth policies for the nation is the availability of an educated, skilled work force (Deaton and Deaton, 1988; Hobbs, 1988; Ross and Rosenfeld, 1987).

Herein lies the link between a strong, healthy system of rural schools and the prospects for needed rural economic development. It is the rural school that can serve as one of the primary instruments for the creation of an educated workforce, and can make its contributions in many ways. In a recent paper, Mulkey and Raferty (1989) summarize a number of key roles that the rural school can play in rural economic development. Especially noteworthy are their reminders that: the schools can become the true community learning resource center by assisting in adult literacy training, community leadership development, and by offering comprehensive adult education programs; and, they can develop instructional programs on the history, social, economic, and political profiles of the community, and alternative futures for the community (pp. 14–20).

A Question of Equity

In our view, the four preceding lines of argument summarized above represent a strong case for the adoption of comprehensive, integrated, and cohesive policies by the federal and state governments for helping resolve the rural education "problem." It is to be noted, however, that they all tend to come down on the side of pragmatic reasons for public policy attention. While this level of argument is important as a rationale for taking action, there is another justification for doing so that is less pragmatic in nature, but equally compelling.

This line of argument appeals to the public's sense of fairness. And before we are accused of wishful thinking here, we are mindful of the thesis of McCloskey and Faller (1984) who argue that equity concerns have been a sustaining part of the American ethos since the very beginning of this nation. It is indeed a powerful force that has in the past helped shape public policy choices and we are confident will continue to do so.

The equity issues associated with the rural school "problem" are numerous in number. For example, why should a child's access to his or her state constitutionally guaranteed right to equal educational opportunity continue to be overly dependent on the accident of geography, as it is in so many instances? Or, why should not government provide assistance to those who of economic necessity live in nonmetropolitan regions rather than being virtually forced to migrate to metropolitan regions to gain access to those public services that have become accepted features of the standard of living of the American populace? Or, is it fair to continue to ask rural communities to support public education (frequently at a level of local effort in excess of urban jurisdictions) with the knowledge that many of the students of rural schools will leave the community upon graduation, a point stressed by Mulkey (1989b)?

A recent quote by J. Norman Reid, Deputy Director, Rural Development, Economic Research Service, U.S. Department of Education (1990) captures a number of the points we have raised here:

> The rough times experienced by most rural areas in the 1980s make it clear that being rural carries with it heavy penalties. Some penalties are due to location: more remote places have been left out of the action in this decade. Others are due to narrow rural economic bases, more limited physical infrastructure, and institutional capacity.

Will these "penalties" continue in the 1990s? We believe they will, and furthermore, are likely to accelerate unless there emerges a new commitment to address the pervasive issues confronting rural America. And, we argue, the centerpiece of this new commitment must begin with the establishment of comprehensive, integrated, and cohesive federal and state rural education policies that are so critical to any sustained revitalization efforts.

Criteria that Should Guide the Development and Selection of Politics at Both Levels

Thus far we have presented an argument for the enactment of comprehensive, integrated, and cohesive policy formulations at both the federal and state levels of government. The next step we undertake here is to briefly discuss the criteria we would use as guides for the development of both strategic goals and tactical objectives of federal and state policies and the relative weight we assign these. A total of six potential criteria are introduced.

There is general acceptance of the need to make use of the first two of the six criteria we identify here: cost-effective and cost-benefit analysis. Levin (1983) defines each as follows:

> Cost-effectiveness (CE) analysis refers to the evaluation of alternatives according to both their costs and their effects with regard to producing some outcome or set of outcomes. (p. 17)

> Cost-benefit (CB) analysis refers to the evaluation of alternatives according to a comparison of both their costs and benefits when each is measured in monetary terms. (p. 21)

A third criterion for which there is widespread acceptance is the need to make use of equity considerations in exploring various alternatives. There seems to be little controversy that the measure of this concept is fairness in the application of the effects and efforts of public policies, although confusion continues to arise from the predisposition of some to equate equity and equality of educational opportunity. The latter is of course judge-made law that has its origin in decisions handed down by the courts and is derived from the Equal Protection Clause of the Fourteenth Amendment (Hogan, 1974, p. 3).

We rely on Dunn (1981) to be clear about the need for the use of three additional criteria critical in the development and selection of strategic goals and tactical objectives needed to implement public policy. The three are adequacy, responsiveness, and appropriateness. Dunn defines the three thusly:

> Adequacy: the extent to which any given level of effectiveness of alternative policies satisfied the needs, values, or opportunities that the policy is intended to address.

> Responsiveness: the extent to which alternative policies satisfy the needs, preferences, or values of those that are to benefit from the policy objective.

Appropriateness: refers to the value or worth of the objective of the policy and whether or not the assumptions underlying these objectives are appropriate for society. (pp. 236–238)

It is the use of these three criteria, that Dunn labels "decision criteria," especially his advocacy of the criterion of appropriateness, that we find particularly useful in the exercise we are engaged in here. We subsequently weight this criterion heavily, along with several others. As Dunn states:

While all other criteria take objectives for granted . . . the criterion of appropriateness asks whether these objectives are proper ones for society. To answer this question analysts may consider all criteria together— that is, reflect on the relations among multiple forms of rationality—and apply higher-order criteria (metacriteria) that are logically prior to those of effectiveness, efficiency, adequacy, equity, and responsiveness. (p. 238)

Dunn continues:

The criterion of appropriateness is necessarily open indeed, since by definition it is intended to go beyond any set of existing criteria. For this reason there is not and cannot be a standard definition of criterion of appropriateness. (p. 238)

We also support Dunn's assertion that "there are multiple rationale bases underlying most policy choices" (p. 225). According to Dunn, these are:

1. Technical Rationality—choices based on a comparison of policy alternatives according to their ability to promote effective solutions to the policy problem.

2. Economic Rationality—choices based on a comparison of policy alternatives according to

their ability to promote efficient solutions to the policy problem.

3. Legal Rationality—choices based on a comparison of policy alternatives according to their legal conformity to established rules and precedents.

4. Social Rationality—choices based on a comparison of policy alternatives according to their ability to maintain or improve valued institutions in the society.

5. Substantive Rationality—choices based on a comparison of multiple forms of rationality in order to make informed judgments in particular cases and under particular circumstances. (pp. 225–226)

We have gone at some length citing the work of Dunn because he has so clearly illuminated the issue of the rural education "problem" as we have conceptualized it. We argue that his definition of adequacy, responsiveness, and particularly, appropriateness be used in the framing of strategic goals and tactical objectives to the dilemmas confronting the still significant rural school component of the public school enterprise in this nation. That is, we believe that while policy choices made for rural education must embrace effectiveness criteria (technical rationality), efficiency criteria (economic rationality), and equity criteria (legal rationality and social rationality), they ultimately must also be based on the use of adequacy, responsiveness, and appropriateness criteria. This is so because values and preferences, indeed the essential worthiness of public policy, must be considered.

The weight we assign to these latter three types of criteria obviously complicates an already complex task. Nonetheless, we see no alternative but to insist that the explicit statement of values, a necessary precondition for the use of the three criteria, but not necessarily for the others, be inserted early in the discussion about strategic goals and tactical choices and not ever lost sight of. As Dunn and many others remind us, values can never be divested from the methodologies employed in policy analyses (Lasswell, 1956; Etzioni, 1961; Young, 1977; Anderson, 1984; Gilliott, 1984). To this we add, nor should they.

The prominence we give adequacy, responsiveness, and appropriateness criteria in the formulation of both federal and state strategic goals will, among other benefits, assure that cost benefit criteria, as critical as these are and of necessity must be, does not dominate strategic choices. Importantly, their extensive use will in our view best promote the attainment of the strategic goals: that is, the restoration of a viable rural America is to be highly valued and a strong rural school system is judged to be the single most critical building block in this effort.

The work of several others greatly influenced our choices of strategic goals that we identify as appropriate for the two levels of government. Kerr's (1976) discussion of the issue of selection criteria is especially helpful. She argues for the use of four tests of justification, or conditions that "must be true to say that a policy choice is justifiable of being supportable on nonarbitrary grounds" (p. 171). The four tests are:

- The desirability test: the policy must promote the development of "beliefs, attitudes, skills, dispositions, values, or tasks" that are viewed to contribute to an attribute of some consensus about the "Good Life."

- The effective test: the choice of a policy is more likely than any other choice to achieve the purpose of the policy.

- The justness test: the purpose of the policy, when achieved, must be just.

- The tolerability test: the costs of the choice, in both resource expenditure and undesirable results, must be tolerable when measured by three additional tests: proportionality, less costly,

> and acceptability (of undesirable side effects). (pp.
> 171–192)

Kerr also discusses the importance of sequencing her four tests of justification:

> The order in which these tasks are introduced is at
> variance with the order in which they would logically
> be applied in that the justness test was found to take
> precedence over the desirability test. Further, it should
> be noted that there is no point in applying the
> effectiveness test if a policy did not pass the
> desirability test. The tests of justifiability would then,
> logically, be applied in this order: (1) the justness test,
> (2) the desirability test, (3) the effectiveness test, and
> (4) the tolerability test. (pp. 172–173)

The Intent of Federal Policy

We enter what Goodlad (1983) has correctly referred to as the "conceptual swamp" of educational goal setting or establishing the intent of policy recommendation with less trepidation than many apparently seem willing to do. For our vision of both the responsibility and the potential of meaningful federal and state roles for improving rural education is relatively clear, as is our view of the function and technical features that ought to characterize such statements.

Considered first are a small number of statements of intent we believe are appropriate for the federal government, followed in the next section by those judged to be necessary for adoption at the state level if a comprehensive, integrated, and cohesive federal and state policy response to the rural education "problem" is to be forthcoming. In both statements, we have attempted to be selective, especially by limiting the foci of our proposals to those viewed to be the most critical building blocks. As a result, many other worthy foci are excluded here.

We believe further that the goal or intent statements as presented satisfy our notion of the function of such pronouncements as well as the technical features that ought to guide their construction. There does seem to be widespread agreement that to be useful in policy debates, an intent or a goal statement should be broadly stated, identify the values sought, be unspecified in its time period or duration, and be nonquantifiable (Dunn, 1981; Lewis, 1983; Walsh, 1985). In our view, the proposed strategic goal statements satisfy these main standards in a reasonably unambiguous manner.

It should be apparent from our earlier discussion of the five lines of arguments offered in defense of our conceptualization of the rural education "problem" that we come down on the side on the activist, not the traditionalist, view of the role of the federal government. The thrust of our proposed strategic goals that the federal government should assume are consistent with this position. We clearly view the rural education issue, and the larger question that it is inextricably linked, the revitalization of rural America, as within the domain of national interest as we define this elusive theory. We are not encumbered here with the frequent legal debates surrounding the admittedly complex issues of national authority vs. national purpose in that we perceive an aggressive, ambitious federal role in rural education to be in the national interest.

The preferred intent of federal policy development is that it focus on these six national priorities:

1. Support for more balanced national growth through the revitalization of rural America and the use of education as the centerpiece of efforts to improve rural community development and rural economic development that are both so essential for the achievement of revitalization efforts.

Subsuming rural education within the broader context of rural revitalization efforts and then subsequently linking it to the two principal foci of any meaningful, long-term revitalization strategies—rural community and rural economic development— is intended to achieve several points. It acknowledges what has been overwhelmingly demonstrated to be always critical for large segments of the American populace in their choices about where to live, raise families, and work; that is, access to quality education is an important determinant of quality of life considerations. Moreover, the shift to this more defensible rationale should help move the debate from the tendency of many to discuss the rural education "problem" as one peculiar to all those (unfortunate and distant!) folks still left in the heartland of the nation or in its outer fringes to one that is of paramount interest to all Americans. That is, it will promote the quality of the debate by pointing out still another near truism; mainly, the interdependence of nonmetropolitan and metropolitan interests and that the welfare of each of these communities of interest should be of paramount concern to the other.

> 2. The creation of a new mechanism with the clear authority to both direct and coordinate policy development and program administration across agencies that have an existing mission for promoting rural interests and services.

> 3. The creation of a new mechanism with the authority to coordinate federal policy development and program administration with state government sponsored rural revitalization efforts.

The emphasis we give these two strategic goals, that could operationally be combined, is based in part on our convictions that there is a desperate need to link social and physical planning in new, more meaningful and productive ways and to concentrate and target available or new resources far better than we heretofore have been able or willing to do.

Recommendation #2 goes farther than any of the four alternatives identified by Knutson, Pulver, and Wilkinson (1988) in their excellent discussion of the need for better coordination of federal rural development policy among the approximately thirty individual agencies engaged in rural development programs. Their four options are: designation of a lead agency, the use of cabinet councils, the designation of a special assistant to the President, and the creation of a new rural development department.

Further, in the case of education, it is clear that fundamental changes are occurring in the demographic make-up and behavioral patterns of the student population attending the schools. Traditionally, the problems of poverty, crime, school dropouts, teenage child-bearing, drug abuse, suicide, and other problem behaviors of adolescents have tended to be examined separately.

The ability of the schools when acting alone, to respond to these changing conditions over which they have little or no control, is greatly limited. A much broader perspective of education policy development that would consider all the conditions of children and youth, as well as the relationship these conditions have on schooling, is required. New relationships must be forged between the schools and other instrumentalities of government if more effective policies and programs are to be realized.

The same concerns and needs exist for other public services as well. It is also recognized the way that the federal government structures its response to an issue tends to influence the way states organize themselves to deal with the same issue. Thus, a breakthrough at the federal level in this regard is likely to be modeled right across the country.

A reconstituted Advisory Commission on Intergovernmental Relations could assume one or both of the functions addressed here. Should this alternative be explored, one of the minimal restructuring needs is that education, presently now excluded, be accepted as one of the domains to come under the preview of this group.

It is likely that recommendations #2 and #3 will be viewed by some as merely another in the long list of efforts to respond to a need by creating another bureaucracy or adding to an already existing entity. We hope this is not the case for our proposal does not rest with the creation of still another organizational entity, or an expanded charter for an existing unit. The operative clause in goal statement #2 is "granting the unit authority to direct and coordinate" appropriate activities of all of the federal government's human and fiscal resources in a concentrated attack on the multidimensional issues confronting rural America. This call for the creation of what some might call a "rural czar" is precisely the kind of bold step required. The track record of past efforts to affect meaningful interdepartmental coordination (to say nothing about intradepartment coordination), with some notable exceptions, suggests to us that creation of a "rural czar" has merit. We acknowledge that it could also be argued that the track record of other federal "czars" (e.g., the so-called drug "czar") hardly warrants enthusiasm for this approach. We think the validity of an analogy such as this is questionable. For example, the resources thus far available for the drug "czar" to direct and coordinate the federal war on drugs pale when compared to the huge resources of existing departments who already have a mission that could, if better directed and channelled, contribute in important ways to any new, broad-based domestic rural policy (e.g., Education, Agriculture, Labor).

Recommendations #2 and #3 are also made for state government. It is through the use of the two parallel mechanisms at both levels where the primary pressure as well as incentives for the development of comprehensive, integrated, and cohesive federal and state policies can be expected to occur, both among agencies at each level, and between the two levels.

The emphasis we give to the two proposed new mechanisms at both levels assumes that conflict between national and state policy goals are inevitable, on the one hand, and that further, this conflict in part is strongly influenced by structural, not substantive, factors present among units of government at each level and between units at both levels. A process and multiple platforms are viewed as minimal requirements needed for the development of consensus and to promote collaboration.

> 4. The vast expansion of current statistics and research on the condition of education to include comprehensive profiles and research on the status of rural education that will inform both federal and state policy makers on the problems and issues, policy implications, and alternative solutions available for their resolution.

The emphasis we place on data collection and analysis of the condition of rural education is appropriate given the significance of rural schools and the meager descriptive data presently available. The need for a substantial expansion of the equally meager, largely nonadditive research literature on the status of rural education has been addressed by many, most recently Stephens (1985) and DeYoung (1987). We stress the need for good, solid data mindful of the cautions of some concerning the use of social science research (Caplan, Morrison, and Stambaugh, 1975; Lindblom, 1986).

We assign primary responsibility for both tasks to the federal government. This is done in part because the federal government represents a huge, unparalleled resource already in place to undertake both tasks. The resources available to the recently expanded National Center for Educational Statistics as well as other units of the Office of Educational Research and Improvement and the regional labs and the research center funded by it in the Department of Education, along with the Economic Research Service of the Department of Agriculture, and the Department of Labor, to cite but a few, are significant, in both an absolute sense and in relative terms. The need of course is for these resources to be better orchestrated, the aim of a previously stated strategic goal.

Moreover, we also assign the primary responsibility for these tasks to the federal level in part for these additional reasons: the need for uniform comprehensive data across the states (that can still acknowledge the great diversity that exists among rural schools!),[10] the near-universal need across all states for studies of the costs and benefits of alternative policy options; and, finally, assigning the primary responsibility to the federal government appears to be the most cost-effective approach.

5. The vast expansion of the investigation, implementation, and assessment of the use of high-cost technology that has potential for addressing multi-state rural school improvement efforts, especially those technologies that will contribute most to the achievement of national educational goals.

The federal government is in the best position to underwrite research on the costs and benefits of technologies that hold promise of enhancing the quality of rural education in the nation, particularly in those curricular areas given prominence in the recently adopted national goals. Moreover, the anticipated high cost of installation of many of the promising technologies can best be borne by the federal government.

6. The federal government should adequately reimburse rural districts for programs and services that it mandates must be offered by all districts that place inordinate costs of compliance on such districts because of their isolation, sparsity of population, fiscal limitations, and other difficulties beyond their control that seriously complicate implementation.

While the past history of federal behavior in this regard is not promising, the fairness of establishing the need for dollars to follow mandates needs to again be stressed. As one example of the inequity of past practice, rural schools were especially handicapped in their attempts to implement underfunded federally mandated programs for exceptional children. It is imperative that they not be again so, especially should federal mandates emerge from the recently adopted national goals.

The Intent of State Policy

The strategic goals that we suggest ought to guide state policy development for rural education are substantially (as well as numerically) more significant than those advanced for the federal government. This is due in large measure to the state's constitutional responsibility to maintain a system of common schools and its plenary authority over them. We briefly review these points below. Also provided as further background for our discussion of the state's preferred strategic goals is consideration of common instruments used by the states to promote the achievement of its policy goals.

The State's Authority Over Public Education

In the United States public education has clearly been established as a state function by the delegated powers of the Tenth Amendment of the U.S. Constitution. Support for the concept of state responsibility for education is to be found in an evolving pattern of constitutional, statutory, and judicial decisions that together form the legal bases of education.[11] There appears to be substantial consensus among students of education law (Hamilton and Mort, 1941; Remmlein, 1953; Edwards, 1971; Reutter and Hamilton, 1976; Alexander and Alexander, 1985) that the following legal principles prevail:

- Local school districts are governmental agencies of the state created as instrumentalities through which the state carries out the constitutional mandate to provide a system of common or public schools.

- It follows that the power of the state over its educational system is plenary, subject only to such limitations as may be imposed by the state or federal constitutions.

- It follows that the state may alter or dissolve that which it has plenary authority to create.

- It is almost universally held that the legislature may delegate the formation and alteration of school districts to subordinate agencies or officials and that this delegation of administrative control does not violate the principle of the separation of power.

- The major constitutional constraints on the plenary authority of the state to delegate to a subordinate agency or official concern possible violations of the impairment of the obligation of contracts (Section 10, Article 1, U.S. Constitution) and to the concern that the exercise of authority may be arbitrary or unreasonable (Thirteenth Amendment of the U.S. Constitution).

• Since the state has plenary authority over the public schools, all local school officials represent the state and serve as officials or agents of the state.

• All local school district property is state property held in trust for the state by local officials.

The legal issues surrounding the state's plenary authority over education, that at one time generated substantial litigation, appears to have been settled by the end of the 1950s. It has reemerged in recent years but the majority of the newer challenges center on the state's authority with regard to the merger of urban and suburban districts for the purpose of achieving court-ordered desegregation or as a response to judicial remedies for affecting fiscal equity among districts in (usually) metropolitan regions. The possible significance of these newer challenges for the well-established legal principles concerning the exercise of the state's plenary authority is not known. It is also true of course that the recent state supreme court decision in Kentucky (The Council for Better Schools et al. vs. Wilkinson, Governor, et al., 1989) has expanded the court's definition of equal educational opportunity for all children and youth in a fundamental, precedent-setting way. Pending legislation in still other states may broaden this definition even further. For the moment, at least, it can be categorically stated that the state has the legal responsibility to ensure that all students, regardless of geography or wealth, have access to an (usually minimally defined) educational program.

Areas of Primary State Interest

While the state's plenary authority over education seems to be largely settled, differences in the manner in which states have exercised their authority are to be noted, and have changed over time, as will be discussed below.

For much of the evolution of the public school system in this nation, the states have tended to allow substantial discretionary authority to local school districts. States have tended to confine their interests to the fiscal operations of the schools (e.g., required budget format, required audit), the certification of personnel, the extent of the education offered (e.g., elementary and secondary programs, vocational education), minimum accreditation standards, and minimum building standards (Campbell, Cunningham, and McPhee, 1965).

In a content analysis of state control over education as expressed in existing statutes, state constitutions, and court opinions in thirty-six states in the early 1970s, Wirt and Kirst (1982) confirmed the tendencies identified by Campbell and his colleagues. They constructed a six-point scale to measure the extent of state control in various content areas: absence of state control, permissive local autonomy, required local autonomy, extensive local option under state-mandated requirement, limited local option under state-mandated requirement, no local option under state-mandated requirement, and total state assumption.

The intense state interest in the quality of education in the recent school reform movement has resulted in a substantial expansion of the scope of areas of primary state interest. However, we believe that Wirt and Kirst's six-point scale for classifying the nature of state interest in the recent expanded state activity still has utility in differentiating the way that the state has continually attempted to accommodate the state-local partnership concept in education.

Common State Policy Instruments

McDonnell and Elmore (1987) developed a conceptual framework for classifying alternative instruments or mechanisms that states make use of in translating strategic policy goals into tactical objectives or action plans. The four generic classes of instruments in their framework are:

- Mandates: rules governing the action of individuals and agencies, intended to produce compliance.

• Inducements: the transfer of money to individuals or agencies in return for certain actions.

• Capacity-building: the transfer of money for the purpose of investment in material, intellectual, or human resources.

• System-changing: the transfer of official authority among individuals and agencies to alter the system by which public goods and services are delivered. (p. 2)

The authors' discussion of the costs and benefits and selected examples of the four instruments are presented in Table 1. Their discussion of the major assumptions that appear to underlie each of the four generic instruments in their typology and the consequences of each are presented in Table 2. In our view, McDonnell and Elmore have correctly captured a number of essential considerations in the choice of criteria and alternative strategies that ought to be considered in an exercise of the type we are engaged.

So, too, is their attempt to frame propositions concerning under what conditions policymakers prefer the use of one or more types of instruments as opposed to others. One of their major hypotheses about this question is that choice is influenced by: how the policy issue is defined, the resources available, and the existing constraints (e.g., institutional context, government capacity, fiscal resources, political support or opposition, available information, and tradition) (pp. 19–26).

In a paper that focused exclusively on strategies used by the states to promote the policy goal of the reorganization of rural school districts, Stephens (1986) identified four major approaches (see Tables 1 & 2) that were used either singularly or in combination in many states in earlier times:

• the enactment of legislation promoting reorganization (three major variants: mandatory legislation, permissive legislation, semipermissive legislation)

TABLE 1
CHARACTERISTICS OF POLICY INSTRUMENTS

Instrument	Primary Elements	Expected Effects	Costs	Benefits	Examples
Mandates	Rules	Compliance	Initiators: Enforcement Targets: Compliance Avoidance	Specific benefits to individuals Diffuse benefits to society	Environmental regulation Nondiscrimination requirements Speed limits
Inducements	Money (procurement)	Production of value (short-term returns)	Initiators: Production Oversight Displacement Producers: Overhead Matching Avoidance	Initiators/producers: Increased budget authority Clients: value received	Grants-in-aid to governments In-kind grants to individuals
Capacity-building	Money (investment)	Enhancement of skill, competence (long-term returns)	Short-term costs to initiating government	Short-term, specific benfits to receiving agency; long-term, diffuse benefits to society	Basic research Preservation
System-changing	Authority	Composition of public delivery system; incentive	Loss of authority by established deliverers	Gain in authority by new deliverers	Vouchers Deinstitutionalization New providers (HMOs, community mental health agencies)

Source: McDonnell, L.M., and Elmore, R.F. Alternative Policy Options. New Brunswick, N.J.: Center for Policy Research in Education, Rutgers University, 1987, p. 8.

TABLE 2
ASSUMPTIONS AND CONSEQUENCES OF POLICY INSTRUMENTS

Instrument	Assumptions	Consequences
Mandates	(1) Action required regardless of capacity; good in its own right (2) Action would not occur with desired frequency or consistency without rule	Coercion required; create uniformity; reduce variation. Policy contains information necessary for compliance; adversarial relations between initiators, targets; minimum standards
Inducements	(1) Valued good would not be produced with desired frequency or consistency in absence of additional money (2) Individuals, agencies vary in capacity to produce; money elicits performance	Capacity exists; money needed to mobilize it; as tolerable range of variation narrows, oversight costs increase; most likely to work when capacity exists
Capacity-building	(1) Knowledge, skill, competence required to produce future value; or (2) Capacity good in its own right or instrumental to other purposes	Capacity does not exist; investment needed to mobilize it; tangible present benefits serve as proxies for future, intangible benefits
System-changing	(1) Existing institutions, existing incentives cannot produce desired results (2) Changing distribution of authoity changes what is produced	Institutional factors incite action; provokes defensive response; new institutions raise new problems of mandates, inducements, capacities

Source: McDonnell, L.M., and Elmore, R.F. *Alternative Policy Options.* New Brunswick, N.J.: Center for Policy Research in Education, Rutgers University, 1987, p. 13.

•   enactment of state aid formulas containing
fiscal incentives/ disincentives.

•   the enactment of new or strengthened
standards for the operation of districts (especially
those concerned with the scope of the program,
personnel, facilities, and the financial aspects of
district operation).

•   the use of extra legal measures to promote
attainment of the same policy goal (especially the
advocacy of reorganization by the professional
communities, by many in the academy, and state
officials). (p. 22)

The first three strategies in particular were drawn from
the work of Campbell, Cunningham, Nystrand, and Usdan
(1975), Knezevich (1984), and Fitzwater (1958), whose
descriptive report that covered sixteen states actively engaged
in district reorganization efforts stands as the seminal
descriptive study on this topic. It is argued by Stephens that
the fourth strategy, seldom considered in the literature, was
perhaps the most influential and effective of all in that it more
than likely precipitated the other three.

Recommended Strategic Goals for the States

We offer eleven strategic goals for the establishment of
comprehensive, integrated, and cohesive policies for rural
education. The eleven are judged to be the most critical building
blocks needed. As discussed previously, many other worthy
foci were excluded in an attempt to identify the most critical
areas of state policy action. It could be argued that many of the
proposals apply equally well to all types of school districts,
urban and suburban as well as rural. While conceding the merit
of this concern, our interest here is on rural systems, districts
that, we have attempted to make a case, warrant the undivided
attention of the policy communities. Moreover, it will be noted
that the themes of a number of our proposals have been
expressed by others. Our interest here is not in the novelty of

the proposals but rather one of pointing the direction and identifying the basic building blocks of a meaningful policy response.

The first three of the proposals closely parallel the first three previously recommended strategic goals for the federal government:

1. The state should support more balanced growth policies for the state through the revitalization of its rural areas and make access to high quality education the centerpiece of its efforts to improve rural community development and rural economic development, both so vital for the achievement of this policy goal.

2. The creation of a new mechanism with the clear authority to both direct and coordinate policy development and program administration across agencies that have an existing mission for promoting rural interests and services.

3. The creation of a new mechanism with the authority to coordinate state policy development and program administration with federally sponsored rural revitalization efforts.

The rationale for promotion of the three is similar to that presented in the early discussion and will not be restated here. The remaining eight of the proposed strategic goals are established below. A brief discussion of each, or series of related goals, is also presented. It is to be noted that the intent of all eight is to put the state in a proactive posture toward rural education, not neutral toward it, nor even just supportive of it.

4. The state should strive to create a meaningful state-local partnership with the citizens of rural communities that will result in the creation of a new social contract that will insure their accessibility to quality education. The social contract should establish the overriding state

interests in education, and provide maximum local discretionary authority to achieve the state interests.

5. The state should provide incentives and technical assistance to rural local communities that will enable them to engage in long-range strategic planning and make informed decisions about alternative futures of their community and their school.

We have multiple reasons for establishing a new state-local partnership (recommendation #4) as a strategic goal. These can be summarized in this way. It is clear that in the 1990s the state will be required to be even more active in its pursuit of meaningful and sophisticated student performance accountability systems, and the complex set of prerequisites and planning that this will require. It is also true that there are a growing number of compelling reasons why the state must also engage the primary delivery system for its imperatives—the local school district—and do so in increasingly creative and sophisticated ways. The numerous centralizing forces afoot in education and in the larger society (e.g., judicial oversight) seem to be matched in number and in significance by decentralizing pressures (e.g., empowerment). The reconciliation of these two factors must center on the creation of a new state-local partnership where the interests of the state are accommodated with both the reality of the need for a (largely local) delivery system, as well as match the preferences of citizens of a community.

6. The state should be committed to the establishment of a common system of schools that will provide each resident school-age child and youth the opportunity to acquire the necessary skills and competencies to function as an informed and contributing member of society as the state, and the larger community, enter the new information age.

7. Closely related, in the establishment of such a common system of schools, the state should be committed to remove the negative consequences of geography, wealth, and other factors that interfere with each resident school-age child and youth's access to the opportunity to develop the competencies and skills necessary to function as an informed and contributing member of the emerging information age society.

The emphasis we give to the need for the state to promote capacity building in local communities (recommendation #5) that will promote their ability to make informed judgments about the future of their schools (and communities) is consistent with our view that the vast majority of individuals will ultimately make correct decisions concerning the welfare of their children when provided with well-documented, objective alternative solutions, and the costs and benefits of these that reflect their values, not someone else's.

The stress we place on access to a quality education in several of the proposed goals (recommendations #6 and #7) is intended to place an important parameter or limit on the state's legal and ethical responsibility for education. For example, access does not necessarily mean that the state is obligated to provide equal funding to every school district that chooses to unilaterally attempt to meet state educational priorities where it can be demonstrated that such a decision is not cost-effective. However, there are instances where geographic, topographical, or sparsity considerations preclude or greatly restrict a student's educational opportunities, unless, for example, they are sent to boarding schools, an objectionable alternative in most instances. Placing an emphasis on access to educational programs also puts a high premium on an investment in alternative delivery systems, particularly the use of technology, for meeting the needs of the state system of schools.

The emphasis given to the creation of a state system of schools that will prepare students for the information age (recommendations #6 and #7) is intended to achieve two objectives. On the one hand, it should serve as a reminder that this statement of strategic goals, like all others, should be concerned about what will be required in the future. The information age requirements will, at a minimum, mean that students will need to develop competencies and skills in information processes, computers, problem solving, and decision making. These must be the centerpieces of the curriculum of the common system of schools. Furthermore, the focus on the future ought to help assure that the interest of the policy communities should always be on the design, and directed toward the establishment of a new generation of rural (and urban and suburban alike!) schools. This focus will help guard against the inclination to strive to preserve an older system that may have a curriculum that is of little or no value in meeting the future needs of the citizens of this nation.

8. The state should establish minimum levels of educational services that are to be accessible to all children and youth and then monitor whether or not rural local communities desirous of maintaining a school make provision for these minimums, not necessarily their production, the standard by which compliance is to be judged.

The first part of this strategic goal addresses what Timor (1989) argues for in his urging that "state policymakers have the responsibility to establish clear expectations and a general educational framework" (p. 27). His views regarding this preferred and needed state role are shared by virtually all students of school government.

The importance we place on urging the state to limit its monitoring practices to whether or not a local district provides a service and not expect each local unit to necessarily produce all services would represent a fundamental paradigm shift (Stephens, 1989). In a recent publication, the Advisory Commission on Intergovernmental Relations (1987), a congressional chartered policy unit, took a position that argues:

. . . a multiplicity of general-purpose and special-purpose governments in a metropolitan area is not an obstacle to good government or to metropolitan governance. On the contrary, a diversity of local

> governments can promote key values of democratic government—namely, efficiency, equity, responsiveness, accountability, and self-governance. A multiplicity of differentiated governments does not necessarily employ fragmentation; instead, such governments can constitute a coherent local public economy. (The Organization of Local Public Economics, 1987, p. 1)

The new ACIR position represents a fundamental change in the way it has viewed the proliferation of local governments in both metropolitan and nonmetropolitan areas. Long an advocate for the reorganization of local jurisdictions, the ACIR has now reversed its traditional posture. The centerpiece of its new position is the insistence that one should make a clear distinction between the provision and production of public goods and services. The ACIR defines these two activities as follows:

> Provision refers to decisions that determine what public goods and services will be made available to a community. Production refers to how those goods and services will be made available. (p. 1)

Distinguishing provision from production allows one to minimize the previous position of many that holds that, in the case of education, each local school district in a state must not only provide all required or needed services, but in addition, produce all those services, a formidable task indeed given the current widespread discrepancies in the wealth and other resources of local school systems. Acceptance of the new position of ACIR will likely promote the greater use of interdistrict coordinating mechanisms (recommendation #11) that can serve as the producers of many educational programs and services beyond the reach of many local school systems in nonmetropolitan areas.

Use of this perspective should also fundamentally change the heretofore heavy emphasis on mandatory rural school reorganization, and allow some of the other strategic goals argued for here to be pursued.

9.   The state should adequately reimburse rural districts for programs and services that it mandates must be offered by all districts in the state system of schools since the rural district, in discharging these responsibilities, is merely acting as an agent of the state.

10. The state should assume responsibility to provide each rural school district in the state system of elementary-secondary education with the resources and technical assistance necessary for it to remain in compliance with the laws, rules and regulations, and standards established by the state.

11. The state should provide incentives that promote collaboration among rural local districts and other service providers that hold promise for the efficient production of both the prescribed minimum levels of educational services as well as the production of enrichment services judged by rural districts to be needed to enhance the quality of their program.

In a recent article on the promotion of interdistrict relations as the preferred state policy option for improving rural education, Stephens (1988) identified seven core propositions that he argued represented a synthesis of what most students of interorganizational relations view as factors that cause an organization to seek out or be receptive to engage in relations with another organization: when the organization is faced with a situation of resource scarcity or other perceived need; when the organizational leadership perceives the benefits to outweigh the costs; when the organization has a common mission and perceives that attainment of its goals is more likely to be realized through interorganizational arrangements than by acting alone; when there is a history of good relations, a positive view of the other, and both are in close geographic proximity; when the organization can maintain its organizational identity; when the organization members can maintain their prestige and authority; and, when the organization has few or no other alternatives (p. 14).

Stephens continued:

> However, there is more to be said regarding the promotion of interorganizational arrangements. One also needs to think about how best to implement this policy choice, once the decision is made to promote its use and design configurations are agreed upon. While implementation considerations are implied in a number of the seven previously cited core propositions, direct reference to this issue has received scant attention by specialists in the field. Therefore, what follows is one additional proposition that is directed to this important phase of public policy development. This proposition in particular flows from my own study and observation of state and local planning and implementation efforts to promote interorganizational arrangements that have extended over two decades: the successful implementation of widespread interorganizational arrangements is dependent upon a strategy of using state-induced external incentives to motivate local decision makers to seek out or be receptive to such efforts. (p. 14)

We stop short here of endorsing the small-town triage strategy advocated by Lapping, Daniels, and Keller (1989). While this strategy is meritorious on many grounds, it also raises troubling questions. According to Lapping and his colleagues, the major issue facing planners "is how to influence the allocation of public funds and resources to create a sustainable pattern of rural settlement" (p. 296–297). To achieve this goal, "planners would seek to provide public funds to the growing towns of 2,500 to 5,000. . . . Second priority would be given to larger growing towns of 5,000 to 15,000" (p. 297).

The small town typology used by Lapping and his colleagues, used economic reliance (independent and dependent) and several categories of both population (growing, stagnant) and economic trends (economically diversified, natural-resource-based communities). The triage strategy would

TABLE 3

STRATEGIC GOALS AND FOCI OF SELECTION CRITERIA

Theme of Strategic Goal	Selection Criteria Primarily Focused on					
	Cost-Effectiveness	Cost-Benefit	Equity	Adequacy	Responsiveness	Appropriateness
1. Use of schools as the centerpiece for revitalization of rural America	X					X
2. New mechanism to coordinate policy development and program administration	X	X				
3. New mechanism to coordinate state/federal efforts	X	X				
4. New state-local partnership created			X	X	X	X
5. Incentives and resources to enable rural communities to do strategic planning		X	X	X	X	X
6. Provide opportunity to acquire necessary skills and competencies			X	X	X	X
7. Remote negative consequences of geography, wealth, and other constraining factors			X	X	X	X
8. Establish minimum standards; monitor provision, not necessarily production	X		X			
9. Reimburse cost for state mandates			X			
10. Resource and technical assistance to remain in compliance		X				
11. Incentives to promote interdistrict collaboration	X	X				

give lowest priority to stagnant towns that are remote and dependent on natural resources for their primary economic activity. The goal of the strategy is "to make public spending achieve economies of scale in the provision of public services and build up population centers that can be self-sufficient in the long run" (p. 297).

And, Finally

Additional discussion of our rationale for advancing the set of strategic goals we argue for here is to be found in the following two overviews. In the first (Table 3), we illustrate the primary criteria toward which each of the eleven is directed. Cost-effectiveness and cost-benefit considerations are embedded in a number of the eleven goals, as they must be, and should be realized. However, greatest weight is given the three criteria of adequacy (the extent to which any given level of effectiveness of policy alternatives satisfies the needs, values, or opportunities that the policy goal is intended to address), responsiveness (the extent to which alternatives satisfy the needs, preferences, or values of those that are to benefit from the policy goals), and the elusive but critical consideration of appropriateness (whether or not the assumptions underlying the policy goals are appropriate for society; see table 3). The heavy weighting we assign the three criteria is consistent with our position on how best to conceptualize the rural school "problem" and our position on the role of government for addressing the issue.

The second overview makes use of Wirt and Kirst's approach to examining state involvement in education, followed by McDonnell and Elmore's discussion of common instruments used by the states for implementing state policy.

Four of the eleven proposed strategic goals are viewed to be examples of Wirt and Kirst's classification of state actions that would allow "extensive local option under state mandated requirement." This is especially true for the following strategic goals: #4 new state-local partnership created; #5 incentives and resources to enable rural communities to do strategic planning; #8 establish minimum standards, monitor provision not production; and #11 incentives to promote interdistrict collaboration.

Others should be viewed as illustrative of the category, "limited local option under state-mandates requirement." Only the first three could be viewed as approaching their classification of "total state assumption." While it is true that responsibility for implementation of the three must rest with the state, even here it is assumed that the state will engage a wide array of interest groups in its deliberations (see Table 3). These assessments are compatible with our overall approach to the rural school issue and, of importance, are consistent with the set of values we bring to this exercise.

It is also to be noted that all four of McDonnell and Elmore's generic classes of policy instruments are reflected in our package of eleven proposed state strategic goals. The use of mandates is explicit in several and implied in others. Inducements, in the form of incentives, are also common. A focus on capacity building is also reflected. The extensive use of interdistrict collaboratives for the production of both required and optional programs and services would represent the use of system-changing, as the two authors define this term, correctly so we add. While not as permanent as some proposed structural changes, such as the reorganization of two or more previously independent school districts, use of a collaborative would ordinarily result in moving some decision authority from a heretofore autonomous unit to the larger group of units engaged in the collaborative.

Concluding Comments

Rural education has been dealt an unprecedented salvo in the 1980s and could well become what some have expressed concern about, the "barnyard" of American education. While we do not have apocalyptic visions such as this swimming in our heads, it is likely that the 1990s could represent an axial point in the history of public education in the nation where some fundamental redefinition of the rural education problem is required and where the nation's table of values must be revisited. We are in the midst of a genuine national and international change that could alter rural education in perhaps irreversible ways unless a comprehensive, integrated, and cohesive federal and state strategic response is forthcoming.

We want to stress that the logic of our conceptualization of the rural education "problem" and of the core strategic goals we have identified has little to do with sentiment for rural education, that is, a blind desire to save the past. This objective is not without appeal. However, in dealing with the "problem" of rural education, whose welfare remains so crucial to the future of this country, sentiment cannot be controlling.

What must matter in public policy choices concerning rural education is the initial framing of strategic goals that pass the tests of adequacy, responsiveness, and appropriateness, while always mindful of the need to also reflect frequently competing economic and legal concerns as well. Our proposed package of core strategic goals for the development of comprehensive, integrated, and cohesive federal and state policies are designed to provide such a framework.

Each of the core strategic goals must be viewed in combination one with another. The outcome of their adoption must remain largely problematic, a feature of course of most public policy choices. We acknowledge this possibility. However, we are confident that the conscious acceptance of the values that shaped the strategic goals put forth here will help assure the presence of a commitment and staying power necessary to arrive at the best course of action needed in the next decade and beyond.

NOTES

1. There certainly is no shortage of synthesis pieces that attempt to track and describe the movement or of critiques of it. See, for example: *The next wave: A synopsis of recent education reform reports* (1987); *School reform in 10 states* (1988); *Results in education: The governor's 1991 report on education* (1988); and

the extensive coverage given the movement in a series of articles in two special issues of *Educational Administration Quarterly*, edited by Bacharach (1988a and 1988b).

2.   A conservative estimate is that approximately one hundred major reports have been issued during the past seven years that advocate a particular position that would add to or alter the mission of the schools. This estimate excludes the hundreds of state legislative initiatives enacted during the same period, many of them either explicitly or implicitly broadening the aims of education.

3.   This estimate of the range of rural school districts was used by Stephens and Turner (1988) who in the process of developing a six-step approach used in their calculations examined over thirty estimates used by federal agencies, state education agencies, professional associations, and writers in the field. For a complete discussion of the six-step procedure, see Stephens (1987).

4.   There were 15,577 operating public school systems in the nation in 1987–88 (Digest of Educational Statistics 1989, p. 90). This same source established the enrollment figure in public elementary-secondary schools as approximately 40,224,000 in 1987 (p. 9).

5.   There is a growing rich literature on the history of the school reorganization movement in this century. See, for example: Cubberly, 1922; Covert, 1930; Commission on School District Reorganization, 1958; Barker and Gump, 1964; Sher and Tompkins, 1976; Sher, 1977; Peshken, 1983.

6.   See especially: *Rural economic development in the 1980s: Preparing for the future* (1987); Bender, et al. (1985); McGranahan, et al (1986).

7.   One of the charges given to a number of the authors of papers presented at a U.S. Department of Education invitational conference held in Kansas City in 1985 requested that attention be given to the hypothesized effects of the school reform movement on rural schools as it was unfolding across the country. See Horn (1985), Augenblick and Nachtigal (1985), and

Forbes (1985). Muse (1984) and Stephens (1988) offer similar perspectives.

8.   The peculiar problems of effecting change in rural schools has not been the focus of extensive study; see especially Rogers and Svenning (1969) and the previously cited reports stemming from the Rural Experimental School Program.

9.   For a good overview of the present federal rural policy coordination mechanisms see Long, Reid, and Deavors (1988).

10.   The recent work of Cohen (1985) serves as another confirmation of a generally accepted conclusion that state policy makers (governors' education aides, chairs of education committees in state legislatures, members of state boards of education, and chief state school officers) rank their number-one information need policy developments in other states. Also ranked high was the need for information on costs and effects of policy options (p. 4).

11.   For a review of early precedents that have established the state's responsibility for public education, see Thurston and Roe (1957).

REFERENCES

Advisory Commission on Intergovernmental Relations. *The Organization of Local Public Economies.* Washington, D.C, 1987.

Alexander, K., and Alexander, M. D. *American Public School Law.* St. Paul, Minn.: West Publishing Company, 1985.

American Association of School Administrators. *Schools in Small Communities.* Seventeenth Yearbook. Washington, D.C., 1939.

Anderson, J. E. *Public Policy-making.* 3rd ed. New York: Holt, Rinehart, and Winston, 1984.

Aronowitz, S., and Giroux, H. *Education under Siege: The Conservative, Liberal, and Radical Debate over Schooling.* South Hadley, Mass.: Bergin & Garvey, 1985.

Augenblick, J., and Nachtigal, P. M. "Equity in Rural School Finance." Paper presented at National Rural Education Forum, sponsored by U.S. Department of Education, Kansas City, Missouri, July 15, 1985.

Bacharach, S. E., ed. "Education Reform: Change and Rhetoric." *Educational Administration Quarterly, 24,* 3 (1988b).

Bacharach, S. E., ed. "Education Reform: Change and rhetoric, Part 2." *Educational Administration Quarterly, 24,* 4 (1988b).

Bailey, S. K., and Mosher, E. *ESEA: The Office of Education Administers a Law.* Syracuse, N.Y.: Syracuse University Press, 1968.

Barker, B. D. "A Description of Rural School Districts in the United States." *The Rural Educator, 6,* 3 (1985): 1.

Barker, Roger G., and Gump, P. V. *Big School, Small School.* Stanford, Calif.: Stanford University Press, 1964.

Beckner, W. "The Case for the Smaller School." Phi Delta Kappa Educational Foundation, Fastback 190. Bloomington, Ind.: *Phi Delta Kappan* (1983): 3–4.

Bender, L. D., ed. *The Diverse Social and Economic Structure of Nonmetropolitan America.* Washington, D.C.: U.S. Department of Agriculture, Economic Research Service, 1985.

Berke, J. S., and Kirst, M. W. *Federal Aid to Education.* Lexington, Mass.: D. C. Heath, 1972.

Butterworth, J. E., and Dawson, H. A. *The Modern Rural School.* New York: McGraw-Hill Book Company, Inc., 1952.

Campbell, R. F., Cunningham, L. L., and McPhee, R. F. *The Organization and Control of American Schools.* Columbus, Ohio: Charles E. Merrill Books, Inc., 1965.

Campbell, R. F., Cunningham, L. L., Nystrand, R. O., and Usdan, M. D. *The Organization and Control of American Schools.* Columbus, Ohio: Charles E. Merrill Publishing Company, 1975.

Caplan, N., Morrison, A., and Stambaugh, R. J. *The Use of Social Science Knowledge in Policy Decisions at the National Level.* Ann Arbor, Mich.: The University of Michigan, Institute for Social Research, 1975.

Cohen, M. "Meeting the Information Needs of State Education Policymakers." Executive Summary. Alexandria, Va.: National Association of State Boards of Education, 1985.

Commission on School District Reorganization. "School District Reorganization." Washington, D.C.: American Association of School Administrators, 1958.

The Council for Better Schools, et al. vs. *Wallace Wilkinson, Governor, et al.* Commonwealth of Kentucky, Franklin Circuit Court, Division T. Civil Action No. 85- CI–1759.

Covert, T. *Rural School Consolidation.* Pamphlet No. 6. Washington, D.C.: U.S. Department of the Interior, U.S. Office of Education, U.S. Government Printing Office, 1930.

Cubberley, E. *Rural LIfe and Education: A Study of the Rural-School Problem as a Phase of the Rural-Life Problem.* Boston: Houghton Mifflin, 1922.

Deal, T. E., and Nutt, S. C. *Promoting, Guiding, and Surviving Change in School Districts.* Cambridge, Mass.: Abt Associates, Inc., 1979.

Department of Rural Education. *Rural Education: A Forward Look.* Yearbook. National Education Association of the United States, 1955.

Department of Rural Education. *Rural Education Today.* Washington, D.C.: National Education Association, 1967.

DeYoung, A. J. "The Status of American Rural Education Research: An Integrated Review and Commentary." *Review of Educational Research, 57,* 2 (1987): 123–148.

DeYoung, A. J. *Economics and American Education.* New York: Longman,1989.

Digest of Educational Statistics. Washington, D.C.: U.S. Department of Education, National Center for Educational Statistics, 1989.

Dror, Y. *Ventures in Policy Sciences.* New York: American Elsevier Publishing Company, Inc., 1971.

Dunn, William N. *Public Policy Analysis: An Introduction.* Englewood Cliffs, N.J.: Prentice-Hall, 1981.

Edwards, N. *The Courts and the Public Schools.* 3rd ed. Chicago: University of Chicago Press, 1971.

Etzioni, A. *A Comparative Analysis of Complex Organizations.* New York: The Free Press, 1961.

Etzioni, A. *Social Problems.* Englewood Cliffs, N.J.: Prentice-Hall, Inc., 1976.

Firestone, W. A. *Great Expectations for Small Schools: The LImitations of Federal Projects.* New York: Praeger Publishers, 1980.

Fitzwater, C. O. "School District Reorganization: Policies and Procedures." Washington, D.C.: U.S. Department of Health, Education, and Welfare, Office of Education, 1958.

Forbes, R. H. "State Policy Trends and Impacts on Rural School Districts." Paper presented at the National Rural Education Forum, sponsored by U.S. Department of Education, Kansas City, Missouri, 1985.

Gilliott, S. "Public Policy Analysis and Conceptual Conservatism." *Policy and Politics, 12,* 4 (1984): 345–367.

"Goals for Public Education in Texas." Operation PEP. Redwood City, Calif.: San Mateo County Board of Education, 1969.

Goodlad, J. I. "A Study of Schooling: Some Implications for School Improvement." *Phi Delta Kappan, 64,* 8 (1983): 552–558.

Hamilton, R. R., and Mort, P. R. *The Law of Public Education.* Chicago: The Foundation Press, Inc., 1941.

"A Hard Look at USDA's Rural Development Programs." The Report of the Rural Revitalization Task Force to the Secretary of Agriculture. Washington, D.C.: U.S. Department of Agriculture, 1989.

Haynes, R. P. "Four Arguments for the Preservation of Rural America." *The Rural Sociologist, 9,* 1 (1989): 14–18.

Herriott, R. E. *Federal Initiatives and Rural School Improvement: Findings from the Experimental Schools Program.* Cambridge, Mass.: Abt Associates, Inc., 1980.

Hobbs, D. J. "Economic Social Change in Rural Communities: Implications for Rural Schools." AASA Small Schools Series #3. Arlington, Va.: American Association of School Administrators, 1983.

Hobbs, D. J. "Education Reform and Rural Economic Health." Paper Presented at Conference, "Risky Futures: Should State Policy Reflect Rural Diversity?" Louisville, Ky., Appalachian Educational Laboratory, 1988.

Hogan, J. C. *The Schools, the Courts, and the Public Interest.* Lexington, Mass.: Lexington Books, D.C. Heath and Company, 1974.

Honeyman, D. S., Thompson, D. C., and Wood, R. C. *Financing Rural and Small Schools: Issues of Adequacy and Equity.* Charleston, W.Va.: ERIC Clearinghouse on Rural Education and Small Schools, 1989.

Horn, J. G. "Recruitment and Preparation of Quality Teachers for Rural Schools." Paper presented at the National Rural Education Forum, sponsored by U.S. Department of Education, Kansas City, Missouri, 1985.

Ingram, M., and Mann, D. *Why Policies Succeed or Fail.* Beverly Hills, Calif.: Sage Publications, 1980.

Jess, J. "The Needs of Rural Schools." *Illinois School Research and Development, 21*, 2 (1985): 7.

Johnson, F. "Assigning Type of Locale Codes to the 1987–88 CCD Public School Universe." Washington, D.C.: U.S. Department of Education, National Center for Educational Statistics, 1989.

Kerr, R. H. *Educational policy: Analysis, structure, and justification.* New York: David McKay Company, Inc., 1976.

Knezevich, S. J. *Administration of Public Education.* 4th ed. New York: Harper & Row, Publishers, 1984.

Knutson, R. D., Pulver, G. C., and Wilkinson, K. P. "Toward a Comprehensive Rural Development Policy. Focus on the Future: Options in Developing a New National Rural Policy." *Proceedings, Rural Development Policy Workshops.* College Station, Tex.: Texas A&M University System, Texas Agricultural Extension Service, 1988.

Lapping, M. B., Daniels, T. L., and Keller, J. W. *Rural Planning and Development in the United States.* New York: The Guilford Press, 1989.

Lasswell, H. D. "The Political Science of Science." *American Political Science Review* (1956): 961–979.

Lasswell, H. D. *A Pre-view of Policy Sciences.* New York: American Elsevier Publishing Company, Inc., 1971.

Levin, H. M. *Cost Effectiveness: A Primer.* Beverly Hills, Calif.: Sage Publications.

Lewis, J. *Long-Range and Short-Range Planning for Educational Administrators.* Newton, Mass.: Allyn and Bacon, Inc., 1983.

Lindblom, C. E. "Who Needs What Social Research for Policymaking?" *Knowledge Creation, Diffusion, Utilization, 7,* 4. 339–366. Beverly Hills, Calif.: Sage Publications, 1986.

Long, R. W., Reid, J. N., and Deavers, K. L. "Rural Policy Formulation in the United States." Washington, D.C.: U.S. Department of

Agriculture, Economic Research Service, Agriculture and Rural Economics Division, 1988.

Lows, R. L. "Rural School Finance: A Critical Analysis of Current Practice in Illinois." Paper presented at Annual Convention of the National Rural Education Association, Bismarck, N.D., September 22–24, 1988.

Mann, D. *Policy Decision-Making in Education: An Introduction to Calculation and Control.* New York: Teachers College Press, 1975.

McClosky, H., and Zaller, J. *The American Ethos: Public Attitudes toward Capitalism and Democracy.* New York: Allyn & Bacon, 1984.

McDonnell, L. M., and Elmore, R. F. "Alternative Policy Instruments." New Brunswick, N.J.: Center for Policy Research in Education, Rutgers University, 1987.

McGranahan, D. A., et al. "Social and Economic Characteristics of the Population in Metro and Nonmetropolitan Counties, 1970–80." Washington, D.C.: U.S. Department of Agriculture, Economic Research Service, 1986.

McLaughlin, M. W. *Evaluation and Reform: The Elementary and Secondary Education Act of 1965/Title I.* Cambridge, Mass.: Ballinger, 1975.

Monk, D. H., and Haller, E. J. *Organizational Alternatives for Small Rural Schools.* Ithaca, N.Y.: Department of Education, New York State College of Agriculture and Life Sciences, Cornell University, 1986.

Mood, A. M. *Introduction to Policy Analysis.* New York: North-Holland, 1983.

Mulkey, D. "Education Policy and Rural Development: A Perspective from the Southern Region." Presented at the Southern Region Rural Development Policy Workshop, Birmingham, Ala.: Extension Service, U.S. Department of Agriculture, December, 1988.

Mulkey, D. "Acknowledging Rural America: The Context for School Participation in Community Development." Presented at "A Working Regional Conference: The Role of Education in Rural Community Development." Roanoke, Va.: Appalachian Educational Laboratory and Southeastern Educational Improvement Laboratory, September, 1989a.

Mulkey, D. "Research Needs in Rural Education: An Economic Perspective." Paper presented at the National Rural Education Forum, sponsored by National Rural Education Association, Reno, Nevada, 1989b.

Muse, I. "Excellence in Rural Education: A Nation at Risk Revisited." *Rural Education Mini Review.* Las Cruces, N.M.: ERIC Clearinghouse on Rural Education and Small Schools, New Mexico State University, 1984.

Nachtigal, P. M. "Improving Rural Schools." Washington, D.C.: National Institute of Education, U.S. Department of Education, 1980.

Nachtigal, P. M., ed. *Rural Education: In Search of a Better Way.* Boulder, Colo.: Westview Press, 1982.

"The National Commission School District Reorganization." *Your School District.* Washington, D.C.: Department of Rural Education, National Education Association of the United States, 1948.

"National Education Goals." Washington, D.C.: Office of the Press Secretary, The White House, 1990.

"New Alliances for Rural America." *Report of the Task Force on Rural Development.* Washington, D.C.: National Governors' Association, 1988.

"The Next Wave: A Synopsis of Recent Education Reform Reports." Denver: Education Commission of the States, 1987.

Peshkin, A. *The Imperfect Union: School Consolidation and Community Conflict.* Chicago: The University of Chicago Press, 1983.

"President's National Advisory Commission on Rural Poverty." *The People Left Behind.* Washington, D.C.: Superintendent of Documents, U.S. Government Printing Office, 1967.

Raferty, S. R., and Mulkey, D. "Rural Education and Community Development: School-Based Initiatives and Policy Implications." *Proceedings of the Eleventh Annual Small Rural School Conference.* Manhattan, Kans.: Center for Rural Education and Small Schools, Kansas State University, 1989.

Remmlein, M. K. *The Law of Local Public School Administration.* New York: McGraw-Hill Book Company, Inc., 1953.

"Results in Education: The Governors' 1991 Report on Education." Washington, D.C.: Center for Policy Research and Analysis, National Governors' Association, 1988.

Reutter, E. E., and Hamilton, R. R. *The Law of Local Public Education.* 2nd ed. Mineola, N.Y.: Foundation Press, 1976.

"Revitalizing Rural America." A Cooperative Extension System Response. Washington, D.C.: U.S. Department of Agriculture, 1986.

Rogers, E. M., and Svenning, L. "Change in Small Schools." Las Cruces, N.M. ERIC/CRESS, New Mexico State University, 1969.

Rosenblum, S., and Louis, K. S. *Stability and Change: Innovation in an Educational Context.* New York: Plenum Press, 1981.

Rosenfeld, S. A. "Rural Vocational Education for a Technological Future." In *States' Agendas for Rural Economic Development.* 21–28. Edited by J. C. Hackett and L. A. McLeamore. Lexington, K.y.: Cooperative Extension Service, University of Kentucky, 1987.

"Rural Economic Development in the 1980s: Preparing for the Future." Washington, D.C.: U.S. Department of Agriculture, Economic Research Service, 1987.

"School Reform in 10 States." Denver: Education Commission of the States, 1988.

Sher, J. P., ed. *Education in Rural America: A Reassessment of Conventional Wisdom.* Boulder, Colo.: Westview Press, 1977.

Sher, J. P. *Heavy Meddle.* Raleigh, N.C.: North Carolina School Boards Association, 1986.

Sher, J. P. "Class Dismissed: Examining Nebraska's Rural Education Debate." Lincoln, Neb.: Nebraska Rural Community Schools Association, 1988.

Sher, J. P., and Tompkins, R. B. "Economy, Efficiency, and Equality: The Myths of Rural School and District Consolidation." Washington, D.C.: U.S. Department of Health, Education, and Welfare, The National Institute of Education, 1976.

Shore, I. *Culture Wars: School and Society in the Conservative Restoration, 1969–1984.* Boston: Routledge & Kegan Paul, 1986.

"Signs of Progress." A Report on Rural America's Revitalization Efforts. Washington, D.C.: U.S. Department of Agriculture, 1989.

Southern Rural Development Center. "Building Partnerships for People: Addressing the Rural South's Human Capital Needs." Atlanta, Ga.: Southern Rural Development Center, 1989.

Spring, J. *Conflict of Interests: The Politics of American Education.* White Plains, N.Y.: Longman, 1988.

State Research Associates. *Education Reform in Rural Appalachia, 1982–1987.* Lexington, Ky.: Author, 1988.

Stephens, E. R. "Toward the Construction of a Research and Development Agenda for Rural Education." *Research in Rural Education, 2,* 4 (1985): 167–171.

Stephens, E. R. "Resisting the Obvious: State Policy Initiatives for Rural School Improvement does not Mean just Another Round of Massive District Reorganization." Paper presented at annual meeting of People United for Rural Education, Des Moines, Iowa, 1986.

Stephens, E. R. "The Rural Small School District Superintendent: A Position at Risk." *Planning & Changing, 18,* 3 (1987): 178–191.

Stephens, E. R. *The Changing Context of Education in a Rural Setting.* Occasional Paper 26. Charleston, W.Va.: Appalachia Educational Laboratory, 1988a.

Stephens, E. R. "Promoting Interdistrict Relations: The Preferred Policy Option for Improving Education in Rural Small School Districts." *Educational Planning, 7,* 2 (1988b): 6–17.

Stephens, E. R. "A Brief History of State-Sponsored Interdistrict Conjectures." San Francisco: Far West Laboratory for Educational Research and Improvement, 1989, pp. 38–39.

Stephens, E. R., and Turner, W. G. "Leadership for Rural Schools." Arlington, Va.: American Association of School Administrators, 1988.

Stoke, H. W. "National Necessity and Educational Policy." *Phi Delta Kappan, 58,* 8 (1959): 552–558.

Thompson, D. C., and Stewart, G. K. "Achievement of Equity in Capital Outlay Financing: A Policy Analysis for the States." Charleston, W.Va.: ERIC Clearinghouse on Rural Education and Small Schools, 1989.

Thurston, L. M., and Row, W. H. *State School Administration.* New York: Harper and Brothers, Publishers, 1957.

Timor, T. B. "Educational Reform: The Need to Redefine State-Local Governance of Schools." Charleston, W.Va.: Appalachia Educational Laboratory, 1989.

Walsh, J. "Goals for Schools, Schooling, and School People: A Framework for Definition, Analysis, and Action." Occasional Paper 109. Charleston, W.Va.: Appalachia Educational Laboratory, 1985.

Wirt, F. M., and Kirst, M. W. *Schools in Conflict.* Berkeley, Calif.: McCutchan Publishing Corporation, 1982, p. 230.

Young, K. "Values in the Policy Process." *Policy and Politics, 5,* 2 (1977):
    1–17.

Rural Grassroots School Organizations: Their Agendas for Education

Paul Nachtigal

> *Grassroots: Society at the local level, especially in rural areas as distinguished from the centers of political leadership. —Webster*

When you dial (309) 254–3444, the answer at the other end of the line is "Elevator." If the voice is not that of Scott Jones, he is usually within hollering distance. In addition to running the Elevator in Industry, Illinois, Jones was one of the founders and the first president of the Illinois Association of Rural and Small Schools. Founded in 1987, it is one of the more recent of a growing number of grassroots organization being formed to defend and support small rural schools. Why the emergence of this organization at this point in time? And, why have such organizations emerged with some degree of regularity over the past 20 years?

The Forces That Spawn Grassroots Rural School Organizations

The emergence of grass roots rural school organizations is a response to the long term urbanization and industrialization trends which have marked this country's history since the turn of the century. Prior to this time, American education was rural. In 1820 only 13 cities of 8,000 people existed in the twenty-three states that comprised the Union. By 1860, the number of cities had increased to 141. While the urbanization trend was already beginning to build, in a country as vast as this one (where rural districts continued to dominate even into the 1950s and 1960s), there was little reason to organize around rural education interests.

Even though most of America was rural during the first part of the century and rural districts continued to dominate in numbers, urban professionals very early on gained control of the leadership of American public education, leadership which felt compelled to address the "rural school problem." By the 1890's, the National Education Association Committee of Twelve prescribed the "consolidation of schools and transportation of pupils, expert supervision by county superintendents, taking the schools out of politics and (employing only) professionally trained teachers." "Don't underestimate the problem of school reform," Ellwood P. Cubberly wrote in 1914, "because the rural school is today in a state of arrested development, burdened by education traditions, lacking in effective supervision, controlled largely by rural people, who, too often, do not realize either their own needs or the possibilities of rural education, and taught by teachers who, generally speaking, have but little comprehension of the rural-life problem . . . the task of reorganizing and redirecting rural education is difficult and will necessarily be slow" (pp. 105–106).

The forces that have resulted in the need for rural grassroots school organizations have evolved slowly and over-time. Only recently have they been perceived to be of sufficient threat to spur action. The more significant of these changes are discussed below.

A Change in Goals and Purposes

Accompanying the urbanization of public education has been a general shift in the purposes of schooling. Gradually, over time, more emphasis was placed on state and national goals as opposed to the more generalized "democratic" goals that local rural communities could interpret as serving their own particular interests. New curricula, often designed with urban needs in mind, was perceived to be in conflict with local values and beliefs. With the shift of emphasis to state and national goals, the message for rural students grew stronger that achieving success meant leaving the rural community: the good life was to be found in urban areas. A wedge was gradually being driven between the school and the local community.

The Pursuit of Efficiency and Effectiveness

Education reformers, impressed with the efficiency and effectiveness of scientific management and mass production sought to achieve similar results by adopting a factory model of schooling. A model which, to be successful, needed larger numbers of students than were typical in small rural schools and more specialized teachers. The comprehensive high school promoted by James B. Conant in the late 50s proclaimed that in order to provide a quality education, a school needed a minimum of 100 students in the graduating class. Policy makers, in pursuit of greater efficiency and effectiveness, continued to push for more and more school consolidation. Over the relatively short period of 40 years, 85% of the school districts of the country were eliminated through school consolidation. The 117,000 of 1940 were reduced to 16,960 by 1972. As we will see later in this chapter, this more than any other issue, has been responsible for the emergence of grass roots organizations.

Erosion of Local Control

The shifting of the purposes of schooling, the emergence of standardized testing, the growing reliance on textbooks published for a national market coupled with fewer and fewer school districts, have all contributed to an erosion of local

control. The redirecting of rural education has been consistent
with the adoption of an urban model of education described in
David Tyack's *One Best System* (1974). The ultimate goal of
these reform efforts, according to Tyack was the deliberate
shifting of power from lay people to educational professionals.
James Guthrie in looking at the consequences of school
consolidation points out that on the matter of public
participation in school organization, prior to the consolidation
movement each school board member represented 250
constituents; now that number averages in excess of 2,000.

Given the centralization that has taken place in public
education, one could argue that local control is a myth, and that
local boards of education have outlived their usefulness. To an
increasing degree, school policy is made in the political arena at
the state level. If this is true, why then do rural people continue
to hang on to the notion of local control?

There are, it turns out, other dimensions to local control
that are valued and can be exercised which go beyond the
policy kinds of decisions concerning such things as the number
of course offerings, the rate of teacher pay, or the mandates for
serving special student populations. Perhaps the most
important of these is that local school boards select who will
administer the school and, either directly or indirectly, who
teaches the children. By controlling the selection of personnel,
the local community, to a large extent, establishes the proper
filters for adapting the centralized/national curriculum to fit the
values and mores of the local community. It is not unusual for
the preponderance of teachers and administrators in rural
communities to have grown-up in communities very similar to
the one in which they teach after having attended a nearby
teacher training institution. Alan Peshkin's book, *Growing Up
American: School and the Survival of Community* (1978),
describes the deliberation of the Mansfield school board in
hiring a new superintendent, a task made necessary by the
death of Mr. Tate who had served in that position for 17 years.
After interviewing the finalists, the board chose ". . . a person
who would administer the school system in their spirit, true to
the prevailing outlook. . . ." "He's country," they agreed, thus
assuring themselves they had made the right choice.

It is the basic need to conserve local values, to maintain social control over the behavior of young people in the community that drives rural communities to maintain as many vestiges as possible of local control. Perhaps the more local control erodes, the more tenaciously one holds on to what is left. Maintaining a school in our community; holding on to our rural values are cornerstones upon which grassroots organizations build their mission.

Importance of School to Community Vitality

Local control has often been seen by policy makers and educational leaders as a roadblock to progress, something that parochial rural people want to hang on to but sacrificed, if need be, for the sake of progress. For many progressives, it carries with it a negative connotation not unlike Cubberly's (1914) statements of 75 years ago. ". . . a state of arrested development, burdened by education traditions, . . . controlled largely by rural people, who, too often, do not realize either their own needs or the possibilities of rural education. . . ." A frequent, and often last stand, argument against consolidation has been that if the school is removed from the community the community will die. The response from the pro-consolidation people is that if that is all that is keeping the community alive, it deserves to die. For those concerned about the broader issues of the vitality of rural America and rural development, this response is being re-examined.

In recent years quality education and economic vitality have become closely linked. Healthy communities require quality schools. Quality schools require healthy communities. This is as true for rural communities as urban communities if not more so. The school is often one of the largest, if not *the* largest, economic enterprize in rural communities. If rural America is to remain healthy, a concerted effort must be made to keep schools in rural communities and find ways to use the resources of the school to facilitate rural development. The National Governor's Association (1988) has given credence to this position by commissioning a background paper *The Role of the Public Schools in Rural Development.* As this notion gains acceptance, grassroots organizations have another important plank in their platform for preserving rural schools.

The Shifting of Political Power from Rural to Urban

A final reason for the emergence of rural education grassroots organizations is the continuing shift of the balance of political majorities from rural to urban. Rural interests historically dominated the legislative process at both the state and national level where rural interests tended to be arguably over-represented. With the coming of one-man one-vote, the continued decline of population in rural areas, and periodic reapportionment, this is no longer the case. And, while seniority has resulted in many elected officials elected from rural areas chairing important committees, it is only a matter of time until these positions will change. As this happens rural interests will no longer be taken care of by virtue of rural political power. Rural interests will need to become better organized and create the necessary coalitions to see that their interests are protected. Grassroots educational organizations will be an important part of this coalition building.

Giving Definition To Rural Education: A Prerequisite

In the beginning was education. There was no differentiation made between rural and urban education. In fact, the one-best-system of public eduction assumes that education is education, whether the setting is rural or urban does not make any real difference. Efforts to begin articulating the unique differences of rural education were undertaken in the mid–50's by educators such as Frank Cyr, Columbia Teachers College. As the initiator of the Catskill Area Project in Small School Design, he used an automobile/train analogy to describe the differences (Cyr, 1959).

The small school should be as utilitarian as the automobile. The small school, like the automobile should be designed as a self-contained unit. It should not be designed as a series of specialized units, as is the railroad train. Like the automobile, the small school should be designed to serve the varied needs and interests of small groups of students. This means there is need for a new design of small schools, a design that will replace the rigidity of specialized big-school pattern with a more flexible pattern. This design rests on several related characteristics.

- The small school serves small groups.
- Human relations are basic.
- Organization and operation are articulated.
- Operation must be flexible.
- Personnel must be versatile.
- Facilities must serve multiple purposes.
- Pupils participate in policy and planning.
- The school is an integral part of the community.

The dialogue about rural education, how it was different and how strategies could be developed specifically to improve rural schools was given further mid-century credibility by a number of special projects funded by such prestigious organizations as the Ford Foundation. The Rocky Mountain Area Project for Small High Schools, followed by the Western States Small Schools Project, added to the work started by the Catskill Area Project. Other efforts such as the Upper Mid-west Small Schools Project initiated by the University of North Dakota, and the Oregon Small Schools Project followed. These and similar programs defined the "IT," giving substance to the concept of rural education. There was now something to organize around. In fact, these efforts were the fore-runners of the grassroots organizations which were to follow.

Grassroots Organizations Come of Age

The issue which is most likely to serve as a catalyst for the forming of a future grassroots rural school organization is the threat of further school consolidation. As policy makers, usually at the state level, turn up the heat on rural schools by developing "more rigorous" accreditation standards better suited for large districts than small; or when certification standards are increased so that teachers are more limited in courses that they can teach, rural educators, rural board members, rural school patrons, complain. When the state threatens to close rural schools, for whatever reason, it is time for action.

People United for Rural Education, a Case in Point

In January 1977, former State Senator Earl Willits, a long time opponent of small schools, introduced a bill in the Iowa legislature to mandate the reorganization of districts with fewer than 300 pupils, K–12. This was to be the first step in a Department of Public Instruction's plan to consolidate Iowa's schools into districts with 1,000 or more students, in keeping with the recommendations of the Iowa-based Great Plains School Organization Study, which concluded that this was the smallest efficient and adequate educational unit. The hearings on the Willits bill drew a range of opponents to school consolidation. Joyce Losure, vice-chair of her county chapter of Farm Bureau Women; Janet Kenney, secretary of her local Parent-Teacher Organization; and James Jess, superintendent of a three community school district from an earlier consolidation, were a few of a growing number who shuttled between North-central Iowa and Des Moines as the hearings continued into the spring. As the bill moved out of committee and was about to be place before the legislature, Kenney and Losure who had become good friends, decided it was time to try and influence individual legislators. Upon the advise of the State House, the two registered as lobbyists, becoming Iowa's newest lobby, the first for rural schools.

As they watched the lobbying process unfold, they suddenly realized that the school administrators were organized, the Department of Public Instruction was organized, but no one was organized to speak for the interests of rural schools. The next day they began sending out letters, twenty-one invitations to an organizational meeting at the Kenney farm on April 27. For the most part they were people they hardly knew, people who they had met at the hearings, or read about in the paper. Sixteen people showed up, twelve homemakers ranging from young married women to grandmothers, and four professional educators, including James Jess. By the end of the meeting a new grassroots organization had been formed, People United for Rural Education, PURE. The organizations purpose: "To promote the qualities that have been inherent in rural education and to pursue educational excellence that will enhance rural community life." Late that afternoon, five housewives drove to the office of a local insurance man who was a notary public to file nonprofit incorporation papers.

Under the threat of legislative action detrimental to rural schools, membership and support for PURE grew rapidly. By October the organization had 312 members scattered across the state. The list of donors could serve as a guide to rural Iowa. By spring of 1978, PURE could point to some small victories. Losure and Kenny, with help from everyone they could muster pushed two House Files through the legislature, one permitting small districts to share employees and resources, the other allocating funds to help cushion the blow of declining enrollments. Both passed in spite of opposition of the DPI. In addition, PURE lobbied hard for changes in legislative language, changing from "It is . . . the policy of the state to encourage the reorganization of school districts" to "It is . . . the policy of the state to encourage economical and efficient school districts which will insure an equal educational opportunity to all children in the state."

While there have been some victories, PURE's battle on behalf of rural schools has been a continual uphill struggle. During the dozen years of its existence, the general position of the legislature and the DPI has not been changed vis-à-vis rural schools. The sharing legislation and the provision for

addressing the problem of declining enrollment (allowing
districts to count "phantom pupils") which were championed
by PURE were major issues to be addressed as a part of the
1989 school finance legislation, because of the costs to the
state. While there have been no recent efforts to mandate
consolidation, the new finance legislation continues the strong
incentives for districts to move toward mergers, the new
accreditation standards increase the difficulty of the smallest
schools to survive. The screws continue to be tightened down
in the name of securing educational excellence. Schools are
required not only to offer certain classes, they must insure that
students are taking those classes. The number of units required
to be taught in high school, for example, will be increased from
27 to 41 and includes four units of foreign language—up from
two; ten units of vocational education—up from five; one unit
of education; and a program for meeting the needs of gifted and
talented. As classes proliferate, rural schools simply run out of
students. There are just not enough to go around. At the
administrative level, boards will be required to employ an
individual to serve as superintendent, this person is not
allowed to serve a dual role as principal. More requirements
also mean larger budgets that cannot be met in a depressed
agricultural economy. (The new requirements are not
accompanied with the new money from the state to meet those
requirements.) And, even if a community elected to do so, tax
limitations prevent this from happening. The impact of the new
standards on rural schools is a major item in the current agenda
of People United for Rural Education.

    People United For Rural Education is in some ways a
unique grassroots organization in that it was started by and the
membership continues to be made up of non-educators.
Professional educators are welcomed but serve in an advisory
capacity only. The leadership has continued to be fairly stable
with Janet Kenney serving as the principal lobbyist. The energy
level of the organization has tended to ebb and flow over the
years depending on the perceived threat to rural schools. The
organization is currently experiencing serious problems as a
result of the agriculture crises. In many rural families both
parents have had to find employment to keep afloat at two and

sometimes three jobs, with a 40 or 50 mile commute each way. The volunteer time which has sustained PURE and made it a success in the past is no longer available. Talks are now taking place with Rural Schools of Iowa, an organization made up of rural educators, concerning a merger. It is a merger which many PURE members approach reluctantly, but they recognize both groups can be more effect if they join forces. Action is scheduled to be taken in November on creating a new organization, the Iowa Rural Education Association.

Other Similar Organizations

While PURE is unique as a group (that is, initiated by lay people), similar organizations with the same purpose (protecting/promoting the interests of rural education) have emerged across the country usually triggered by the same set of circumstances: the consolidation of schools. Schools for Quality Education (SQE), for example, is a grassroots rural education organization in Kansas, came into existence eleven years before PURE. It formed in response to a mandatory school unification bill that reduced the number of districts to just over three hundred, and gave them all a new USD (Unified School District) identity. The schools in Linn County, Mound City, Blue Mound, and Prescott became Jayhawk USD 346. The purpose of SQE was to "champion the interests of small schools" and "deter any further consolidation without the vote of the local communities." The "big four" (the four large Kansas city districts) each had their own lobby and appeared to be benefiting from action taken by the state legislature. The state school boards association, which represented districts of all sizes, was unable to take on the cause of small rural schools. The only choice was to create their own organization.

Formalizing a grassroots school organization in Kansas turned out to be a bit of a problem. In attempts to discourage the use of public money for lobbying purposes, state law restricted school districts in the number of membership organizations to which they could belong. Which meant if they belonged to the state school boards association, they could not pay membership fees with public money to a group like SQE. So, SQE was not set up as a membership organization. Instead, districts paid for membership services. This issue has now, 20 years later, been resolved by the legislature when they voted that public funds could be used for lobbying activities. It is now legal to pay dues to SQE and the school boards association at the same time.

The agenda for SQE, since consolidation has not been a critical issue in recent years, has instead focused at the state level primarily on school finance related issues. Severance taxes and the reappraisal of property, along with the perennial issue of how the school finance formula treats schools of different size, are currently at the top of the organizations agenda. SQE fought for and was successful in getting legislation passed which would allow for contract arrangements with neighboring districts.

SQE has taken a proactive stance in promoting the strengths of rural schools, co-sponsoring with the Center for Rural and Small School, Kansas State University, *A Study of the Perceived Effectiveness of Kansas Small Schools.* Data were collected from a random sample of small schools on 31 variables which students, educators, school board members and the community considered to be the most important indicators of school quality and effectiveness. This study represents a significant effort by a grassroots organization to begin to assemble evidence in support of its mission to influence policy makers to be more supportive to the schools which they represent.

At the current time, approximately one-third (97 of 304) of Kansas school districts are members of Schools for Quality Education, a gain of 20 districts in the last 8 years. This represents approximately 70% of the districts of the state enrolling fewer than 500 K–12.

The Illinois Association of Rural and Small Schools, like the majority of rural school organizations, was formed in response to actions of the state legislature, in this case the Educational Reform Package of 1985. Once again, within this package was a section on mandatory school reorganization. A study by the State Board of Education had concluded that Illinois had too many schools, over half of which should be closed. The report went on to say that an optimal learning environment would have high schools of 500 to 1250 (grades nine through twelve) or a combined unit district enrollment (K–12) of 1500 students. This, more than any of the other provisions which included the development of state-wide standards to assess performance, caused individuals like Scott Jones to mobilize on behalf of their schools and communities. In the foreword to a publication *Is School District Reorganization Necessary? A Study of 34 Small Illinois School Districts*, Jones writes "As Illinois cannot survive without its cities, towns and villages, they in turn cannot survive without their schools." The foreword ends with "Take a school from an urban neighborhood and you insure urban decay. Take the school from a rural community and you guarantee its death. My plea to you is: PLEASE SAVE RURAL ILLINOIS, PLEASE SAVE OUR SCHOOLS" (Rogers, 1986).

At least in part due to the efforts of the Illinois Association of Rural and Small Schools, the state backed off the compulsory school consolidation effort and in its place put in a system of financial incentives to encourage school mergers. Here, as in other states, school finance is the next issue to bubble to the top of the agenda. The ongoing battle is the fight between Chicago and down state for what is perceive to a fair share of the education budget.

The membership in the organization, which consists of board members, administrators as well as community people, now numbers approximately 150 and is growing gradually. The Association has the attention of the State Board of Education and is now consulted on rural education issues.

The North Dakota Small Organized Schools (NDSOS) is a state-wide organization representing over 100 school districts. In a flyer outlining its legislative program for 1989, NDSOS states that ". . . it exists for the purpose of obtaining legislation for the benefit of the association: providing quality educational opportunities for all children of North Dakota; opposing further North Dakota unified school district consolidation without the approval of the patrons involved; pursuing the quality of excellence in education; giving identity, voice, and exposure to the particular quality of rural schools; and enhancing the quality of life unique in the rural community." The brochure then goes on to outline 10 legislative priorities which relate to school finance, transportation funding, support money for distance learning technology, incentive payments for district cooperative and shared services, teachers salaries, the state responsibility for special education costs, and maintaining the local districts prerogative for establishing the school calendar.

The organization, which is most active during the biennium when the legislature meets, hires a part-time lobbyist who, in addition to working for the NDSOS agenda, publishes a weekly newsletter to keep the membership informed of legislative developments. The *NDSOS Legislative Report* provides an ongoing summary of proposed legislative action along with admonitions such as "THIS MEASURE SHOULD BE OPPOSED. PLEASE CONTACT MEMBERS OF THE SENATE EDUCATION COMMITTEE AND REQUEST THAT THEY REJECT THIS PROPOSAL" or "THIS IS HARMFUL LEGISLATION AND NEEDS TO BE OPPOSED! PLEASE CALL YOUR LEGISLATOR AND ASK THAT HE OR SHE NOT SUPPORT THIS MEASURE!"

The New York Rural Schools Program, based at Cornell University, claims 40 of the 350 districts in the state as members. The $200 annual dues supports a newsletter, an annual conference along with projects designed to provide information to legislative committees considering action which might impact on rural schools. At the encouragement of the Rural Schools Program, the Legislature of the State of New York commissioned the study *Organizational Alternatives for Small Rural Schools: Final Report to the New York State Legislature* conducted by two Cornell University professors, David H. Monk and Emil J. Haller. As in the other states described above, school finance is a continuing agenda item. Other recent concerns have included legislative initiatives concerning teacher tenure and school governance.

Themes and Variations

Similar organizations with similar agendas exist across the country in (at least) such states as Minnesota, Michigan, Arkansas, Utah, Nebraska, Colorado, Missouri, Oregon, Texas, and Pennsylvania. Most of the organizations have organized in response to legislative action at the state level. Rural schools are threaten by school consolidation, urban schools are perceived to be getting more than their share of the school finance budget, accreditation standards are designed so that they are difficult, if not impossible, to meet by smaller schools. The Minnesota Rural Education Association mission is a bit more general, seeking to secure a fair share of the political process for its rural constituency and promoting the value of rural education and rural life. What is different across the country is who took the leadership to get the organization started and who makes up the membership of the organization. PURE has been pure about it being a community membership organization; Schools for Quality Education and New York's Rural Education Program have district membership which includes both board members and administrators. North Dakota's Small Organized Schools is made up of school administrators; most other groups such as the Colorado Association of Rural Educators (CARE), the Illinois Association of Rural Schools, and the Minnesota Rural Education Association welcome all interested in the welfare of rural education.

There are also themes and variations about how the different organizations go about their work. Some of the organizations provide financial support for at least a part time lobbyist, e.g., Kansas, North Dakota, Iowa, and Minnesota. Others, like New York, Colorado, and Nebraska use other approaches to influence the outcomes of the legislative process. New York provides information to legislative committees, and Colorado holds a CARE Fair at the state capitol during the legislative session in which rural programs are showcased.

Each organization has also developed its unique leadership and governance structure. The governing board is usually selected on a regional basis. Schools For Quality

Education requires that the president be a school board member, the Colorado Association of Rural Educators makes sure that the presidency is rotated among teachers and administrators. In Illinois the president of the organization has been a lay person.

Support Structures

There does not exist at this point in time a national agency that provides a coordinating function for all of the grassroots organizations. The National Rural Education Association comes closest to that function. Having become independent of its long-time parent organization (the National Education Association) in 1980 and establishing headquarters in Fort Collins, Colorado, it has become quite active. It now claims 12 state affiliates along with many individual members who are active in grassroots organizations. A similar regional organization, the Southern Rural Education Association, serves groups in that section of the country. SREA came into existence, at least in part, because rural educators in the Southeast did not feel they were being adequately served by the National Rural Education Association.

There appears to be an emerging pattern in which institutions of higher education are providing formal support to grassroots organizations in the form of a part-time executive secretary and a central repository of organization records. For example, The Center for Rural and Small Schools at Kansas State University performs this function for Schools for Quality Education; Cornell University is headquarters for the New York Rural School Program; and Dr. Frank Sorenson, Western Illinois State, serves as Executive Secretary for the Illinois Association of Rural and Small Schools.

With the advent of federal funding for the Rural Initiative, the Regional Educational Laboratories have emerged as an additional resource for these organizations. They provide a clearing house for information on rural issues, speakers for annual gatherings and in some cases upon request from state education agencies, technical assistance in preparing proposed legislation which might be viewed as favorable for rural schools.

Summary

Grassroots organizations, because they form in reaction to a series of forces beyond their control, tend to disappear once those forces are no longer seen as a threat. Rural grassroots school organizations are likely to become more numerous and be with us for some time to come. Dale Jahr in *The Rural Political Economy: Change and Challenge* (1988), documents the decline of political strength of rural interests at the Federal level, a situation which will see further deterioration as the result of the 1990 reapportionment. A parallel shift in power is taking place in most states. This loss of political influence will result in a growing discrimination in funding programs designed to address problems in rural areas. In order to surface the rural agenda, whether it be education, economic development, or other human service programs, it will take more grassroots organizations, not fewer. Furthermore, coalition building among the grassroots organizations will become increasingly necessary for securing the necessary response at either the state or federal level. The viability of the rural life option cuts across the special interests of education, health care delivery, economic development, and securing a future for agriculture. Rural grassroots school organizations could be catalysts and leaders for such a broader rural agenda.

REFERENCES

Cubberly, E. *Rural Life and Education: A Study of the Rural-School Problem as a Phase of the Rural Life Problem.* Boston: Houghton Mifflin, 1914.

Cyr, F. *Catskill Area Project in Small School Design.* Oneonta, N.Y.: State University Teachers College, 1959.

Dunne, F. "Have You Considered Reorganization? Iowa's People United for Rural Education." In *Rural Education: In Search of a Better Way.* Edited by P. Nachtigal. Boulder, Colo.: Westview Press, 1982.

Jahr, D. "The Rural Political Economy: Change and Challenge." Washington, D.C.: Joint Economic Committee of the U.S. Congress.

Monk, D., and Haller, E. *Organizational Alternatives for Small Rural Schools: Final Report to the New York State Legislature.* Ithaca, N.Y.: Cornell University, 1986.

National Governor's Association. "Rural Development: The Role of the Public School." Washington, D.C.: National Governor's Association, June 1988.

Peshkin, Alan. *Growing Up American: Schooling and the Survival of Community.* Chicago: University of Chicago Press, 1979.

Rogers, R., et al. "Is School District Reorganization Necessary? A Study of 34 Small Illinois School Districts."

Tyack, D. The One Best System: A History of Urban Education. Cambridge, Mass.: Harvard University Press, 1974.

Why Reform Doesn't Apply: Creating a New Story About Education In Rural America

Toni Haas

Introduction

Its all a question of story. We are in trouble just now because we do not have a good story. We are in between stories. The Old Story—the account of how the world came to be and how we fit into it—is not functioning properly and we have not learned the New Story. The Old Story sustained us for a long period of time. It shaped our emotional attitudes, provided us with life purpose, energized action. It consecrated suffering, integrated knowledge and guided education. We awoke in the morning and knew where we were. We could answer the questions of our children. We could identify crime, punish criminals. Everything was taken care of because the story was there. It did not make men good, it did not take away the pains and stupidities of life, or make for unfailing warmth in human association. But it did provide a context in which life could function in a meaningful manner. (Berry, 1987)

Education reform effort are reactions to changes in The Story. Called story, or world view or paradigm, what we are talking about in this chapter is a fundamental shift in basic beliefs and assumptions about the nature of things and the human condition (Kuhn, 1970; Ford, 1975; Schwartz and Ogilvy, 1979). Reform is the process of moving from the Old Story to a New Story. The Old Story guided education, provided us with life purpose and energized action. That action has proven disappointing to policy makers and frustrating to educators and parents, particularly those in rural settings. This chapter discusses current reform efforts, their intended and unintended consequences for education in general and their particular impact on education in rural America. The chapter concludes with a section suggesting that the failure is more fundamental than a failure of reform, it is a failure of the Old Story. Rural Education could tell a New Story, one with promise for reforming all of education.

Educational Reforms of the 1980s

Identifying the Problem

Current reform efforts, while quietly underway on local and state levels, burst on the national political agenda in 1983 with the publication of The National Commission on Excellence in Education's report on *A Nation At Risk*. The Commission was an outgrowth of the Reagan administration, which targeted education as a place that the conservative agenda could have greatest impact (Heritage Foundation, 1980). The Commission's report was quickly followed by *Making the Grade* by the Twentieth Century Fund Task Force on Federal Education Policy (1983), *Action for Excellence* from the Education Commission of the States' Task Force for Economic Growth (1983); *Educating Americans for the 21st Century* from the National Science Board Commission on Pre-College Education in Mathematics, Science and Technology (1983); *High School* by Ernest L. Boyer of the Carnegie Foundation for the Advancement of Teaching; *A Place Called School* by John

Goodlad (1983); *Horace's Compromise* by Ted Sizer (1984) and *Our Children at Risk* (National Coalition of Advocates for Students, 1985).

The rationale for change was remarkably consistent between these reports. Students' academic performance is poor and should be improved to improve the country's declining competitive position in the international economy. The focus on economic competitiveness overtook reform efforts that had been building since the 1960's, and which were focused on other "reforms," removing the predictive power of race, gender, national origin, handicapping condition and socioeconomic background in school success. Blame, for the current state of affairs was, of course, assigned to teachers and principals who fail or are unable to exercise their proper leadership roles. The 1980s reports agreed that changing education depends on teachers and asserted that better teaching would result from improved working conditions, more compensation, better training and more rigorous certification requirements. Finally, reformers claimed, the structure of education isolates schools from other agencies and forces in the community, particularly business. The very structure of education must also be changed.

Improving the Product: Focus on Students

Education has traditionally been a state function. The New Federalism of the Reagan years, coupled with growing power of the Governors, placed education for economic development on the political agendas of the states. State legislatures reacted and by 1992 all 50 states will have increased graduation requirements (Education Commission of the States, 1989).

Reforms in science and math education have received most of the attention, and early in 1989 both the House and Senate introduced resolutions calling for a high priority to be placed on science and math instruction. William Baker, former chairman of AT&T Bell Telephone Laboratories maintains, "Science and math are the substance of this age, just as

exploration and warfare were the substance of other ages"
(Tifft, 1989).

This policy response on a state level was, as Reich (1988)
noted, more of the old story: More standards, more
regulations, more money, more courses, more time spent in
school, more homework. Early reformers assumed, and many
policy-makers concurred, that more of this and more of that
would translate into higher test scores, higher literacy rates and
higher graduation rates (Hargesheimer et al., 1988).

However, results have been disappointing. Standards are
up everywhere while performance has leveled off, lagged
behind or stagnated; and the era is being called "A decade of
failed education reform" (Lezotte, 1989). The National
Assessment of Educational Progress showed recently that while
98 percent of high school students can read signs, only
36 percent can read and understand passages from
newspapers; only 4.7 percent can read a railroad or airline
timetable; only 28 percent can write an acceptable letter to a
prospective employer; and only 27 percent can do a two-step
math problem (NAEP, 1987). International comparisons are
even more depressing (NAEP, 1987).

Improving the Workforce: Focus on Teachers

In addition to setting higher curricular and graduation
standards (improving the product), policy makers attempted to
improve productivity in education through attention to
teachers. Conditions of the workplace and quality of the
workforce were of equal concern (Boyer, 1983; Goodlad,
1983; Sizer, 1984; "A Nation Prepared," 1986; The Holmes
Group, 1987). The early part of the decade saw dire
predictions about the numbers and quality of people entering
the workforce. After more than a decade of teachers surplus,
the trend began to reverse in 1984 as public enrollment rose.
In 1985, the National Center for Education Statistics projected
that more than 2.7 million teachers would be needed to staff
schools by 1993 (NCES, 1985). This meant, according to Emily
Feistritzer, "nearly one and a half times as many elementary

teachers will need to be hired in the next eight years" (Feistritzer, 1985).

To attract more teachers to the profession, policy makers began with salaries. Teacher's salaries were undoubtedly low in some areas. The NEA reported teacher's actual purchasing power had steadily decreased since 1971. Low entry and career salaries were considered one barrier to attracting good people into the profession, and the specter of teacher shortages (and perceptions of teacher's political clout) resulted in salary increases amounting to just under 10 percent from 1983 to 1987 on average for all teachers (NEA, 1987). Overall, from 1969 to 1987 teachers' salaries rose 4.4 percent in constant dollars (NCES, 1988).

Keeping teachers in the workforce was also a concern and simple salary increases, it was feared, wouldn't be sufficient. Attention shifted to motivator variables. More than half (52 percent) of the teachers who were polled by the Harris organization reported themselves seriously considering leaving teaching to go into some other occupation in 1987, and 22 percent reported they were likely to leave within the next five years. Since 1983, twenty-five states have funded career ladders or other teacher incentive programs (NGA, 1989).

A third concern was with the quality of the teaching workforce. Research findings on the preparation of teachers were dismaying. Most prospective teachers view the teacher's role as telling the students what they need to know and giving them practice in it, a view that has dominated classrooms from the inception of the common school (Cuban, 1984; Jackson, 1986; McDiarmid et al., 1989). Prospective teachers tend to focus on making learning fun, not on creating learners who make meaning of new material (Ball, 1988). This approach to teaching encourages students to rely on memorization (Anderson and Smith, 1987; Nickerson, 1985). Poorly prepared students entering the teaching profession, and being greeted there by inadequate programs with little opportunity to either gain a deep understanding of content areas or wide experience in a variety of real life classrooms, depend heavily on programmed curriculum and texts to survive their first several years (and perhaps continue this pattern throughout their careers). To address the problems of teachers not expert in content areas, a consortium of leading research Universities proposed that teacher preservice education take place on the graduate level at major research Universities (Holmes Group, 1987).

Proposals to restructure the curriculum also abound, most recognizing a wider range of skills to be acquired, featuring integration of a number of bodies of knowledge, incorporating experiential learning, problem-solving and critical thinking skills and more cooperative learning (Bloom, 1971; Costa, 1985; deBono, 1983; Good et al., 1983; Guskey, 1985; Hunter, 1982; Johnson and Johnson, 1987; Joyce and Weill, 1986; Marzano and Arredondo, 1986; Resnick, 1987; Slavin, 1983, 1986; AASA, 1989; NCTM, 1989).

Rethinking the Process: Restructuring Education

The second wave of reform shifted to the currently widely held belief that nothing short of fundamental change, restructuring of schools, will suffice if the economic and social health of the nation is to be assured (Schlecty, 1988; McCune, 1988; Hutchins, 1989; Nachtigal and Hobbs, 1988; Cohen, 1988; Education Commission of the States, 1987; Nachtigal and Haas, 1988; National Conference of State Legislatures, 1987). Dennis Doyle characterized this phase as "business-led school reform (1987). Personnel practices such as quality circles, site-based management and shared decision-making were proposed, as were closer ties to the clients or parents. Forty-one states have suggested, expanded or instituted initiatives to increase parental involvement, and a number of states have set up plans where the free marketplace model permits parents to chose the schools their children attend (NGA, 1989).

Why Current Reforms don't Apply

For the most part, the thrust of all these just listed reforms continue to be standardization, a search to find ways to fix America's educational system as if it were a monolithic entity. This assumption was never more evident than in the fall of 1989, when George Bush summoned the country's Governors to a summit meeting to set national goals for improving education.

Yet, in my opinion, it is the assumption that remains, i.e., that there is a single American education system, and that policy pronouncements will fix it, which is in error. Education in America takes place in a variety of settings and the organizations that deliver education, the public schools, represent a variety of circumstances and opportunities.

Rural schools in particular are different from other schools, distinct because of their size, the scale on which education takes place, their isolation from one another and from the infrastructures of support present in more populated areas. Experience in this decade of disappointing reform suggests that not only is there not "one best system", but that current reform efforts are inherently flawed, limited in their ability to create conditions of positive change for rural students. These limitations are outlined in the next section.

Why the Old Story Doesn't Work Now: Limitations of Current Policy Approaches to Improve Rural Education

Five interconnecting factors limit the potential of current reform efforts for improving rural education, and some are downright dangerous for the continued existence of rural schools. These five factors include:

1. We don't have good definitions of what constitutes rural education.

2. Rural is not valued in American society.

3. Generic policy impacts differently on rural schools because they ignore implications of scale, isolation and diversity.

4.   Resource allocations based on per capita
     formulas without regard to student circumstances
     are inherently inequitable.

5.   Policy outcomes require implementation that
     rural schools may not have the capacity or will to
     deliver.

1. We don't have good definitions of what constitutes rural
education.

There are serious problems defining what is rural
education. Identifying which districts are rural presents a
conceptual, definitional problem, noted by all serious observers
of rural education (Commission on Schools in Small
Communities, 1939; Butterworth and Dawson, 1952;
Department of Rural Education, 1957; Sher, 1977). The United
States Department of Agriculture (USDA) identifies population
areas at the county level. There are two rural designations,
those counties with no places of 2,500 or more in population
that touch a Standard Metropolitan Statistical Area (SMSA) in
more than one place and have at least one percent of the labor
force commuting to the central county of the SMSA for work;
and those counties with fewer than 2,500 people in a single
place that are not adjacent to an SMSA (McGranahan et al.,
1986). Education adapted this definition but it has not proven
useful, for it masks rural diversity; provides no information on
the scale on which schooling is taking place; and does not
account for geography or distance nor isolation from
educational, government and economic support systems found
in metropolitan areas.
     Every list of criteria to define rurality incorporates
assumptions and exceptions. Yet, taken alone, none is sufficient
to provide consistent guidance for policy.
     Size. Size alone is not a useful discriminator in identifying
rural districts. If size were the only issue, small towns that are
bedroom communities for major metropolitan areas would
qualify. Population statistics alone can be very misleading, for
based on population, the most urbanized state in the U.S. is
Nevada!

Distance. Distance from a standard metropolitan population center is likewise not a good test of rurality. Grand Forks, North Dakota and Cheyenne, Wyoming are the largest cities in their states. While they are not rural in comparison with other North Dakota or Wyoming areas, they are certainly not urban by East or West Coast standards.

Isolation. Size and proximity to urban areas are two proxy measures, a third is isolation. In the west, people regularly drive more than 50 miles for groceries, but the Iowa and Minnesota schools that serve small towns six and ten miles apart are certainly rural.

Economic base. The economic base of the community is another criteria that provides little guide for action. While there is growing understanding that rural is not synonymous with agriculture, there remain vast differences within communities based on farming, ranching, forestry, mining, fishing, and recreation.

Self-designation. Official U.S. policy around racial identification has begged the question by resorting to self-designation. This strategy is not going to work in identifying rural areas, partially as a result of the anti-rural bias. Many residents of communities which would be called hamlets or villages in other parts of the world define rural as exclusively unincorporated areas and themselves as "living in town." Many areas that are rural by USDA definitions in terms of size, isolation and distance from metropolitan areas are not typically rural, for example, Aspen, Colorado, or Edgartown, Massachusetts.

One way around the lack of a single satisfactory definition has been the development of topologies that categorize rural districts. Tom Gjelten (1982) makes use of socioeconomic, cultural and demographic definitions to come up with five categories: stable, depressed, high growth, reborn and isolated. Paul Nachtigal (1982) uses socioeconomic factors, the significant political structures and the local values to consider districts that are rural poor, traditional middle America and communities in transition. A third typology is that of Don Croft (1986) that describes student outcomes, behaviors, district enrollment patterns and finances to label districts as remedial, decremental, incremental, major expansive and exemplary based on the independent variables of isolation, population density and county economic base.

Michael Weiss, in *The Clustering of America* (1987), uses the target marketing system developed by the Claritas Corporation to describe lifestyles and values (as reflected in purchases people are likely to make) for 40 neighborhood types, including 14 different rural settings. The Northwest Regional Education Laboratory focuses on the identification of districts based on family poverty, low expenditure per pupil, low student outcomes and limited curriculum offerings to identify schools and students who are "at risk" (*End of the Road*, 1988). An excellent discussion of the need for a valid taxonomy for rural schools is available in the work of Stephens (1985, 1988).

The issue of rural diversity is of more than academic interest. Diverse rural areas reflect different traditions and expectations about how school will be kept. They give rise to different governance and administrative structures and are the cause and result of much political turmoil. For purposes of this analysis, understanding of the diversity represented by the notion of rural is crucial because generic policies have an uneven impact on different types of school settings, and because different areas have developed very different notions of the purposes of schooling.

2. Rural Is Not Valued in American Society

There is a wide spread anti-rural bias in this country. We are accustomed to assuming rural means backward and behind the times. The story around rural has, for this century at least, equated rural with inferior. This trend is evident in the language that we use to describe rural residents, as explained by Cosby and Charner (1978). Just as other minorities are stereotyped by the larger society, knowledge about rural folk is remarkably stereotypical in nature. Labels generally carry a negative connotation and represent an urban "put down" of rural people in rural life. This is readily evident in the slang terms "hicks," "red necks," "plo-boys," "hillbillies," "crackers," "clodhoppers," and, of course, "good ole boys," "cowboys," and "folk.". . . For those who feel that the notion of rural-urban differences is simply an artifact of the misguided imagination of a few sociologists, we challenge you to construct a comparable list of stereotypical terms for urban folk.

A second paradigm that operates even for many rural advocates is "local generalizing." Cosby (1980) explains this happens when people assure that all of rural America is basically like the rural area they know. Local generalizing prevents a rural constituency from forming because of competing perceptions of what rural really is. The South, for instance, has been short circuited by perceptions of limited potential of Southerners (Howell, 1989) which they, themselves, may incorporate.

> Once people are labeled, they find themselves being rewarded in various ways for behaving as the label demands, or being punished for falling short. . . . In the extreme case, the role associated with a social type can become part of and individual's identity, part of his sense of who he is. I suppose that few would object to someone's thinking of himself as a gentleman and trying to act like one, but what about someone who has been told he is a redneck and believes it? . . . We make our character, but we must make it out of the material at hand. (Reed, 1986)

When legislators and others make rural policy from an urban perspective, or from an inappropriate rural generalization, they fall prey to a subtle, yet powerful form of what we would call "cultural imperialism," dominated by the paradigms they hold.

> The regulators of our society and the school system itself, perhaps for want of a clear new vision, are intent on revitalizing the old vision. The latest waves of educational reform . . . are pushing more of the same industrial age paradigms . . . more classical European curriculum content introduced earlier and to be covered faster; new ways of tracking kids toward the same old ends; more standardized tests,

measuring rote memory tasks instead of thinking.
(Washington Education Association, 1988)

The policy makers in northern, urban industrial areas
who often devise programs for rural locales frequently do not
recognize this problem in general, which is made more complex
by the diversity of rural America (Cosby, 1980; Howell, 1989).

3. Generic Policies That Treat All Schools Alike Have Differential, Usually Negative Impacts on Rural Schools

State and national policies that treat all schools alike have
a differential, often negative impact on rural schools because
they ignore the effects of scale, isolation and diversity. For
instance, standardization of graduation requirements, increasing
specialization in teacher certification and centralization of school
accrediting policies in State Departments of Education penalizes
schooling conducted on a small scale by requiring discrete
courses taught by specialist teachers. To offer advanced
physics, for instance, or two years of a foreign language to a
student body of 400 may mean hiring part time teachers
(difficult in some rural areas), having teachers teach out of their
area of specialization (frowned upon by state accreditation
standards) or paying for a full time teacher who teaches less
than a full load.

Special education provides another case in point. Public
Law 94–142 (now PL 99–457) mandated public education for
all students with handicaps without regard to district financial
capacity. The federal share of special education provides
minimal support. In a small district in Montana, appropriate
placement of a single child born with severe handicaps has
required as much as eighty percent of the districts' operating
budget. Since the birth or movement of students into districts
cannot be predicted or controlled, small school administrators
have no way to plan or control costs.

The standardization, specialization and centralization
trends are invested with tradition but there is no scientific data
that suggests more discrete coursework results in greater
student learning. Regardless of how many courses are offered,
student's ability to take courses is limited by the number of

class periods in a day. Students in schools offering 200 courses and in schools offering 24 courses attend school the same number of hours and are confined by the length of the school day. Increased course taking requires expanding the school day. Because few states collect student achievement scores by size of district, there is no reliable evidence that students in small schools taking fewer courses suffer. Indeed, since rural students do at least as well as their urban and suburban counterparts on ACT and SAT tests that are intended to cover the entire curriculum, a case could be made that rural students receive more in-depth, integrated educations.

Generic teacher preparation programs also impact negatively on the ability to attract well qualified rural faculties. Specialization for teachers presents a twofold problem for rural schools. First, currently a large percentage of teachers hired to teach in rural schools are, themselves from rural areas. Rural School Boards prefer to hire teachers they refer to as "country" (Peshkin, 1978). By controlling the selection of personnel, the local community believes it establishes necessary filters for adaption the centralized/national curriculum to fit the values and mores of the local communities (Nachtigal, 1989). Their training tends to take place in regional public colleges, formerly state normal schools, that have a long history of teacher training (Bagenstos and Haas, 1987). If the pattern of students attending colleges near their homes continues, confining teacher preservice training to major research universities makes the profession less appealing to students from rural areas.

If the profession continues to depend heavily on female workers, then the longer distance from home and required post-baccalaureate work argue against female labor force participation, particularly in light of the number of other options now available. Many rural schools now have excellent staffs because it is convenient for their families (e.g., husbands who are farmers, small business or professional people in small towns). As these women reach retirement age, there may not be a pool of qualified people to replace them.

Finally, the barriers to female participation are even more serious for both male and female minority candidates. In addition to the economic and geographic disincentives, state mandated testing without provision for remediation for those who do not pass the tests may provide an insurmountable barrier to entering the teaching workforce. Serious questions can be raised about student's exposure to highly qualified minority teachers, a rural as well as urban issue.

If preservice education takes place only on the graduate level, the cost/benefit ratio of investment in professional training is less attractive, particularly to people of middle and low incomes. Current economic dislocations in agriculture and energy extraction industries have placed significant limits on the abilities of rural students to attend colleges and universities, and student loan programs often are not available for families who are land poor and already have significant debt loads.

Finally, teacher preparation programs pay inadequate attention to preparing teachers for rural schools. A survey of teacher preparation programs in twenty seven rural states suggested the only ten percent of the 208 public and private institutions responding offered a preservice program to prepare rural teachers (Jones, 1987). Fewer than two percent of 14,000 faculty surveyed by Barker and Beckner (1987) reported they were engaged in research and/or publications on rural education or small schools. Preparation particularly important for training rural teachers includes course work directly related to rural school teaching, exposure to a course in rural sociology, practicum or student teaching in a rural setting, experience in teaching two or more grade levels in the same room, and an emphasis on multicultural issues of schooling (Barker and Beckner, 1987, Miller, 1988). There are a few notable exceptions, programs for which the specific requirements of rural teacher preparation is not invisible. Information about these programs tends to travel via a rather informal network of involved rural educators and researchers (Miller, 1988).

4. Resource Allocations Based on Per Capita Formulas Are Inadequate

The Old Story, based on mass production models, allocates funding on a per student basis. Per pupil expenditure calculations inherently, and inevitably, discriminate against rural school systems. Comparing per pupil costs is an unfair, inaccurate and scientifically unsound method for measuring the relative efficiency of schools. There are simply too few young people in most rural areas to make rural schools look good on the per pupil cost yardstick. In a rural context, this yardstick is measuring a lack of fecundity, not efficiency (Sher, 1988).

Rural states have always been the poorest in the nation. A rural family in which the head of the household works is nearly twice as likely to be poor as a comparable city family, and this dire finding applies to whites as well as blacks, full time as well as part time workers (Center on Budget and Policy Priorities, 1989). Compounding the problem, many rural states fund their schools through property taxes, a strategy that has strapped the schools because much of rural America has been in a recession since 1980. School finance formulas based on property taxes are increasingly the focus of court challenges. Unfortunately, this situation may not improve in the near future. The performance of a public finance system depends on underlying economic conditions and the tax structure employed to raise needed revenues. Three major problems face states in general and rural schools in particular, according to Chicoine and Hoke (1986).

A. Expenditures, necessary to maintain and improve the educational system as advocated in the numerous reform documents, will increase. State fiscal capacity to is limited, particularly in states where school funding is dependent on property tax and land is being severely and regularly devalued.

B. Increased budged demands come on top of several years of state budget pressures. It is unlikely that states will raise tax rates in the near term causing state revenue growth to depend on general improvements in the economy.

C. Finally, there is likely to be little help from outside. Federal inter-governmental aid is expected to continue to decline.

Further darkening the fiscal picture for schools are two demographic trends. While the numbers of rural residents has remained relatively constant, what they look like has and will continue to change. The first trend suggests that rural communities are growing older. Transfer payments are the major source of income in almost a fourth of the rural counties (Dillman and Beck, 1988). Older citizens bring their own capital and are prime clients for increased services. However, they may see their needs for public services in direct competition with the tax investment in public schools. This can result in lessening support for the schools, since older citizens have a very high voting rate. The second trend is increasing numbers of students entering school at risk for failure, whose educational needs tend to be expensive to serve (Sher, 1988).

The traditional solution, consolidation to achieve economies of scale and reduce costs of schooling, is no longer the answer. Over the course of nearly a century, consolidation slowly supplanted local control as the cornerstone of the status quo in rural education. Consolidation, centralization and urbanization were transformed from substantive political issues into technical and administrative problems (Augenblick and Nachtigal, 1985), based on assumptions about economy, efficiency and quality. As we shall see below, those assumptions no longer hold.

Economy. As a policy option, consolidation has largely reached the limits of its usefulness. By and large, the round of consolidations in the 1950s and 1960s reaped the cost savings that could be made without paying an unacceptably heavy political price (Zymelman, 1973; Guthrie, 1980; Sher, 1976; 1988). Transportation costs, typically overlooked by zealous consolidators, add substantially to the costs of larger districts farther away from student's homes, and if a price were attached to the time students spend on busses, cost savings in larger rural districts decline substantially (Guthrie, 1980).

Centralized purchasing was another cost savings assigned as a benefit to larger rural schools, but the added costs of distribution, possibilities of delays and the administrative, managerial costs of a centralized system eliminate the hoped for benefits (Zymelman, 1973).

Efficiency. The argument for efficiency refers to the relationship between cost and quality. There are two basic ways efficiencies can be achieved: first, by holding the quality/output constant while lowering the cost; or second, by holding the cost constant by raising the quality/output. It's hard to prove efficiency in education, especially given both the limited outcome evidence and inherent ambiguities of measuring "yields" in service-producing institutions (Sher, 1988). Just as there is no good evidence that further consolidation can be justified as an economic issue, there is mounting evidence that further consolidation may have a deleterious effect on school quality (Haas and Nachtigal, 1988; Hobbs, 1988; Sher, 1977; 1988; Walberg and Fowler, 1988).

Quality. A final argument for consolidation was that students in rural schools received educations of inferior quality. The body of research that most recently addressed the quality of schooling has come to be known as the effective schools research. The consistent elements found in effective schools are both institutional and interpersonal and are present in many rural schools as a function of their unique characteristics, size and the strong links between rural schools and their communities. These elements include a safe, orderly climate, clear and focused mission, instructional leadership, high teacher expectations and monitoring systems that assess student performance (Edmonds, 1979, 1981); purposeful leadership, participation in leadership by teachers; consistency among teachers; structure in instructional sessions with a limited focus; intellectually challenging teaching; work centered environment; and maximum communication between teachers and students, record keeping, positive climate, and parental involvement in the life of the school (Rudder et al., 1979). While there are limits to this correlational research (Hutchins, 1989), what is important to this discussion is that these characteristics are readily available to students and schools in rural America.

Current reform efforts are beginning to look at the outcomes of education. Researchers are now suggesting that small scale schools (those enrolling no more than 400 students in high school, for instance) may provide better educations than their larger counterparts, as a function (at least in part) of their small size (Monk and Haller, 1986; Walberg and Fowler, 1988). Solutions to funding questions require a New Story, one that depends not on per pupil formulae but rather is sensitive to the needs of students. Some states, notably Colorado, have implemented differential funding formulas that include multiple categories of schools. The next step in the evolution is attention to kinds of schools and needs of students and identification of new sources of income.

5. Policy Outcomes Require Implementation that Rural Schools May Not Have the Capacity or Will to Deliver

The fate of small, rural schools is a significant matter, on ethical grounds. Children should not be subjected to inferior educations if we know how to provide more adequate ones. It is also significant on equity grounds. Children should not be disadvantaged by where their parents chose to live. Finally, small rural schools are important on economic grounds. Rural schools educate more than 20 percent of the country's students and a vital rural sector is essential to the overall economic health of the nation (Sher, 1988).

Crafting reforms that will make a positive difference for rural education is more difficult now than it was at the beginning of this century because control of the schools has moved out of the hands of local residents to the more distant state and federal levels, both formally and in practice. Rural educators and the citizens who support rural education know they are paying for a system in which they have little say, and that the ideal of local control of education has become a myth.

While it was true in the early days of the country when local Boards of Education set local policies and local budgets for which they were responsible, the Common School Crusade of the 1850s marked the beginning of both centralization (first at the county and then state levels) and of professionalization of schooling. By the beginning of this century, State Departments of Education were a fixture on the landscape and had gathered to themselves a powerful monitoring role which included credentialling teachers and teacher preparation programs, setting standards for curriculum (through universal courses of study and graduation (through examinations) and determining the length of the school year.

Indeed, while lip service is paid to the notion of local control, the reality is that there is a national curriculum, arising from standardized textbooks, standardized tests and inadequate teacher training and professional development practices. The economics of textbook publishing are that the content of texts is determined by the several large states (California and Texas, most prominently) which have state adoption systems. Textbook publishers gear their content to be acceptable to the adoption bodies, which determine what students in the rest of the country will learn. This reality also has resulted in what's been called the "dummying down" of textbook content (Mirel, in press) and the distancing of rural students from curriculum that mentions or respects their local realities (Hobbs, 1987, Postman, 1988, Barone, 1989).

Standardized tests, given periodically to all the students in a particular grade, are required by many states. They have gained new prominence as accountability measures of school effectiveness, a trend exacerbated by public comparisons across states that are touted as tools for attracting new economic development, no less. Standardized tests coerce a standardized curricula, for which teacher is willing to have her or his students not seem to perform well in public comparisons? And in some areas, teacher assignments and salaries are linked to student performance on standardized tests.

Should a school escape the temptation to administer standardized tests to entire classes of students, students themselves are forced to purchase the opportunity to take national examinations if they wish to attend colleges and universities on both the undergraduate and graduate levels. ACT and SAT tests are a multimillion dollar industry (as is special preparation for taking those tests) which is only recently being called into question. The questions that are arising, however, are not about the value of the examinations, just their reliability and the potential hidden sorting function they perform.

> The argument can best be summed up as the difference between standardization and standards. Standardization assumes that there is broad and irrefutable agreement on what is the most educationally appropriate way to provide an education. In fact, there continues to be serious debate about different learning styles and the relative value of alternative instructional approaches. There is only broad agreement that students come to schools with different needs and respond individually to instruction. Policy makers often confuse what is easy to measure (numbers of books in a library, size of facilities, teacher and specialist to student ratios) with the more subtle and complex questions about how well specific schools and teachers are meeting individual education needs. (Sher, 1988)

The subtle and complex questions that Sher describes include questions about the purposes of education. Reforms of the 1980's to date have equated increasing the excellence of education with increasing the numbers of students who attend college. They totally disregard non-college bound students, that half of the population that the Grant Foundation calls "forgotten" (1988). Even more complex is the reality that to be college educated (and reap the economic benefits of a college education) means to rural students that they are exiled from their homes, since the jobs requiring college educations are not being created in rural areas, according to statistics from the Departments of Agriculture and Labor (see Howley, this volume). It is little wonder that rural educators and rural citizens find it not in their interests to support reforms that are aimed at, on the one hand, fixing things that "ain't broke," and on the other, stripping them of their most precious resource, their children.

Educational policies that return some real sense of local control to communities, that value the rural experience and use the community as a focus of study are beginning to emerge. With them is emerging a new sense of local commitment to education, a surprising willingness to experiment with nontraditional approaches to curriculum and instruction and a redesigned, restructured school organization that meets the needs of all the students, not just those who are college bound, and that links the resources of the schools to the redevelopment of rural communities (Haas et al., 1989).

Summary: It's a Story of Story

Policies that mandate standardization, centralization and specialization dilute the power of local citizens to set the course for the education of their children. The notion that professionals know best and that the country is served with a national curriculum, national standards and a national educational system comes from the Old Story. A New Story is arising, one that may nurture education in rural America. It is a story that allows for variation and diversity, for many power centers rather than one, and for multiple purposes of schooling.

The purposes of American public education traditionally were represented by two contrasting views. They were commonly cast as the Athenian vs. the Spartan, education for the well rounded individual or education for its own sake vs education for the purposes of the State, which included education as a means to an end (productive employment, for example, or well-informed electorates). Variations arose from adaptations of French and Prussian schooling practice and were played out by theorists such as Cubberly, James, Dewey, Skinner and Neill.

The roots of the philosophic debate are found in the basic argument between those who believe in the intrinsic values of knowledge and those who believe in the instrumental values of knowledge. The former tend to reside philosophically in the idealist camp and to promote an education geared to intellectual development, the acknowledged artistic and scientific works of humankind, and the fostering of disciplined habits of character. The latter tend to reside in the pragmatist camp and to promote an education geared to social as well as intellectual development, useful knowledge from contemporary life, and the expansion of creative individual potentialities (Noll and Kelly, 1970).

However, the terms of the argument changed with the advent of a new kind of analysis in the late sixties involving the structural, political and economic purposes of schooling (Katz, 1970; Bowles and Gintis, 1975; Tyack, 1982; DeYoung, 1989). In this view, both goals may be simultaneously pursued by a democratic capitalistic state. On the one hand, goes this theory, the state must socialize and train labor for capitalistic production. This is a reproductive role, "creating and imposing an ideological representation of dominant male business culture." On the other hand, the schools are intended to serve a democratizing role, inculcating children with democratic ideals and "equalizing access to material goods and services, particularly education itself" (Carnoy and Levin, 1985).

Yet, a third view, and New Story, begins to emerge. The purpose of equalizing access is a very different notion than creating citizens who function well in a democracy, citizens who are productive or citizens in whom class and power differentials are preserved. Beginning in the 1960's, schools once again became crucibles for social reform, the laboratories that would eliminate racism through desegregation and insure the equal participation of all members of society through inclusion of persons with disabilities (PL 94142, 1974) and non-English speakers (bilingual and ESL programs).

Equalizing access has evolved into a mission of reducing the predictive effects of race, gender, national origin, handicapping condition or socioeconomic class, that of equalizing outcomes ("Our Children at Risk," 1985; Carnoy, 1989). Teaching students about cultures different from the dominant culture and the growing interest in students performing public service as part of their school experience are trends that move to yet another purpose. The difference is between a transmitting purpose (preparing individuals to function well in the society as constituted, as it currently exists) and a transforming purpose (preparing individuals who will/are expected to change the existing system).

The world view or Old Story common at the beginning of the century arose from the Enlightenment and glorified science in a rational, positivistic universe. The dominant model was a machine or clock. Physics seemed to be headed toward a kind of closure. All the fundamental problems seemed solved or close to resolution. Chemistry dealt with relatively simple and stable substances, well defined by equations describing closed systems that tended toward stability (equilibrium). Mathematics used differential calculus to describe phenomena that changes smoothly and continuously. Darwin described an evolutionary system that occurred as a result of random mutation and competition. New possibilities are introduced by random mutation and the "fittest" survived.

The changes in this century in these patterns or paradigms are most eloquently described by Schwartz and Ogilvy (1979) as the shifts from simple toward complex, from hierarchy toward heterarchy, from mechanical toward holographic, from determinate toward indeterminate, from linear toward mutual causality, from assembly toward morphogenesis, and from objective toward perspective. The New Story opens the possibility of shifts away from the simple, one best system model to system of complex variations that reflect rural diversity. The New Story sees raising up children as the job shared among parents, the school and the community, a holistic approach to creating the next generation of Americans. The curriculum under the New Story would be flexible and adapting, more focused on problem solving and discovering strategies than on memorizing facts. It would allow for mutual causality and mutual influence, with teachers and students, parents and administrators all having a say in the process of education. Learning, under the New Story, would be shared and the contributions and perspectives of all would be welcome.

Historically, rural education has been viewed as education for emancipation. Educational programs were designed to equip rural young people with the skills and attitudes to leave rural communities. With the decline of ready employment opportunities in larger urban areas and the deterioration of the quality of life, increasingly, rural people and rural communities seek education for empowerment, that is an education that enables them to make choices. If they chose to move to the city, they have the skills to successfully do so. However, if they wish to remain, their education has prepared them to create their livelihood, if need be, to stay in the rural community (Ford Task Force, 1987). The challenge to policy makers will be to devise flexible policies that support education for both purposes.

REFERENCES

American Association for the Advancement of Science. "Science for all Americans: A Project 2061 Report on Literacy Goals in Science, Mathematics, and Technology." Washington, D.C.: AAAS, 1989.

Anderson, C., and Smith, E. "Teaching Science." In *Educators' Handbook: A Research Perspective.* Edited by V. Richardson-Koehler. New York: Longman, 1987.

Augenblick, J., and Nachtigal, P. "Equity in Rural School Finance." In mimeo, available from Mid-continent Regional Educational Laboratory, 12500 East Iliff Ave., Suite 201, Aurora, CO 80014, July 1985.

Bagenstos, N., and Haas, T. "Alternative Systems for Accreditation: National and McREL State Responses to Issues of Teacher Quantity and Quality." Aurora, Colo.: Mid-continent Regional Education Laboratory, 1987.

Ball, D. "Knowledge and Reasoning in Mathematical Pedagogy: Examining What Prospective Teachers Bring With Them to Teacher Education." Unpublished doctoral dissertation, College of Education. Michigan State University, East Lansing, Michigan.

Barker, B., and Beckner, W. "Preservice Training for Rural Teachers: A Survey." *The Rural Educator, 8,* 3 (1987): 1–4.

Barone, T. "Ways of Being at Risk: The Case of Billy Charles Barnett." *Phi Delta Kappan* (October 1989).

Beale, C. L. "People on the Land." In *Rural U.S.A.: Persistence and Change.* Edited by Thomas Ford. Ames, Iowa: Iowa University Press, 1978.

Berryman, S. "Shadows in the Wings: The Next Educational Reform." New York: National Center on Education and Employment, 1987.

Bloom, B. S. "Mastery Learning." In *Mastery Learning: Theory and practice.* Edited by J.H. Block. New York: Holt, Rinehart & Winston, 1971.

Bowles, S., and Gintis, H. *Schooling in Capitalist America.* New York: Basic Books, 1976.

Boyer, E. *High School.* New York: Harper & Row, 1983.

Brown, D. "Demographic Trends Relevant to Education in Non-metropolitan America." In *Rural Education, A Changing Landscape.* Washington, D.C.: U.S. Government Printing Office, 1989.

Butterworth, J., and Dawson, H. *The Modern Rural School.* New York: McGraw-Hill, 1952.

Callahan, R. *Education and the Cult of Efficiency.* Chicago: University of Chicago Press, 1962.

Campbell, R., Johnson, D., and Stangler, G. "Return Migration of Black People to the South." *Rural Sociology, 39,* 4 (1974): 514–528.

"Cardinal Principles of Secondary Education." Report of the Commission on the Reorganization of Secondary Education. Appointed by the National Education Association, Bureau of Education (Bulletin No. 35). Washington, D.C.: U.S. Government Printing Office, 1918.

Carnoy, M. "Education, State, and Culture in American Society." In *Critical Pedagogy, The State and Cultural Struggle*. Edited by H. Giroux and P. McLaren. New York: State University of New York Press, 1989.

Carnoy, M., and Levin, H. *Schooling and Work in the Democratic State*. Stanford: Stanford University Press, 1985.

Chicoine, D., and Hoke, G. "Rural Economies, Tax Structures, and Meeting the Demand for State-Local Government Services: A Focus on Local Schools." In *New Dimensions in Rural Policy: Building Upon on Heritage*. Studies prepared for the use of the Subcommittee on Agriculture and Transportation of the Joint Economic Committee, Congress of the United States. Washington: U.S. Government Printing Office, 1986.

Cohen, M. *Restructuring the Education System: Agenda for the 1990s*. Washington, D.C.: National Governors' Association, 1988.

Commission on Schools in Small Communities. *Schools in Small Communities*. Seventeenth Yearbook. Washington, D.C.: American Association of School Administrators, 1939.

Cosby, A. "The Urban Context of Rural Policy." *Interstate Compact* (Fall 1980): 38–39.

Cosby, A., and Charner, I. "Education and Work in Rural America: The Social Context of Early Career and Achievement." College Station, Tex.: Texas A&M University, 1978.

Costa, A. "How Can We Recognize Improved Student Thinking?" In *Developing Minds: A Resource Book for Teaching Thinking*. Edited by A. Costa. Alexandria, Va.: Association for Supervision and Curriculum Development, 1985.

Council for Educational Research and Development. "End of the Road." Washington, D.C.: CEDAR, 1988.

Croft, D. "Rural Taxonomy." Unpublished working paper presented at a meeting of the Consortium of Higher Education Rural Program Administrators, Reno, Nevada, 1986.

Cuban, L. *How Teachers Taught: Constancy and Change in American Classrooms.* New York: Longman, 1984.

Cubberly, E. *Rural Life and Education.* Cambridge, Mass.: Riverside Press, 1914.

Cubberly, E. *Public Education in the United States.* Boston: Houghton Mifflin, 1919, 1934.

deBono, E. "The CoRT Thinking Program." In *Thinking and Learning Skills: Vol. 1. Relating Instruction to Research.* 363–388. Edited by J. W. Segal, S. F. Chipman, and R. Glaser. Hillsdale, N.J.: Erlbaum, 1985.

Department of Rural Education. *Administration in a Small Community School.* Yearbook. Washington, D.C.: National Education Association, 1957.

Dillman, D., and Beck, D. "Information Technologies and Rural Development in the 1990s." *The Journal of State Government, 1,* 1 (1988).

Douglass, H. *The High School Curriculum.* New York: The Ronald Press, 1964.

Doyle, D. "Business-led School Reform: The Second Wave." In *Across the Board,* 1987.

Edmonds, R. "Effective Schools for the Urban Poor." *Educational Leadership: 37,* 1979.

Edmonds, R. "Focusing on Research into Effective Schools." Paper presented at the annual meeting of the Association for Supervision and Curriculum Development, March 1981.

Education Commission of the States. "The Evolving Reform Agenda." The ECS Policies and Priorities Committee, Denver, Colo.: ECS, 1987.

Feistritzer, E. *The Condition of Teaching, 1985.* Princeton, N.J.: Carnegie Foundation for the Advancement of Teaching, 1985.

Ford Foundation Western Rural Task Force Meeting, June 14–16, 1987, Denver, Colorado.

Ford, J. *Paradigms and Fairy Tales: An Introduction to the Science of Meanings.* Vols. 1 & 2. London: Routledge & Kegan Paul, 1975.

"Forgotten Half: Non-College Youth in America." Washington: Youth and America's Future: The William T. Grant Commission on Work, Family and Citizenship, 1988.

Gjelten, T. *Ensuring Excellence in Rural Education.* Arlington, Va.: American Association of School Administrators, 1982.

Good, T. L., Grouws, D., and Ebmeier, H. *Active Mathematics Teachings.* New York: Longman, 1983.

Goodlad, J. *A Place Called School.* New York: McGraw-Hill, 1984.

Guskey, T. R. *Implementing Mastery Learning.* Belmont, Calif.: Wadsworth Publishing Co., 1985.

Guthrie, J. "Organizational Scale and School Success." In *Education Finance and Organization: Research Perspectives for the Future.* Edited by C. Benson, M. Kirst, S. Abramowitz, W. Hartman, and L. Stoll. Washington, D.C.: National Institute of Education, 1980.

Haas, T., Nachtigal, P., and Parker, S. "What's Noteworthy on Rural Schools and Community Development." Aurora, Colo.: Mid-continent Regional Education Laboratory, 1989.

Hahn, R., and Bidna, D. *Secondary Education: Origins and Directions.* New York: Macmillan, 1965.

Hargesheimer, D., Sherer, L., and Kamas, D. "Restructuring Schools: The Second Wave of Education Reform. Lincoln, Neb.: Nebraska Legislative Research Division, 1988.

Hobbs, D. "Rural School Improvement: Bigger or Better?" *The Journal of State Government, 61,* 1 (1988).

Hobbs, D. "What Will Rural America Look Like in the Year 2000? "Office of Social and Economic Data Analysis, University of Missouri, Columbia, Missouri, 1988.

Howell, F. "Rural Education Reform and Rural Youth in the United States: Some Thoughts With Special Reference to the South." In *Rural Education, A Changing Landscape*. Washington, D.C.: U.S. Government Printing Office, 1989.

Hunter, M. *Mastery Teaching*. El Segundo, Calif.: TIP Publications, 1982.

Hutchins, C. "Strategic Planning Overview." Unpublished paper available from the author. Aurora, Colo.: Mid-continent Regional Education Laboratory, 1989.

Jackson, P. *The Practice of Teaching*. New York: Teachers College Press, 1986.

James, T., and Tyack, D. "Learning from Past Efforts to Reform the High School." *Phi Delta Kappan, 64*, 5 (February): 400–406.

Johnson, D. W., and Johnson, R. T. *Learning Together and Alone*. 2nd ed. Englewood Cliffs, N.J.: Prentice-Hall, 1987.

Johnson, N., and Beegle, J. "The Rural American People: A Look Backward and Forward." In *Rural Society in the U.S. Issues for the 1980s*. Edited by D. Dillman and D. Hobbs. Boulder, Colo.: Westview Press, 1982.

Jones, B. "Preservice Programs for Rural Environments: Survey and Recommendations." *Research in Rural Education, 4*, 1 (1987): 3–8.

Joyce, B., and Weil, M. *Models of Teaching*. Englewood Cliffs, N.J.: Prentice-Hall, 1986.

Katz, M. *The Irony of Early School Reform*. Boston: Beacon Press, 1970.

Keely, C. "Immigration Composition and Population Policy." *Science 1985* (August 1985): 587–593.

Kuhn, T. *The Structure of Scientific Revolutions.* Chicago, Ill.: University of Chicago Press, 1974.

Lee, E. "Internal Migration in the United States." *Population: The Vital Revolution.* Edited by Ronald Freedman. Garden City, N.Y.: Basic Books, 1964.

Lezotte, L. "Base School Improvement on What We Know About Effective Schools." *The American School Board Journal* (August 1989).

Lindert, P. "American Fertility Patterns Since the Civil War." In *Population Patterns of the Past.* Edited by R. Lee. New York: Academic Press, 1977.

Marzano, R. J., and Arredondo, D. E. *Tactics for Thinking.* Alexandria, Va.: Association for Supervision and Curriculum Development, 1986.

McCune, S. "Policy Notes." Aurora, Colo.: Mid-continent Regional Education Laboratory, 1988.

McDiarmid, G., Ball, D., and Anderson, C. "Why Staying One Chapter Ahead Doesn't Really Work." Issue Paper 88–6. East Lansing, Mich.: National Center for Research on Teacher Education, 1989.

McGranahan, D., Hession, J., Hines, F., and Jordon, M. "Social and Economic Characteristics of the Population in Metro and Nonmetropolitan Counties." Rural Development Research Report No. 58. Washington, D.C.: Department of Agriculture, Economic Research Service, 1970–80.

Meeker-Lowry, S. *Economics as if the Earth Really Mattered: A Catalyst Guide to Socially Conscious Investing.* Philadelphia, Pa.: New Society Press, 1988.

Miller, B. "Teacher Preparation for Rural Schools." Portland, Ore.: Northwest Regional Educational Laboratory, 1988.

Mirel, J. *The Rise and Fall of an Urban School System: Detroit, 1907–80.* Ann Arbor: University of Michigan Press, in press.

Monk, D., and Haller, E. *Organizational Alternatives for Small Rural Schools*. Ithaca, N.Y.: Cornell University, 1986.

Nachtigal, P. *Rural Education: In Search of a Better Way*. Boulder, Colo.: Westview Press, 1982.

Nachtigal, P. "What's Right With Rural Schools." Aurora, Colo.: Mid-continent Regional Educational Laboratory, 1987.

Nachtigal, P., and Haas, T. "The New School Finance Research Agenda: Restructuring Rural Schools." Paper prepared for the National Conference of State Legislatures. Denver, Colo.: Mid-continent Regional Educational Laboratory, 1988.

Nachtigal, P., and Hobbs, D. "Rural Development: The Role of the Public Schools." Paper prepared for the National Governor's Association, Washington, D.C., 1988.

"A Nation Prepared: Teachers for the 21st Century." New York: Carnegie Commission on Education and the Economy, 1986.

National Center for Education Statistics. *Digest of Education Statistics, 1988*. U.S. Department of Education. Washington, D.C.: U.S. Government Printing Office, 1988.

National Council of Teachers of Mathematics. "Curriculum and Evaluation Standards for School Mathematics." Washington, D.C.: NCTM, 1989.

National Governor's Association. "Results in Education: 1989." Washington, D.C.: NGA, 1989.

Nickerson, R. "Understanding." *American Journal of Education, 93* (1985): 201–239.

Noll, J., and Kelly, S. *Foundations of Education in America*. New York: Harper and Row, 1979.

"Our Children at Risk." Cambridge, Mass.: National Coalition of Advocates for Students, 1985.

Peshkin, A. *Growing Up American: Schooling and the Survival of Community.* Chicago: The University of Chicago Press, 1978.

Peterson, W. *Population.* New York: Macmillan, 1961.

Postman, N. *Conscientious Objections.* New York: Knopf, 1988.

Presseisen, B. *Unlearned Lessons: Current and Past Reforms for School Improvement.* Philadelphia: The Falmer Press, 1985.

Rapeer, L. *The Consolidated Rural School.* New York: Scribner, 1920.

Reed, J. *Southern Folk, Plain and Fancy.* Athens, Ga.: University of Georgia Press, 1986.

Reich, R. "Education and the Next Economy." Washington, D.C.: National Education Association, 1988.

Resnick, L. B. *Education and Larning* [sic] *to Think.* Washington, D.C.: National Academy Press, 1987.

"Restructuring Public Education: Building a Learning Community." The Report of the Education Task Force, Washington Education Association, 1989.

Rosenfeld, S., and Sher, J. "The Urbanization of Rural Schools, 1840–1970." In *Education in Rural America: A Reassessment of Conventional Wisdom.* Edited by Jonathan P. Sher. Boulder, Colo.: Westview Press, 1977.

Ross, D., and Usher, P. *From the Roots Up: Economic Development as if Community Mattered.* Croton-on-Hudson, N.Y.: Bootstrap Press, 1986.

"Rural Economic Development in the 1980s: Prospects for the Future." Rural Development Research Report No. 69. Washington, D.C.: U.S. Department of Agriculture, Economic Research Service, 1988.

Rutter, M., et al. *Fifteen Thousand Hours: Secondary Schools and Their Effects on Children.* Cambridge, Mass.: Harvard University Press, 1979.

Schlecty, P. "Schools for the 21st Century: The Conditions for Invention." Paper presented to the ECS annual conference, Baltimore, Md., 1988.

Schumacher, E. F. *Small is Beautiful: Economics as if People Mattered.* New York: Harper and Row, 1973.

Sher, J. "Class Dismissed: Examining Nebraska's Rural Education Debate." Nebraska Rural Community Schools Association, P.O. Box 2003, Lincoln, NE 68502, 1988.

Sher, J. "Propositions for Rural Education in 2020." In *What's Noteworthy on Rural Schools and Community Development.* Edited by T. Haas, P. Nachtigal, and S. Parker. Aurora, Colo.: Mid-continent Regional Education Laboratory, 1989.

Sher, J., and Tompkins, R. "Economy, Efficiency and Equality: The Myths of Rural School and District Consolidation." In *Education in Rural America A Reassessment of Conventional Wisdom.* Edited by J. Sher. Boulder, Colo.: Westview, 1977.

Siegel, P. "Education and Economic Growth: A Legislator's Guide." Denver, Colo.: National Conference of State Legislatures, 1988.

Sizer, T. *Horace's Compromise.* Boston: Houghton Mifflin, 1984.

Slavin, R. E. *Cooperative Learning.* New York and London: Longman, 1983.

Slavin, R. E. "Using Student Team Learning." Baltimore: Center for Research in Elementary and Middle Schools, Johns Hopkins University, 1986.

Stephens, E. "The Changing Context of Education in a Rural Setting." Occasional Paper 26. Charleston, W.Va.: Appalachia Educational Laboratory, 1988.

Stokes, C. S., Schutjer, W. A., and Nelson, M. R. "Land Availability and Human Fertility: Toward a Synthesis of Agricultural and Demographic Development Policy." University Park, Pa.: Pennsylvania State University, 1979.

Taeuber, C., and Taeuber, I. *These* [sic] *Changing Population of the United States.* New York: Wiley, 1958.

Tifft, S. "A Crisis Looms in Science." *Time,* September 11, 1989.

Tyack, D. *The One Best System.* Cambridge, Mass.: Harvard University Press, 1974.

Tyack, D. *Managers of Virtue: Public School Leadership in America, 1820–1980.* New York: Basic Books, 1982.

Uhlenberg, P. "Non-economic Determinants of Non-migration." *Rural Sociology, 38,* 3 (1973): 296–311.

Walberg, H., and Fowler, W. *Expenditure and Size Efficiencies of Public School Districts.* Chicago, Ill.: Heartland Institute, 1988.

Weiss, M. *The Clustering of America.* New York: Harper and Row, 1988.

Willits, F., Bealer, R., and Crider, D. "Persistence of Rural/Urban Differences." In *Rural Society in the U.S. Issues for the 1980s.* Edited by Don Dillman and Daryl Hobbs. Boulder, Colo.: Westview Press, 1982.

Zymelman, M. *Financing and Efficiency in Education.* Boston: Nimrod Press, 1973.

INDEX

ACT tests, 425, 431
absenteeism, 278, 279
accelerated learning, 277
accountability systems, 195
accreditation standards, 272,
    402, 404
acquisitiveness, in education, 98,
    103
administration of rural schools,
    xix, 189, 190, 192, 250
adult education, xviii, 27–72,
    270
adult literacy, 42, 43, 351
advanced placement, 221
advertising and adult education,
    28
Advisory Commission on
    Intergovernmental Relations,
    360
Age of Reason, 8
agrarian: economy, 3, 8; lifestyle,
    4, 7, 14, 16, 29; myth, 29,
    30, 36, 37
agribusiness, 52
agriculture: commercial, 36;
    crises in, 404; economics of,
    x, 82, 87; 92, 347, 404,
    426; in education, 29, 30,
    32, 100; experimentation in,
    34; goods, 273; and
    literature, 28; and southern

blacks, 41; and technology,
    18
alienation, 28
American Association of Adult
    Education, 49
American Council on Rural
    Special Education's Rural Job
    Referral Service, 246
American Farm Bureau
    Federation, 30
American Federation of Labor,
    39, 40
Anglo-Saxonism, 8–10, 14
animal husbandry, 28
anti-intellectualism, 6, 16
anti-rural bias, 421, 422
Appalachian Kentucky, 274
apprenticeship, 39
Arkansas, 409
artistic works, 433
Asian American labor, 18
at-risk students, 277–279, 422,
    428
attitudes: 109; Middle Western,
    17; of students, 278, 279
audiographics, 204, 206–208,
    208, 218, 221–230
Axtell, James, 6, 7

balanced growth policies, 358,
    369
Baptists, 11

Bible, 10
bilingual programs, 434
blacks: 10, 11, 13, 17, 28, 31, 276; and adult education, 53; as county agents, 34; educational activities for, 41; and philanthropy, 41
block grants, 270
Boards of Cooperative Education Services (BOCES), 187, 188, 224–226, 284
bureaucracies, 3
burnout, 250
business, isolation from education, 415
business incubation, 108
business school partnerships, 52
Butterworth, J.E., 342

CARE. See Colorado Association of Rural Educators
CCC. See Civilian Conservation Corps
CETA. See Comprehensive Employment and Training Act
cabinet councils, use of, 359
cable transmissions, 191, 205
Caldwell, Charles, 10
California, 19, 431
Calvinism, 5
capacity-building, 367
capitalism, 96, 98, 113, 116, 434
career education, 51, 99, 100
Carlyle, Thomas, 9
Carver, George Washington, 34
Catholicism, 8
Catskill Area Project in Small School Design, 400
Center for Rural and Small Schools at Kansas State University, 410
centralization, xvii, xx, 98, 424, 428, 430, 433
certification, 245, 402, 415
Chapter I, 276
Chateaubriand, François René, 9

Chautauqua movement, 31
childhood, developmental stages of, xviii
Chinese Americans, 19
church, and education, 5, 8, 20, 30, 37
citizenship, 28, 44, 77, 340
civic education, 42, 44, 45, 47, 49
Civil War, 18
Civilian Conservation Corps (CCC), 38, 40
class, social, 109
class size, 223, 234, 349
classroom management, 231
clearances, of labor, 91, 93
clearinghouses, 314–317, 321
coalition building, 400, 411
cognitive stages, xviii
Coleman, James, 74, 75
Coleridge, Samuel Taylor, 9
collaborative agreements, 207, 254
college-bound students, 276, 433
colleges and universities, 32, 52, 150, 285, 425, 426, 431, 432
colonial life, 4, 5, 7
Colorado, 409, 430
Colorado Association of Rural Educators (CARE), 409, 410
Committee of Twelve, 396
common school movement, 8, 16, 19
communism, 113
communities, role of, x, xi, 7, 14, 28, 38, 48, 50–53, 98, 104, 105, 108, 115, 116, 150, 162, 163, 183–186, 218, 269–273, 281–283, 342, 349, 351, 398–400, 408, 415, 420, 428, 432, 435
community colleges, 48, 52
compensatory education, 100, 275, 276
competitiveness, xv, 76–81, 85

mercantilist class, 4
Methodists, 11
metropolitan systems, 150
Mexican-Americans, 18, 19
Michigan, 409
microcomputers. *See* computer-
    assisted education
microwave telecommunications,
    191, 205, 208, 209, 220
Mid-Continent Regional
    Educational Laboratory, 187
Midwest, the, 14, 17, 90
migrant workers, 51
migration to cities. *See*
    urbanization
minorities, 50
mining, 87, 93
Minnesota, 409
Minnesota Rural Education
    Association, 409
minority children, 28, 270, 425
Missouri, 409
mobility of settlers, 15
modernization, xv, 36, 39
monitoring, by state, 431
Moonlight schools, 44
moral training, 4, 340
Morris, Robert, 12
Mountain Women's Exchange,
    53
multicultural issues, 426

NDSOS. *See* North Dakota Small
    Organized Schools
NYA. *See* National Youth
    Administration
Nachtigal, P. M., 335
National Assessment of
    Educational Progress, 416
National Center for Educational
    Statistics, 346
National Clearinghouse for
    Professions in Special
    Education, 246
National Commission on
    Excellence in Education, 414
national curriculum, 431, 433

National Education Goals, 341
national necessities, 341
national origin, 434
national policies, 424
national priority, and rural
    dependency, 81
National Rural Education
    Association, 410
national standards, 433
National Youth Administration
    (NYA), 38, 39
nation-building, 84
Native Americans, 10, 11, 17–
    19, 51, 96, 321–323
natural law, 5
nature, 115
Nebraska, 409
Negro Conferences, 35
Neighborhood Youth Programs,
    53
neoclassical economics, 85, 95–
    97, 106, 113
networks, 426
New Deal, 38–41
New England academies, 12
New South, 44
New York, 409
New York Rural Schools
    Program, 408, 410
New York State College of
    Agriculture, 35
nineteenth century schooling, 3
non-college-bound students, 432
nonmetropolitan counties, 93
normal schools, 425
North Dakota, 282, 407, 408
North Dakota Small Organized
    Schools (NDSOS), 407, 408
Northeast, the, 4, 90
Northeastern Utah Telelearning
    Project, 218–222
Northwest, 19
novelty, 100, 103
nutrition lessons, 44

occupational roles, 273
occupational therapy, 243, 253

Promotion of Agriculture in the
    South, 32
propaganda, 28
property, reappraisal of, 406
property taxes, 427
Protestantism, 14, 16, 17, 19, 20
Public Law 89-313, 240
Public Law 94-142, 240, 241,
    276
public policy, 336, 339, 345
public schools, 52
publications, general education,
    319–320
purchasing, centralized, 429
Puritanism, 4–6, 9

Quakerism, 11
quality of education, 407, 429
quality of schools, 283

RCEC. *See* Rural Communitites
    Educational Cooperative
race, 10, 19, 14, 30, 33, 34, 36,
    39, 85, 86, 89, 90, 109,
    273, 415, 434, 434
railroads, 82
rates of return, 102
rationality, economic, 354, 355
reading rooms, 31
reapportionment, 400
reason, 5, 10
recreation, 3
recruitment of teachers, 28, 150
redevelopment of rural
    communities, 433
reform, educational, xvi, 100,
    340, 398
Reform tradition, 19
regional colleges, 425
regional delivery of services, 187
Regional Educational
    Laboratories, 410
regional issues, neoclassical
    economics and, 96
regulations, educational, 415
relevance, 76

religion, 3–7, 14, 28, 37, 41, 43,
    341
Renaissance, 6
reorganization, educational, xviii,
    178, 183–189, 192, 193,
    196, 336, 346, 347, 367,
    396
reproductive role of education,
    434
research, educational, x, 35, 79,
    151, 180, 235, 261, 274,
    282, 362, 429
resettlement programs, 38
residential schools, 193–195
resource allocation, 49, 242,
    256, 258, 270, 427–430
resource development, and
    extension centers, 51
resources, xviii, 343
resources, in rural education,
    313–329
responsiveness of educational
    policy, 353, 379
restructuring of schools, 360,
    417
retirement-dependent counties,
    93
revitalization of rural America,
    358, 359, 369
revivals, religious, 28
rewards, ix
Rocky Mountain Area Project,
    401
Romantic movement, 9, 10, 11,
    14, 18
Rosenwald Fund, 12
rural agenda, 411
rural areas, perceived as
    peripheral, 88
rural areas, penalties of, 352
Rural Communitites Educational
    Cooperative (RCEC), 53
rural "czar," 361
rural development, 342, 344,
    350, 358, 399
Rural Development Act of 1961,
    51